Understanding Terrorism and Political Violence

This book explains the life cycle of terrorist organizations from an innovative theoretical perspective, combining economics with social psychology. It provides a new approach to understanding human behavior in organized society, and then uses this to analyze the forces shaping the life cycle of violent political movements.

Economic and rational-choice theorists assume that human beings are motivated only by self-utility, yet terrorism is ultimately an altruistic act in the eyes of its participants. This book highlights the importance of the desire to belong to a group as a motivating factor, and argues that all of us face an eternal trade-off between selfishness and community concern. This hypothesis is explored through four key groups: al-Qaeda, Hamas, the IRA in Northern Ireland, and the Naxalites in India. Through this, the book analyzes the birth, growth, transformation, and demise of violent political movements, and ends with an analysis of the conditions which determine the outcome of the war against terrorism.

This book will be essential reading for advanced students of terrorism studies and political science, and of great interest to students of social psychology and sociology.

Dipak K. Gupta is the Fred J. Hansen Professor of Peace Studies and the Distinguished Professor in Political Science at San Diego State University, California. He is author of seven books.

Series: Political Violence
Series Editors: Paul Wilkinson and David C. Rapoport

This book series contains sober, thoughtful and authoritative academic accounts of terrorism and political violence. Its aim is to produce a useful taxonomy of terror and violence through comparative and historical analysis in both national and international spheres. Each book discusses origins, organizational dynamics and outcomes of particular forms and expressions of political violence.

Understanding Terrorism and Political Violence

The life cycle of birth, growth, transformation, and demise

Dipak K. Gupta

 **Routledge**
Taylor & Francis Group

LONDON AND NEW YORK

First published 2008 by Routledge
2 Park Square, Milton Park, Abingdon, Oxon, OX14 4RN

Simultaneously published in the US and Canada
by Routledge
270 Madison Ave, New York NY 10016

*Routledge is an imprint of the Taylor & Francis Group,
an informa business*

Transferred to Digital Printing 2008

Typeset in Times New Roman by
RefineCatch Limited, Bungay, Suffolk

British Library Cataloguing in Publication Data
A catalogue record for this book is available from the British Library

Library of Congress Cataloging in Publication Data
Gupta, Dipak K.
Understanding terrorism and political violence : the life cycle of birth,
growth, transformation, and demise / Dipak K. Gupta.
p. cm.—(Case series on political violence)
Includes bibliographical references and index.
ISBN 978–0–415–77164–1 (hardback)—ISBN 978–0–415–77165–8
(hardback) 1. Terrorism—Social aspects. 2. Political violence—
Social aspects. I. Title.
HV6431.G856 2008
363.325—dc22
2007036617

ISBN10: 0–415–77164–1 (hbk)
ISBN10: 0–415–77165–X (pbk)
ISBN10: 0–203–93027–4 (ebk)

ISBN13: 978–0–415–77164–1 (hbk)
ISBN13: 978–0–415–77165–8 (pbk)
ISBN13: 978–0–203–93027–4 (ebk)

To Andy, Anurupa, Sanjiv and Rajiv

Contents

Figures

Tables

Foreword

Dipak Gupta's excellent study of terrorism offers a unique combination of rigorous interdisciplinary analysis, personal experience, and both historical and theoretical scope. It is a most welcome addition to the field. The argument benefits from a unifying framework and consistency of approach not always found in the literature on terrorism, large though it is. The work is firmly grounded in theories of social movements. The basic precepts are clear and well illustrated, making the book direct and accessible. Both specialists and non-specialists will profit from reading it.

The analysis integrates economics, social psychology, and biology. It does so by expanding the basic concept of rationality to include altruism as an incentive for behavior. Individual actors move to violence both for themselves and for others, and it is not unreasonable for them to do so. Rationality should not be defined narrowly as selfishness.

Dipak Gupta stresses the critical role of entrepreneurs in movements toward violence. Such leaders are able to build on long histories of frustration and grievance to motivate followers to shift from ideas to action. They are an essential ingredient in the process of activation of emotions and mobilization to violence.

While nationalism, religion, and Communism provide context and impetus for terrorism, these ideologies are more alike than different in that they are vehicles for the expression of identity. The boundaries among categories of purpose are fluid. Gupta argues persuasively that it is a mistake to attribute terrorism to religious belief in itself rather than its political expression in a specific time and place.

The book is valuable for its focus on the interactive dynamics of the process of terrorism—the life cycle of the subtitle. Groups emerge, flourish, and decline. They change strategies and tactics according to circumstance and opportunity. They are, however, rarely successful in the long run, and the current jihadist movement embodied in al-Qaeda and its affiliates, associates, and imitators is no exception. Gupta warns against excessive government responses to terrorism that play into the hands of extremists and often prolong rather than reduce terrorism. A military response, in his view, is invariably counterproductive. Policy-makers would be wise to attend to his admonition against overreaction and to the sensible recommendations with which he concludes his analysis.

The work provides thoughtfully chosen illustrations of the argument, drawn principally from the histories of the IRA, Hamas, the Naxalites, and al-Qaeda. Many readers will find the discussion of the Naxalite movement in India especially interesting, since generally little is known about these groups in the West. It is especially here that Dipak Gupta's empathetic personal vantage point enlightens our understanding of individual motivation.

Martha Crenshaw

Preface

"The years that try a man's soul": a personal narrative

"Terrorists?" The elderly man looked up in puzzlement. I was explaining to my uncle, one of the gentlest souls I have ever met, the areas of my academic research. In his mid-eighties, he could not reconcile the loathsome figures of the crazed terrorists that he sees in the Western media with his own image from his boyhood days. "I was a terrorist myself," the frail gentleman told me with a faint smile that did betray a certain pride. My uncle, like many of his generation, was involved in fighting the British colonial rulers of India. They joined secret organizations, carried illegal firearms, and helped carry out attacks not only against the foreign occupants but also their "agents" from the indigenous population. The latter group included many of my other relatives, some of whom were judges, magistrates, government-employed physicians, and even police officers. In fact, I come from a long line of terrorists and their adversaries.

Around the beginning of 1900, when Bengal was fast becoming the hotbed of Indian resistance to colonial rule, my paternal grandfather joined a small band of men with the daunting aspiration of driving the foreigners out of his native land. Since it was nearly impossible for them to acquire firearms at that time, my grandfather joined groups who trained in Indian martial arts and dreamed of fighting the armies of the British Empire with nothing more lethal than heavy bamboo sticks. Decades later one of his relatives threw a home-made bomb at the infamous Police Commissioner of Calcutta, Sir Charles Tegart, but the inefficient device blew up leaving him writhing in a pool of his own blood.[1]

Indian nationalism, a process by which the disparate people of the vast country started to look upon themselves as a single political entity, began in Bengal nearly fifty years before my grandfather embarked on his quixotic mission. Like everywhere else in the colonial world, it was some of the best and brightest of the British-trained intelligentsia, which, in the process of getting exposed to the Western world, developed nationalistic yearnings. But not all. Several members of my immediate family (in the Indian sense of the term) distinguished themselves as public prosecutors, police detectives, and judges. Quite interestingly, when my paternal grandfather was charting his revolutionary course, my maternal grandfather was studying hard to get a law degree and eventually became a judge under the British Raj and, no doubt, handed down sentences to the likes of my paternal grandfather.

My family's involvement on both sides of the law did not disappear after the independence of India. My father was a magistrate in the provincial Civil Service, while one of his cousins was a noted leader of one of several revolutionary Communist parties in Bengal.

The American revolutionary leader and polemicist Thomas Paine described his days as "the years that try a man's soul." So it was in the crowded streets of Calcutta when I went there to college. The tumultuous sixties rocked Europe and America with rebellious ideas, which left its imprint even on the relatively insulated part of the world where I lived. As the news of student protest and the rise of left-leaning ideologies in the far-away continents started arriving in India, it touched my own life. By the middle of the decade, when I arrived in Calcutta from a remote town in the foothills of the Himalayas to attend a prestigious private college, the air around me swirled with excitement of new ideas and intoxicating ideologies of making the world a better place. A new movement had started. It began as an act of rebellion by a small band of illiterate peasants, led by a small cadre of urban revolutionaries against the oppressive landlords and evil moneylenders in a poor, dusty, and utterly unremarkable village, called *Naxalbari*, not too far from my home in North Bengal. Books and pamphlets filled the streets of Calcutta with romantic tales of the unlikely heroes. They were the true sons of the soil, who would have the courage to look social injustice straight in the eye and challenge the entrenched power of the establishment. And there were songs; those long lugubrious melodies, which could take you away to a land awash with blood, tears, and sweat of those you have never known in your comfortable middle-class lives, but with whom you felt an inextricable, yet inexplicable, kinship. You have known them through innumerable stories, novels, movies, and plays. You could almost see their darkened faces, hear their sobs, and feel their outrage. Attending endless discussion groups, fraternizing with factory workers and slum dwellers in the depressing city, made me feel alive the way I had never felt before. "Empowerment," a word that I would come to learn many years from then, was how I would have described my feelings at that moment. The absolute clarity of our collective vision stood in front of me like the mighty Himalayas for everyone to see. It flowed like the holy Ganges in its obvious logical sequence from its beginning to its end. Those who could not see the evident truth were either ignorant or were blinded by the narrow interest of their economic class. I felt myself being part of a much bigger, and an incredibly coherent picture in an otherwise chaotic landscape. A sense of self-ordination into a higher cause imbued me with a feeling of strength that I did not know I—a small-town boy lost in a big city—possessed. My moral certitude painted the world in stark contrasts of black and white, good and evil, right and absolutely wrong! It enveloped me like a mother's womb, with a ready community of those who agreed with me. My community was formed not only on the basis of our common faith but also in our resentment toward those we agreed to hate.

As I look back and question my motivations for aligning myself with the movement, I ask if there were reasons other than the need to belong, facilitated through bonds of friendship. I realize that there were other reasons as well. Belonging to a group not only accorded me with psychological comfort, it also provided me with physical security. Calcutta at that time was bubbling with energy and it was dangerous for a young man not to belong to a group. The name Naxalite was itself a deterrent to others from assaults.

I simply do not know how far my youthful zeal would have taken me down the path of revolution had it not been for a friend of mine, a comrade in arms, who showed up at my doorstep with a big satchel. "There is a gun in here," he mentioned in a matter of fact tone that almost made me jump. "You have orders to carry out. You will go to a village that we have already scouted out. The man who is the village moneylender goes to the field every morning to relieve himself. You are to shoot him." He paused to survey my reaction and added in a deep whisper, "You should be happy because you have been chosen to carry out this 'action.' It is an honor." I stared blankly at the messenger and his frightful cargo. The message hit home. I could quickly see the abyss in front of me and I recoiled. I declined the "honor." A few months later, I was on my way to the US to get a Ph.D. But by that time, many of my close friends and relatives were caught up in the storm. Some were killed, some sent to prison, some went into exile, and some others—including a number of the most brilliant minds I have known in my life—simply disappeared into the black hole of the massive Indian urban jungle.

After a school bombing that produced far more noise than any damage to property or person, police arrested and then tortured my younger brother, a mere boy, yet to use his first razor blade. His inopportune youthful bluster brought him to the attention of the law enforcement. Ironically, the officer in charge of the police station was distantly related to us. So was the mighty Calcutta Police Commissioner, who brought down the rebellion with brutal force.

I saw first hand the devastating effects of political violence not only on individual lives and families but also on the nation as a whole. Indescribable violence and cruelty mixed freely with rampant corruption and degradation of everything we uphold as humanity. The primal emotions, unleashed by an overwhelming sense of threat along with a general breakdown of law and order, depraved every fiber of civil life. Its poison spread through every vein, infected ever sinew and exposed the worst of human nature like never before. Slowly, the entire society grew accustomed to the lowest common denominator of social behavior, as if it were the most normal part of everyday life.

During my brief foray into the world of violent political action, I also experienced first hand the motivations of those who took part in the rebellion against an essentially unjust system. Many were totally dedicated to the cause. However, not all "revolutionaries" were inspired by the call of creating a brand new world. They were drawn to the movement by far baser instincts: the prospect of money, mayhem, and every other kind of criminal mischief.

Many street thugs promptly learned the revolutionary lingo and climbed the organizational ladder to assume leadership position within the movement. Quickly—for some of the leadership—hunger for money and power replaced concern for those who were hungry for food and justice.

My personal story, typical of so many across time, culture and geographic space, points to a number of important points of this book. Since the September day of 2001, when the US woke up to the most horrific sight of the destruction of the Twin Towers of New York, the word "terrorism" has entered our vocabulary as an overused and ill-defined term, both in public and private discourse. It has indeed become a label of convenience. Anything that threatens us around the world we can label as "terrorism." However, the term "terrorism" suffers from a terminal dose of ambiguity. Sowing terror in the minds of the adversaries has been part and parcel of statecraft from the very beginning when individuals formed groups and established territorial claims. Throughout history, groups have attempted to threaten others by deed. The sight of severed heads on the bridges of London were warning to those who might contemplate disobeying the Crown or the Church. The cruelty of Attila the Hun made him memorable in history and prevented others from rising up in arms against him. By this standard the Nazi genocide would qualify as terrorism, as would the Allied firebombing of Dresden and the dropping of the atomic bombs in Hiroshima and Nagasaki. By this definition, the acts of 9/11 would be seen as terrorism, as would the actions of my uncle, fighting an unjust colonial ruler. During the 1980s the US supported the *Mujahideens* in Afghanistan and the *Contras* in Nicaragua. The dictatorships in Latin America and elsewhere—often supported covertly or overtly by the US and the Soviet Union—in the so-called Third World nations ruled their civilian population by the threat of extreme violence and also by systematic surveillance and repression of their political opponents. These acts would be considered terrorism as well.

While in the West we describe the murderous orgy spread through the acts of self-immolation as "suicide bombing," in the Arab/Muslim world they are called acts of martyrdom. The difference between the two terms is as wide as the gulf that separates the two sides. My own uncle's puzzlement is a reflection of this ambiguity of the term "terrorism."

I mention my personal story to illustrate a number of important points presented in this book. First, my story points to the need for a careful and differentiated definition of terrorism. The old adage "one man's terrorist is another man's freedom fighter" is indeed true. It is imperative to remember that the language of discourse in part determines the policy prescribed to remedy the "disease"; how we describe a certain event has a lot to do with how we choose to deal with it. It is perhaps more useful to think of terrorism as an *epiphenomenon*, a minor sideshow of a larger social problem. Terrorism, in this sense, is simply a choice of strategies, tactics, and methods by groups to achieve a common good. Some movements, such as the ones led by Mahatma Gandhi and Martin Luther King, Jr., used non-violent methods to achieve their political goals. Gandhi called off his movement as soon as violence broke out. In contrast, the leaders of groups we generally call "terrorists" deliberately use violence directed at non-combatant, civilian populations as parts of their larger strategy. And all of these are parts of what in the academic literature is known as collective action, designed to achieve public goods for some particular "community." Thus, to Gandhi the public good was national independence, to Mao and Lenin it was the establishment of a Communist society, and to Osama bin Laden, it is to establish a global Islamic Caliphate, based on a specific interpretation of Islam. This is an important qualification since we must recognize that the term "terrorism" is essentially derogatory. It is a political label attached by those who are opposed to these groups and/or are harmed by their activities. This political nature of terrorism is amply reflected in the shifting annual lists of terrorist groups published by the US State Department.

Yet, despite all the shortcomings and confusion, there is a problem of not using the term "terrorism." Unless we are firm believers of ends justifying the means, there is no other alternative but to accept the disparaging term in describing the horror and grief that are caused by indiscriminate killing and maiming of people. Therefore, in this book, I will use the term terrorism mindful of its full implication.

As I reflect upon the days long past, I ask myself, how did I get involved in the movement? There is a simple and astonishing answer, which I presume is true for most people who join violent terrorist groups all around the world. It came slowly, naturally, and even unconsciously. I was drawn to the movement even before I knew much about Karl Marx and his writings. Of course, I knew the names of Lenin and Mao from the cursory glances at the morning newspapers. At first, I simply tagged along with my good buddies in the college who seemed altogether "cool." These urbane young men were so worldly, so much more in tune with pulse of metropolis, than I was. Through them I became exposed to the revolutionary literature. Through them I came to know the underclass: the slum dwellers, the workers, and the thugs. And through them I met some of the leaders, older men who were already involved in the Communist movement. What struck me most about these men was their level of self-assurance in knowing the "right path." There was no doubt in their minds about the past, present, or the future of the society. I learnt how India had come out of pure feudalism and colonialism and was in the grip of a semi-feudal, semi-colonial system, which would be overcome only when the peasants and the workers would rise up against the pervading injustice so deeply imbedded in the very fold of the society. What struck me most was the rigidity of their conviction in an otherwise vacuous world. I was attracted to the assuredness of their vision and desperately wanted to believe in it.

My friend and noted psychologist John Horgan is absolutely right in pointing out that in the analysis of terrorism, the question of how one gets involved is far more interesting and instructive than wanting to know *why*. The question "how?" leads to the process of recruitment and retention. No one wakes up on a fine morning and signs on the dotted line, or even makes a conscious Faustian contract with a violent group. Most are recruited from the hangers-on, those who come in contact with active members through kinship or friendship. Over time, step by step, their involvement gets deeper. Like soldiers in the battlefield, the bond among them sustains them. Their loyalty becomes a collective code that binds them inextricably. We see that among the suicide bombers, such as the team that carried out the 9/11 attacks or the attacks on the London underground in 2005. These men had ample opportunities to defect (a predicted outcome in any economic game-theory model), but they did not.

Finally, as my story shows, everyone has a choice. My involvement in a violent movement was minimal until the time I came face to face with a fundamental decision. I chose not to pick up the weapon and carry out my assigned task, but some of my friends made a different choice. The streets of Bengal in the early 1970s were full of tales of death, violence, and torture. When the test of time tries a man's soul, some go one way, some go the other. As social scientists it is our job to find out how and why people make their choices at the crucial junctures of their lives.

This book is about understanding the life cycle of dissident organizations. In my youth I saw a movement develop, degenerate, and die. I left India, but could not leave the desire to understand the causes and effects of violence that leave lives shattered and a society in utter chaos. This volume is the outcome of my lifelong quest for answers. Therefore, although the book is written primarily for a scholarly audience, its subject matter remains intensely personal to me.

Acknowledgments

For this project I have taken a truly audacious path by traversing many academic disciplines. In the academic world walled by strict disciplinary boundaries, the perils are many. The destruction of the Tower of Babel in academia has made interdisciplinary communication nearly impossible; the methodologies are different, the assumptions are different, and even the language is different. Therefore, it would not have been possible for me to undertake this task without a lot of help from some of the best-known experts from various fields. I am particularly grateful to John Horgan, Alex Schmid, Jerrold Post, Andrew Silke, Mia Bloom, Taradas Bandyopadhyay, Ariel Merari, Michael Stohl, Brian Loveman, Ranjit Gupta, Andy Ray, N. Monoharan, James Dingley, M. Narayan Swami, Partha Ghosh, Brian Adams, Lei Guang, Ajay Mehra, Niaz Shah, Ignacio Sanchez Cuenca, Rogelio Alonso, Leonard Weinberg, and many others. Khaleel Muhammad's help in understanding Islamic tradition is much appreciated. Apart from the help I received from the scholars and the experts in the field, a number of friends kept me honest by constantly raising extremely difficult questions during many social gatherings. Among them, I must mention Pradip Sur.

Help from friends and colleague cannot fully compensate for deep understanding of each discipline. I can simply hope that in trying to develop a coherent story from fields afar, I have not made too many egregious errors.

I am grateful to Andrew Humphrys of Routledge for keeping up the pressure to complete this work. I am truly honored that Martha Crenshaw agreed to write a foreword to this book. It is impossible to conduct serious research in the field of terrorism without Crenshaw's path-breaking work.

The research for this book was funded by a generous gift from the United States Institute of Peace. During the course of my research, I traveled to a number of troubled spots of the world. I interviewed a large number of prominent terrorism experts, academics, journalists, police, and intelligence officers. Their insights have formed the backbone of this volume. In this book I will not present this information in a systematic way, but it will be subsumed in the discussion.

Finally, I must acknowledge my wife, Munia. Without her active help, support, and love this book simply could not have been written.

1 Introduction

This Treason doth want an apt name.
Edward Coke, Chief Justice of Common Pleas Regarding the Gunpowder
Plot (1605)

Introduction

The President of the US looked visibly haggard on the eve of the fifth anniversary of the 9/11 attacks. George W. Bush's speeches in the immediate aftermath of the horrendous acts that claimed the lives of nearly 3,000 people were noted for their defiance. The self-assured man, enjoying an unprecedented popular support—nearly 90 per cent by some opinion polls—promised the country a quick resolution of the problem of terrorism. His swaggering speeches were peppered with such phrases as "rooting out" terrorism and "hunting down" those who were responsible for such a reprehensible crime. He boldly promised a nation hungry for revenge to deliver Osama bin Laden, the leader of al-Qaeda, "dead or alive." In a most grandiose scheme, the US counter-terrorism efforts were quickly dubbed as the "global war on terror." In an effort to eradicate the scourge of terrorism from the face of the earth, the Bush administration opened a two-front war in Afghanistan and in Iraq. The emergent Bush Doctrine put the entire world on notice: "You are either with us or against us." Any nation that would harbor terrorists or give aid and comfort would be held directly responsible for the actions of these groups. And if any foreign government was found supporting a terrorist group that targeted the US, its allies, or its global interests, it could expect unilateral actions by the US military disregarding any question of international legitimacy of such actions. According to the Bush Doctrine, the security of the US must override all other concerns and diplomatic niceties. The President, in his first speech immediately after the attacks, by drawing copiously from Christian imageries, declared America's fight against terrorism as the modern-day "Crusade."

Five years later, at the time of writing this book, with bin Laden still at large, the wars in Iraq and Afghanistan grinding on, and fresh attacks by the al-Qaeda still looming large in the mind of every American, President Bush appeared much more circumspect as he talked about a long, hard, ideological combat. The tone of his speech left no doubt in the minds of many that he was warning the nation of a generation-long struggle.

With the spectacular attacks, the trickle of literature on terrorism turned into a torrent. The need to know more about the people who would commit such an atrocity from a stunned populace was nearly insatiable. Not only was the general public hungry for information, but also various government agencies started contacting the experts in the field. Some of the best academic institutions quickly initiated new curricula on terrorism.[1] In keeping with this exploding demand, the number of studies on terrorism has registered an exponential growth. As the discourse on terrorism grew, so did the need to put this burgeoning literature within a consistent theoretical perspective.

It is interesting to note that the Anglo-American scholarship was not interested in studying social conflicts. In 1964, facing an analogous situation of rising mass violence, Harry Eckstein, a prominent political scientist, lamented: "When today's social science has become intellectual history, one question will certainly be asked about it: why did social science, which had produced so many studies on so many subjects, produce so few on violent political disorder?"[2]

Although the attacks of 9/11 shook the country to its core, terrorism had been on the radarscope of the experts for decades prior to that fateful day. The rising concern over the capability of a relatively small group of non-state actors to inflict pain on a large segment of the population has been amply reflected in the number of books and articles that started coming out after 1940. A search in the University of California systems library catalog, MELVYL, shows the number of published books with the term "terrorism" in the title. I have presented the information in Figure 1.1, which amply demonstrates the exponential increase in the importance placed by the academic community on the study of terrorism.[3] The number of books with terrorism in their title published in the six and a half years since 2000 was more than ten times the total number of publications for the past six decades.

This overwhelming addition to our knowledge poses the challenge of putting this vast literature in a conceptual framework. After providing a new approach to understanding human motivation in organized societies, this book is concerned about understanding the forces that shape the life cycle of violent political movements. How are these movements born? How and when do they grow rapidly? Under what conditions do some of these politically motivated groups lose their ideological bearing and become criminal in their orientation? When do they face defeat, disintegration, and political death?

In order to address these questions I will begin by taking stock of the existing literature on the theories of mass movements and terrorism. This burgeoning literature is the product of many scholars from many academic disciplines, journalists, policy analysts, and former intelligence officers, among others. Each group of authors follows its own set of objectives. While

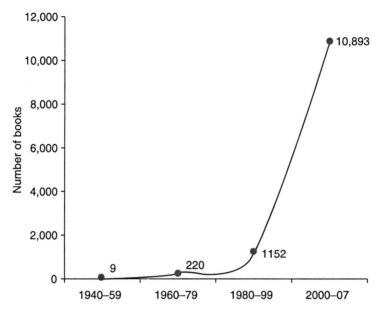

Figure 1.1 Published books with "terrorism" in the title.

the academics tend to theorize about human behavior and analyze the long-term trends, the motivations of the journalists, policy-makers, and former intelligence officers are more immediate. In the second chapter, I have attempted to provide an analytical scheme with which to classify this burgeoning literature.

Despite the impressive number of books and articles, the literature leaves a significant gap in providing us with a consistent theoretical structure for understanding the motivations for terrorism. This inadequacy stems from the poverty in the Western epistemological tradition, which does not allow us to completely grasp the motivations behind collective actions. Hence, in this book, by drawing from various fields, particularly by expanding the rational-choice arguments to include the findings of social psychology, I propose a new set of postulates for analyzing the motivations of the terrorists and their organizations.[4] In Chapter 3, by combining insights from various branches of social sciences and social psychology, I posit my own hypotheses regarding motivation of individual members for joining a dissident group. I argue that economic theories, which equate human rationality with striving to maximize self-utility, miss another important motivational factor: the desire to further the welfare of the group in which we claim our membership. The desire to belong, which membership in a group offers, is just as strong and is inextricably intertwined with our self-love. Since terrorism is inherently an altruistic act, at least in the mind of the participant, we cannot fully comprehend it without the help of group motivation, the principal preoccupation of social psychology. Therefore, without properly understanding the motivations behind acts of altruism, we cannot differentiate between politically motivated violent actions from ordinary criminal enterprise.

By extending the factors of individual motivations to the group, therefore, Chapter 4 explains the dynamics of mass political movements. The evolution of a movement is deeply influenced by the responses of the target government. In this chapter I develop a theoretical perspective on the dynamic interactions with the society at large that shape the life cycle of a terrorist organization.

Based on this theoretical perspective, the next four chapters analyze the birth, growth, transformation, and demise of violent political movements. Although I draw upon examples of many dissident groups around the world, in my explanation I specifically concentrate on four political movements: Hamas, al-Qaeda, Irish Republican Army (IRA), and Naxalites. These four disparate groups were chosen for specific methodological reasons. They represent the diversity of ideology, chronology, and their relative positions on their particular life cycle. Let me explain.

If we look at the world of violent political movements, we can see that these four groups are organized around three, often overlapping, ideologies: nationalism, religious fundamentalism, and Communism. The forces that create nationalistic identity with which a segment of the population defines itself separately from the rest of the society often follow the contours of religious and/or economic class divisions. In the post-colonial world sub-national separatism is inevitably associated with a feeling of deep exploitation by the majority of the minority population. A deep sense of injustice, the inspiration for many of these movements, stems from differential rates of economic growth, lack of political opportunities for specific groups, or the presence of oil and other natural resources to which the indigenous population feels a certain sense of entitlement. From Biafra to Bangladesh, from Croatia to East Timor, these separatist movements have often caused bloody civil wars, where two regular armies or organized militias have waged bloody warfare. Although many of these conflicts are labeled as "religious," "nationalistic" or "class warfare," these three seemingly distinct ideologies are often impossible to completely distinguish from each other.

If we look at our selected groups, we can see that they represent the entire ideological spectrum. While Hamas and the IRA are primarily nationalistic, al-Qaeda's goals are millenarian in nature. Hamas is fighting to establish a Palestinian state along the ideals of Sunni Islam, whereas the IRA, at least in the earliest periods of its history, was waging a war to unify the entire island of Ireland under a Catholic rule.[5] In contrast, al-Qaeda is not aiming at establishing a single state, but wants to create an Islamic Caliphate stretching from Spain to Indonesia. The Naxalites, an insurgency group in India, in contrast, aim at establishing a Communist regime according to the ideals of China's erstwhile Communist leader, Mao Zedong. Yet the Naxalites in India, for instance, are flourishing only in the tribal regions where ethnic divisions are deep and abiding. Similarly, the IRA, a primarily nationalistic group based on Catholic identity, evolved to embrace socialist ideology. The Islamic millenarian movements, such as al-Qaeda, give expression to Islamic identity along with a strong economic egalitarian message. Moreover, in defining their fight against the West, they cannot often escape Arab/Islamic nationalistic aspirations.

These groups also offer a perfect diversity in terms of where they are in the life cycles of their movements. Thus, Hamas and al-Qaeda, barely a decade into their lives, have shown impressive strength in shaping the history of the twenty-first century. The IRA, the longest surviving dissident group in the world, after nearly 100 years of its existence is currently facing the prospect of a political death. Finally, the Naxalites in India, having been comprehensively defeated in the early 1970s, have come back with renewed vigor.

From time immemorial political extremists have been laying a trap for the state to overreact in a way that alienates those who were happy taking a moderate stance. The objectives of the terrorist groups are served when the government acts in a way that is perceived as immoral and uncalled for by a large section of the population. Although the motives of the terrorists are fairly clear on this, the state cannot give up its addiction to the failed policies of the past. In the final chapter I ask the question: why do we follow the same path of mutual destruction? Although terrorism has been a part of human society from its very inception, what has changed is the ability of a small group to inflict catastrophic amount of death and destruction. If the history of modern terrorism began with the invention of dynamite, in this age of advanced technology the risks of deaths of unimaginable magnitude is a real possibility. The question is: when we face attacks that would make the 9/11 incidents pale in comparison, will we collectively have the wisdom to separate myths from reality and move forward in a judicious manner? By drawing from areas of social psychology and cognitive sciences, I attempt to provide an answer to this puzzle and then address the question that is on everyone's mind: is the war against terrorism winnable?

Defining terrorism

In 1605, a plot was hatched by a group of provincial English Catholics to kill King James I of England, his family, and most of the Protestant aristocracy. The plotters tried to smuggle barrels of gunpowder into the vaults underneath Parliament House. The conspirators planned to blow it up during the State Opening, when the king was going to be in the House. The members of the "Gunpowder Plot" had also plotted to abduct the royal children, and incite a revolt in the Midlands. The enormity of the conspiracy left Edward Coke, the Chief Justice of Common Pleas, searching for an appropriate word to describe it. The "reign of terror" (*la Terreur*) following the French Revolution, which gave birth to the term "terrorism," would have to wait for almost two hundred years to be coined. Coke was at a loss to find a suitable sobriquet, which would adequately capture the revulsion, scorn, and disgust the hatched plot evoked in him. He expressed his bewilderment by stating: "This Treason doth want an apt name." President Bush would similarly look for an appropriate term to describe those who could plot mass murders on such a scale. He would use term such as "Islamic terrorists" or "Islamo-fascist" to express his indignation toward the radical Islamic groups that threatened his nation. Others have similarly tried in vain to coin terms, such as "suicide murderers" and "suicide terrorists," to capture their feelings toward the perpetrators of these attacks. In contrast, those who perpetrate these acts always see them as legitimate responses to their longstanding grievances, taken as the last resort in self-defense. In the Arab/Islamic world, the sympathizers of their ideological aims refer to them as "*Shahid*" or "martyrs." The chasm that separates the connotations of the two sets of terms are as wide as the view that separates the two worlds. In the blame game both sides of a terrorist attack see themselves as the victims.

Although the condemnatory epithet of "terrorism" has become a part of our everyday political lexicon, Rapoport points out that in the past many "terrorists" did not mind the label and, in fact, wore it as a badge of honor.[6] Since the anti-colonial movements had a wide support base among their own people, their armed struggle to sow terror in the minds of their colonial lords was seen as legitimate; they proudly wore the name "terrorist." However, with time the anti-colonial organizations realized the need for "a new language to describe themselves, because the term terrorist had accumulated so many negative connotations that those who identified themselves as terrorists incurred enormous political liability."[7] Lehi (acronym for *Lohamei Herut Israel*, "Fighters for the Freedom of Israel"), the Jewish extremist group operating in the British Mandate of Palestine, was perhaps the last self-identified terrorist group in history. Menachem Begin, the leader of the Irgun gang, categorically rejected the label and instead called the occupying British force the real "terrorists."[8] This new-self-description as "freedom fighters" quickly received global acceptance and no group since the Lehi has called itself "terrorist". The members of dissident organizations are acutely aware of the negative image conveyed by the term. A member of the IRA, despite being convicted of several attempted murders, kidnapping, and arms possession, vehemently denied the label: "To me, 'terrorist' is a dirty word and I certainly don't . . . nor have I ever considered myself to be one, but ah, I remain an activist to this day."[9] To him these were political activities separate from those of a common criminal or a loathsome terrorist.

Furthermore, as Rapoport observes, while the dissident organizations eschewed the term, governments around the world realized the political value of calling a dissident organization "terrorist".[10] The media in the US, particularly prior to the 9/11 attacks, in order to maintain its neutrality, alternately called the same individual a terrorist, a guerrilla fighter, an insurgent, or a soldier.

Leo Tolstoy in one of his short stories tells the tale of a man who wanted to know everything about the sun. As he continued to stare at the sun, his eyesight started getting affected. He saw the sun getting dimmer and, eventually, one day he could not see it anymore. Frustrated, the man concluded that there was no such object as the sun after all. Those of us who have attempted to study and define terrorism can very well relate to this man's frustration.

The term "terrorism" has been a source of confusion, contradiction, and controversy from the first time it slipped into our political vocabulary. The word itself was coined during the terrible days of the French Revolution. From the beginning, the word had different meanings for different people. The Revolution was the product of the class-ridden French society, which caused miserable poverty for the common people. Although ordinary people in eighteenth-century Europe lived in abject poverty, the lives of the poor in France were particularly miserable.[11] On 14 July 1789, the people of Paris stormed the most hated symbol of oppression, the Bastille prison, and destroyed it brick by brick. Just as Americans celebrate the Fourth of July as the beginning of the American Revolution, so the people of France celebrate Bastille Day, which marked the beginning of the French Revolution.

Yet after achieving power, the French Revolution, similar to most upheavals without a coherent goal, began to focus its fury inward. On 26 July 1794, the revolutionary leader Maximilien Robespierre announced to the National Convention that he had in his possession a list of names of traitors who were plotting to overthrow the revolutionary government. That started the "Reign of Terror" when nearly 40,000 men and women were publicly beheaded by the use of guillotine. These gruesome acts were carried out in order to instill fear in the minds of the "enemies" of the revolution and to assure the common people that the old, unjust system of monarchy was not going to return. These acts were designed to terrify an aristocrat or a supporter of the French monarchy into submission. On the other hand, to a commoner and a supporter of the revolution, these were necessary acts to bring about a new and just French society. The feared prosecutor Georges Danton assured the fellow citizens, "Let us be terrible, so that people will not have to be."[12]

It is interesting to note that from its inception, the connotation of the term, at least in the minds of general public, has changed radically. In the early days it was equated with state repression, while these days the term is associated more with the acts of non-state actors, particularly those who target a civilian non-combatant population for political goals. After two hundred years of use and abuse, the *Oxford English Dictionary* still gives two definitions for terrorism: 1) "government by intimidation as directed and carried out by the party in power in France during Revolution of 1789–94," and 2) "policy intended to strike with terror those against whom it is adopted." The first definition clearly associates the term with an organized state, while the second offers a very broad characterization, which can include both state and non-state actors.

The term has, therefore, always meant different things to different people. The old saying "one man's terrorist is another man's hero" still holds true.

Given the ambiguity of the term from its very inception, it is no surprise that there is no consensus about its definition. Schmid and Jongman, in their often-cited work, considered 109 definitions offered by governmental agencies, think tanks and academic scholars, and saw a singular lack of uniformity.[13] This confusion amply reflects the fact that terrorism is a political term. All of us use it as a tool to label those with whom we are in conflict. Therefore, it should be no surprise to learn that while Osama bin Laden is despised as a crazed killer and a quintessential terrorist in the West, he is revered as a hero by many in the Islamic world. Strolling through the streets of many Muslim countries, a foreign visitor might be offended by the sights of vendors doing a brisk business in posters bearing his likeness. Similar to the image of Che Guevara in the West, the white-turbaned image of the scion of one of the wealthiest families in the world peers at us from ramshackle tea stalls and the side of the rickshaws. Judging from the preponderance of his likeness on the streets of Karachi to Cairo, it is clear that bin Laden has truly achieved his iconic status in the Muslim world and has become a mythical hero to the multitude.

Social scientists, however, cannot study something without first defining it. By culling the diverse definitions presented by Schmid and Jongman,[14] it is possible to see the preponderant (but not universal) use of the terms "violence," "civilian," "non-state actors," and "political." Without getting too bogged down in the analyses of the various definitions,[15] let us take a simple definition of terrorism offered by the US State Department, which defines terrorism as "politically motivated violence perpetrated against non-combatant targets by sub-national groups or clandestine agents, usually intended to influence an audience."[16]

Although this definition appears to be quite neutral at first glance, there should be no doubt about its political and conceptual implications. This definition of terrorism rests on four factors, which relate to the acts themselves (violent), the actors (non-state groups), the target (non-combatant), and motivation (political). This definition is significant not only in what it includes but also what it leaves out.

To be considered as an act of terrorism there must be an actual act of violence or its threat. For instance, if a bomb kills people and damages property it is clearly an act of terrorism. Similarly, if there is a specific threat, such as a phone call announcing the planting of a bomb, it will be considered as terrorism by this definition. Thus, the Gandhian movement or the Civil Rights movement led by Martin Luther King will not qualify as terrorism. Neither will a group be considered as "terrorist" if it simply espouses a radical ideology but makes no specific threat.

The second criterion defining terrorism involves the presence of "groups of non-state actors." By concentrating solely on the non-state actors, it would leave out the handiwork of many dictators around the world, where they suppressed political dissent through brutal acts of repression and gross violation of human rights. It would also not include the bombing of Dresden by the Allied forces during the World War II, or the dropping of the atomic bombs in Hiroshima and Nagasaki. By this definition, therefore, the "reign of terror" after the French Revolution, which gave terrorism its name, will not be considered as terrorism. This definition would, therefore, exclude by far the largest source of civilian death in the world: governments.[17]

Third, this definition makes it clear that we are not interested in acts of a single individual, the so-called "lone wolves." Although these individuals, such as Theodore Kaczynski (the "Unabomber"), can cause a lot of damage and spread terror in a community or an entire nation, they are of less importance to us, since we are primarily interested in the life cycle of terrorist organizations and not of a single, disgruntled, often psychologically unstable person.

Fourth, the US State Department definition defines acts of terrorism by their selection of targets. This is the most ambiguous aspect of this definition. The term "non-combatant" covers civilians, but should it also include members of the armed forces not engaged in active combat? If we exclude targeting of the military personnel and infrastructure, in the series of the 9/11 attacks, we will have to classify the crashing of the hijacked planes, United Airlines flight # 175 and the American Airlines flight # 11, which struck the World Trade Center towers, and the United Airlines flight # 93, which crashed in Pennsylvania, clearly as acts of terrorism. However, what about the American Airlines flight # 77 that hit the Pentagon building? Since the Pentagon is the headquarters of the US armed forces, this definition would not be regarded as terrorism. If we relax the definition of non-combatant a bit to include military personnel during periods of active hostility, targeting the US patrols by al-Qaeda in Iraq and Afghanistan should not be considered as terrorism, but the attack on the USS *Cole* off the coast of Yemen will. In that case, what about attacks by groups, such as Hamas, the Palestine Islamic Jihad, or the al-Aqsa Martyr Brigade within Israel, which target off-duty members of the Israeli Defense Force? Since there is conscription in Israel any public place where young men and women congregate can be seen as a gathering place for active duty personnel of the IDF. It is therefore clear that any definition of target selection is going to be arbitrary. To call one attack terrorism and another a guerrilla attack may serve political purposes, but such distinctions do not offer any insight for policy-makers or add clarity to academic discourse.

The final, and perhaps foremost, criterion for an act of violence to be considered as terrorism is that it must have a political aim. A politically motivated act is undertaken in the name of an entire community. Therefore, the instrumental goal of a violent act of dissidence is a public good that must be shared with the entire community regardless of the levels of participation by an individual member. The significance of this public-good aspect of a terrorist organization's motivation becomes abundantly clear when we compare their goals with those of organized-crime syndicates,[18] or the motivations of a single person embarking on acts of violence for personal revenge. From a behavioral standpoint, a terrorist group attempts to achieve public goods, the benefits of which must be shared with the entire community that the group claims to represent irrespective of an individual's participation *in the endeavor to procure it.*[19] In contrast, a criminal gang does not operate out of any apparent "higher calling." Their predominant motivation is the provision of private and/or quasi-public goods, *which are shared only among the immediate members of that group.*

History is replete with examples of men and women embarking on acts of violence against important state officials for reasons of personal passion. Despite the fact that these acts may have had significant political implications for a nation, since the motivations behind such acts are not political, we cannot accept them as terrorism. For instance, on 4 June 2001, the Crown Prince Dipendra Shah of the Himalayan nation of Nepal, in a fit of drug-induced rage, killed most of the royal family.[20] Although there is doubt about the exact circumstances of these killings, if we accept the veracity of the official version, they set in motion a chain of events that had a profound impact on the history of Nepal.[21] However, if the acts of violence had no political aim, nobody would classify them as "terrorism."

Today, there is a fierce debate regarding the definition of the terms terrorism, insurgency, guerrilla warfare, civil war, genocide, etc. Shakespeare once rhetorically asked, "What is in a name?" The fervor of the current debate clearly demonstrates that, in the final analysis, a name we attribute to an act reflects our political motives. Charles Tilly is correct when he points out:

> Some vivid terms serve political and normative ends admirably despite hindering description and explanation of the social phenomena at which they point. Those double-edged terms include *riot*, *injustice*, and *civil society*, all of them politically powerful but analytically elusive. They also include *terror*, *terrorism*, and *terrorists.*[22]

While defining terrorism we came full circle. Looking for precision, we systematically chipped away at the definition of terrorism, and in the end we were left with a rather general statement. The reason for this confusion is similar to that in Leo Tolstoy's story; indeed, there is nothing that can be defined specifically as "terrorism." It is a label of convenience that we attribute to the activities of which *we* do not approve. In the final analysis, among all the non-state groups that are actively involved in a conflict against a much stronger state apparatus, attacks against civilian populations are simply one of many strategies. Their strategies may involve non-violent protest demonstrations or, at times, attacks against the "soft" targets of an assembled civilian population or the symbols of a nation. Depending on their strategic assessment, a group's tactics would evolve, and, at any single time, may contain many different types of actions. In this book, therefore, I will use the terms "terror," "terrorism," and "terrorist" in one of their broadest possible connotations, as "politically motivated violent attacks by non-state actors", being clearly mindful of its political implications and the corresponding sundry shortcomings.

2 Theories of the origins of movements

Poverty is the parent of revolution and crime.

Aristotle (384 BCE–322 BCE)

Those who would commit suicide in their assault on the free world are not rational.

Senator John Warner[1]

The puzzle

The clean-shaven men, looking no different from all other passengers, must have said their prayer in preparation for the ultimate sacrifice. As the hijackers sprung into action soon after the plane took off from Boston's Logan Airport, they moved with deliberate premeditation. They had taken training in flying very large aircrafts and had meticulously practiced every move in taking over control from the crew during the past several years to successfully guide the airplanes through the twin towers of the World Trade Center and to the Pentagon building. The spectacle of the first successful attack on the US mainland since the war of 1812, when British soldiers torched the White House, stunned the world. The images of the collapsing skyscrapers and the desperate people jumping from the inferno became seared into our collective memories. The coordination and organizational skills demonstrated by the 9/11 hijackers were so great that many in the Arab/Muslim world actually refused to believe that a handful of their own could pull off something like this. The conspiracy theorists were in full swing suggesting that it was in fact the handy work of the CIA and the Israeli intelligence agency, Mossad.[2] As the nation tried to grapple with the grief and anger over the attacks, these acts of self-sacrifice threw many into confusion in their attempt to understand the motivations of the perpetrators.

Since self-preservation is at the core of the entire organic world, the sight of young men deliberately taking their own lives to inflict death and misery on others created a widespread conundrum as to how to categorize these people. Scholars and commoners alike have tried to understand the motivations of those who would risk it all and rise up against the most formidable of enemies. Predictably, instantly after the attacks, there were four overlapping lines of perceptions. Some blamed it on poverty, some on unreasonable religious fanaticism, some on lack of democratic freedom, and others on psychological disorder.

Writing around the fourth century BCE, Aristotle blamed acts of political violence on the time-honored suspect, poverty. His accusation of poverty as the most potent generator of political ill-will still resonates strongly among many in today's world. To most of us, the link between poverty and terrorism (or more broadly, sociopolitical violence) seems almost self-evident. The quote at the beginning of this chapter from Aristotle shows that poverty as the root cause of political violence has been taken for granted for at least two thousand years of recorded scholarship. As a result, the sight of these horrific killings prompted many well-meaning people to appeal for a less inequitable distribution of global resources. Like Aristotle, the South Korean winner of the Nobel Peace Prize, Kim Dae-Jung, in his acceptance speech, stated that: "At the bottom of terrorism is poverty."[3] His view was widely accepted by other members of the exclusive community of Nobel Laureates.[4] Some in the US, such as Laura Tyson, the former Chief of Presidential Council of Economic Advisors under the Clinton Administration and Dean of the Haas School of Business at Berkeley, called for a new Marshall Plan as part of a frontal assault on terrorism.[5]

Like poverty, religious fanaticism has also been a prime suspect for political violence and terrorism. The term "zealot" originated with the incidents of terrorism carried out by the members of a Jewish political movement of the first century AD.[6] The ancient historian Josephus chronicled their daring acts of violence, designed to draw the reticent Jewish community into a war against the occupying Roman forces. The popular press[7] as well as the political decision-makers quickly resorted to the image of irrational individuals carrying out desperate acts. They must have sacrificed their lives for the glory of God and for personal salvation.[8] And many others assumed a much more salacious reason: these men have killed themselves to fulfill some sort of sexual fantasy.[9] From cartoonists to late-night comedians, the media became full of jokes about having sex with 72 virgins in paradise.[10]

If these people were not prodded by poverty or inspired by religion, then there was only other possible explanation: they were crazy. The comment of John Warner, the powerful Chairman of the Senate Armed Services Committee, quoted at the beginning of the chapter, amply demonstrates this perception of terrorism.[11]

Despite the persistent stereotype of terrorists being poor and less educated than the rest of the population, quantitative evidence shows little direct causal link between economic deprivation and terrorist activities. A spate of empirical studies spanning the past three decades has failed to show any consistent pattern between terrorism and poverty.

When we examine the evidence, while some of these hypotheses offer partial explanation, none of the above factors offers a compelling rationale for an otherwise rational actor to participate in such acts of terrorism targeting innocent civilians. Although poverty and humiliation may play some part, contrary to the popular images, those who study terrorism, particularly the psychologists and psychiatrists who have interviewed the terrorists, are nearly unanimous in their assertion that these people show no hint of psychosomatic disorder.[12] The extensive documentations of hours of interview also demonstrate that most of the perpetrators were not whom we may call irrational religious zealots. While some of the participants in suicide attacks were inspired by religious reason,[13] there are many others who were not. For instance, while the Hizbullah in Lebanon is widely credited with the starting suicide attacks, the Sri Lankan Tamil Tigers perfected the use of humans as the weapons delivery system.[14] The Tigers (LTTE) were not, however, inspired by any religious vision. Neither was the Kurdish Workers Party, the PKK, or the Marxist Palestinian dissident group, the PFLP.[15] All these secular groups were able to use their human bombs without any promise of eternal afterlife.

The implosion of the Soviet Union in 1991 brought an end to the Cold War. As the threat of global Communism passed into distant memory, the US needed a moral anchor for its foreign policy. Quickly, the zeal to prevent Communism from spreading was replaced by a new mantra: the spread of democracy. The expedient policy of supporting some of the worst dictators and tyrants in the name of fighting the Cold War was now to be replaced by a new policy doctrine of democratic reforms. The introduction of democratic system was seen as the panacea of many social and political problems, including international terrorism. In the euphoria scholars and policy-makers alike embraced the new doctrine with evangelical zeal. Respected economist and philosopher Amartya Sen bravely termed democratic freedom as a right.[16] The idea of freedom of choice was germane in his discussion of functioning and capabilities, with which Sen analyzed the process of choice among competing goods.[17] Torn from its moral and philosophical moorings, the so-called "neo-cons" in the Bush White House took it as an article of faith that democracy was the best antidote against the spread of the most virulent forms of terrorist violence.[18] Unfortunately, despite the hope and the hype, democracy—liberal or illiberal—failed to deliver its promised goods.[19] The elections in occupied Iraq, with its much-touted pictures of the Iraqis flashing their purple-stained fingers, were quickly followed by a huge explosion of the incidents of terrorism. Even deeply democratic nations, from Great Britain to Spain, spawned homegrown suicide terrorists.

Aristotle famously said that real progress in knowledge is marked not by what we know but by defining more carefully what we don't know. New research redefining the expanding contours of ignorance leaves us with the need to reconcile the theories with deeply held suppositions. However, before we delve into the question of the root causes of terrorism, let us take a systematic view of the various theories of social behavior.

Analysis of terrorism and political violence: a theoretical perspective

Although terrorism has posed a problem for organized societies throughout history, until quite recently many academics refused to study it seriously. Among many social problems terrorism was perhaps considered at best a nuisance. Or, in some cases, some academics—particularly in the realm of social sciences—might have bought into the idea of the terrorists being crazed fanatics on quixotic missions to change the world. Having little to explain in terms of a generalized theory of terrorist behavior, social scientists, with the exception of political theorist David Rapoport,[20] economist Todd Sandler *et al.*,[21] and political scientist Martha Crenshaw,[22] showed little interest in terrorism research.[23] The pioneering efforts of these scholars sought to dispel the notion that acts of terrorism were random events, reflecting the deep emotional distress of the perpetrators. Among the policy analysts, the work of Brian Jenkins of RAND Corporation and Paul Wilkinson of University of St. Andrews, Scotland provided other notable early examples of systematic analysis of terrorism from a much more practical point of view. Their diverse work firmly established the fact that these are premeditated strategic actions, demonstrating a process of rational thinking. Over the next two decades, as the world started to experience the increasing impacts of terrorism, the academic world also began to pay attention. Yet, for many mainstream American scholars, these events took place in distant lands, resulting from forces that were of little interest to all but those who specialized in those areas of the world. For the academics, the study of terrorism remained relegated to special cases of the larger question of social movements.

The fateful September day of 2001, however, caused a radical shift as the coordinated attacks riveted the world's attention to the threats that such acts pose to the social, political, and economic order. Every generation defines its time with the help of some momentous event. Those who were alive at the time remember the VE Day, 8 May 1945, when the forces of Nazi Germany unconditionally surrendered to the Allied forces. Those who were old enough to remember would always recall the exact moment they heard the awful news that an assassin's bullets had taken the life of John F. Kennedy on 22 November 1963. Similarly, the images of airplanes going into the Twin Towers of the World Trade Center and people jumping from the skyscrapers on 9/11 will forever be seared into our memories.

The 9/11 attacks took the lives of nearly 3,000 people and altered the course of history. After the initial shock was over, the entire nation wanted to know who were these terrorists and why did they hate us so? Overnight, terrorism was everyone's concern, including the academics. The federal government started pouring substantial sums of money into the study of national security. Due to the increased demand from a nation thirsty for answers and the government providing the necessary funds, the number of books and articles that started to come out on the subject became almost mind boggling.

As trickles turn into a torrent, it is natural to take stock of the accumulated knowledge. A number of books and articles have done a great service to the readers by putting the burgeoning contributions to the understanding of global terrorism within a manageable framework.[24] The vastness of the existing literature requires an overall scheme of classification. In the following section of this chapter, I will present such a scheme from a behavioral perspective.

Before we begin this discussion, it is important to start with two important and interrelated caveats. As noted above, although terrorism has a long history, its systematic analysis has a short past. In fact, the earlier scholarly writings concerned themselves with social movements rather than terrorism. However, from my definition it should be clear that what we call "terrorism" is merely a strategy used by some dissident groups as a part of a larger social movement. Some choose non-violent methods, such as civil disobedience, others take up armed struggle. Within this latter group are some which target non-combatants, whom we call "terrorists."

The second caveat relates to my attempt to put the burgeoning literature on terrorism in a schematic form. It is useful to note at this point that these classifications are not airtight and, therefore, are merely heuristic ideal types with a considerable degree of conceptual overlap, both in the concept and in the approaches taken by individual scholars. Thus, many theories discussed in this chapter often transcend one single discipline. There is an inherent danger in attempting to pigeonhole diverse ideas. Yet, this tendency to generalize must be tempered with the need to have an overall road map of the vast literature on collective movement and terrorism.

A classification scheme of theories of collective movement and terrorism

Terrorism being a social phenomenon of extreme importance to a nation's concern for security, it is natural that the issue will be approached from a wide variety of standpoints with different objectives. For instance, when academic scholars write about terrorism, their goals include a systematic analysis of the problem, its root causes, and a rigorous investigation of its long-term trend. The journalists are much more existential in their pursuit and attempt to assess the current conditions through direct observation of the ground reality. The security experts typically concern themselves with a particular organization and/or its leadership to predict their immediate future actions. The high-level policy-makers write about the relative efficacy of policies dealing with terrorism. Any classification of a vast field of literature requires a specific perspective. My classification scheme reflects a behavioral perspective.

I have presented my classification scheme for analyzing social movements in general, and terrorism in particular, in Table 2.1. I start out with a broad

Table 2.1 Classification of theories of social movements and terrorism.

No specific theoretical foundation	*Studies based on theoretical paradigm*		
	No explicit behavioral assumption regarding human nature		*Explicit assumption regarding human nature (rational-choice models)*
Historical case studies	**Psychological theories**	**Marxist theories**	Rational-actor hypothesis
Journalistic studies	• Psychopathology	**Western sociological theories**	Game-theoretic models
Case studies by security experts and former intelligence officers	• Social psychology		
	• Social learning	• Modernization	
	• Identity theory	• Structural imbalance	
	• Narcissistic personality	• Relative deprivation	
	• Paranoia hypothesis	• Resource mobilization	
	Social psychological theories		
	• Social learning		
	• Frustration–aggression hypothesis		
	Cognitive theories		

dichotomy between those scholars who do not use any broad social-science theoretical framework to analyze the causes of terrorism and those who do. The vast majority of the books and articles do not use any specific theoretical structure. For instance, Walter Laqueur's classic study of terrorism is a historical analysis.[25] So are the works of eminent social and political historians such as Theda Skocpol[26] and David Rapoport.[27] Similarly, terrorism specialists, such as Paul Wilkinson,[28] Brian Jenkins,[29] Alex Schmid,[30] Bruce Hoffman,[31] Rohan Gunaratna,[32] and Jessica Stern,[33] have made valuable contributions to our understanding of the various issues of terrorism, yet none of these are grounded in any particular social theory. There are also numerous books and articles by eminent journalists[34] and former intelligence officers[35] which do not base their analyses on any particular assumption regarding human nature or subscribe to any sociological theory.

Among the works that are based on theoretical paradigms, where an author analyzes terrorism by using a set of generalized rules and then proceeds to corroborate their validity with empirical observation, there is yet another set of dichotomies. Some of the theories are based on an assumption of fundamental human nature, which guides an individual's decision-making process, while others make no assumption about individual rationality.[36] Those who do not begin with an assumption of human rationality develop theories of social movement from either the disciplinary distinctions of psychology or social sciences. Psychological theories once again can be directed toward the motivations of terrorists as individuals or as members of a particular group. While clinical psychologists and psychiatrists dominate the first sub-group, the latter is the primary preoccupation of social psychologists. Finally, those who analyze terrorism based on a specific assumption of human nature are economists and their progeny, the "rational choice" theorists.

By looking at Table 2.1, it is possible to inject yet another distinguishing characteristic between those who attempt to understand human behavior within a theoretical perspective but do not make any explicit assumption regarding human nature, and the economists who do. We may consider the first group of writings as "demand side" and the second group as "supply side." In other words, the demand-side theorists see rebellion arising out of a "need for rebellion" created by imbalances and injustices within the society. In contrast, the rational-choice theorists assume that rebellions occur because of the incentives and opportunities open to each group. The rational-choice theorists may not search for the "root causes" of dissent because the root causes inevitably stem from individuals' and groups' efforts at maximizing their self-interest. Therefore, a dissident group will choose to violently confront the government when it finds sufficient incentives (possibilities of reward) and opportunities (lowering of costs). Let us examine more closely the various theories of social movement and terrorism.

Psychological perspective

Psychologists analyze individual personalities to get a glimpse of their motivations for joining terrorist organizations. The early attempt at using psychodynamics to explain violent political behavior started with Freud himself. All his life, he had studied the problems of individual patients. To Freud, the human mind shows the interplay between id, ego, and superego. In Freudian psychology, each person is born with various instincts, which include the need to satisfy hunger and sexual urges. The id, however, does not distinguish between the internal mind and external environment. Thus, id only recognizes being hungry or being lustful. Id stimulates the drive to eat, for instance, but makes no distinction between the image of food and the food itself. The ego distinguishes between the two and bridges the gap between the initial drive and its satisfaction. Thus, ego would recognize the hunger for a specific food, say a hamburger. But ego does not consider the morality of action, which is left to the superego. Superego represents the social norms and checks the primal drives of the id. Thus, if I am an observant Hindu, I must not eat beef, just as Jews or Muslims must not eat pork, regardless how hungry I may feel. That I must restrict my food habit is a social and religious norm, which the superego imposes on my impulses.

In his psychoanalysis, Freud puts his patients on his famous couch and delves deep into their repressed sexuality as a result of various social norms. His analysis by its very nature is individual-centric. Through his clinical observations he had developed his theories of psychodynamics. In the later stage of his life, Freud became interested in applying his theory to a larger context of the society. In his book *Civilization and Its Discontents*, he argued that unresolved sexual issues motivate a revolutionary to act against the national authority figures.[37] Thus, when anarchists strike against the leaders of a nation, they are subconsciously acting on their hostility toward their father figure, out of an Oedipus complex.

Although the use of Freudian psychodynamics[38] has been waning in other areas, in the field of terrorism research it has found its wider use.[39] Taylor[40] recognized the conceptual problems associated with the Freudian approach, yet it remained one of the most important sources of psychological analysis of the terrorist personality, particularly in the 1970s and 1980s.[41] However, since psychiatry and psychoanalysis are driven by observations of individual behavior, the Freudian approach to the analysis of political violence was quickly picked up by scholars attempting to understand the motivations of the leaders. In this area, the work of Jerrold Post is most noteworthy.[42]

Psychopathogy

Reflecting the popular perception, the idea that many of those who take part in terrorist activities are, in fact, insane found its root in several psychological studies.[43] However, insanity is not only a medical term but also carries legal implications, since clinically insane persons are not sent to regular prisons but are sent to mental institutions.[44] As Victoroff points out, "insanity" in modern Western psychiatry is defined on a multi-axial scale, where axis I measures diagnosable clinical illnesses, such as schizophrenia, deep psychosis, and severe depression, while axis II measures personality disorder.[45] Thus, on the axis I, we measure individuals' ability to distinguish right from wrong (loss of reality), while the axis II scale measures their ability to empathize with their victims with full knowledge of right and wrong. Although systematic evaluation of clinical psychosis of perpetrators of terrorism is rare, those who have studied a significant number of terrorists have come to a near unanimous conclusion, a rarity in any field of academic research: while terrorist groups are sometimes led by people who may be classified as "insane," "psychopathic" (axis I), or "sociopathic" (axis II), the foot soldiers of terrorism are rarely diagnosed as such.[46] Recently, a number of studies have been conducted on the basis of detailed interviews of the terrorists and participants in the violent social movements by eminent psychiatrists or psychologists. Their collective work has significantly enhanced our knowledge base regarding the motivations of not only the leaders[47] but also the followers in the global campaigns of terrorism.[48]

Narcissism theory

The theory of Narcissistic personality as an explanation of terrorism is derived directly from Freudian psychoanalysis. Kohut extended Freud's original explanation of ego by asserting that when an individual's ego is damaged in childhood as a result of lack of maternal empathy, children develops a Narcissistic personality, whereby they experience persistent grandiose fantasies and become unable to grasp the full implications of their actions on others.[49] Based on the detailed analysis of a number of West German leftist radicals[50] and a number of other extremist group members,[51] scholars have extended this notion of a damaged ego from parental lack of empathy to a feeling of humiliation experienced through the political process. As a result, there "might be a pathological exaltation of self (the genesis of the leader), the abandonment of independence to merge with the archaic omnipotent figure (the genesis of the follower), or a combination of these impulses, as seen in the egotistical yearning for glory under the mask of selflessness."[52] Eyad Sarraj, the noted Palestinian psychologist, having treated a number of those who have participated in the killings of Israeli civilians, has argued for the feeling of humiliation as adults as the primary motivating force for joining radical groups.[53]

Social psychological theories

Psychological theories, derived primarily from Freudian psychology, are dominated by the clinicians and psychiatrists who attempt to understand individual personality traits. In their many-faceted research they often look for diagnosable disorders, such as paranoia, delusion, schizophrenia, or severe depression. In their analysis, the society enters as the backdrop. In contrast, social psychologists focus primarily on the interaction between an individual and the society. They see their field of study as "the systematic study of social behavior. It deals with how we perceive other people and social situations, how we respond to others and they to us, and in general how we are affected by social situations."[54]

Frustration–aggression theory

Among scholars looking for the root causes of violent rebellion, frustration and anger have the longest lineage, going back to Aristotle.[55] In more modern times, in the field of non-Freudian psychology, frustration–aggression hypothesis has generated a large number of studies. The idea, first proposed by Dollard *et al.*, causally linked frustration—defined as interference with goal-directed behavior—felt by an individual to violent actions, designed to remove the source of frustration.[56] The direct off-shoot of this age-old supposition found a solid footing in political science during the late 1960s and early 1970s within the rubric of "relative deprivation" theory. We will have a chance to discuss it later when we consider the social-science literature on collective movement.

Identity and paranoia theories

One branch of psychodynamic theory treats prejudice (leading to group violence) as a personality disorder. In the best-known work, which is often credited with starting the field of social psychology, a group of scholars funded by the American Jewish Committee in the immediate aftermath of World War II began an impressive project to understand how an entire German community could participate in something so horrendous as the Holocaust. The extensive report, published in 1950,[57] came to the conclusion that German anti-Semitism developed from a particular personality type called the "authoritarian personality." They argued that authoritarian pro-clivity is the result of four factors: (1) rigid adherence to conventional values and patterns of behavior, coupled with harsh punishments for slight deviations; (2) an exaggerated need to submit to, and identify with, strong authority figures; (3) a generalized environment of hostility; and (4) a mystical, superstitious frame of mind.

In the subsequent years the idea of wanting to belong to a group and assume a collective identity became the focus of many scholars in the nascent field of social psychology. In a series of experiments, researchers expanded on and demonstrated the overall validity of Erik Erikson's[58] theory that adolescents reach a stage of identity formation at which point group affiliation assists in their self-definition. For instance, famous experiments by Sherif[59] and Sherif and Hovland[60] clearly demonstrated the importance of groups in the human decision-making process and learning to be prejudiced against others. Stanley Milgram (1974) showed our proclivity to follow orders from an authority figure. Henri Tajfel revealed our fundamental desire to form bonds with members of the "in-group" (friends and allies) and act against those whom we consider as our enemies ("out-group").[61] These studies in experimental psychology advanced our understanding of collective movements in general, and terrorism in particular. Psychologist Jerrold Post moved the analysis of the formation of collective analysis an important step forward by establishing a link between leaders and their followers. Through his many studies, he showed that the proclivity of followers to act violently toward the members of the out-group is particularly pronounced when their leaders espouse a paranoid ideology of hate.[62]

Social-learning theories

In contrast with the identity theories, where the authors speak of the followers' identification with a larger group on the basis of preordained ascriptive or birth characteristics,[63] the proponents of the social-learning theory, originally proposed by social psychologist Bandura,[64] claim that violence toward another group is a learned behavior. Thus, to them, the reason young men and women join violent dissident groups is not because of any innate aggressiveness but for cognitive reconstruction of moral imperative inculcated by the social milieu within which a child is brought up. Thus, a child growing up in the Palestinian refugee camps in Lebanon or in Gaza is surrounded by pictures of the martyrs, those who gave their lives for the glorification of God and for trying to drive the Israelis out of the occupied land. In such a situation, children internalize the value system, and learn to differentiate between good and evil, rightful owners and the occupiers, oppressed and the oppressors. The children—similar to all others in the world—reflect the cultural, political, and religious values imbued in the environment surrounding them. In Pakistan, for example, the recent hub of Islamic extremism, students are indoctrinated through the Madrassa (religious school) system from their early childhood.[65] Nearly all of these students come from the lower economic strata of the Pakistani society, where the parents send their children to get at least some rudimentary education and, more importantly, perhaps, to get them fed through the school system. As a result, it becomes natural for an Catholic child growing up in the mean streets of Belfast to join the IRA, a Palestinian to join Hamas, a Tamil growing up in the Jaffna peninsula to enlist in the LTTE, or a Pakistani to join groups espousing *jihad*.

Cognitive theories

The cognitive theories aim at understanding the ultimate frontier of human understanding, the process by which our brains process information to arrive at a decision. In the Western tradition, we assume a complete separation between emotion and reasoning. What is emotional cannot be rational. Yet, in the recent developments in the process of cognitive decision-making, we are confounded by the complexity which shrouds the path through which we make our decisions from mundane, everyday matters to momentous decision that shape our lives. How do we decide which toothpaste to buy, for instance? Is it the price, the color, the taste, or the impact of a recently viewed advertisement, which equates its use with something magical? Or, is this process significantly (and qualitatively) different from the way an individual decides to become a suicide attacker?

Recent scientific discoveries have produced some highly significant counter-intuitive results. In the Western tradition, reason is seen as strictly separated from emotion. The sixteenth-century French Philosopher René Descartes proudly proclaimed: *cogito ergo sum*—"I think therefore I am." The idea that the essence of humanity rests with its ability for dispassionate reasoning has since been the bedrock on which the Age of Reason is founded. Yet, Damasio showed that contrary to the fundamental assumption of Western rational thinking, there is no wall separating reason from emotion.[66] Damasio narrates the case history of a patient who underwent brain surgery to remove a benign tumor and woke up with a completely new personality. Although he had all his analytical faculty in tact, there was an important difference: he had no emotion. An irreversible damage to the prefrontal cortices had robbed him of his emotional responses. As a consequence, he became a perfect analytical machine with no emotion or feeling.[67] He was thus the embodiment of human rationality, where decisions could be made without any passion. Unfortunately, this man was a miserable failure in life. Given a number of options, he could do excellent analyses pointing out their respective costs and benefits, but in the end, did not know which one he wanted the most. Thus, Damasio, in his provocative book, pointed out that rational thinking cannot be separated from emotional responses; Descartes was wrong, after all. Based on findings such as these, a new branch of analytical writings has sprung up in political science and economics, where the researchers are literally putting under the microscope the way our brains process information.[68]

Aggregate social-structural theories

Sociologists and political scientists hypothesize that social and political movements take place as a result of imbalances within the social structure. The vast sociological literature on social movements can be broadly dichotomized into Marxist and non-Marxist.

Karl Marx and Marxist theories of revolution

Karl Marx argued that the capitalist system of production dissociates laborers from their own fruits of labor. As a result, they feel alienated. Their alienation gives birth to political actions ("class struggle") against the capitalist socio-political and economic superstructure.[69] Practicing Marxists throughout the world based their revolutionary activities on the theory of class struggle. In this struggle it is not important to focus on the psychological aspects of an individual since their participation is the outcome of the manifest destiny of the flawed system. Therefore, although "alienation" is a psychological term, Marx and his followers were by no means interested in the psychological state of an individual. They assumed that the proletariats were already frustrated and angry due to their inability to control their own means of production. However, because of the presence of religious beliefs ("the opiate of the masses") and other epiphenomena, such as nationalism and ethnic identity, they are unable to recognize the true source of their angst. As soon as the true nature of the production relationship is revealed to them, the proletariat would take up arms against the capitalist system, which is based on their exploitation by the bourgeoisie. To Marx, the role of the revolutionary leadership is to educate the proletariat of their only true identity: their economic class. The practitioners of Marxist politics agreed with his broader analysis but differed as to how this "realization" could be brought about. While Mao[70] and Lenin[71] proposed extensive "education" for the "politicization of the masses," Guevarra,[72] Marighela,[73] and other Marxist revolutionaries, such as the leader of the Naxalite movement in India, Charu Mazumdar,[74] argued for armed insurrection to serve as the catalyst force to ignite the fire of class hatred.

Non-Marxist theories

At the root of all social movement there is the presence of a collective identity. Among the non-Marxist writers, Max Weber was among the earliest writers to point out the nature of socially constructed ethnic identity, which he called the "human groups." These groups were constructed on the basis of a mythological belief in a common ancestry.[75] Although Weber held that the basis of ethnic nationalism is fictitious, this belief provides a strong motivating force for large-scale mobilization.

The question is, how are these identities formed? The *primordialists*, mostly anthropologists, argue that identity is based on ascriptive or birth characteristics; these are "biologically given" at birth.[76] The primordialists pointed out that children born in a particular ethnic, linguistic, or religious group grow up with a definite sense of community, which not only provides them with a shared belief in a number of areas of social existence, but also accords them a sense of psychological comfort of belonging.[77] Clearly, not all collective identities are based on racial, ethnic, linguistic, or tribal identity,[78] and many of these identities are formed around perception of cultural differences within these sources of ascriptive characteristics.[79]

In contrast to the primordialists who often seem to be arguing for the formation of groups for their own sake, the instrumentalists contend that groups are formed to obtain certain specific political or economic advantages. In other words, these groups are formed to extract some instrumental rewards from a larger community.[80] From the perspective of instrumentalists, aspects of collective identity are invoked and manipulated by political entrepreneurs to create a political pressure point to extract some economic or political benefits or to respond to a situation of threat.

The constructivists, on their part, categorically reject that idea that collective identity is either inherited at birth or manipulated by political entrepreneurs for a stated political or economic purpose. Instead, by extending Max Weber's original claim, they contend that these identities are socially constructed and take on a life of their own.[81]

Modernization and grievance

Having discussed the sources of group identity from a societal perspective, let us now turn our attention to the factors that bring two groups to a violent conflict. A number of scholars see sociopolitical conflicts as the outcomes of an inevitable clash between the traditional values and the forces of modernization. Much of the literature on modernization stems from the writings of the late nineteenth-century French scholar Emile Durkheim. In his defining book *The Division of Labor in Society*, Durkheim called the advanced indus-trialized societies "mechanically integrated."[82] In these technological societies the economic roles are divided along multiple roles, which renders the trad-itional divisions of ethnicity, class, or caste irrelevant. As a result, every citizen becomes dependent on every other citizen, and each one becomes a small part of a large jigsaw puzzle that can only be contemplated when each performs his or her particular role.[83] When the traditional role comes in conflict with the new challenges of the modern times, mass movements are generated.[84]

Along similar lines, James Berber, for instance, calls the conflict *Jihad versus McWorld*.[85] The world of jihad is defined by the adherence of strict codes of conduct, where conformity is valued and expressions of individualism are suspect. When this world comes in contact with the McWorld, where the golden arches compete with spires of churches and the domes of the mosques, the culture clash upsets not only the traditional values but also undermines the traditional authority structure, which inevitably produces violent outbursts of protest. Within this theoretical perspective, sociopolitical conflicts are viewed as the unintended consequences of the modernization process, a birth pang for the deliverance of truly industrialized societies.

Theories of social-structural imbalance

A number of prominent sociologists and political scientists have sought reasons for political instability and rebellion within the folds of social struc-ture. Social-structural imbalances take place when a society fails to assimilate a group of people within it, and conflicts are generated from social-structural strains due to widespread poverty, inequality, etc. Some have argued that conflicts are essentially the outcome of lack of political legitimacy of those in power, while others contend that when the demands on the polity outstrip its ability to deliver, social order tends to break down.

Among the social-structural theorists, the work of Deutsch and Smelser is most prominent. Mass movements do not just take place simply because some people are alienated since they cannot cope with the demands of the modern times. Mass movements take place when there is a mobilization of disaffected individuals. Karl Deutsch developed the concept of "mobiliza-tion," where mobilization does not mean gathering of a large number of people, but the creation of a national identity.[86] He theorized that mass movements and ethnic conflicts are produced when a nation fails to assimilate a portion of its population. These people facing a gap in assimilation develop a separate national identity based on their desire to belong to a group in order to cope with the fears of economic, political, and psychological insecurity. When mobilization outpaces assimilation, according to Deutsch a violent movement is born.

Neil Smelser draws on a large canvas to explain violent social movements.[87]

Smelser identifies six conditions that lead to structural strain. These are *structural conduciveness* (the regime's response to protest), *structural strain* (factors of economic grievances), *growth of generalized belief* (spread of belief among the people linking the grievances to its source), *precipitating events* (historical events that serve as the trigger for launching a movement), *mobilization of participants* (organizational efficacy in developing a large-scale mobilization), and *ineffective social control* (ability of a regime to suppress dissent). Smelser argues that these six factors create what he called "value added," which leads to conflict.

In contrast to Smelser, who stresses largely economic factors, Lipset and Huntington identify the political aspects of social conflict. Lipset argues that at root of a civil society is the acceptance of the rulers by the ruled.[88] This is the essence of political legitimacy. Violent conflicts are born when the state authorities lose political legitimacy among a segment of the population. Thus, I may not agree with the policies of the President of the US, but as long as I do not question the occupant of the White House's legal authority to preside over the nation, the Administration enjoys political legitimacy in my view. However, if a number of us question the occupant's political legitimacy, a social movement appears.

In a similar vein, Samuel Huntington saw social unrest as an imbalance between demand and supply of political goods.[89] As citizens we demand a host public goods—reduction of poverty, corruption, protection from threat, etc.—from our government. However, when the demand outstrips the government's ability to supply, violent protests erupt.

Relative deprivation

Insightful as they were, the early efforts at linking sociopolitical and economic inequalities to rebellions and insurrections did not address the critical question of testing the hypotheses with the help of empirical investigations. In the post-World War II political and sociological literature, internal social conflicts are often assumed to be the phenomena of poverty-stricken countries. The structural theorists were happy attempting to explain rebellion in the rapidly changing Third world nations, the decades of 1960s and 1970s saw a rising tide of dissident activities in the affluent West, where the structural inequities were supposed to be low. Davies,[90] Feierabend and Feierabend,[91] and Gurr[92] attempted to provide an answer to this puzzle by attempting to fuse an essentially individual-based theory of aggression, proposed by Dollard *et al.*, to the structural conditions of a society.[93] They argued that when expectation outstrips achievement—regardless of the absolute levels of economic consumption or the provision of political rights—frustration is generated. The collective frustration turns to anger and, hence, to violence.

Concerns over mass rebellion and terrorism in Europe and North America led to a significant increase in government funding for collecting quantitative data on various aspects of political violence.[94] The accumulated numerical information gave a shot in the arm for quantitative research into mass movements and allowed researchers to test hypotheses with statistical techniques.

By culling the existing literature, we may define poverty-induced deprivation in one of three ways. First, we may define "poverty" as a source of individual or "egotistical deprivation," where an individual takes part in violent political activities out of his personal feeling of anger. Much of the information for these studies is gathered from direct face-to-face interviews of the participants in terrorist activities[95] or from other secondary sources, such as arrest reports.[96] The second group of studies focuses on "fraternal deprivation" or deprivation felt by individuals as members of a group. This is a situation where individual actors might feel that while they may not have personally experienced discrimination, poverty, or humiliation, their intense sense of deprivation is the product of a shared concept felt by an entire community or group.[97] Third, empirical studies examine whether the macro structural variables such as per capita income, rate of poverty, or inequality in income distribution are causally correlated with terrorism and other forms of sociopolitical violence.[98]

Most of the studies of individual (or egotistical) deprivation find the contrary result that the ranks of the violent revolutionaries are not filled by those from the poorest segments of the population but by scions of the middle- and upper-middle class families. The macro-level studies linking aggregate measures of poverty and deprivation, similarly, show a mixed bag of results. When it comes to international terrorism, there is little evidence that the poorest countries export attackers, particularly to the Western nations. Similarly, while many poor countries experience widespread violence and outbreaks of civil wars, many others do not.

A group of scholars, journalists and academics have conducted highly influential studies examining the importance of scarce natural resources in generating civil wars among the poorest nations on earth.[99] Fearon and Leitin show that, when started, particularly in the poorer parts of the world, these civil wars continue to spawn violence for decades to come.[100] They also claim that when controlled for per capita income, the more ethnically or religiously divided societies are no more prone to violence than those which are more homogeneous. Unfortunately, their analysis does not shed light on protracted conflicts in the developed worlds, such as the IRA and ETA.[101] Although Collier and others bring important issues to the fore, it is important to note that the notion of scarcity of resources is a relative concept and is a socially constructed condition. For instance, in Saudi Arabia water is much more of a scarce commodity than oil. The chances of violence escalate when a society attributes value to a particular scarce resource and fails to find a way to distribute it fairly.

Among these studies, only those looking for a shared feeling of deprivation ("fraternal deprivation"), for instance the Palestinians, the Maghreb Arabs in Europe, find a more consistent set of results linking poverty among a specific ethnolinguistic or religious group with acts of terrorism.[102] Some point out that more than economic poverty, it is the sense of humiliation and injustice that a group feels gives birth to acts of political violence.[103]

Another group of scholars attempt to establish a link between social movements and factors of economic inequality within nations. For instance, several examined its causal link with land distribution.[104] Gupta shows that political violence is generated in societies where income is concentrated in the hands of a few, particularly when such redistribution comes at the expense of the middle class.[105] Unfortunately, the results, based on cross-national analyses, often produce a mixed bag of relatively weak correlations, demonstrating the fundamental weakness of the macro theories of revolution. Social, economic, and political inequalities do provide the necessary conditions for violent uprising, but they are not sufficient causes. In other words, acts of rebellion do not take place simply because there is widespread frustration. For that they need additional factors.

Resource-mobilization theory

The search for the sufficient causes of political violence propelled a number of prominent sociologists to offer theories of resource mobilization.[106] Their theory points to the need of social networks to channel the individual frustrations and alienations into a coherent collective action. In this theory the community institutions and social networks become effective mobilization vehicles for collective action when the dissident leadership can draw on shared beliefs and worldviews that motivate individual actors and legitimize the acts of rebellion. Although the resource-mobilization theory attempts to bring about a synthesis between social-structural theories and psychological theories, the problem it faces is that a theory of rebellion based on leadership and social networking is not amenable to the testing of hypotheses based on statistical techniques. Therefore, those who have attempted to offer quantitative evidence have faced a number of serious methodological problems.[107]

Models of individual behavior: the rational-choice theory

The triumphant march of individualism that saw human beings separate from an overarching collective started with the onset of the Protestant Reformation.[108] The Age of Reason allowed each one in the society to evaluate his or her own relationship with God and, in the process, firmly established the primacy of individualism.[109] However, its culmination saw its ultimate manifestation in the work of a Scottish customs officer. The publication of Adam Smith's book *The Wealth of Nations* in 1776 coincided with the revolution on the other side of the Atlantic. Yet the impact of this epochal work on our philosophical tradition was no less revolutionary. In his book, Smith chose an essentially selfish, perennially self-utility maximizing the individual as the sole building block of his theoretical edifice. Being born in the market place, the assumption of self-utility maximization was so intuitively obvious that nearly a hundred years after the publication of Smith's book, Edgeworth, one of the founding fathers of neoclassical economics, asserted that "the first principle of Economics is that every agent is actuated only by self-interest."[110] This basic assumption of human motivation has since been the fundamental building block of economics as a social science.

The reduction of a complex being into one single motivational force allowed Smith to systematically analyze people's market behavior.[111] The readily understood mono-motivational force became the driving engine for the later development of economics as a "social science" much the same way as the Newtonian theory of gravitation contributed toward the understanding of the movement of the celestial bodies.

The end of the seventeenth century shook up the world of astronomy with the gradual acceptance of Isaac Newton's theory of gravitation and mechanics. Since the earth goes around its axis as it orbits the sun, with all other planetary bodies having their own orbital path, the movements of the planets look chaotic indeed to an earth-bound observer. Therefore, the medieval astronomers had to specialize in a single planet. They would track its path over the years and, based on decades of observation, could predict its movement. The Venus specialist, for instance, would have little to say about the movement of Mars. It all changed when Newtonian mechanics, ranked among humanity's greatest achievements in abstract thought, made their specialized job obsolete. With the help of his laws of gravitation, a model could be created which would generalize the theories of planetary movements. By using his formulae one could explain complex movements for all the revolving bodies around the sun.

The quick success of physics in developing models based on universal laws of nature placed it at the top of scholarly disciplines. The beauty of the argument in physics rests with its ability to express a seemingly complex behavior with the help of a very small number of explanatory variables. The exalted position of physics after the publication of Newton's work in the 1680s was matched by a revolution in the discipline of economics (often known as "moral physics" in those days) nearly a hundred years later with the publication of Adam Smith's *The Wealth of Nations*. Although it is a matter of some controversy as to how much Adam Smith was influenced by the intellectual revolution wrought by the Newtonian discoveries,[112] most scholars see a definite connection. Thus, Hetherington points out that "Adam Smith's efforts to discover the general laws of economics were directly inspired and shaped by the examples of Newton's success in discovering the natural laws of nature."[113] Analogous to the Newtonian physics, Smith reduced human behavior to a single source of motivation, self-interest.[114] By using such a truncated view of human nature, economists were able to develop intricate mathematical models for analyzing human behavior. Economics, originally conceived to explain behavior in a market place, was blessed by the fact that many of its outcomes are readily quantifiable. Thus, the aspects of demand and supply of tangible goods provided the much needed empirical evidence for statistical verification of the proffered hypotheses. What we cannot measure, however, is the driving forces behind this demand, which the economists conveniently call "utility."

The concept of utility, which is so germane to the development of the discipline of economics, has been a source of controversy from the beginning. Can utility be measured in units? The utilitarians, such as Jeremy Betham, around 1815, theorized that it could. They assumed (and held as self-evident) that the utility of a single dollar given to a rich person will be less than that of a poor destitute. Thus, finding a $100 bill will have a far less significant impact on the life of a billionaire than on the lives of a homeless family. The pursuit of this line of argument led some of the utilitarians to a radical policy prescription. Since this money will do more good to the latter, the total utility of a society would go up if wealth is redistributed from the rich to the poor, until the point where everyone is equally well off. To counter this argument, economists, and particularly a Swiss Italian named Wilfredo Pareto, insisted that the marginal (an additional unit) utility of money is non-measurable. Therefore, no social good could come through a redistribution of wealth. Since the source of demand for a good remains buried in individual psychology, economists had to overcome the "contaminating" effects of myriad psychological factors. This issue was resolved in the 1950s, when economist Paul Samuelson offered his theory of *revealed preference*. He argued that there is no need to measure utility or preferences, since when we demand a certain product, we essentially reveal our preferences. Economists, therefore, could theorize about human actions without having to explain the sources of their motivations.

The need to explain motivation was further diminished with the publication of a seminal paper by two stalwarts in the field. George Stigler and Gary Becker, in their seminal article "De Gutibus non est Disputandum" ("There is No Disputing about Taste"), argued that an individual's preferences should be judged solely on his self-interest.[115] What about culture, social norm, historical, and individual idiosyncrasies? Stigler and Becker answered that they could all be seen as "taste," which we take for granted and do not need to include in the economic models.

Unfettered by the need to explain individual differences of "taste," economics could now claim to be a true dispassionate science, unencumbered by history or culture. Similar to the Newtonian physics, economists could now concentrate on developing elegant mathematical models and test their hypotheses with sophisticated econometric techniques. Philosopher of science Karl Popper argued that a science must be able to offer hypotheses that are "falsifiable" with empirical evidence. Since theories of metaphysics (beyond physics or the physical world), such as god, soul, or spirit, cannot be proven or disproven with empirical data, any assertions about them cannot pass as matters of scientific inquiry. Economics, the first among the social sciences, could pass the test of a true science by criteria laid down by the noted epistemologist.[116]

The success of economics in developing a scientific analytical structure did not remain confined within its disciplinary boundaries. Although born out of the need to understand market behavior, it quickly spilled over into other sister disciplines of social sciences, particularly political science and sociology by the name of rational-choice theory. Exchange at the market place lies at the heart of economics. Finding the rules of such controlled conflict is the essence of economics. Similarly exchange is also at the core of all our social political intercourse. Therefore, the rules established in economics found ready acceptance among many in political science and sociology. Thus, rational-choice theorists, by assuming that each individual is a self-motivated actor, sought to generalize rules for forming alliances or engaging in political conflicts and in social interaction.[117] Therefore, Stigler and Becker may be forgiven for their imperial hubris when they asserted: "Our hypothesis is trivial, for it merely asserts that we should apply standard economic logic as extensively as possible."[118]

This success soon allowed economics and its progeny, the rational-choice theories, to impose their hegemonic control over other branches of social sciences.[119] The popularity of rational-choice theory in the realm of political sciences began with the publication of Anthony Down's seminal work and quickly became a recognized discipline.[120]

The name "rational choice" is loaded with a number of overt and covert important implications. To begin with, the rational choice not only models an actor's decision-making calculus, it proceeds to define *rationality* itself. It tells us that rational people take decisions based on the assessment of expected benefits and costs of each action to the actor alone and that to do otherwise is "irrational," or, a bit more charitably, "a-rational."

The precept of economic rationality can be applied to the action of a single participant in an act of political rebellion,[121] or a rebel organization,[122] or to a state actor.[123] These analyses of human behavior are based on the ubiquitous assumption of self-utility maximization by a "rational" actor, where rationality is strictly interpreted as following the dictates of maximization of narrowly defined self-interest.

Understanding behavior of a rational group

The economic concept of "rational" behavior of an individual can easily be extended to the motivation of a group. When we consider the group as a single entity, we can assume that it behaves "rationally," that is, it aims at maximizing its own welfare. In economics, the advancement in the field of game theory has enhanced our knowledge in situations when two rivals face off in a strategic game.[124] Although there are numerous types of games, including ones that can include multiple players, the most famous is what is known as "prisoner's dilemma." The fundamental contribution of this game is that it provides insight into how two parties facing each other often settle for a solution that is not in the best interest of either. This happens fundamentally because the two do not trust one another and, as a result, instead of reaching a point of negotiated settlement, which would have been the best, settle for suboptimal solutions.

In sum

In this chapter I have presented the vast literature on social movements, political violence, and terrorism within a schematic classification. Needless to say, such pigeonholing can lead to oversimplification of a rich scientific tradition. Yet I believe that my classification allows the reader a bird's eye view, which is essential to a multidisciplinary understanding of social conflict. In light of this discussion, I will present my hypothesis in the following chapter.

3 Selfish altruist

Modeling the mind of a terrorist

> Perhaps the worst impairment comes from the neglect—and denial—of the role of reasoning and choice, which follows from the recognition of our plural identities.
>
> Amartya Sen[1]

Accounting for action: the problems of working for a common good

Acts of terrorism and political violence originate in every corner of the earth spanning history, culture, and ideological orientation. Yet, the only common thread that binds the diverse acts of those who take part in terrorism and other politically motivated violence is their professed claim of striving to achieve a common good for their community. This common good stems from an effort to alter the prevailing power position along the principles of a specific religious view, ethno-nationalism, or economic class. Kellen, therefore, is entirely correct in pointing out that a "terrorist without a cause (at least in his own mind) is not a terrorist."[2] This ubiquitous pursuit of altruistic goals separates a terrorist from a common criminal. Hence, without understanding the source of this altruistic motivation, we simply cannot comprehend terrorism. Yet, similar to every human being, those who engage in altruistic behavior are not without their selfish motivations. The Western social sciences tell us precious little about this complex being with mixed motives. Therefore, in this chapter I will propose a theoretical perspective to understand and analyze collective actions, such as terrorism.

Toward this goal, in this chapter, I will first briefly examine the three main philosophical traditions: the neoclassical economics, the Darwinian theory of evolution, and the Freudian psychology that have shaped the me-centric view of mainstream Western thought, where acts of altruism are often unrecognized, suspect as a cynical ploy for some other ulterior motives, or are pushed outside the realm of analysis altogether as anomalous behavior. In the second section, I will offer my own hypothesis based on an expanded view of human rationality. By bringing in recent work in social psychology with economics, I will attempt a fuller explanation of human as social animals. I will argue that in order to understand human motivations, we must include our proclivity to join groups and to work toward its welfare along with the standard assumption of economics, which views human beings as perennial pursuers of self-utility. This expanded view of rationality will allow us to take a fresh look at collective actions, in general, and terrorism, in particular.

The one-dimensional being

In the Western liberal tradition, which holds individualism at its core, we can readily understand behavior prompted by greed and passion; we can even fathom sudden impulses. What we have trouble understanding is well-planned acts of self-sacrifice, which are seen as the outcome of "rational calculation" by the human mind.

Today we take the liberal values of individualism for granted. Similar to breathing in oxygen, we are rarely mindful of its all-encompassing existence. Thus, the French philosopher of science Michel Foucault calls the assumption of me-centric individualism "positive consciousness of knowledge," which he defines as "a level that eludes the consciousness of the scientists and yet is a part of scientific discourse."[3] Although, according to Foucault, the primacy of individualism emerged fitfully from the penumbra of the collective around the seventeenth century,[4] similar to any revolutionary shift in paradigm—from faith to reason—it evolved slowly over many generations of scholarship.[5] For instance, the early strings of individualism can be traced back to the thirteenth century Catholic theological writings of St. Thomas Aquinas, who saw human intellect as independent of divine revelation.[6] These ideas took a more definite shape in the works of Thomas Hobbes. While his conclusions of needing the Leviathan, an all-powerful beast of national government under a benevolent Christian prince, can hardly be regarded as liberal, Hobbesian postulates were highly individualistic. Hobbes explicitly rejected the traditional theories based on religious interpretation and deduced societal obligations and political rights from the self-utility of the essentially dissociated individuals. This is the notion of a value-neutral being "essentially the proprietor of his own person or capacities, owing nothing to society for them," that served as the stepping stool for the philosophy of individualism.[7]

The quick success of physics in developing models based on universal laws of nature placed it at the top of scholarly disciplines. The beauty of the Newtonian logic in physics rests on its ability to express a seemingly complex behavior with the help of a very small number of explanatory variables. As I discussed in the previous chapter, the exalted position of physics after the publication of Newton's work in the 1680s was matched by a revolution in the discipline of economics nearly a hundred years later with the publication of Adam Smith's *The Wealth of Nations* in 1776.

The perennially self-serving individualism, which forms the foundation of

Western philosophical thought, was reinforced by the development of two other powerful intellectual traditions. Nearly a hundred years after the publication of *The Wealth of Nations*, Charles Darwin published *On the Origins of Species by Means of Natural Selection, Or the Preservation of Favoured Races in the Struggle for Life*. His primary premise—particularly as understood by the public at large as well as many in the academic community—was that the incommutable law of nature compels each living organism, from a single cell amoeba to a human being, to submit to the law of survival of the fittest. Therefore, through all our actions, consciously or unconsciously, we strive to outbid others in order to make sure that not only we survive, but also that we are able to leave our genetic materials in our offspring. Thus, in the animal world each animal tries to be the alpha animal, often through brutal fights, so that they can have the right to mate with the fittest female(s). This is the iron law of nature. By extending it to its fullest stretch, Dawkins argues that in the ultimate analysis, all of us are nothing more than receptacles of the DNA molecules.[8] These molecules attempt to survive by making every organism preserve their own strands. Thus, Dawkins argues that to be selfish is in our genetic makeup.

The Darwinian theory produced two unintended consequences. First, among some biologists, it promoted the myth that evolution was a linear process.[9] Second, to many others, particularly to those in the then nascent field of social sciences, evolution implied progress. After all, with nearly every stalwart in the Western intellectual tradition for the past two centuries directly or indirectly mentioning "natural law," the Darwinian theory of evolution provided a perfect basis to introduce it to social sciences. Moreover, it contained a strong moral message. The influence of Darwin's findings quickly spilled over into the realms of social sciences through the works of Herbert Spencer.[10] The Social Darwinists saw in the market process the reflection of the law of nature, where the fittest are rewarded with riches and the unfit are relegated to poverty.[11] Needless to say, such a theory became instantly popular with the Nuevo riche of American society, who started sponsoring academics professing Social Darwinism. Many top universities benefited from such benevolence, particularly the University of Chicago. Through their effort, the essence of Social Darwinism, however flawed, became part of Western consciousness. The basic congruity between natural selection and economic process caused a natural fusion between biology and economics. A number of biologists took some of the basic economic models and attempted to understand the process of evolution.

The other stream of influence that placed the individual in its exalted position in the Western intellectual tradition is the result of the overwhelming influence of Sigmund Freud. Although Freudian psychology is based on clinical observations of individual patients, toward the end of his life Freud aimed at explaining social violence and violent rebellions. In his book *Civilization and Its Discontents*, Freud uses the same tools for individual psychoanalysis and, in effect, puts the whole of society on the couch. His macro-level study of conflict was also based on an individual's primal needs based on id, ego, and superego. Freud saw in rebellion against authority figures by men an expression of the subconscious Oedipal complex, where the multitude rise up in arms as a result of their urge to slay their father figures, the rulers of a nation. The women revolutionaries join the forces of dissidence out of their penis envy.

The confluence of these three great philosophical traditions—in Neoclassical economics, Darwinian biology, and Freudian psychology—paved the way for the universal acceptance of the logic of individual utility maximization as the sole definition of human rationality, and ultimately it became what Foucult calls "positive consciousness of knowledge." While we may disdain criminal and other deviant acts, we can readily recognize their perverse logic. However, what truly baffle us are the acts of extreme altruism and self-sacrifice; in our bewilderment we find it convenient to regard them as "irrational" or, a bit more charitably, "a-rational."

The precept of economic rationality can be applied to the action of a single participant in an act of political rebellion,[12] or a rebel organization,[13] or to a state actor.[14] These analyses of human behavior are based on the ubiquitous assumption of self-utility maximization by a "rational" actor, where rationality is strictly interpreted as following the dictates of maximization of narrowly defined self-interest. There are several important analytical problems with the assumption of individual short-term *selfish* utility maximization.

The list of critics of the truncated view of human nature since its very inception, however, is indeed long.[15] The penchant to place all human actions within the confines of a restrictive view of human motivations saw two movements. While Western social sciences saw the development of the rational-choice school, starting in the 1950s, a contrasting view resulting from an effort to understand how people *actually behave* as opposed to how they *ought to behave* was shaping up under a broad and extremely loose rubric of behavioralism. In his presidential address to the American Political Science Association, Robert Dahl began by noting that "Perhaps the most striking characteristic of the 'behavioral approach' in political science is the ambiguity of the term."[16] The behavioral approach in the US was started by the "radicals" in academia and was greatly aided by the infusion of new ideas from Europe as well as the development of survey methods as a tool of analysis, which gave researchers a window into the minds of the people. Yet, at the end, the reductionist view of human nature triumphed despite the fact that its orthodoxy came under fire from a long list of luminaries.

Economist Amartya K. Sen in his influential essay "The Rational Fools" emphatically states that "universal selfishness as *actuality* may well be false, but universal selfishness as a requirement of *rationality* is patently absurd" (emphasis in original).[17] Others, such as philosopher Herbert Marcuse, saw a much more sinister implication of this assumption.[18] To him the assumption of economic rationality was pregnant with motives of class oppression and the maintenance of the status quo by the elites of the society. However, the most important demonstration of the shortcomings of this fundamental assumption of human rationality came from the work of Mancur Olson.[19]

The American political-science literature, in the decades immediately following World War II, was awash with celebratory writings of the democratic achievements based on voluntary association of free citizens to further their own interest. The triumph of democracy over its totalitarian alternative was seen through its bedrock principle of freedom of association, where every citizen is free to form groups to redress grievances and shape public policy. Yet, in 1965, in one of the most influential publications, Olson pointed out the logical pitfalls of using economic rationality in explaining the emergence of voluntary associations. His original intent was to explain why people did not automatically form collective organizations and mobilize to provide public goods.

In order to fully appreciate Olson's reasoning, we must understand the concept of public goods. Economist Paul Samuelson developed the concept of public goods.[20] The public goods are generally defined with two important attributes: excludability and exhaustibility.[21] Public goods are for the enjoyment of every member of the community, regardless of their level of involvement in the effort at procuring these goods. For instance, tax dollars pay for clean air, yet a destitute person who does not pay any taxes is free to enjoy the benefits of a pristine environment. Second, the benefits of public goods do not get exhausted with the increase in the number of users. Therefore, when a new child is born, nobody worries about his or her share of the clean air.[22]

Olson introduced the term "free rider" into the social-science lexicon, where "rational" individuals would argue that since the benefits of a public good are not restricted to those who participate in the attempt to procure it, it would make sense for each individual to free ride and let others pay for it. With everybody reasoning this way, no public goods would be produced. In other words, suppose there are two individuals both of whom would benefit from a political change resulting from the removal of a tyrant from power. However, one has decided to participate in an act of political dissidence, while the other has decided to do nothing. We can see that the two actions would mean the following to the two members of the community:

Participant = benefit − cost

Non-participant = benefit

As we can see from the above formulations, since a non-participant does not have to pay any cost (loss of time or income, or even loss of life) to get benefits from a collective good, there is no reason for any rational human being to participate in a collective action. Furthermore, as the group size increases, a single participant's contribution to the cause becomes increasingly insignificant. A single voter cannot affect the outcome of a national election. Nor can a single suicide bomber expect to establish a global Islamic state with his or her sacrifice. Therefore, nobody would have any reason to contribute to a collective cause. As a result of this impeccable logic, no collective action will ever be undertaken, no war will be fought (and won), and much of what we see around us as public goods within an organized society will cease to exist. While the free-rider problem is acute for large groups, the presence of selective benefits—where each member can equate his effort with the outcome—can explain an individual's participation in a small-group initiative, such as a *coup d'état*, far better than it can a grass-roots involvement in a mass movement.[23]

The logical lapses in economic arguments happen when we assume that every rational being is motivated only by his/her self-utility. In that case, knowing fully well that I can get the benefits even when I don't pitch in, what is my incentive to contribute to the collective effort? Therefore, in a society full of economically "rational" actors, where everybody would want to free ride, no public good will ever be produced, no war will be won and there will be no terrorism. Elinor Ostrom unequivocally points out the absurdity of the economic assumption of human rationality in her Presidential address to the American Political Association meeting:[24]

> Let me start with a provocative statement. You would not be reading this article if it were not for some [of] our ancestors learning how to undertake collective action to solve social dilemmas. Successive generations have added to the stock of everyday knowledge about how to instill productive norms of behavior in their children and to craft rules to support collective action that produces public goods and avoids "tragedies of commons." What our ancestors and contemporaries have learned about engaging in collective action for mutual defense, child rearing, and survival is not, however, understood or explained by the extant theories.

History, however, often has a way of injecting irony into academic discourses. While the scholarly community was busy discussing the theoretical implications of Olson's paradox, much of the Western world saw an explosion of participation by ordinary citizens in demonstrations against the unpopular war in Vietnam. To the astonishment of the proponents of the rational-choice school, noted economist Albert Hirschman observed:[25]

> Astoundingly large numbers of citizens, far from attempting to get a free ride, have been taking to the streets, to the nation's capital, or to other places where they expect to exert some influence for change. In this connection, it is interesting to note that while economists keep worrying about the free rider problem, political scientists have become increasingly concerned about the "paradox of participation." What began as a

methodological explanation for political inactivity quickly turned into a methodologically driven puzzle questioning why political participation should be as high as it was.

Facing the prospect of a direct affront to the fundamental building block of their discipline, economists and the proponents of rational-choice theory reacted in a predictable way. Some questioned the motives of participants of collective actions and found hidden sources of hedonistic motivations. Thus Tullock flatly asserted that those who take part in a revolutionary movement out of altruistic concerns are either irrational or have ulterior motives of personal gains.[26] Thus, they are either insane, or are basically criminals. Sadly, by following the strict definition of economic rationality, these are the only two choices we have to understand the motivations of a terrorist.

Others, such as Lichbach, attempted to show that partial payments (private gains) and/or coercion by the community (or peer pressure) for participation were behind people's decision to participate in collective actions.[27] However, the problem is that if an actor gets any special payment for participation, then what this person is attempting to achieve is no longer a public good. The same is true for participation induced by coercion. Neither of these two acts would then qualify as "altruistic." In that case, how do we explain many terrorist attacks, where the assailants take grave risks to their person and sacrifice everything with the intention of achieving some political goals? Some may indeed participate out of a desire of personal salvation or reward in the afterlife. Yet, there are groups such as the Sri Lankan Tamil Tigers which are secular. Furthermore, the vast majority of those who take part in rebellious activities do so voluntarily, without much evidence of coercion.

In sum, we cannot understand altruism within the framework of economic rationality. The assumption of a selfish actor itself stands in the way of understanding altruism. Webster's Dictionary defines altruism as "devotion to others or to humanity, as opposed to selfishness."[28] That is, individuals are altruistic when the primary beneficiary of their conscious acts is someone other than themselves. Yet, the very notion of rationality, based on the economic assumption of self-utility, causes circular reasoning in its definition. Economist Andreoni, for instance, claims that a "pure altruist" is one who gets no pleasure or utility out of participating in a collective action, since even a small amount of pleasure or utility would make her an "impure altruist."[29] However, as Rose-Ackerman correctly pointed out, such a rarified being would have no reason whatsoever to take part in a collective action.[30] Therefore, according to Andreoni, the only person who would participate is an impure altruist who derives pleasure out of sheer participation, which he calls the "warm glow effect of having done the right thing." In other words, under the assumption of economic rationality, Andreoni cannot even define an altruist without getting entangled in circular reasoning.[31] For us, however, he makes an important point that while it is impossible to define altruism under the assumption of economic rationality, in the final analysis, each one of us, even in our most sincere effort at being altruistic, derives some pleasure. In other words, all of us operate from mixed motives.

Despite the obvious shortcomings of such a truncated perception of human motivations, the assumption of economic rationality has become something of a "sacred cow," a sacrosanct concept that nobody dares to challenge. Some who have come tantalizingly close to attempting a different explanation of the motivations behind participation in collective actions have, in the end, carefully avoided the issue. Thus, Schuessler, skillfully showing that much of our collective behavior is the outcome of "expressive choice" as opposed to "instrumental choice," begins his book by sidestepping the issue by stating that: "The purpose of this book is not to 'solve' the paradox of participation, but to demonstrate how the paradox itself rests on a methodological foundation of outcome orientation that is inappropriate in many instances of large-scale collective behavior."[32] Olson himself was keenly aware of the illogic of collective action under the assumption of economic rationality and observed:

> It is not clear that this is the best way of theorizing about either utopian or religious groups ... Where nonrational or irrational behavior is the basis for a lobby, it would perhaps be better to turn to psychology or social psychology than to economics for a relevant theory. The beginnings of such a theory may already exist in the concept of "mass movements."[33]

In the end, many scholars like Fiorina realize that the collective action dilemma is the "paradox that ate the rational choice theory,"[34] yet accept the notion of a self-utility maximizing *homoeconomicus* as the only game in town. Ostrom, for example, after pointing out the problems associated with the fundamental assumption of rational choice theory, insists: "While incorrectly confused with a general theory of human behavior, complete rationality models will continue to be used productively by social scientists, including the author."[35]

There is no denying, of course, that economics has been able to fulfill many of its promises. Its preeminent status within social science as the sole hegemonic discipline is well-deserved.[36] Economics has truly brought a Newtonian revolution through its truncated view of human motivation, particularly in the areas of personal decisions from market behavior to marriage to criminal activities. As Nobel Laureate economist Gary Becker has amply shown, many of these acts can be accurately understood and predicted by using economic logic.[37] Another Nobel Laureate economist, Milton Friedman,[38] in his spirited defense of positive economics, famously argued that: "Truly important and significant hypotheses will be found to have assumptions that are wildly inaccurate descriptive representations of reality, and, in general the more significant the theory, the more unrealistic the assumption."[39] However, the problem for the economic logic is that it fails by its own rule offered by Friedman: it fails to predict the emergence of collective movements, particularly when the group size is very large.

Since the preoccupation of political science is collective behavior, where the logic of economic reasoning leaves us ruefully wanting, the adherents of rational-choice hypotheses have offered weak defenses for its continual use. Thus, Lichbach argues that although nearly all groups have grievances, "at least ninety-five percent of the time, in at least ninety-five percent of the places," they do not rebel.[40] Thus, while the logic of self-interest cannot explain why people rebel, we should be happy knowing that it can explain people's preponderant proclivity to free ride. In many ways, Lichbach's claim makes sense. It is extremely important to know the barriers to participation in collective actions. However, I argue that if we agree with Ostrom's claim that the economic rationality model should not be taken as a general theory of human behaviour,[41] we only settle for an incomplete theoretical perspective. Thus, Rose-Ackerman is quite categorical in admitting that "Altruism and nonprofit entrepreneurship cannot be understood within the standard economic framework."[42]

The problem, however, is that, as Ostrom points out, there is no alternative being offered to systematically explain collective behavior.[43] Given this intellectual void, Becker felt justified in claiming that

> our assumption of stable preferences (based on self-utility alone) was intended not as a philosophical or methodological "law," but as a productive way to analyze and explain behavior. We are impressed by how little has been achieved by the many discussions in economics, sociology, history, and other fields that postulate almost arbitrary variations in preferences and values when confronted by puzzling behavior.[44]

There are two aspects to Becker's objection to the altering of the concept of self-utility as the fundamental assumption of human rationality. First, he is correct in pointing out that in order to save the theories from tautological reasoning we must assume stability of preferences. It is of course true that while self-interest is stable and permanent, collective interests are unstable and ephemeral.

Witnessing such seemingly chaotic choices, we may assume that the actor's "tastes" have changed, or there is some logical inconsistency ("irrationality") in the decision-making process. If we assume that there is something irrational about the actor's choice, then we exclude such decisions outside of our explanatory capabilities. On the other hand, if we argue that the actor's preferences have changed, it runs counter to our methodological necessity of assuming a stable preference.[45] There is, however, a wide schism among economists about whether preferences and beliefs either exist as mental states or play an important role in the choice process.[46] Although most economists would prefer to remain agnostic regarding the origins of beliefs and preferences, it is fair to state that a minimal independence between preferences and choices must be maintained in order to save theories from tautological reasoning. We all recognize that reality is too complicated to be properly encapsulated. If we are interested in building models of the mind, we must make reductionistic assumptions. Otherwise, any theory that attempts to explain everything can become what Lichbach calls, a "vague and unfalsifie-able sponge," which in the end adds nothing to the explanation.[47]

Second, Becker's objection to altering the unitary source of motivation is the inclusion of an "arbitrary" variation of tastes and preferences. Alongside the question of arbitrariness, we must also address the question of falsifi-ability. These are extremely important methodological questions. Therefore, I would like to hold them in abeyance till I have had a chance to offer my alternate paradigm for analyzing our social behavior.

Janus's children: the doorway to the mind of a social being

Janus, the Roman god, is shown with two heads. Symbolizing the beginning— the Roman calendar starts with January, bearing his name—the ancient deity whose symbol would adorn the doorway to many Roman homes perhaps also serves as the representation of the duality of our motivations and the funda- mental inner conflict between the two. This conflict is between the welfare of our own self and the welfare of the group in which we claim our membership. We all strive for our personal welfare, wealth, prestige, power, love, respect, and rectitude. At the same time, we want to do good for our community, even at the cost of our personal wellbeing. In our actions we are sometime selfish and sometime altruistic. This conflict can sometimes pull us in the opposite directions; and at other times the two faces can merge into a single confusing overlap. I posit that if we are to understand the root motivations of terrorism, we must do so within the context of this eternal duality.[48] Thus, I assume that rational beings do not pursue a single goal but, by having a dual motivation, face an eternal trade-off between trying to attain private goods for themselves and public goods for their communities (for a more formal presentation of my model, see Appendix A).

Although the idea of expanding the fundamental assumption of rationality may seem fairly reasonable to those outside the realm of economics, for the economist the idea of self-utility is held as sacrosanct. As we have noted before, many prominent economists have questioned the validity of the assumption of self-utility maximization, but none has offered an alternative. Thomas Kuhn pointed out that a scientific paradigm that is accepted as "normal science"[49] cannot be shaken up simply by exposing its conceptual weaknesses. A scientific paradigm is replaced only when a new theory can conclusively prove its superiority over the accepted one. In social sciences paradigm shifts have come at dictates of a radically changed political, sociological, or eco- nomic reality. The advent of the Industrial Revolution made mercantilism obsolete and gave birth to Adam Smith and the neoclassical economics. The Great Depression produced Keynesian economics, which placed the govern- ment in the driver's seat of the national economic engine. The overregulated 1970s saw the resurgence of liberalism. Today, when we face an intellectual challenge in the shape of global terrorism, I believe that it is time to reexamine the basis of some of the fundamental assumptions upon which the current "normal science" of social inquiry is based.

Before making a case for an expanded view of human rationality, which includes group welfare as a separate argument in the utility function of a rational actor, I must address the objections raised by Becker and other stalwarts in economics. These involve the questions of arbitrariness, identifiability, and falsifiability.

Arbitrariness

Becker objected to the inclusion of "arbitrary" factors in the preference structure of a rational being. In that case, we need to ask, how fundamental is the group psychology in human psyche?[50] I argue that the human need to belong to a group is just as strong as a source of preference as is self-utility. This need has been biologically imprinted in us from our long evolutionary past. Therefore, while it may be efficient to assume a uni-dimensional being for the analyses of preference for private goods, it is singularly impossible to understand our preference for public goods, even at the cost of our own welfare, without resorting to the notions of group preference and collective identity.

The evolutionary process has imbued in all the herding animals a strong need to form bonds within the group, act on its welfare even at the cost of personal loss, and regard non-group members as "outsiders" or even as "enemies." This is the only way the early hominids could survive. As a result, the need to belong to a group has perhaps been biologically programmed deep within our brain structure.

When we belong to a group, the membership costs a part of our individuality. The price of belonging to a group is the sacrifice of selfish needs. Sometimes, we need to sacrifice little, and at other times, our allegiance to the survival as a group calls for a total submersion of individual identity to the collective. In the primate world, cooperation within groups and acting on its best interest comes naturally. Although chimpanzees cannot swim, there are documented cases where some have drowned in zoo moats trying to save others.[51] Having observed the higher primates, both in the wild[52] and in captivity,[53] biologists have firmly established the fact that these animals not only show empathy, but also have developed a keen sense of ethical behavior in accordance with their own group norms. For instance, among similar ranked animals, the grabbing of disproportionate amounts of food can bring swift retribution. As a result, every member is likely to share food when the distribution is unequal.[54] Many such examples of altruistic behavior in the simian societies have led a number of prominent primatologists and evolutionary biologists to claim that the seeds of morality lie deeply imbedded in our evolutionary past. Edward O. Wilson boldly claims that the study of ethics should be taken away from the philosophers and be trusted in the hands of the biologists.[55] In fact, some[56] have claimed that the process of evolution has made our brains hard-wired for understanding and acting upon moral codes of conduct. This hard-wiring (based on instinctive understanding of group needs and reflexive participation in altruistic behavior) and soft-wiring (based on social learning) has made all of us both selfish and altruistic at the same time. We should not, therefore, be surprised when we encounter a Palestinian youth, Sahmoud Sleyman Abu Hasanein, who, before undertaking a dangerous mission which killed him, left a written message for his family seemingly anticipating the question of free ridership. In it he pointedly asks his father:[57] "Dear father: If I do not defend my religion, my land and holy sites, and another person does not, and another, then who will liberate the land and the holy places?"[58]

Yet, along with altruism, the selfish needs of the individual are ever present in our psychological makeup. While every animal acts instinctively to preserve the group's interest, at the same time each is biologically programmed to strive to become the alpha animal. A lonely male lion after driving out the dominant male, for instance, kills off all of his rival's offspring. The top lioness of the pride, after making token efforts at saving her cubs, submits to the victor's sexual advances to produce the fittest progeny.

In the end, a group is just as strong as the commitment of its members to its collective goals. In biology, this is known as "inclusive fitness". This conflict between individual fitness and group fitness was not lost on Darwin himself. Thus he notes:

> It must not be forgotten that although a high standard of morality gives but a slight or no advantage to each man and his children over other men in the same tribe, yet that an increase in the number of well-endowed men and advancement in the standard of morality will certainly give an immense advantage to one tribe over another. There can be no doubt that a tribe including many members who, from possessing in a high degree of patriotism, fidelity, obedience, courage, and sympathy, were always ready to aid one another, and to sacrifice themselves for common good, would be victorious over most other tribes; and this would be natural selection.[59]

Thus, while selfish behavior favors an individual over others within a group, altruistic behavior by individual members favors a group against other groups.[60] Thus, what we call morality, idealism, and altruism are often rooted in our preference of group welfare over our narrowly defined selfish interest. Darwin made clear the equation of morality with group-favoring behavior, as he further adds:

> At all times throughout the world tribes have supplanted other tribes; and as morality is one important element in their success, the standard of

morality and the number of well endowed men will thus everywhere tend to rise and increase.[61]

Our short-term individual interest often clashes with the long-term group interest, which we recognize as moral dilemma. Zoologists studying animal behavior see a strong parallel between the animal world and human society. Thus, Wyne-Edwards observes:

> Where the two (individual interest and group needs) conflict, as they do when the short-term advantage of the individual undermines the safety of the race, group-selection is bound to win, because the race will suffer and decline, and be supplanted by another in which antisocial advancement of the individual is more rigidly inhibited. In our own lives, of course, we recognize the conflict as a moral issue, and the counterpart of this must exist in all social animals.[62]

In sum, I argue that group preference is not trivial or arbitrary. The need to belong is as fundamental to human social existence as the pursuit of self-utility. The importance of groups in our decision-making process is recognized in many disciplines. For example, Abraham Maslow, in his classic exposition of psychological needs, placed the need to belong immediately after the physical needs of food and shelter.[63] Similarly, the entire body of social psychology, beginning with the path-breaking work of Henri Tajfel, clearly establishes the importance of groups in the ways we see the world.[64] Even the Nobel Laureate economists Daniel Kahneman and Amos Tversky (and their associates) have shown how belonging to a group can alter our preference pattern.[65] In other words, contrary to the standard rational-choice assumption a group is not a simple amalgam of isolated individuals. When we join a group, it creates its own dynamics in how we perceive costs and benefits of each action. We not only form a bond with other members, we also adhere to its rules, written and unwritten, sublime and trivial, clearly articulated and implicitly understood.[66] For instance, contrary to the image of a perennially selfish actor, we automatically tip after a meal, often abiding by an unwritten rule of percentage of the total bill even when we are in a totally unfamiliar place or by ourselves, where the embarrassment of a chance meeting with the server or being served by the same person in the near future, or the peer pressure in front of others in the party, is non-existent. We may not eat the last piece of cake at a gathering even when there is no explicit prohibition against it and even though we are really tempted by it. And when our self-restraint crumbles, we often speak out aloud about our less than savory intention of helping ourselves to the last piece, or make some other self-deprecating comments as if to absolve ourselves of breaking the rule of social conduct. I may donate anonymously to National Public Broadcasting knowing full well that my getting the signals is not predicated upon my contribution of a small amount of money.[67] Many of these activities reflect our need to live by the explicit or implicit norms laid down by the society.

Thus, in their path-breaking work, Kahneman and Tversky demonstrate that individuals make distinct choices depending on whether the outcomes are "framed" in terms of gains or losses. The flood of subsequent studies has firmly established the effects of "framing" on the basis of group affiliation in the diverse fields of cognitive science, communications studies, law, political science, psychology, and economics.[68]

Identifiability

People have joined collective movements throughout history, from the Minutemen of yesteryears to today's Islamic fundamentalists, and have made their ultimate sacrifice out of concern for their communities or groups. Similar to today's jihadis going to Iraq and Afghanistan to fight the infidels by rejecting their comfortable middle-class living in the Islamic world, adventurers and left-wing ideologues became involved in the Spanish Civil War against the forces of General Franco. Gentiles have risked their lives and the lives of their families to save Jews during the Holocaust.[69] Even in our everyday lives we engage in acts of altruism. People jump into freezing rivers to save a perfect stranger, while others take up the cause of children suffering in far-away lands, or contribute generously to alleviate the plight of the neighbors. Yet, in most of these cases, as Monroe points out, when people save others at the risk of their own lives, they do not often recognize their acts as altruistic.[70] Therefore, being altruistic comes just as naturally to all of us as being selfish. In that case, are the two acts distinctly identifiable?

On the flip side, do we not often engage in altruistic behavior to gain personal recognition or at least to satisfy our need to have adventure or some fun? There are numerous examples of young men joining violent dissident groups, attracted by the possibility of carrying sophisticated arms, to satisfy their needs of adventure and even to impress young women. In that case, are these acts not a reflection of a participant's need for self-utility maximization?

The conceptual separation between self-utility and group utility is indeed difficult since they both stem from our need for self-preservation. Therefore, like two petals of a flower, they are indistinguishable at the root. Nevertheless, I argue that such a conceptual distinction is necessary for a fuller understanding of human motivations as a part and parcel of our social existence.

I posit that perhaps every conscious human action is a mixed outcome of both individual and collective identity. Although for the most part the two cannot be separated, we are on a safe ground when we look at the extreme ends of our motivational spectrum. For instance, when I am investing my money in the stock market, I am acting solely on the basis of my self-interest. On the other hand, when suicide bombers sacrifice their lives, their actions reflect the total submersion of their individual identities in the collective.

However, even in these extremes, we can detect the possibility of a mixed motive; if I invest only in those companies which conform to my moral ethical standards, or I blow myself up with the hope of personal salvation,[71] or I fulfill some sexual fantasies[72] through my act of ultimate sacrifice, I may be following a mixed motivational directive. However, if I am not constrained by any such moral considerations in my investment decisions or if I sacrifice my life for a secular cause (or without any conviction for rewards in the afterlife), then these may be assumed to reflect the purest forms of motivations of the two ends of the spectrum. It would seem absurd to assume that we will be able to classify any single act, much less an actor, as purely self-serving or purely altruistic. We do not even comprehend our own motivation; the essence of Hindu philosophy puts quest to "know thyself" as the highest form of knowledge, an essentially unattainable journey toward nirvana. However, economics faced a similar dilemma by asserting that individuals maximize their own utility. Without any way of measuring utility (or preference), Samuelson argued that our actions reveal our true preferences. In economics, it is known as the "revealed preference" hypothesis. Similarly, I argue that although pure motivations are never known, we may be able to analyze our actions through our "revealed preferences."

Falsifiability

The hallmark of scientific inquiry is the falsifiability of the proffered hypotheses. The important question, therefore, is whether the expansion of the standard assumption of economic rationality makes it an unfalsifiable sponge that explains everything, and in the process it explains nothing. In defense of this objection of tautological reasoning, it is important to note that the assumption of self-interest is also not falsifiable. It is merely used as a guidepost. In fact, as Popper points out:

> No natural history can be interpreted in the absence of at least some implicit body of intertwined theoretical and methodological belief that permits selection, evaluation, and other criticism. If that body of belief is not already implicit in the collection of facts—in which case more that "mere facts" are at hand—it must be externally supplied, perhaps by a current metaphysic, by another science, or by personal and historical accident.[73]

The fundamental assumptions can, thus, be beyond proof. The assembled evidence must provide support for the central assumption, which itself may not be falsifiable. The assumption of self-utility allows us to develop hypotheses linking outcomes to a set of incentives or independent variables. The inclusion of group-utility by no means lessens our ability to develop cogent models of social behavior.

Furthermore, self-utility is stable and unfalsifiable by itself. The aspects of group-utility, in contrast, are unstable and contextual. Therefore, such behavior is amenable to empirical verification. In fact, Gupta, Hofstetter, and Buss have shown that indicators of collective identity measured directly from survey can explain collective action far better than the measures of an individual's economic abilities (self-utility).[74] The entire field of social psychology is constantly expanding our knowledge with cogent experiments, which are shedding lights on our group-motivations.

Sources of collective identity

In the animal world, group affiliation comes instinctively through biological linkages. The primate groups are often built around a dominant male, hierarchically structured females and a number of lesser males, all of whom are genetically connected. Association among humans takes a much more complex form. People form associations based on birth characteristics or through personal interest.[75] I call the first group *ascriptive*, where people band together because of common religious faith, national identity, language, or caste. This is the essence of the *primordialist* perspective, where collective identity is seen as "biologically given" or is the result of some other "natural phenomenon."[76] This is the environment in which a child is born, kinships and neighborhoods are established, religion and culture imbue the child her identity. Depending on the context, this identity can be religious, ethnic, cultural, linguistic, or simply tribal or familial. The expressions of these identities can take the form of custom, tradition, food, attire, and music.[77] At times of intense competition, these differences play a major role in defining in-group and out-group affiliation. Psychologist John E. Mack calls these "cultural amplifiers."[78] These amplifiers are designed to create mountains out of molehills by magnifying minute differences in culture to an absurd level; after all, in Jonathan Swift's political satire *Gulliver's Travels*, the two groups of Lilliputians fight over which end of the boiled egg to crack.

We also form groups on the basis of a common concern, such as animal-rights, the environmental, etc. I call these *adoptive* groups, where people adopt these collective identities, often later in life. These adopted group identities can also involve religion, where people convert to a different religion voluntarily and take part in collective actions based on its imperatives.

However, the problem with considering group-identity is that, unlike individual identity, it is not invariant. A collective identity, after all, as Benedict Anderson points out, is an "imagined community." As social beings in complex societies we carry literally innumerable collective identities. Many of these identities are *ascriptive*, based on birth characteristics (e.g., nationality, or ethnic, linguistic, or religious affiliation) and others are based on *adoptive* identity. The *ascriptive* identities, with their quintessential images of "good" and "evil" create a mindset, which Post calls "hatred bred in the bone."[79] These are images through which a baby gets inculcated from birth.[80] In these societies, where widespread socialization into the politics of extremism also offers an extensive social network, joining a terrorist organization become synonymous with the rites of passage for many young men. Thus, children born into the hate-filled world of the working-class Catholics and Protestants in Northern Ireland, the Palestinian refugee camps, or the territories controlled by the LTTE in Sri Lanka, or the FARC in Colombia, ensure a steady supply of recruits into the extremist organization.

Basis of collective identity

Collective identity can be based on three main sources of group formation: religion, ethno-nationalism, and Marxist economic class.[81] According to Anderson, these are imagined because although nobody knows every member of the community yet, they imagine a common horizontal bond of fraternity regardless of actual differences in income, status, or life experiences. On the basis of these constructed concepts, some will be included and others excluded. The first two are primarily *ascriptive*, while the Marxist class identity is adoptive.[82] When rational people act, they act upon not only what they believe is best for them individually but also what they perceive to be in the best interest of their community. The pursuit of individual welfare is defined as selfish, while the quest for group welfare is the basis of altruism. As Anderson points out: "Ultimately it is this fraternity that makes it possible, . . . for so many millions of people, not so much to kill, as willing to die for such limited imagining."[83] Anderson, of course refers only to nationalism; however, he sees this as a part of a larger cultural root that subsumes all three sources of collective identity. Let us examine this a bit more carefully.

Religious identity

Scott Atran asks an interesting question: why do we trust in gods?[84] This heretical question goes to the heart of evolutionary logic. In a primitive society, without much surplus food, where every individual must devote every waking hour to hunting and gathering, why should anyone take time off for seemingly unproductive religious observances? If one group imposes a certain restriction on the behavior of its members, which prohibits them eating certain readily available food, participating in productive activities on certain days, or engaging in unrestricted pleasurable sexual activities, then does not another group that is unfettered by such restrictions have an evolutionary advantage over the one that imposes such prohibitions? Furthermore, religion presents a counterfactual, counterintuitive world of supernatural agents who manipulate peoples' existential anxieties caused by an unpredictable future. Therefore, religion apparently poses this evolutionary puzzle: would a group not abiding by any religious constraint not have a greater inclusive fitness?

The adherence to religious rites increases a group's inclusive fitness. This is because religion provides a society full of disparate self-serving individuals a coherent structure. All herding animals adhere to their group norms, which can vary among prides, pods, and cackles. This allows them to settle disputes and maintain group cohesion based on clear distribution of labor and codes of conduct. Similarly, in human groups, religion provides the grist which holds a society together by clearly identifying those who are the members of the community through attire, norms, and rituals.[85] It also singles out those who are outside the group. This process of identification allows members to be altruistic toward their own group while providing justification for extreme violence against the non-believers. For these reasons religion has been one of the most potent sources of collective identity. In the name of God we are not only ready to make the ultimate sacrifice, we are also ready to kill. Religion promises rewards, which may even be construed as instrumental in the minds of the strict adherents.

The case against religion is indeed formidable. Since religion is about faith, to those with unquestioned fealty to every word of the sacred text, there is no compromise. The distinction between faith and reason is recognized universally in every religion. While it is not clear whether the need for God is hard-wired in the folds of our mysterious brains, there is no question of its allure to most of us.[86] All religious-inspired movements define a millenarian concept to its followers. The unquestioned faith in working toward facilitating the returning of the Messiah immensely empowers the adherents. The rewards for the temporal toil come, if not in this life, in the afterlife. This heady notion of the quintessential good and evil allows people to engage not only in the ultimate acts of self-sacrifice but also in the direct involvement of the most gruesome killings of the enemies of the ultimate good.[87]

The suspicion that religion in general and Islam in particular causes terrorism became reinforced at the sight of the religious zealots crashing airplanes to cause widespread death and destruction. Furthermore, it is apparent that despite the repeated denials by President George Bush and many others in position of power, to many it seems like the enactment of Samuel Huntington's work, a "clash of civilizations."

Facing this question, several lines of arguments have surfaced. Some have argued that, above all, religion and its many violent interpretations create mindsets that breed extreme religiously sanctioned violence. Others have pointed their finger squarely at Islam as the most intolerant religion of our times. Another group of writers have posited that it is not religion that gives birth to violence; concealed underneath the religious pronouncements are goals that are essentially political or territorial. They simply manipulate religious symbols and utilize the language of religion to achieve their true objectives.

Some authors argue that religion, by its very nature, creates an imaginary world of the sacral and the profane, the believers and the non-believers.[88] It also provides its followers with a supply of religious resources, such as God's blessings, eternal life, Paradise, and salvation. To the strict adherents of religion, the supply of these resources dwindles as people move away from the "true path" shown in the sacred texts. The leaders of the fundamentalist religious movements claim that these resources were in abundance at some specified "golden time" in the religion's history; their goal is to bring back those days of the Paradise on earth. The only way to achieve this goal is through self-sacrifice and by meting out punishment to the heretics and the other polluters of religious faith, who are the enemies of God.

Some point out that it is not religion but religious practices that play an important role in preparing the mind of a terrorist for making the ultimate sacrifice. An al-Qaeda manual for the 9/11 attackers instructs the operators to "keep busy with repeated invocation of God." Holmes points out:[89]

> Prayer is behaviour, not thought. Indeed prayer is ritual designed to block thought, to prevent the spontaneous upsurge of disobedient impulses and inclinations. Prayer is anesthesia. Chanting, supplications, and religious songs and reciting scripture act as a sedative. It can even induce a trance. And, unlike daydreaming, it is a *regulated* behaviour. Reading the Koran into one's palms and then rubbing one's hands all over one's body, in a ritual self-blessing, takes time and crowds out other thoughts. Mantras, like counting sheep, are standard techniques, recommended by psychotherapists, for managing anxiety and keeping demons at bay. . . . The danger of last minute faltering can be minimized by shutting down most cognitive functions.[90]
>
> (Emphasis in original)

Other influential scholars, such as Bernard Lewis, have pointed out that not all religions are the same in provoking violence.[91] Some religions, like Islam, are much more prone to produce aggression and carnage than others. They argue that this is because, within its sacred text, Islam supplies justification of violence against the non-believers. Taking a slightly different perspective, Selbourne argues that the current economic and political conditions are creating conditions within the Islamic nations and in the broader Islamic community, where a virulent form of the religion can flourish.[92] Unless we can take corrective measures in time, we in the West are bound to lose our battle with Islam.

Writing a month after the deadly 9/11 attacks, author Salman Rushdie holds Islam, or how the religion is understood by the multitude of its adherents, directly responsible.[93] In his provocative article in the *New York Times*, Rushdie took aim at the prevailing "mantra" among the Western intellectuals: "This isn't about Islam." He flatly asserted that "[t]he trouble with this necessary disclaimer is that it isn't true." Rushdie explains:

> For a vast number of "believing" Muslim men, "Islam" stands, in a jumbled, half-examined way, not only for the fear of God—the fear more than love, one suspects—but also for a cluster of customs, opinions and prejudices that include their dietary practices; the sequestration or

near-sequestration of "their" women; the sermons delivered by their mullahs of choice; a loathing of modern society in general, riddled as it is with music, godlessness and sex; and a more particularized loathing (and fear) of the prospect that their own immediate surroundings could be taken over—"Westoxicated"—by the liberal Western-style way of life.[94]

Rushdie's criticism, however, does not make a distinction between what the religion truly preaches and how it is understood by many of its followers. The sacred books in every religion speak in mysterious words; the antiquated texts are open to wide variations of interpretation. The term jihad, for instance, has been in the limelight due to the current wave of Islamic violence. To the outsider, it conjures up the images of a holy war, fought by wild-eyed fanatics. Within Islam, however, a distinction is made between Greater jihad (conquering the inner weaknesses within one's own self) and Lesser jihad (taking up arms against an outside force when Islam is at risk). Even in the latter case, there a wide-ranging debate within the Muslim world regarding who can call (fatwa) for an armed response. Facing this new global wave of terrorism it is not uncommon to blame the religion itself,[95] yet we can readily see that killing in the name of God is not the exclusive domain of Islam. The cruelty of the Crusaders toward nearly everyone they encountered is legendary and, in the Islamic world, the term "Crusade" evokes fear and revulsion. The excesses of religious zealotry gave birth to centuries long fratricide between the Catholics and the Protestants. In the Hindu religion, which is generally seen as peaceful and meditative, the revelation of Lord Krishna in Bhagavad Gita exhorts Arjuna, the warring hero of Mahabharata, to engage in the slaying of his kinfolks in the name of *Dharma yuddha* (holy war). The Buddhists monks in Sri Lanka have shown little compassion for the Tamils and have been most vociferous in pressing for war against them.

In contrast to those who hold religion itself responsible for violence, Pape, after studying patterns of suicide attacks all over the world, is convinced that religion per se is not at the root of conflict.[96] Since suicide attacks are carried out by secular Arab/Muslim groups such as the PFLP, the al-Aqsa Martyr Brigade, the Chechens, as well as secular Hindus, such as the Tamil Tigers of Sri Lanka, there is no reason to hold religion or, in particular, Islam responsible for these acts. Underlying all these acts of self-sacrifice is the presence of political and territorial claims.

When we dig deep into our motivations we quickly discover that it is not religion per se that causes mass violence, but the fact that religion readily offers one of the building blocks of collective identity. Thus Juergensmeyer points out:

> In looking at the variety of cases, from the Palestinian Hamas movement to al-Qaeda and the Christian militia, it is clear to me that in most cases there were real grievances: economic and social tensions experienced by large number of people. These grievances were not religious. They were

not aimed at religious differences or issues of doctrine and belief. *They were issues of social identity and meaningful participation in public life that in other contexts were expressed through Marxist and nationalist ideologies.*[97]

(Emphasis mine)

A strong collective identity is a tool that can be used by skillful leaders to serve practically any kind of cause—noble or reprehensible.

Tribalism and ethnic identity

There is a sad fact of life. In the US, where obsession with professional football teams runs deep, the police departments across the nation report that after each game the number of calls for domestic abuse shoot up.[98] The game of football, played by groups of millionaires employed by billionaires, evokes such a sense of group loyalty that ordinary people take out their disappointments on their own families. This strong identification with sporting teams all over the world simply reflects our evolutionary need to form community bonds and fight against the "enemies."[99] The roots of our national, ethnic, tribal, and clan identities are similarly rooted in our primordial desire to form a group and act upon its interest. Such groupings provide another most potent sources of collective identity. This identity embraces everyone born within a defined community. The members do not have to do anything special to be included in its membership and, once included, can share in its past glories and its humiliations—factual or mythological. By looking around the world, we can see nothing permanent in these groupings. The identities that once propelled groups to engage in extreme savagery are often relegated to history, while new identities are born. In today's world the ancient enmity between the Scots and the English, the Swedish and the Fins are largely considered anachronistic, reduced to infrequent snide remarks or demonstration of cultural pride. Today we do not even know the identity of the Canaanites and the Philistines, who were much reviled in the Bible. Few rise up to defend the honor of the Austro-Hungarian Empire. Yet, we see bloody struggle for freedom by the East Timorians and the Bangladeshis, who did not exist as separate nations until recently. Once again, similar to religion, ethnicity and tribalism only serve as material for constructed identity.

Along with religion, nationalism serves as the most common source of violent upheavals, where the battle lines are drawn by some vaguely understood definition of who is included and who is not. Similar to all other herding animals, humans—since their simian days—have lived in small groups along bloodlines and have competed with others for scarce resources. The indelible psycho-biological need to form groups caused the familial lines to merge into clans, and clans into tribes. Over time the advent of technology brought a broader view of the community by facilitating transportation and communication. By the end of the eighteenth century—particularly in Europe—the consciousness of a larger entity of nationalism began to permeate ordinary people.[100] In a relatively short period of time, ethno-nationalism, where a sovereign statehood is claimed in the exclusive name of an ethnic or linguistic group, swept the entire continent, culminating in the two catastrophic global wars. Hyper-nationalism, the most virulent form of nationalism, continued to take its heavy toll in human lives even after the wars, giving birth to terms such as ethnic cleansing and other kinds of mass violence. The advent of technology in transportation and communication along with weapons of large-scale destruction exponentially increased the capacity to inflict harm on others.

Yet what is nationalism? When does a group of people start to think of themselves as different from the rest? History shows that while nearly the entire world lives in multiethnic, multilingual, multicultural societies, some define themselves solely on the basis of a certain "national" identity. Anderson points out that a deep division develops between the champions of separate nationalism and those looking from the outside.[101] This division involves

(1) The objective modernity of nations to the historian's eyes vs. their subjective antiquity in the eyes of nationalists. (2) The formal universality of nationality as a socio-cultural concept—in the modern world everyone can, should, will "have" a nationality, as he or she "has" a gender—vs. the irremediable particularity of its concrete manifestations, such that, by definition, "Greek" nationality is *sui genesis*. (3) The "political" power of nationalism vs. their philosophical poverty and even incoherence. In other words, unlike most other isms, nationalism has never produced its own grand thinkers: no Hobbeses, Tocquevilles, Marxes, or Webers.

This conceptual ambiguity of nation and nationalism led a noted scholar, having studied the phenomenon for decades, to ruefully conclude: "Thus I am driven to the conclusion that no 'scientific definition' of the nation can be devised; yet the phenomenon has existed and exists."[102] Nationalism, therefore, is truly a mental construct, which creates an imagined community inhabited by like-minded individuals."[103] In its most volatile cocktail, nationalism and religion often mix into a deadly concoction of "holy nationalism."

Marxist class identity

Marxist class identity is based on the ownership of the means of production. Marx saw the world in the binary terms of those who owned the means of production (capital) and those who toiled without owning them. To him the conflict between these two classes was the fundamental dialectic that propelled the evolution of capitalism and led to its inevitable destruction. Karl Marx rejected the conceptions of identity based on nationalism, religion, culture, or ethnicity as epiphenomena, a false identity. He essentially argued that belonging to an economic class is determined by birth. In the Marxist writing, the class-based identity becomes indelible, which the revolutionary leaders attempt to unmask by revealing the "true nature" of the eternal conflict created as a result of the establishment of the capitalist system to the masses. Indeed, the first organized government set up along the lines of Marxist ideology, the Soviet Union, steadfastly refused to give itself a nationalistic name. Thus, it was not the Socialist Republic of Russia, but a large conglomerate of Soviet Republics.[104]

Despite claims of economic class being the true identity, one of the biggest failures of Marxist theory is its inability to grasp the draw of other ascriptive sources of identity. As soon as the Soviet Union imploded, like the Russian doll, a new sub-national identity came out of the larger national entity in a seemingly endless series of division; the Abkakhsians, the Chechens, the Ingushetians began claiming their place in the sun as separate nations. Similarly, in India the Communist movement could find its footing along the contours of tribal lines.

Political entrepreneurs and the imagined community

To anyone living within a multicultural society, the basis for forming groups is innumerable. We can form groups on the basis of religion, nationality, economic class, language, gender, culture, or common interest. Yet, at the end, only a few inspire us to take part in collective actions. The question then is: how do we choose the most predominant identity from all others? For that we need the work of an external agent. Although the ingredients for the formation of collective identity are all around us, it takes someone special to tell a coherent story by drawing from religion, history, and mythology, which resonates with a number of people. The noted economist Joseph Schumpeter in a seminal book showed that it is not enough to understand the forces of demand and supply to analyze the market process.[105] For that we need to recognize the role that a group of leaders play to shape the course of the economy. He called them the "entrepreneurs." The entrepreneurs are not the people who invent; rather these are the individuals who take other people's inventions and innovate. These entrepreneurs act as the catalytic agents to make the market take its shape. Take, for instance, the case of Bill Gates. He did not invent anything, but took the existing bits of technology, created the corporate giant Microsoft, and changed the course of the entire field of computer technology. In the political arena, these political entrepreneurs come in the form of George Washington, Hitler, Gandhi, Martin Luther King, Jr., and bin Laden. Through their vision these innovators "connect the dots" for their followers, which not only suddenly allow them to see who they are in terms of a larger entity, but also a way out of their current predicament. Thus, under the leadership of George Washington, a new nation was formed. Hitler gave a common purpose to fellow Germans. King showed the African-Americans the promised land of racial equality. We cannot understand collective action without understanding the process by which a motley group of individuals are suddenly bound together for a common purpose, good or evil.[106]

Our collective identities firmly establish our membership in mentally constructed communities. Since there are infinite numbers of collective identities that an individual can assume, the process of developing a compelling identity on the basis of which a large number of people would act is one of the most intriguing questions that faces us. I argue that the development of a collective identity depends upon the abilities of "political entrepreneur(s)" to develop the necessary collective identity by "faming" the issues that produce anxiety among people. The importance of framing, particularly by the authority figures in the human decision-making process, is well recognized in the field of psychology and cognitive sciences.[107] The concept of "entrepreneur" as a catalytic agent for change has been around at least since economist Joseph Schumpeter introduced it in 1912.[108] In my formulation, while aspects of absolute and relative deprivation provide the necessary condition, the presence of a political innovator provides us with the sufficient condition for producing collective movements, in general, and terrorism, in particular.

If leadership is crucial for collective action, the logical question to ask is, who are these leaders? In a set of famous experiments Stanley Milgram clearly demonstrated that even a marginally recognized authority figure can play a significant role in influencing people to do things they would normally not do.[109] In these experiments, the male volunteers, drawn through newspaper advertisements, were told that they were taking part in an experiment to study memory and learning. The subjects were told that they were the "teacher" and were to ask a series of questions to a "student" in the next room. The "teachers" were to administer an electric shock to the "student" if he made any mistake. With a repeated mistake the extent of shock would increase. As the level of shock increased, the "teacher" heard the man on the other side of the wall first grunt and then scream in agony, complaining about a heart condition. If the "teacher" refused to administer shock, he was simply told by a man in a white lab-coat to go on. If he refused to go on after three such instructions, the experiment was halted. To the horror of those who have faith in human judgment, two-thirds of the subjects (the "teachers") went all the way, administering the highest level of shock with clearly marked switches, supposedly "killing" the unseen "student" in the next room. Milgram also included women volunteers to see if they would react any differently from their male counterparts. Alas, the level of obedience among women was no different than among men, although they seemed to be more conflicted about their task. The most striking feature of the Milgram experiments is that the authority figures that the subjects were obeying were not known national figures. They were simply assistants wearing white laboratory coats. Given human proclivity to follow leaders, it is hardly surprising that people will adhere to instructions not only by the likes of Osama bin Laden, but also of the village mullahs and the heads of small neighborhood cells, such as

Muhammad Siddique Khan, the leader of the group responsible for the 7/7 train and bus bombings in London.

Human history, in fact, is replete with examples of crimes of obedience,[110] from the Holocaust to the Mai Lai massacre, where otherwise rational, highly educated people have engaged in acts that defy every norm of civilized society. This proclivity to subject oneself to a group norm can engulf an entire nation, such as in Nazi Germany, where most people became Hitler's willing executioners.[111] Such madness can similarly afflict a small community of people. In 1978, the world came to know of a collective suicide/murder of nearly one thousand of Reverend Jim Jones' followers in the far-away jungle of Guyana.[112] In an episode eerily reminiscent of the grizzly scenes of Jonestown, another cult group, Heaven's Gate, committed an act of mass suicide in 1997. When the police entered the mansion the group had rented in the most expensive part of San Diego, they discovered 39 bodies of men and women. As a testimony of the power of the leader, the autopsy revealed that several men in their twenties had had themselves surgically castrated to prepare their bodies to directly ascend to the alien spaceship, which they were told was waiting for them.

When we form groups, we inevitably form a bond, which often requires us to subsume our individuality to the needs of the group. This is not only true of a nation under charismatic leadership such as Hitler's Germany, Mao's China, or Habyarimana's Rwanda, it also serves as the driving force of small terrorist cells. Sageman, a trained psychiatrist, after a careful study of the cell in Germany that brought about the 9/11 attacks, calls the phenomenon "a bunch of guys" hypothesis.[113] These men, all from various parts of the Arab world, living in an alien culture in Hamburg, Germany, congregated in a mosque, perhaps for the most mundane of reasons: they were looking for familiar culture, language, and Halal (Kosher) food. Although they came from different countries, the young men were also united by their animosity toward the West, in general, and the US, in particular. Through their many hours of animated discussions, the bunch of guys were looking for actions against their perceived enemies. The opportunity arrived when they made contact with the operatives of al-Qaeda. A plan was hatched, necessary funds were transferred, and the members followed through with the plan to their ultimate destruction; despite numerous chances, contrary to the predictions of the "rational choice theory" and the game theorists, none of the participants defected.

Phillip Zimbardo, in his most recent book, asked the question, how do good people turn evil?[114] By extending the results of his experiments conducted on prisoners and prison guards nearly four decades ago, he answers the question by stating that there is nothing sinister or even mysterious about the way such a transformation takes place. Given the right set of circumstances, which cause people to form a destructive collective identity, practically any one of us is able to become "evil." Thus, Horgan, having interviewed many terrorists, comes to the conclusion that in order to understand their motivations, it is not important to know "why," rather, the more pertinent question is, "how?"[115] Since the need to belong to a group is rooted in the need to survive, the question why anyone joins a group becomes less meaningful than understanding the process which compels many to turn to violence.[116]

In sum, groups are not established randomly. The existence of a separate cultural, religious, or ethnic identity does nor necessarily create a group that would rise up to procure public goods through collective actions. While all of the forces of identity, backed by a widespread feeling of deprivation, serve as the necessary condition, for sufficient condition we must turn to the rise of a political entrepreneur.

The problem of including political entrepreneurs within an analytical framework is that a theoretical paradigm must always have predictive capabilities. Unfortunately, the rise of a charismatic leader cannot be predicted. The debate whether environment produces a leader or a leader shapes the environment cannot be settled with empirical testing. Since the emergence of a political entrepreneur is crucial to our framework, we have to accept the shortcoming of predictive capabilities of social-science theories in anticipating revolutions and mass movements.

Spread of ideology

In the end, terrorism and social conflicts are the products of ideas. After understanding the basic motivations and the process by which terrorist organizations are formed, we must look at the contagion of ideas that bind a large number of people from diverse parts of the world to a common cause. David Rapoport, after examining the history of terrorism, finds a pattern of four different waves, where the flow of ideas swept much of the world through loosely connected groups, bound only to a common adherence to an ideology.[117] He argues that, viewed from a global perspective, acts of terrorism tend to come in clusters, almost like ocean waves. That is why history often seems like a repetitive process. In fact, Rapoport points out that exactly 100 years prior to the 9/11 attacks, in September 1901, William McKinley, the 25th president of the US, was assassinated by an anarchist. Theodore Roosevelt, who succeeded McKinley, declared a crusade to exterminate terrorism, much like President George W. Bush did in September 2001. Roosevelt declared war against terrorism because then, as it is today, the idea of using acts of terrorism to achieve political goals was stirring people all over the world.

Based on the history of the past 125 years, Rapoport identified four waves of global terrorism. The first wave of terrorism was fueled by the "anarchists" in the 1880s and started in Russia. All ideologies are rooted in some real social or political injustice, which the leaders of the movement want to solve by creating a utopian ideal. The leaders claim that these ideal societies existed in the past and can be re-created if only the followers carry out their orders.

The word *anarchy* comes from the Greek *anarchos*, which means "having no ruler." The anarchist movement was started by Mikhail Bakunin (1814–1876). The indescribable misery of the common Russians at the hands of the powerful inspired the anarchists to kill people of authority in order to create a society where everybody would be treated equally. The extreme inequality in the European societies of the time made such an ideology extremely attractive, especially to young men and women. Anarchism spread quickly to the Balkans, Western Europe, and, from there, through the newly arriving immigrants to the US. Anarchism became the first truly international wave of global terrorism.

Europe at the turn of the twentieth century was a virtual tinderbox, with every major power competing for global supremacy. During this period of extreme tension and political rivalry, it was the act of an anarchist that triggered the greatest war the world had ever seen. In 1914, Serbian nationalist Gavrilo Princip assassinated the Austrian Archduke Franz Ferdinand and thereby precipitated World War I.

Anti-colonial movements inspired the second wave of terrorism. The end of World War I produced the Versailles Peace Treaty in 1919, by which the victorious European powers divided up the world among themselves as colonies. However, almost immediately, the new wave of terrorism, which was inspired by the ideals of political independence from the foreign rule, became active.

In 1922, after a long and bloody struggle, the British ended its domination of Ireland but divided the country along religious lines. The Irish provinces with a Catholic majority became an independent nation, the Republic of Ireland, while the northeastern part of the island, where there was a Protestant majority, remained under British rule. The partition of the country saw the rise of the Irish Republican Army (IRA), which aimed to destroy the last vestiges of British colonialism by unifying the island under one (presumably Catholic) rule.

The weakening of the victorious powers after World War II gave new strength to the anti-colonial movements in the 1940s and 1950s. In Palestine, the Stern and Irgun gangs, Jewish terrorist groups dedicated to the ideals of creating an independent state of Israel, started a campaign of attacks against the British and the Arabs. In the mid-1950s, the Greek nationalist group EOKA (*Ethniki Organosis Kyprion Agoniston*) led a successful campaign of violence against the British and Turkish authorities. Terrorist groups sprung up all over the colonies from Southeast Asia to North Africa. The second wave of terrorism ended when the European empires broke up after World War II and the former colonies gained independence. However, as the second wave of international terrorism ended, the third wave of terrorism was beginning to gather momentum.

Advancements in science and technology have brought the world closer together. As we learned more about each other, it became possible not only to communicate with people from distant lands but also to allow revolutionary ideals to spread quickly around the globe. The persistent problems of poverty and social injustice, which spawned anarchism in the late 1800s, saw a resurgence of Marxist and other left-wing movements in the 1960s and 1970s.

After World War I, anarchism as an ideological force declined in strength throughout the world. However, old ideas do not get totally discredited or destroyed unless the social and economic conditions that created them are altered significantly. The ideals espoused by the anarchists did not include an important component, which was added by the Marxist revolutionaries. Following the writings of Lenin and then Mao, those who wanted to change the fundamental order of the capitalist system by force realized the importance of the leadership of a hierarchical party structure in bringing about a revolution. The spread of their ideas manifested as the third wave of terrorism.

The defining moment for the third wave of terrorism came with the Vietnam War. The daily sight of violence on television screens revitalized the leftist movement. The fact that an ill-equipped ragtag band of Viet Cong guerrillas could defeat the US armed forces caught the imagination of many around the world. The Weather Underground in the US, the Red Army Faction in West Germany and Japan, the Red Brigade in Italy, and *Action Directe* in France started planting bombs and staged shooting attacks.

In Northern Ireland, the IRA was able to transform its religion-based movement into a part of the global leftist movement, which renewed the strength of the IRA. A similar transformation reinvigorated the Basque separatist group ETA in Spain. In the Middle East, the secular and left-leaning Palestine Liberation Organization (PLO) and its affiliates, such as the Popular Front for the Liberation of Israel (PFLP), began a campaign of terror by hijacking airplanes. In Latin America, the popularity of Marxist ideologues and strategists such as Che Guevara and Carlos Marighela proved irresistible to many youthful followers. Che even became a cultural icon for the time. The Tupamaros guerrilla groups in Uruguay, the Shining Path in Peru, and the FARC in Colombia became active at this time. In India, inspired by the Communist ideology promoted by China's Mao Ze-dong, the Naxalite movement started its urban guerrilla attacks.

Once again, as with the other waves in the past, this wave of global terrorism saw its decline. In the 1980s, many of these groups had suffered military defeats at the hands of the security and armed forces of the countries in which they were operating. The lack of popular support dealt a devastating blow to the radical groups in Europe and the US.

Finally, in the 1990s, the stalwarts of Communism faltered: the Soviet Union collapsed from within and Revolutionary China became a bastion of hyper-capitalism. Being robbed of the champions of left-wing radicalism, many of these terrorist groups found it impossible to carry on. However, as I mentioned before, the old ideas do not totally disappear unless the conditions that gave rise to such ideas go through radical changes—the leftist ideology is currently staging a comeback in parts of India and in the neighboring mountain nation of Nepal.

Rapoport argues that we are currently in the fourth wave of global terrorism, which started around the last decade of the twentieth century. This wave is fueled not by Marxism or even nationalism—the primary driving force of this wave of terrorism is religious fundamentalism. Ethnic and national identity of a minority group within a large country often coincides with religious differences. For example, the Catholic minority in Northern Ireland, the Hindu minority in Buddhist Sri Lanka, or the Sikh minority in Hindu India are cases where religion and national aspirations are closely intertwined. However, the central force of the fourth wave is different: today's fundamentalist movements aim not only at replacing the current governments but also at transforming their nations into their own image of religious purity.

Few countries in the world are free of these kinds of religious extremist movements. In the US, the "Christian Identity" movement inspired a number of loosely formed groups or clusters of individuals. In 1985, a Sikh extremist group in India planted a bomb and brought down an Air India 747 in mid-air, killing 329 passengers and crew members. In 1994, a Jewish physician, part of a radical terrorist group, murdered 29 Arab worshipers in the tomb of Abraham, located in the city of Hebron. The 1995 Oklahoma City bombing was carried out by members who were at least ideologically associated with the Christian Identity movement. In the same year, the Japanese religious sect Aum Shinrikyo released the deadly nerve gas Sarin in the Tokyo subway, killing 12 and injuring over 3,000 people.

However, in terms of destructive capabilities, none of these religious groups can come close to the Islamic groups operating in many parts of the Arab/Islamic world. No group in history has been able to kill so many as the al Qaeda attacks of 9/11. Similarly, no other groups can match the ability of the Hamas, the Palestine Islamic Jihad, and other groups in continuing a sustained attack of lethal suicide bombing in Israel. We will discuss the causes of Islamic terrorism later in the book.

While ascriptive identities are part of an individual's socialization process often from infancy, there are identities that people choose to adopt at a later stage of life. They may include belonging to an environmental group, a new religious cult, or even developing a Marxist class identity. These identities are to be taught since they do not come naturally.

The dual motivations

If we assume that people are motivated by both ideology and personal rewards, we can rewrite the standard cost/benefit equation as:

Benefit to the self + benefit to the group + net cost of participation > 0

In this formulation, I not only divide up the benefits into individual and collective, I also view the cost as a net of participation versus non-participation. That is, if an individual takes part in a dissident activity, he risks punishment from the state. However, if he remains neutral, he incurs the possibility of retribution by the insurgent forces. If the fear of government is higher than that of the rebel group, without any ideological imperative, an individual will remain passive. However, if the fear of the rebel group exceeds the fear of the government, the same individual will take part in dissident activities.

I argue that in any political movement we are likely to find those who join for personal gains.[118] I call them *mercenaries*. Their motivations are no different from those who join criminal gangs all over the world. However, I call those who join primarily out of their desire to do good for their group *ideologues*. Finally, there are those who join out of fear. For them the cost of non-joining may be too high. I call these individuals *captive participants*. Hence, the motivations for joining a group can be *greed, ideology,* or *fear*.

An organization—terrorist or legitimate—thrives by being protean in its goals and objective.[119] However, once a group is established, it develops an organizational structure. It acquires funds and firearms and gains power. Money, guns, and power inevitably draw many whose interests are primarily personal. Furthermore, when a group gains enough power, it derives the ability to coerce those who might not otherwise have joined. Although it is not possible to peer into the minds of anybody and classify an individual into this motivational scheme, I argue that a proper set of public policies must begin by distinguishing among the ideologues, mercenaries, and captive participants (see Figure 3.1).

Mass communication and expressive choice: gaining vs. being

When we purchase something or join a collective action, why do we do it? Economics has traditionally linked the demand for a good with its utility value. This is known as "instrumental rationality," where I purchase a commodity for its intrinsic value. However, our purchases not only allow us to *enjoy the utility* of the products we buy, but also to *become a certain person* through our consumption.[120] In other words, my choice has an instrumental component, where I want a certain product for its specific functionality, I also covet it for its symbolic value. Thus, I demand a product for what it *offers me*, but also my demand for it is influenced by what *it says about me*. For instance, when I buy a car, I buy it as much for its technical specification (the

		Collective identity	
		High	Low
Economic incentive	High	Mixed motive	Mercenaries/thugs
	Low	True believers	Non-participants

Figure 3.1 Collective identity.

instrumental component of "gains") as for the image of me that it projects. My driving a particular automobile allows me to be a certain individual.

Mass marketing, like political communication, has always depended on the expressive or symbolic aspect of the message.[121] Perhaps the most successful advertisement campaign in history is the "Marlboro Man." The most striking aspect of this ad is that the character does not say or does anything remarkable other than quietly lighting up a cigarette. An analysis of this powerful image suggests that the ad conveys a very important message of rugged individualism, which resonates deeply with the American psyche. Therefore, when I light a cigarette, I not only *enjoy* the taste, but also *become* my own person. In the area of political communication, the 1988 advertising campaign in the presidential race featuring an African-American convict named Willie Horton similarly stands out as a prime example of appealing to a large segment of the population's quintessential image of a threatening figure.[122]

Research on political communication also demonstrates the importance of the use of symbolic words in mobilizing people. For instance, in the US the conservative Republican Party had been trying to eliminate the estate tax, tax on large sums of bequeathals. However, they realized that to the public, the term "estate" evokes images of large inheritance. As a result, they found little public support for it, until they started calling it the "death tax." Suddenly, common people started to associate the tax with the ultimate injustice of having to pay taxes even in death.[123]

If we want to understand the primary recruiting tool for many terrorist organizations, we must pay attention to the message that the leaders send out, which taps into the deeply held religious or cultural ethos of the people. The image of Osama bin Laden, for example, has been carefully crafted by the al-Qaeda. Having shunned a life of extreme privilege, the carefully monitored pictures show him living an ascetic life, sharing simple food with his comrades in a tent from a common plate. These images cut a highly potent symbol in the minds of those who live in societies plagued by corruption and extreme economic inequalities. Also, the attire, the demeanor and the underlying message of the Saudi fugitive conform to the godly images of a holy man in the Islamic world. Therefore, when young men follow bin Laden's path, they become part of this mythological image of Islamic life. It is, of course, important to note that the power of the image is specific to culture, history, and socio-economic condition of the audience. For instance, the image of bin Laden, which works so well in the Islamic world, creates an opposite impression in the Western world. The media plays an important role in creating the image of a hero or a villain and, increasingly, the Internet is becoming the most potent tool of the mass marketing of terrorism. The motivations of extremes of human acts confound us. For example, it is impossible to fully comprehend the mental process that produced the suicide missions of the 9/11 attackers. It will be impossible to put such action within the framework of instrumental rationality. Yet, such actions make more sense as a choice based on the logic of expressive rationality. Perhaps the reason the attackers chose their destiny has less to do with *achieving something as a result of their action*, and more to *be somebody in their own eyes*. To the participants in jihadi movement, the acts of self-sacrifice transform them into god-like creatures, much beloved by God himself. Yet, being a human being, none of them can ignore the calls of self-interest. Some consciously, and many others quite unconsciously, act in their self-interest, craving earthly rewards of money, power, prestige, etc. This quintessential human nature, I submit, makes the job of profiling a terrorist such an impossible task. In their motivations, terrorists remain indistinguishable from all of us.

In sum

In mainstream economics rationality is defined as the drive to maximize an actor's self-utility. This extreme reductionsitic assumption of human nature has an intractable problem: it cannot explain altruistic behavior, the primary basis of collective actions including the decision to participate in an act of terrorism. Therefore, in this chapter I have argued that the inclusion of maximization of group welfare along with self-utility is a way out of this logical quagmire. The proponents of rational-choice theory argue against altering the fundamental assumption of economic rationality since such attempts might render a theory tautological by introducing factors that are "arbitrary." By drawing from biology and social psychology, I have demonstrated that the inclusion of group-based utility is as fundamental to our humanity as the pursuit of selfish utility. Furthermore, since collective identity—from which group-based utility is derived—is contextual and is behaviorally determined, its inclusion in the explanation of altruistic behavior is eminently falsifiable. Finally, the generation of collective identity, however, is not automatic. It is produced, shaped, and promoted by the political entrepreneurs, who, by selectively borrowing from history, religion, and mythology, create the images of enemies and allies.

4   The dynamics of dissent

A theoretical perspective

Our war on terror begins with al-Qaeda, but it does not end there. It will not end until every terrorist group of global reach has been found, stopped, and defeated.

President George W. Bush (2002)[1]

We are in strong and brutal battle, between us and the Jews, with Israel being the spearhead, and its backers among the Zionists and the Crusaders. So we have not hesitated to kill the Jews who conquered the sanctuary of the Prophet (Jerusalem, the third holiest shrine of Islam). And those who kill our children, women, and brothers day after day, and whoever stands in the aggressor's ranks, has only himself to blame.

Osama bin Laden[2]

The puzzle of the "root causes"

The search for the root causes of terrorism has been both controversial and confusing. It is controversial because some argue that given the reprehensible nature of the acts, where terrorists target non-combatants including innocent men, women and children, there is no need to understand the causes that led them to commit these heinous crimes. In fact, the critics fear that any attempt at understanding the root causes may lead to sympathy for the perpetrators. For instance, in June 2005, the presidential advisor Karl Rove criticized the liberals for trying to "understand" the reasons for the 9/11 attacks.[3] In fact, Rove's argument is typical of regime supporters facing threats of terrorism all over the world. This view, however, does not have much credence in the academic community since the steps separating understanding, sympathizing, and advocating are well marked.

The confusion over the search for the root causes arises because none of the usual suspects, such as poverty, religious devotion, or lack of political opportunities, seem to explain fully the outbursts of terrorism. When such hypotheses are tested empirically, they almost always produce weak correlations. On 11 March 2004 a series of bombs exploded in and around the central train station Atocha in the heart of Madrid, which took the lives of nearly

200 commuters during a busy rush hour. On the first anniversary of this 3/11 attack, 65 of the best-known scholars and terrorism experts in the world were assembled in Madrid. Their combined effort was published in a book. Reflecting the collective frustration of this august gathering Louise Richardson was frank in her assessment:

> the search for the underlying accuses of terrorism is a complicated endeavor. The difficulty of the task must serve as an inducement to sustained and rigorous research on the subject—not as an invitation to throw in the towel and deal simply with the symptoms that present themselves.[4]

Poverty

To most of us, the link between poverty and terrorism (or more broadly, sociopolitical violence) seems almost self-evident. Beginning with Aristotle, poverty has been the prime suspect in fomenting political violence for at least two thousand years of recorded scholarship. Yet Krueger and Maleckova, in a thorough study, examined the issue with a great deal of precision and found little correlation between poverty and terrorism.[5] The problem of establishing a correlation between poverty and political violence, however, is that it is not very clear how we should define poverty. Does poverty mean individual poverty, where the poor being tired of not having its fair share of the national wealth starts a violent rebellion? In that case, information on those who take part in violent movements—gleaned from police reports or face-to-face interviews—should clearly demonstrate that the ranks of the revolutionaries are filled by frustrated men and women mired in economic destitution. In psychological terms this is known as "egotistical deprivation." Much of the information for these studies is gathered from direct interviews of the participants in terrorist activities[6] or from other secondary sources, such as arrest reports.[7] Empirical evidence, however, does not establish the case that those who take part in terrorism are from the poorest segments of the community. In 2002 the Pew Research Center conducted a survey of public opinion in the Muslim world.[8] From this survey, Ethan Bueno de Mesquita correlated the following question:

> Some people think that suicide bombing and other forms of violence against civilian targets are justified in order to defend Islam from its enemies. Other people believe that, no matter what the reason, this kind of violence is never justified. Do you personally feel that this kind of violence is often justified to defend Islam, sometimes justified, rarely justified, or never justified?[9]

By using the answer to this question to the various economic, demographic, and political indicators, Bueno de Mesquita found that a person's perception of the economy (either from personal standpoint or in the aggregate) "is essentially uncorrelated with his or her support for terrorism."[10]

The accumulated information from this and other empirical works is fairly clear. Most of the studies of individual (or egotistical) deprivation find the counter-intuitive result: those from the poorest segments of the population do not typically fill the ranks of the violent revolutionaries. Rather it is the scions of the middle- and upper-middle-class families who get disproportionately involved in politically motivated violence. The profiles of the most recent attackers, the participants of the 9/11 attacks, the London underground train bombing (the "7/7 attacks"), along with the involvement of the doctors in the failed plot to bomb various targets in the UK, provide strong anecdotal examples of the involvement of the middle class as opposed to the poor in acts of terrorism.

We can also attempt to establish a correlation between poverty and terrorism by measuring poverty with aggregate data within nations. Thus, we can hypothesize that the nations with the highest percentage of people under the official poverty line would produce the most deaths and injuries from terrorism. I have plotted the log of fatalities and injuries from terrorism in the vertical axis and the percentage of people under poverty from 110 countries (Figure 4.1). As can be seen from this diagram, the plot does not show a strong pattern. A simple statistical test also corroborates this observation.[11]

We may also define poverty as a national phenomenon, where poorer coun-

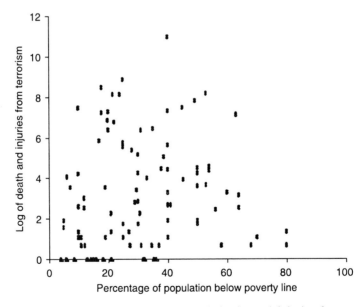

Figure 4.1 Plot of national poverty rates, and deaths and injuries from terrorism (2002–2007).

Source: MIPT database and CIA *World Fact Book.*

tries with low per capita GDP are expected to produce more terrorism. A large number of empirical studies have examined this hypothesis and have generally found a weak correlation between the two.[12] Figure 4.2 plots the casualties of terrorism against per capita GDP, and once again, as can be clearly seen, the correlation between the two is weak.[13]

Another group of studies focuses on "fraternal deprivation" or deprivation felt by individuals as members of a group.[14] This is a situation where individual actors might feel that while they may not have personally experienced discrimination, poverty, or humiliation, their intense sense of deprivation is the product of a shared concept felt by an entire community. For instance, the plight of the Palestinians in Israel has spawned frustration and anger in the Muslim communities throughout the world and has prompted many to take up their cause even when they themselves have not faced poverty or other forms of economic deprivation.[15] A number of studies have found close links between this aspect of deprivation and terrorism and political violence.[16]

In sum, despite the age-old suspicion linking poverty to political violence, empirical evidence draws a much more complex picture.

Lack of democratic freedom

Immediately after the devastating attacks of 9/11 the following question was on everybody's mind: why do these people hate us more than they love their own lives? The quick response that came from President Bush, which

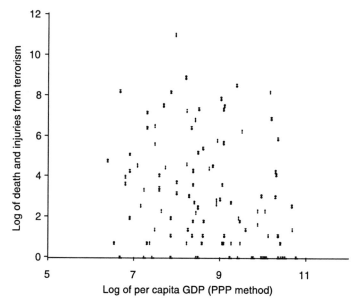

Figure 4.2 Plot of GDP per capita and deaths and injuries from terrorism (2002–2007).

Source: MIPT database and CIA *World Fact Book.*

resonated well with the grieving US public, was that "*they* hate us for our freedom." These terrorists are from freedom-deprived nations and our ability to choose our own destiny has somehow evoked a deep sense of envy among these people. Unfortunately, this line of reasoning allowed the Bush administration to embrace the cause of spreading democracy around the world with the zeal of a religious crusader.[17] Democracy was seen as the perfect antidote for the citizens of the despotic nations. The result of this unquestioned understanding of the root causes of terrorism saw the invasion of Iraq. The transplanted seeds of democracy in the deserts of Iraq were going to sprout and eventually cover the entire Arab/Muslim world, making us safe from terrorism for ever.

Alas, like all other supposed causes of terrorism, this too failed us. The democracies of Great Britain and Spain not only suffered the devastating effects of terrorism, but what shocked many the most was that the perpetrators, unlike the ones who took part in the 9/11 attacks, were not foreigners, but homegrown. Even a number of US citizens were found to have strong links with the al-Qaeda abroad. Although it is a matter of folk wisdom that democracies don't go to war against each other, no such assertion can be made about terrorism. Even if we forget the anarchists, the new left groups in the 1970s, the recent experiences of India, Israel, and Sri Lanka, and the partially democratic nations of Russia, Pakistan, and many others around the world should dispel any myth about democracy as an antidote to terrorism. In fact, based on Pew Research Center's survey data, Bueno de Mesquita found that "attitudes toward democracy as a system of governance for the respondent's home country, and support for terrorism are close to uncorrelated."[18] For a clear demonstration of this overall lack of correlation, I have plotted terrorism data against index of democracy and, once again, as we can clearly see, there is no discernable pattern between the two (Figure 4.3). A statistical test demonstrates the apparent lack of correlation.[19]

What about the hypothesis that democratic nations are the primary targets of the terrorists? Pape[20] has generated controversy by claiming that the democracies are the primary targets of suicide bombing.[21] Although democracy is not a binary concept and nations fall on a continuum of democratic values, many countries with questionable democratic roots are the biggest targets of suicide attacks. These countries would include Pakistan, Afghanistan, Iraq, Morocco, and Russia. Despite having very low democratic values and institutions, these countries have suffered enormously from suicide terror.

Geography

Does geography influence the course of an insurgency? Fearon and Laitin argue that civil wars are not explained very well by the levels of grievances, such as income inequality, poverty, or discrimination in the society.[22] Nor is the lack of democratic freedom or the extent of ethnic or religious differences or any other form of "clash of civilizations" an excellent predictor of civil

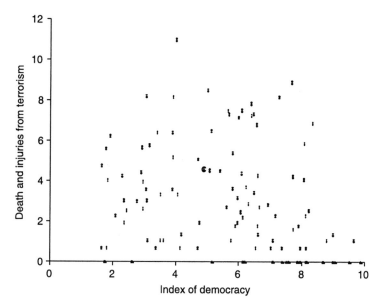

Figure 4.3 Democracy and deaths and injuries from terrorism.

Source: MIPT database and *The Economist*, Democracy Index (2007).

wars, insurgencies or protracted low-intensity warfare. Rather, they demonstrated that these events are best explained by a number of physical attributes such as bad roads and rough terrains. Civil wars are also prevalent in weak nations, without a strong military or bureaucratic infrastructure.

The findings of Fearon and Laitin suggest that the armies of the poor nations with crumbling or non-existent infrastructure offer a weak presence.[23] Furthermore, since the population is not dependent on the government for livelihood it has low opportunity costs for joining the forces of violent opposition, who might provide them with not only security, but also with all the rudimentary public goods that all of us grow accustomed to expect from our governments. From their research we can deduce an interesting conclusion: while insurgency, guerrilla warfare, and civil war, where at least some form of an assembled rebel force collectively challenge the government, are the products of rural, mountainous nations with poor infrastructure, terrorism, whereby a small group of non-state actors carry out attacks against non-combatants, is the more prevalent in the relatively wealthy urbanized nations.

State failure

One of the most dreaded events in a nation's history takes place when the power of the central government weakens or becomes close to non-existent. The hallmark of an organized society is that the state carries the monopoly of the right to use power.[24] In the face of a prolonged armed conflict, many countries around the world become "a mere geographic expression, a black hole into which a failed polity has landed."[25] Countries like Lebanon during its civil war, and Somalia, Afghanistan, and Iraq are prime examples of failed states, at the time of writing this book.[26]

Although the term "state failure" may imply that an entire country has descended into anarchy, it also may happen that an otherwise functioning state with ample central control will contain parts that are lawless. For instance, the "wild west" of the Western Frontier Provinces has only nominally been part of the political structure of Pakistan since her independence. Even the much-vaunted Pakistani army, much less the police and civilian bureaucrats, dare not venture into these areas. O'Donnell calls these the "brown areas" of state control.[27]

Napoleoni aptly describes the failed states and the "brown areas" as follows:

> They are ravaged by internal flights, torn apart by savage conflicts between communities (as has happened in Kosovo); their borders are uncontrolled and undefined; the ruling power (either warlords or dictators, such as Mobutu, or the ruling political elite, such as the Taliban) prey on their own citizens; corruption is endemic; per capita as well as regional GDP is falling rapidly; violence and crime are rife and uncontrollable. Anarchy is the norm.[28]

In a failed state or in a "brown area," the calculation of costs and benefits of terrorist organizations goes through a radical shift. Since the government is

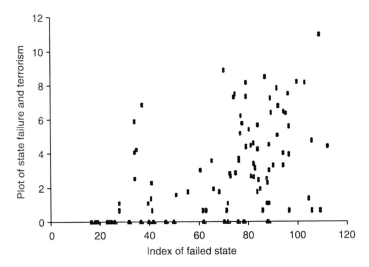

Figure 4.4 Plot of state failure and terrorism.

Source: MIPT database (2002–2007) and State Failure Index, *Foreign Policy* (2006).

Note: the higher the index, the greater is the extent of state failure.

unable to enforce the law, terrorists and all other organizations that operate outside the legal structure carry on their activities with impunity; the costs of participating in illegal activities plummet and all kinds of nefarious activities, including terrorism, flourish. In 2006, the journal *Foreign Policy* developed a cross-national index of state failure, based on 12 factors of governmental control.[29] As we can see, Figure 4.4 shows a clear positive relationship between the extent of state failure and terrorism. The regression results also corroborate this strong relationship.[30]

Solving the puzzle

So, now we are back to square one in our quest for the root causes of terrorism. If it is not poverty or lack of democracy, then what are the causes of terrorism? Surely, physical geography is a facilitating factor for insurgency, but it cannot be seen as the root cause. Moreover, rough terrain and broken-down infrastructure may promote civil wars, but they are not causally linked with terrorism.

The reason the measures of economic deprivation—relative or absolute, egotistical or aggregate national—do not show a strong correlation with the occurrence of political violence is because of the presence of the so-called "collective action" problem.[31] That is, just because an individual feels deprived does not mean that a rational actor will automatically join a dissident movement. In fact, I argue that the factors of deprivation only provide the *necessary condition* for mass violence. For *sufficient condition*, we need to look at the role that political entrepreneurs play in framing the issues to produce a strong enough collective identity. The strength of collective identity, which clearly identifies the "in" and the "out" groups—the "community" and its "enemies"—prompts people to take part in violent actions in the name of their group. In other words, it is not enough for an individual to turn to terrorism because of the frustration resulting from his own economic condition until he is certain that his misery is caused by the machinations of a well-defined group whom he identifies as his enemies. Unlike an individual's self-identity, collective identity is not stable. It is contextual and multiple. The political entrepreneurs bring about violent collective actions by "connecting the dots" for their followers by creating a consistent story by borrowing from religion, history, and mythologies. When this story resonates with a large number of people, they adopt such a collective identity and a mass movement is born.

There are numerous examples of abject poverty and deprivation that did not bring out violent political movements. For instance, Gupta argues[32] that the achievement gap between the Euro-Americans and the African-Americans remains as wide as in the days when Martin Luther King Jr. was marching, the major metropolitan cities were ablaze with widespread race riots, and black radicalism was rampant among groups, such as the Black Panther[33] and the Symbionese Liberation Army.[34] Yet, after the assassination of King, Malcolm X, and other radical leaders, and the dismemberment of the SLA and Black Panther movement, black political movements, both peaceful and violent, came to an end. The Los Angeles riot of 1992 was a disorganized, free-for-all expression of anomic frustration rather than a cohesive action against a racist society.[35] Even the Nation of Islam, under the firebrand leadership of Louis Farrakhan, eschewed all kinds of violent collective actions. In October 1995, when a large number of African-American men assembled for the Million Man March in Washington D.C., Farrakhan urged them to take personal responsibility in the face of a long litany of economic grievances. The need for collective action, radical or otherwise, was simply forgotten. To be sure, there have been small regional issue-oriented protests against racism, often led by Rev. Al Sharpton or Jesse Jackson, but they have been episodic and did not produce any nation-wide movement.

The absence of radical political movements is the result of not having a strong enough collective identity within the African-American community after the passage of the Civil Rights legislation and the abolition of signs of overt discrimination. In the absence of the water cannons, police dogs, and club-wielding white county sheriffs, the community saw a slow dilution of the notion of both "us" and "them" factors of collective identity.

There is no doubt that the African-American community has a distinct identity or a separate worldview. The nature of the chasm in perception was laid bare during the trial of O.J. Simpson.[36] Similar to the divergent worldviews that came out in the Simpson trial, there is also a gap in the black voting pattern. By all measures, the vast majority of the community (often over 90 percent) vote in favor of the Democratic Party.

Yet, there are a number of factors that have contributed to a weak collective identity for the African-American community. Throughout history the most potent generator of conflict has been claims over territory. Few images produce a strong bond of collective identity than the idea of a motherland of a fatherland. Even when a group, such as the Jews in their Diaspora, did not have a territory, they shared the notion of entitlement based on the biblical promise to the land of Israel. In contrast, being brought in as slaves in an immigrant nation, the African-Americans did not have a specific territory they could claim as their homeland. Second, during the Jim Crow era, particularly in the South, the African-Americans were compelled to live in segregated communities regardless of income or social status. After the passage of the Civil Rights legislation, the middle and upper middle class left the poor in the urban ghettos or in abject rural poverty for the suburbs. Therefore, an examination of income distribution of the community shows a U-shaped distribution, where most of the African-Americans are either in the bottom quintile or in the top.[37] These factors have contributed to a physical as well as psychological separation between the leaders and the followers in the community.

A similar picture emerges when we consider the image of the "enemy" or the "out-group" for the African-Americans. In the pre-Civil Rights legislation days, the binary world was painted with broad strokes of black and white. The mid-1960s also saw a huge increase in non-European migration. Today, the African-Americans are another minority group within a multicultural, multilingual, multihued society. In the center-cities of urban America, even those who claim African heritage are divided along myriad national, ethnic, and tribal lines. The Somalis, the Ethiopians, the Haitians, the Jamaicans, compete with the descendants of those who came mostly from West Africa on slave boats. The national debate over the "blackness" of the Presidential candidate Barack Obama is symptomatic of this complex maze of identity in the African-American community. Furthermore, with the disappearance of overt signs of racism, as many surveys have revealed the gradual recession of "racial discrimination" from the list of complaints of the black community, especially among the young.[38] Also, in a society which is firmly established on the bedrock notion of extreme individualism, the perception of a strong collective identity finds a very difficult footing. Finally, and perhaps most importantly, Martin Luther King Jr. never promoted the image of a racial enemy. By framing his struggle against injustice, King took away the sharp edge of a dissident movement that is prevalent among most other parts of the world out of the racial politics in America.

On the other side of the world, there is another important puzzle. Very few groups, if any, have suffered as much in the hands of a larger society as the so-called "untouchable" castes in India. The humiliation and a total degradation that the society imposed on the hapless people remain unparalleled in human history. Yet, as we will see in the following chapter, until the Maoists gave them leadership and fomented a violent insurgency, in the long history of the Indian subcontinent such movements are conspicuous by their near total absence.

As I mentioned above, the answer to the puzzle appears to be simple. All of the factors of actual grievances provide the *necessary* condition for collective actions of all sorts, including terrorism. For *sufficient* condition, we must look for the formation of a strong enough *collective identity, which is formed through the framing of a grievance by political entrepreneurs by expressing them in the context of religion, nationalism or economic class.* The rise of political entrepreneurs remains largely a matter of historical chance; the random occurrence of charismatic leaders with organizational capabilities who can channel the frustration and anger felt by an entire community into sustained collective actions.

Although nobody can predict the rise of a charismatic leader, it is clear that when there is an intense feeling of grievances, the chances of someone utilizing the widespread feeling and frustration increases.[39] Moreover, once these leaders emerge, their basis for constructing collective identity—religious, nationalistic, or economic class—depends on the existing sociopolitical environment. Thus, in an Islamic society, the strong sense of *Ummah* or community, defined by religion, provides a ready launching pad. In contrast, where there has been a strong tradition of political activism based on the language of economic class struggle, Communist movements will flourish. And, where the historic grievance is against another ethno-linguistic group, aspirations of nationalism are likely to sprout.

Along with the work of political entrepreneurs, there is another important aspect of the formation of collective identity, which is most often ignored in social sciences. This involves the role played by literature, music, and art in defining the in- and the out-groups. Every organized government, long before the invention of writing, has engaged in building monuments and sculptures to establish the symbolic identity of a nation. A king's crown is much more than an article of formal wear, it is the embodiment of an entire nation. Every nation today has a national anthem, whose regular singing instantly evokes pride among the audience by promoting the idea of a single community united in its purpose. Similarly, every social movement is shaped by the symbols it uses, the songs that are sung, the poems and the novels that are written, and plays that are staged. It is indeed impossible to quantify the impact of songs such as "we shall overcome someday" on the hearts and minds of those who took part in the acts of civil disobedience against an unfair society. Yet, any examination of people's collective choice will reveal the importance of the symbolic contributions of art and literature to the formation of a dissident movement.

Contagion of ideas

Since these identities, in the final analysis, are "imagined," the contagion of ideas plays a huge role in creating "waves" of terrorism and violence across the world. The local grievances are accentuated when they are linked to a larger global movement. This is the effect of contagion. In David Rapoport's (2006) terminology—discussed in the previous chapter—the global contagion of ideas is called the "waves." The ills of early industrialization produced the anarchists. Through disjointed individual acts, they hoped to change the world. The emerging media covered their acts and provided the much-need publicity which the former British Prime Minister Margaret Thatcher called the "oxygen of the terrorists." The anarchists did manage to shake up the world, until the end of World War I, which saw the beginning of nationalistic aspirations in reaction to the exploitative colonial system. When this second wave died down with the granting of independence to the colonies in the 1950s, a new wave started where the anarchists left off. The emergence of the Soviet Union as a Super Power and China as a source of ideological steward-ship provided the leadership and the resources to begin uprisings led by organized Communist parties. The US involvement in the Vietnam War added fuel to the fire by creating a vast cadre of activists and sympathizers for the third wave of global terrorism. As this wave subsided in the late 1970s and early 1980s, a fourth wave of international terrorism started mostly around the ideals of Islamic fundamentalism. The inability to find a solution to the Palestinian problem has been a source of deep frustration in the Arab/Islamic world. For the past half a century nearly every action from military invasion to terrorism had produced few tangible results for the Palestinians. In the Arab eyes, the West and the US, in particular, had increasingly shed their status as "honest brokers" and moved ever closer to the interest of the Jewish state. To some, the only possible redeemers to this continuing humiliation came in the shape of a defiant Saddam Hussain and, later, in Osama bin Laden. The quick capitulation of Saddam Hussain and his much feared Republican Guards in the two Gulf Wars and the rapid destruction of the Taliban regime in Afghanistan only added to the collective frustration and anger in the Arab/Muslim world. In a series of instructive reports, the United Nations Development Program (UNDP, 2002) painted a picture of a region increasingly failing to keep pace with the economically dynamic South and Southeast Asian nations.[40] Together, in a vast region of Islamic community the series of setbacks created a psychological miasma, from which the ideology of al-Qaeda provided an alternative to some. Thus, the present jihadi movement, representing a concoction of liberation theology, socioeconomic aspirations, and a search for identity in a rapidly changing world, was able to spread rapidly throughout the world as the fourth wave of international terrorism.

Finally, why do we find a strong correlation between state failure and terrorism? Every action is an outcome of motivation and opportunity. The relationship between terrorism and state failure is less of a motivational link and, instead, addresses the issue of opportunity. An organized government's central control and political legitimacy depend on its ability to deliver public goods, such as security, law and order, and physical infrastructure. However, when the central government gets weak a power vacuum is created, which is quickly filled by various extra-legal groups. They provide all the public goods that people in these areas need. For instance, a Brooking Institution report (2007) points out that the Hizbullah's "power resources stems not only from its demonstrated military capabilities to be able to withstand an all-out attack by the Israeli Defense Force, but also from its ability to generate social capital and political legitimacy through their ability to deliver essential services to the devastated areas." Similarly, the Taliban came forward with its Pakistani-supported organizational hierarchy, which was able to provide a modicum of law and order in the war that ravaged Afghanistan in the late 1980s, which gave it a good deal of political legitimacy among a large segment of the war-weary population.

Furthermore, an organized government is characterized by its monopoly of imposing sanctions. If that monopoly is compromised, the ranks of the terrorists are going to be filled with those who otherwise might have been fence sitters. Among them, a significant portion may be called captive participants. Popkin (1979), in his much-cited work, clearly demonstrated the coercive impact of the Viet Cong on the decision-making process of the South Vietnamese peasants to join the forces of the North. Every group attempts to maintain its monopoly over its own territories. As a result, groups such as the LTTE, al-Qaeda, and IRA engage in killing and maiming members of their own community through a systematic process of intimidation. Through such activities, they recruit activists, whose only motivation for joining is the fear of retribution. In sum, any violent movement will comprise the true believers, the mercenaries, and the captive participants.

Birth of a movement

While studying the history we must recognize that no mass movement can be studied as a single event. If we look into the evolution of any movement, we will find its links to a distant past, which will link to an even more remote precedent. Thus, we may study the American Revolution, yet this epochal set of events was simply a culmination of other rebellions, such as the Sons of Liberty, which mobilized the shopkeepers in Boston in 1765 to protest against the Stamp Act.[41] By tracing its history we can go back to the Franco-British rivalry in Europe till the path is lost in the dim antiquity of unrecorded history. Therefore, any narration of the history of a mass movement must start from an arbitrary cut-off date.

A quick look around the world will show that among the multitude of minority groups included in Gurr's *Minorities at Risk*, only a handful take up arms in the name of their community to redress current or past injustices. Whatever the immediate cause that triggers an upheaval is, it is incumbent upon a political leader(s) to take the historic grievances and give them a political character through framing of the issues in a way that resonates with a sufficient number of people within the defined community. The political entrepreneurs, by attracting a core group of followers, establish an organizational structure. When there is a huge asymmetry of power a dissident movement adopts terrorist strategies and carries out propaganda by deed to attract others from a larger base of sympathizers and free riders. I have presented the process by which a movement is born (see Figure 4.5).[42]

Any current movement—except perhaps some idiosyncratic millenarian groups, such as the Japanese Aum Shinrikyo and the East African Lord's Resistance Army—can trace its roots to the history of past struggles and the rise of a charismatic leader. Thus, the current Maoist movement in India has its beginning in the failed movement of the 1970s, which, in turn, carried the remnants of the uprisings in the 1950s, and these to an endless series of peasant rebellions during the British colonial rule.[43] The same is true for the present-day Islamic movement and the rebellion by the Irish Catholics against their Protestant adversaries.

The group and the base

The birth of a movement is characterized by the formation of a dissident group by a small band of ideologically motivated men and women. The reason behind a strong ideological bond among the initial members is because they need to go against an established order, often taking enormous risks to their

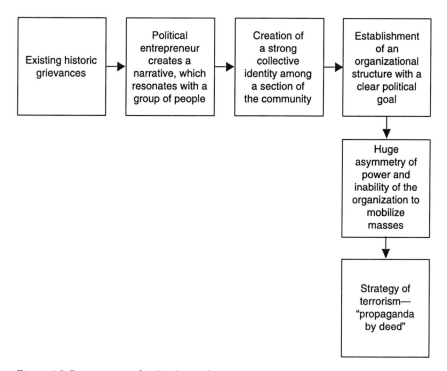

Figure 4.5 Root causes of collective action.

person. Furthermore, since the nascent group is weak, it cannot offer its members special privileges or any other kind of special reward. In order to be viable, the group almost immediately develops a hierarchical structure with a charismatic leader at the helm. Since a dissident movement is created around a set of historical grievances, a larger base of sympathizers usually supports its core membership. These are the free riders, who share the group's core beliefs and feel that their entire community would benefit if the group is able to achieve its political goals. Yet, because of a number of "selfish" reasons they refuse to take activists' roles. Most often this support base is surrounded by an even larger group, which, typically, does not share the ideological orientation nor is it included within the perimeters of the dissident group's perceived "in-group." As a result, the larger society is either apathetic or hostile to the group's political aims (see Figure 4.6).

Al-Qaeda was established in the 1980s and, after the defeat of the Soviet Union in the Afghan war, transformed itself into a fighting force against the Saudi royal family and then against their principal benefactor, the US. The innovation of the idea of the near enemy (the "apostate" regimes of the Islamic nations) and the far enemy (the US and the West) was based on a long struggle, which goes back to the establishment of the young religion and its quick expansion, which brought it directly into confrontation with the

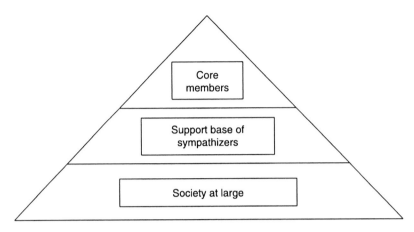

Figure 4.6 The group and the base.

established Christian Europe. Yet, al-Qaeda could bring only a fraction of the world Muslim community to its core.[44] The image of the pious bin Laden has enlarged its support base far and wide, yet many in the Arab/Islamic world still remain either apathetic to his message or are hostile to it. Therefore, public support is absolutely essential in the politics of terrorism. Without public support a dissident organization cannot recruit volunteers, raise money, operate safe houses, or avoid infiltration and destruction by the target government.[45]

The mixed motives of individuals and groups

Reliability of cross-group data on various dissident groups is always open to criticism. Yet, a researcher often needs to work with imperfect information. By using such a data set, collected by the Israeli group ICT, in Table 4.1 we can clearly see that most terrorist groups engage in only a few types of violent activities; they seem to specialize in no more than three activities.[46] As can be seen, nearly all of these ten groups shown in the table are highly specialized in their activities. This table presents a thumbnail portrait of these groups indicating the clustered nature of activities of the terrorist groups. Each cell of the table indicates the percentage of each activity for the groups. The last row presents the sum of the three most prevalent acts of violence as a percentage of each group's total activities. From this list we can easily discern the concentrated nature of the various groups. Thus, for instance, the Basque Homeland and Freedom Party (ETA) and the IRA's activities are primarily concentrated on bombings, car bombings, and shootings (96 percent and 94 percent of their total activities). The Peruvian group Sendero Luminoso (the Shining Path) prefers car bombing, shooting, and hostage taking (90 percent). The Islamic rebel group of the Philippines, the Abu Sayyaf group, and the Revolutionary Armed Forces of Colombia (FARC), on the other hand, specialize in kidnapping and hostage taking. They comprise 91 percent and 82 percent of

Table 4.1 Comparison of profiles of ten terrorist groups (1980–2002) (percent of total activities).

Activities	Hamas	Abu Sayyaf Group	al-Qaeda	Basque Homeland and Freedom (ETA)	Rev. Armed Forces of Colombia (FARC)	Liberation Tigers of Tamil Eelam (LTTE)	Palestinian Islamic Jihad (PIJ)	Irish Republican Army (IRA)	Kurdistan Workers' Party (PKK)	Sendero Luminoso (Shining Path)
Bombing	6.1	27.3	13.3	37.3	7.9	20.7	9.3	25.0	27.6	5.0
Car bomb	4,3	0	33.3	35.3	5.3	10.3	18.5	37.5	0	45.0
Hand grenade	2.6	0	6.7	2.0	0	0	1.9	0	3.4	0
Highjacking	0	18.2	6.7	0	2.6	0	0	0	3.4	0
Hostage taking	0	9.1	0	0	7.9	0	0	0	0	5.0
Incendiary devices	0	0	0	0	0	0	0	0	10.3	0
Kidnapping	5.2	45.5	0	0	65.8	6.9	1.9	0	20.7	10.0
Knife attack	7.8	0	0	0	0	3.4	1.9	0	0	0
Letter bomb	0	0	0	2.0	0	0	1.9	0	0	0
Mortar attack	0	0	0	0	5.3	3.4	0	6.2	0	0
Rocket attack	0	0	6.7	0	2.6	3.4	0	0	0	0
Shooting	37.4	0	6.7	23.5	2.6	10.3	27.8	31.5	13.8	35.0
Suicide bombing	34.8	0	26.7	0	0	41.4	35.2	0	13.8	0
Vandalism	0	0	0	0	0	0	0	0	3.4	0
Arson	0	0	0	0	0	0	0	0	3.4	0
Chemical attack	0	0	0	0	0	0	0	0	0	0
Stoning	0	0	0	0	0	0	0	0	0	0
Vehicle attack	1.7	0	0	0	0	0	1.9	0	0	0
Lynching	0	0	0	0	0	0	0	0	0	0
Total	100	100	100	100	100	100	100	100	100	100
Top three activities as a percent of the total	83.6	91.0	73.3	95.6	81.6	72.4	82.0	94.0	62.1	90.0

Activities of terrorist organizations, 1980–2002. Originally published in Bjørgo (2005).

Source: www.ict.org.il/.

their respective activities. Similarly, only a handful of the world's terrorist organizations engage in suicide bombings. Of the 52 major groups listed by the ICT, only nine engage in suicide bombings. Of them, the ones that are active in the Middle East (eight out of nine) have committed 89 percent of all suicide bombings during the 12-year study period. From this table, it is apparent that Hamas and the PIJ follow the path of violence by choosing to concentrate on suicide bombings, shootings, and knife attacks. Thus, we can clearly see that violent opposition groups do not choose their weapons of terror in a random fashion but are guided by their internal organizational logic. It is also interesting to note that among the major groups listed in table 4.1, only the Kurdish Workers' Party (PKK) comes close to offering a full slate of terrorist activities. Their top three activities comprise a relatively low 62.1 percent of their total activities.

Since all of these groups appear to be highly specialized as parts of a deliberate strategy, the question arises, what does their choice of activities say about the motivations of these groups? I have discussed in the previous chapter that although we can never demonstrate a group's motivation, by following Samuelson I can assume that their choice reveals their preference and motivation.[47] In order to find out how these various activities are associated with each other, I ran a Factor Analysis. I have arranged the components

Table 4.2 Factor analysis of violent activities by selected terrorist groups (1991–2002)

Activities	Component factors				
	I Ideological terrorists	II Professional terrorists	III Anomic terrorists	IV Hooligan terrorists	V Vigilante terrorists
Suicide bombings	**.777**	−.228	.05	.322	.414
Shooting attacks	**.759**	.173	.338	.05	−.245
Grenade attacks	**.678**	.377	.302	.391	−.187
Bombing	.274	**.631**	−.444	.307	.313
Car bombings	.403	**.621**	−.590	−.112	.105
Letter bombings	.344	**.452**	−.698	−.021	.195
Mortar attacks	−.561	**.384**	.301	−.438	.191
Rocket attacks	−.495	**.364**	.292	−.362	.064
Vehicle attacks	−.301	−.012	**.938**	.055	.071
Kidnapping	−.357	−.06	**.898**	−.053	−.008
Hostage taking	−.631	.314	**.391**	.247	.110
Vandalism	−.331	−.005	.074	**.928**	.076
Arson attacks	−.331	.005	.074	**.928**	.076
Incendiary devices	−.387	−.05	.01	**.887**	−.003
Highjacking	−.659	.312	.252	**.344**	.105
Stoning	.267	−.299	.100	−.320	**.804**
Lynching	.134	−.630	−.100	.115	**.736**

Source: Originally published in Bjorgo (2005).

Note: Cumulative percentage of explained variance 89.0%.

according to their highest factor loading in the five categories and have presented them in Table 4.2. This table further bolsters the argument that dissident groups do not choose their activities randomly, but do so with careful consideration; they pick those which are closest to their ideology, expertise, opportunity, and the general modus operandi. Let us look at the logic of association of violent activities as identified by Factor Analysis. We may have a deeper understanding of the categories by focussing on the activities that load the highest within each category. Thus, suicide bombings define the first category and we can call it the ideological terrorists, since these are inspired by ideological fervor (Hamas), religious extremism (the PIJ and al-Qaeda), and personal charisma of a leader (the LTTE). I call them "ideological" because, apart from the technical know-how and complex logistics needed to carry out a successful suicide attack, the act needs supremely dedicated cadres who would be willing to give their lives for the cause. This is so rare in the world of violent conflict that only a handful of the groups can have a ready supply of suitable candidates. If we examine the other activities within this factor, we see that shootings and grenade attacks require being physically close to the target, which indicates the assumption of considerable personal risk by the attacker.

In contrast, groups with specific professional skills carry out the second category of attacks. They include bombings and car bombings, which involve a number of specialized skills. Although seldom motivated by acts of religious zealotry, religion may be one of their principal reasons for conflict. These attacks are usually done with remote control devices, which accord the attackers time to escape. The IRA and the ETA fall into this category. Jessica Stern, having interviewed numerous members of terrorist organizations all over the world, notes:[48]

> Over time, however, militants have told me, terrorism can become a career as much as a passion. Leaders harness humiliation and anomie and turn them into weapons. Jihad becomes addictive, militants report, and with some individuals or groups—the "professional" terrorists—grievances can evolve into greed: for money, political power, status, or attention.

I, therefore, call these groups "professional" terrorists.

The third category of activities are promoted primarily by the groups who need to make a financial gain, such as FARC and the Abu Sayyaf Group. Their preferences for monetary gains are revealed through their preponderant emphasis on hostage taking and kidnapping. Their vehicle attacks are usually related to the attempts of taking hostages. Since the hostages are held for ransom, and usually for quite a large amount, we may conjecture that those taking part in these acts are motivated also by their personal pecuniary considerations. In other words, we may expect to find a larger proportion of what I call "mercenaries" among these groups. We may call them anomic terrorists, since they attempt to operate within an environment of anomie or lawlessness and thrive in failed states or in nations with weakened central control. Dissident organizations thus come with various forms of motivation. For the purpose of careful analysis and subsequent policy prescription, it simply does not stand to reason to paint all groups with a broad brush. We must understand the qualitative difference that separates the original al-Qaeda, founded by Osama bin Laden, from the likes of FARC and Abu Sayyaf.

Escalation and de-escalation

A dissident group becomes more powerful as its base gets strengthened. As shown in Figure 4.7, a group gets stronger when it gains popular support. As a group gains political legitimacy its core group increases in size taking new recruits from the pool of erstwhile free riders. I call them "easy riders" because in Olson's exposition[49] the free riders are those who would not take part in a collective action. The term implies a cut-and-dried absolute categorization.[50] However, as Horgan and others have shown, participation is a seamless process, where someone might take part in a terrorist action and then not do anything in the name of the group.[51] Furthermore, participation can take numerous forms, from passing on a code word to providing a safe passage or a safe house to actually taking part in a violent action designed to kill or injure members of the enemy group. Through the process of escalation, those who did not pay much attention to the dissident group become increasingly attracted to its messages. As a result, a group gains strength and the forces of violent resistance increase.

When a group increases in size, importance, and power, it also develops the capability to recruit another group of activists, the captive participants. In every social movement, particularly those which espouse violence, there are activists who join out of fear of retribution or simple peer pressure. Among

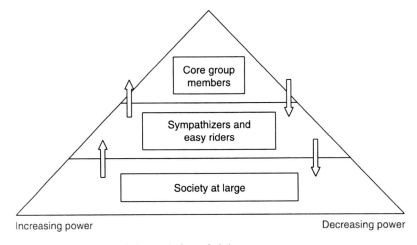

Figure 4.7 Escalation and de-escalation of violence.

the IRA in Ireland, there are numerous examples of young men joining the group due to explicit threats.[52] Although there is no reliable information on how many join these groups out of fear, it is safe to conjecture that the proportion would depend on the strength of the group. Thus, the three types of participants form the core group: the true believers, the mercenaries, and the captive participants.

The opposite takes place when a group loses its political legitimacy and its core membership gets depleted through attrition, desertion, or arrest by the authorities. If the flow of new members is not enough to fill the void, the group starts losing ground. Dissident organizations fight for their political causes. Their choice of violence reflects their strategy to gain strength.

Choice of strategy

When viewed from outside, a particular terrorist action may often seem foolhardy, since many attacks do not appear to have any military significance. For instance, the 9/11 attacks were of no consequence to the military imbalance between the wounded superpower and the Islamic radicals. In fact, these attacks virtually ensured a huge US armed response against al-Qaeda. With Osama bin Laden and Ayman al-Zawahiri on the run, the top echelon of al-Qaeda either killed or arrested, it is hard to imagine what instrumental rationality might have prompted the attacks against the US. As a result, there is often a pervasive assumption of irrationality on the part of the participants as well as the perpetrating terrorist groups.[53] Yet, a careful examination of the terrorist strategies reveals considerable planning and forethought.

By examining terrorist activities, we can divide them into two categories: those that are designed primarily as military actions and those which are symbolic actions, undertaken to produce a number of psychological, political, and, eventually, military results. Thus, those groups that are locked in a territorial struggle stage attacks including suicide missions to gain military advantage. Thus, Hopgood, having studied the use of the elite Black Tigers by the LTTE, saw their use usually for territorial gains.[54] Hopgood clearly states that "Black Tiger attacks aim primarily to win the war, not to spread terror." Similarly, Ayman al-Zawahiri, the leader of the al-Qaeda movement, is clear in his assertion of the efficacy of suicide attacks: "The method of martyrdom operation, [is] the most successful way of inflicting damage against the opponent and least costly to the Mujahidin in terms of casualty."[55]

In contrast, through its activities a group often attempts to send symbolic messages. In their insightful work Schmidt and de Graaf point out that to a terrorist group participation in a violent activity is a form of communication.[56] In the parlance of economics, this is known as "signaling." As they play out a macabre mix between violence and theater they send a message to a number of important adversary and client groups.[57] To the adversaries, it sends a message of threat, the shape of things to come, unless their demands are not met. Pape demonstrates the strategic use of suicide attacks against democracies by various terrorist organizations.[58] Through their acts of public cruelty terrorist groups also signal their commitment to the larger "cause." In their analysis of Hamas, Mishal and Sela argue that part of the motivation of the terrorist group was to provoke the Israelis into imposing draconian measures on the larger Palestinian community.[59] For instance, Bloom argues that Hamas and the Palestinian Islamic Jihad have carefully chosen their strategies to coincide with the ebb and flow of the Palestinian public opinion.[60] When suicide attacks became unpopular they refrained from attacks. When opinion favored the Palestinian Authority to achieve a separate statehood through negotiations with the Israelis, the more radical groups came to a *hudna*, or truce. Similarly, in the immediate aftermath of the 9/11 attacks, when the global public sympathy was clearly in favor of the US, there were no suicide attacks. Through these acts, the dissident groups aim at increasing their political legitimacy and solidifying their support base. Based on econometric analysis Gupta and Mundra showed that suicide attacks in Israel were also caused by inter-group rivalry among the various Palestinian dissident groups.[61] When a government responds with excessive force deemed by the target community, the perpetrating group only increases in stature.[62] Similar to a firm which tries to increase its market share thought advertisement, the various terrorist groups attempt to increase their popular support through acts of wanton violence.

The literature on the strategies of terrorism focusses on its impact on public opinion (both of the target society and the group's own community), the demonstration of the target government's lack of moral standing, inconsistency of application of force, and its offensive weakness in the face of the growing strength of the dissident group. Finally, the groups aim at discrediting the moderates who might be interested in coming to a negotiated settlement with the government.

A dissident group engages in strategic use of violence, which is reflected not only in its timing but also in the choice of activity. For instance, the use of stone-throwing children against the heavily armed Israeli army created worldwide sympathy for the Palestinians living under occupation.[63]

A dissident group may engage in violent activities to demonstrate weakness or inconsistencies of the target government. The ability of a group to expose government weakness increases when it has information on how it might react to the acts of provocation.[64] Empirical findings of Lichbach[65] and Moore[66] corroborate such behavior.

All types of governments are not equally equipped to respond to violence by non-state actors within its own borders the same way. Gupta *et al.* demonstrate that though non-democratic regimes are able to quell rebellions by using brutal force, the democracies are much more constrained in their response.[67] As a result, the democracies must rely on political accommodation rather than sheer repression in their response to violence.

Extremist groups often undertake acts of violence to spoil the middle ground of compromise. Kydd and Walter show that suicide attacks increased in frequency whenever the Israeli and Palestinian authorities were close to an agreement.[68] The Israeli government interpreted the campaigns of suicide attacks by Hamas and the Palestine Islamic Jihad as weakness (or even acquiescence) of the moderate Arafat regime to curb violence by the extremist groups.[69]

Finally, when do terrorist groups employ their biggest weapons, suicide attacks? The smartest weapon in the arsenal of a group is its cadre of suicide attackers.[70] The defining characteristic of suicide attack is that the attackers know that the mission will not be considered a success unless they die in the process.[71] Therefore, as Elster points out, for a group to engage in suicide attacks, it must have volunteers for whom the motivation must shift from "reason" to the "cause."[72]

Evidence from around the world suggests that those groups that are imbedded in a community are typically inspired by nationalistic or irredentist sectarian aspirations, even when they profess religious or Marxist ideologies. These groups develop bases within the society and are much more sensitive to the cultural mores of the base. In contrast, those groups which are filled by the "outsiders," inspired by a millenarian vision, or are supported mostly by foreign countries, are less sensitive to the community's wishes. Similarly, groups that are criminally oriented tend to be less constrained by the community.

Transformation

Terrorist groups are not equal in their devotion to ideological goals. And, over time, some of these groups become more criminal in orientation than political. I distinguish between a terrorist group and a criminal organization by assuming that a terrorist group aims at achieving a set of public goods, the benefits of which will flow to all members of the community, regardless of participation. On the other hand, a criminal gang is motivated by the prospect of quasi-public good (or common pooled resources), the fruits of which are restricted only to the core members of the group.[73] These two goals are often incongruent and, despite the widespread belief to the contrary at the extreme ends of the ideological spectrum a clear division between the two is maintained. As we will see in Chapter 7, these two groups may occasionally develop some cooperative ventures, but they eye each other with unease and suspicion. As a result, their relationship becomes much more complex than is generally assumed.

Terrorism increasing and attenuating forces: the dynamics of terrorism

Terrorism and the strength of a movement follow the dynamic interactions between the state and the dissident group. Facing challenges from a dissident group the state reacts in a predictable way. Since much of what a violent protest group does falls outside the legal system of any organized society, the state portrays these as ordinary acts of criminal behavior. However, when the political nature of these acts becomes apparent, the authorities try a number of time-honored techniques of quelling the rebellion.

During the course of the life of a movement it goes through a number of peaks and troughs when levels of violence escalate and when they subside. We can now develop a conceptual picture of this dynamic relationship by bringing together the accumulated knowledge of the vast literature. We can look at the dialectic relationship between a state and a dissident organization through the interaction between two broadly defined forces: terrorism increasing force (TIF) and terrorism attenuating force (TAF). Let us examine what would constitute these two forces.

In our everyday lives we allocate our available time to the pursuit of activities that promote self-interest as well as our group-interest. The forces that strengthen our collective identity or deepen our conviction that our selfish interests are best served by joining the forces of the opposition make the dissident movement stronger by attracting more activists. On the other hand, if people come to the opposite conclusion, the movement loses ground. Beside the calculations of benefits each rational actor faces a cost factor. If the cost of participation goes up, fewer people join the terrorist movement and vice versa. Beside these three factors of rational decision-making, there are a few facilitating factors. These factors help strengthen the TIF or, in their absence, make the TAF stronger. Let us examine the three factors that determine the escalation and demise of organized dissidence.

Strengthening of collective identity

The notion of "us" and "them" is predicated upon an essentially moral ideological perception, which pitches good against evil, religious against profane, rightful owners against invaders and interlopers. In the process the charismatic leaders frame the issues by defining the in-group and clearly singling out the enemies. The universal message from the leaders is that their community is under attack; without active and violent resistance ("the only language that the enemy understands") its future is doomed.

Rise of charismatic leaders

I have argued that the factors of economic political deprivation do not provide the sufficient causes for the development of systematic opposition to an organized government. For that we need a dissident organization, which can strategically shape the frustration that is widely felt in a community. And, for a successful organization to develop, we need the rise of a charismatic leader(s). This is the biggest un-knowable in history, which ultimately makes any prediction of the rise of terrorism and mass movements problematic. Yet, if we examine the causes of the rise of the fundamentalist movement in Islam, we can see that Muslim grievance against the West has been around at least since the breakdown of the Ottoman Caliphate in Turkey. However, it took a series of political entrepreneurs such as Hassan al-Banna, Sayyid Qutb, Abdul Azzam, Osama bin Laden, and Ayman al-Zawahiri to give it a shape through al-Qaeda by framing the existing grievances in the context of political Islam. Therefore, it should come as no surprise that Fair and Shepherd,[74] by using the Pew Research Center survey data, would find that the largest correlate of support for terrorism comes from those who perceive a threat to Islam.[75]

Overreaction by the government

From the earliest days of the Sicarii, the Jewish zealots who waged wars against the Roman occupiers,[76] to the current day's Islamic suicide attackers, terrorists have always laid a trap for the authorities to overreact and engage in such a manner that would clearly demonstrate their "true nature." Their inhumanity would enrage those who had preferred to sit on the fence and prompt them to take up an active role in the dissident organization. The opponents—often the forces of the target government—reinforce these sentiments through acts that further alienate and provoke the members of the support base. The memories of the atrocities are kept alive through songs, plays, and literature, and the political leadership use these as tools for mass mobilization: the pictures of the tortured and killed serve as the most potent recruiting tool for years to come. In the history of many mass movements, by simply visually inspecting the casualty figures, one can pinpoint the junctures of history when a movement came to life as a response to overreaction by the authorities.

Acts of political/religious provocation by the government

In the final analysis every dissident group lays its claim to moral high ground vis-à-vis the target government. They do it through resorting to religious justification, evoking the images of past glories, and/or demonstrating the immorality of the prevailing economic injustices. Through their strategic moves, the dissident groups attempt to bolster their moral claims. For every movement there are areas of symbolic importance. When the government transgresses these points, public sentiment is instantly inflamed. These arousals of public ire quickly get manifested in terms of higher levels of deaths and injuries.

Strengthening of self-interest

Self-interest rests at the heart of perceived political legitimacy of a government. Through their actions, political authorities strive to engender belief among the citizens of the benefits of staying with the existing political system. However, when there are cracks in the political legitimacy of a regime, the forces that increase terrorism get a boost.

Demonstration of ability to provide public goods

Hearts and minds are not swayed solely by the prospect of ideological reward. Almost all successful dissident groups want to demonstrate their ability to provide material goods for the welfare of their community. The mythical story of Robin Hood exemplifies how a small group of outlaws could gain political legitimacy not only through the demonstration of moral superiority to the existing social structure, but also by distributing their booty to the non-participant population in and around Sherwood Forest. Hamas in the Palestine, Hizbullah in Lebanon, and the Naxalites in India have gained loyalty within their communities by providing public goods from healthcare to the rule of law.[77]

Costs

There are two aspect of costs of participation to an actor in anti-systemic violent actions. The first is the opportunity costs of time, and the second is physical costs imposed by the state in preventing terrorism.

Opportunity costs of participation

Opportunity cost is an economic concept which measures the amount of income that one must give up to engage in a time-consuming activity. To a prospective participant this is a very important consideration. That is why when an economy goes into a deep recession there is a greater propensity for political violence. For that reason, we find more young men and women joining mass movements. Yet to join the workforce on a full-time basis, and still be dependent on parents for room and board, the student population of the world has the lowest opportunity costs of participation.[78] For a similar reason, we find that those living in extreme poverty and eking out a meager existence cannot join dissident movement, since any time taken from their subsistence living would mean starvation. The high opportunity cost also prevents peasants, dependent on strict plant cycles, from joining dissident movements.[79] Although there is little systematic data in this area, a casual perusal of the biographies of the terrorists would reveal that a vast majority of them did not hold jobs in the formal sectors of the economy or were underemployed at the time of their participation.[80] Since it is generally accepted that the activists in political violence are better educated than the rest of the population, their inability to find, or in some cases unwillingness to hold, formal employment commensurate to their educational achievement may signal a low level of opportunity cost for missing work.

Actual costs of participation: government coercion

In contrast to the opportunity cost, which is an indirect measure of forgone income, the actual costs of participation is the price one must pay for getting involved in an extralegal activity. These costs are exacted by the government and come in the shape of loss of income (fines) or liberty (prison time), pain (torture), and even life itself. It can also spill over to the actor's loved ones. For instance, the friends and family members can be targeted. In many cases they may lose their government jobs and, as is the case in the West Bank and the Gaza Strip, the Israelis may destroy the family homes of those who take part in suicide attacks.

Under the standard economic model,[81] an increase in cost would lower the level of participation in the extra-legal activities. However, when it comes to ideological goods, such an assumption is sometime problematic. Thus Gurr argues for a quadratic relationship between government coercion and political violence. In other words, up to a certain threshold, which Gurr calls "high violence, high coercion," increase in government sanction only solidifies the opposition.[82] However, after the threshold is crossed and a set of draconian measures has been implemented, protest movements tend to decrease. A number of studies have empirically shown the existence of this quadratic relationship and have argued that while the democratic regimes, having to work within the limits of law and a biding constitution, are rarely able to cross the threshold of high coercion, the non-democratic nations can often impose such brutal retribution on the protesting dissidents.[83]

Facilitating factors

The factors of my expanded benefit–cost analysis, the ideological or group benefit, individual benefits, and the cost of participation are helped by two important facilitating factors: the presence of a network and the group's ability to raise money. Together they help a group of non-state actors to develop an organizational network and support their activities.

Network and organizational structure

Communication is at the heart of all organizations. The terrorist organizations are no exception to this rule. The way an organization communicates within itself[84] and to its clients through networks has been a subject of intense scrutiny by the theorists for nearly half a century.[85] Research into the process by which grass-root organizations in urban America have developed has shed important light on mobilization of the masses by overcoming the collective action problem.[86] Specifically, a number of scholars have explored the way terrorist and other dissident organizations develop their network.[87]

Dissident movements require the spreading of ideas and a means to mobilize a large number of people. Contrary to the traditional approach, where organizations are seen as hierarchical, elitist, and ahistorical,[88] the non-hierarchical organizations show definite cultural and historic patterns.[89] In their ability to adapt to the local conditions, some movements can tap into their traditional networks. Thus, the Iranian Revolution was greatly aided by the network of Shīa mosques, which distributed illegally taped sermons of the exiled Ayatollah Khomeini and was able to mobilize the masses against the Shah's regime.[90] It is not only the Shītes who have been able to take advantage of the existing network through the mosques; Islamists in general have been able to get their radical message across through the mullahs and the mosques. The Islamic tradition of daily prayer at the calls of the local mullah allows the recruiters to spread their messages and to recruit activists.[91] However, not every city or every country offers the same opportunity. With differing history and socioeconomic, cultural, and historical backgrounds, mosques in London, Milan, Madrid, and Hamburg became hotbeds of radical politics yet they did not in Sydney, Berlin, Chicago, or Geneva, for example.[92]

In the private and public sector there is a wide variety of organizational structures. Some are strictly hierarchical, while others are franchises, with a much looser matrix of operational duties. Each type of organization has its strength and weaknesses. While a strictly hierarchical organization can be much more coherent and have a single vision, non-hierarchical organizations have the advantage of flexibility to adapt to regional conditions. The dissident organizations in a similar fashion demonstrate a wide range of typology. Sageman provides a picture of the al-Qaeda network, where a group of like-minded people across the world is seen as a network with a cluster of nodes.[93] In this framework, a mosque in London, where the volunteers to the global *salafi* movement are actively recruited and plots are hatched for future attacks, is a node. The entire movement may be seen as a network connecting these nodes. This is analogous to the network of air traffic with each airport serving as a node. However, not every airport is equal in status. Some, due to their size of population or geographic location, are the hubs, where the traffic volume is much larger than in the regional airports. Thus, Chicago, New York, Boston, Minneapolis, Atlanta, and Los Angeles are the national and international hubs, while Albany, San Diego, and Pittsburgh are more regional nodes. Similarly, in a fluid and constantly evolving architecture of terrorist networks, we can clearly identify the nodes and the hubs. By plotting these links of communication, Sageman identified the Central Staff, Core Arab, Maghreb Arab, and Southeast Asia as the four clusters built around "hubs" such as Osama bin Laden, Khalid Shaikh Mohammed, Abu Zubaydah, and Abu Bakar Baasyir. The Western journalists and policy-makers, unaccustomed to this fluid and rapidly changing organizational structure, often make the mistake of assuming a strict pyramidal structure of organization.[94] Thus, the respected London newspaper the *Observer* quotes an unnamed security official saying:

> If you look at the structure of al-Qaeda, what you basically have is a
> pyramid. . . . If you see the see the two groups of bombers [who carried

out the 7/7 London bombings] as two separate teams of footsoldiers on the very bottom, then there is a possibility they are linked by command structure in the level above. This is the level we are trying to identify and track down . . .[95]

Unfortunately, the salafi movement is not a top-down system with a strict chain of command going down from bin Laden to Muhammad Sidique Khan (the ring leader of the group) to the teenager Hasin Hussain. As Robb points out, today's radical Islamic groups are not like the old-fashioned PLO with Yasser Arafat as the undisputed head of the organization. Instead, modern jihadi terror groups are linear, open-sourced, decentralized conglomerations of small, quasi-independent groups drawn more by inspiration from bin Laden than a direct instruction from him.[96]

Along the lines of Sageman's[97] understanding of the network, I have presented the structure of a hypothetical terrorist organization (Figure 4.8). In this diagram, a group of nodes make a cluster. I have represented "hubs" as dark nodes. In this hypothetical case, the core group is characterized by the presence of more hubs than the peripheral clusters.

These nodes and hubs should not be viewed simply as points of information exchange, such as "how to make a bomb." Rather, together they represent what is known as a "small-world" of virtual community on the web.[98] Through their interactions, they develop social capital, provide ideological and emotional support, raise money, keep the fire of hatred burning, and plan for future actions. For instance, Robb points out that there are between 70 and 100 groups that make up the Iraqi insurgency, which are organized

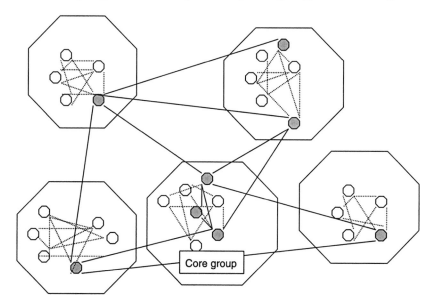

Figure 4.8 Hypothetical representation of terrorist network.

like a "bazaar," where ideas are traded, and they all learn from each other's experience.[99] Through their communications the insurgents perfect their weapons, improve surveillance system and, sometimes, coordinate attacks. This is what Stern calls "inspirational terrorism."[100] Stern contends that their malleability of mission and the ability to create a "virtual family" gives groups like al-Qaeda its strength. As a result of this non-hierarchical organizational structure, they become the true multi-headed Hydra.

In the summer of 2004, the police in London discovered what was quickly dubbed by the media a "sleeper cell." In a diabolical plan, Dhiren Barot, a converted Muslim from India, led a group of men to bomb, among other places, the London Underground. The group planned to stage a huge explosion in the tube tunnel under the River Thames. If they had succeeded, thousands of commuters would have drowned in the subterranean labyrinth of the underground network. What surprised the investigating detectives was the apparent professionalism that these men exhibited; they submitted a business plan to the al-Qaeda operatives minutely detailing every aspect of the project along with a cost estimate for carrying it out.[101] In contrast to this London group, which sought financial help in carrying out these proposed attacks, the Moroccan group that bombed the Atocha train station in downtown Madrid around the time Barot was arrested were even more independent of bin Laden's operation. Unlike the British group, they did not have any direct contact with al-Qaeda nor did they seek funding from any outside sources.[102] The Madrid cell's only contact with al-Qaeda was through the Internet.[103] They raised their own money from selling drugs and other illicit methods.

While al-Qaeda is largely decentralized, other terrorist groups are not. The difference between the two types of groups can be seen when its organizational structure is compared with the PKK (Kurdish Workers Party). The PKK was hierarchical under the leadership of Abdullah Ocalan. After he was arrested in 1999, the group went dormant for a while and changed its name to the Kurdistan Freedom and Democracy Congress in 2002, then to the Kurdistan People's Congress in 2003, in order to distance itself both from Ocalan and from his Marxist ideology.

Although there are groups that are strictly hierarchical and those that are not, within the latter, a group may have a cluster that is non-hierarchical, with another one exhibiting more of a Weberian pyramidal structure. The Southeast Asian network, for instance, exhibited much more of a hierarchical structure.[104] Abdullah Sungkar and Abu Bakar Baasyir created Jemaah Islamiyah from top down along a much more Weberian pyramidal organizational pattern.

Funding terror

Waging a violent campaign against an established social and political order is an expensive proposition. Money is the lifeblood of any organization. To run a modern terrorist campaign a group must be economically savvy. While every group must raise money for their operations, the larger groups, such as al-Qaeda and the LTTE, have developed an incredibly intricate web of legitimate and illegitimate businesses. The very clandestine nature of terrorists makes it doubly difficult to raise enough money to sustain a group's activities. The problem for researching this area is that much of the information on the financing of terrorism is shrouded in secrecy. However, a growing number of important books and articles are filling this need.[105] Based on these published reports, Figure 4.9 presents a scheme for terrorist organizations' avenues for raising money.

The first and foremost source of funding, especially for some of the Islamic groups, is charitable contributions by their support bases. The religious duty of *zakat* or alms is one of the five pillars of Islam. Every faithful is obliged to give a certain portion of his wealth to charity. These contributions are often collected at the mosques. In Saudi Arabia, there is no income tax. Instead, the Saudi citizens are obliged fulfill their religious duties on a voluntary basis. Beside these personal contributions, Saudi banks also collect 2 percent of each transaction as zakat.[106] Since this money, paid by Muslims all over the world, is part of the religious tradition, there is hardly a strict assessment of its volume. However, journalists Pallister and Bowcott estimate that the 6,000 strong Saudi royal family alone is worth $600 billion, making their yearly zakat about $12 billion.[107] Beside zakat, there are many reports of wealthy benefactors supporting terrorist organizations. In fact, bin Laden may have invested most of his fortune in the creation and expansion of al-Qaeda. The role of contributions from the diaspora has been an essential factor in the

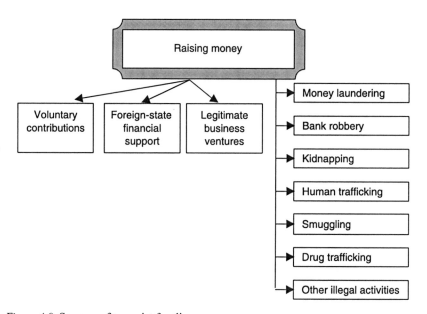

Figure 4.9 Sources of terrorist funding.

sustenance and expansion of many groups. The Irish Catholic diaspora, particularly in Boston, have long supported the IRA, the Canadian Sikhs the Khalistan movement, and the Tamils in India, Australia, and Europe have sent money to the LTTE.

In the process of the development of a violent dissident movement, the crucial role that a foreign state plays in providing financial support cannot be overestimated. An organized government often supports a terrorist group operating in a different country for ideological or for political reasons. Thus, to the Pakistani governments, the support for the Mujahideens infiltrating the Kashmir valley has been a moral issue from the very beginning.[108] The problem for Pakistan has been that, without any history of its own, its national identity had to be artificially crafted. Hence, in order to maintain its separate identity, its political imperative required it to lay claims to the Muslim-majority state of Kashmir. Furthermore, from the point of view of military strategy, the geography of the subcontinent obviated the need for Kashmir to be part of Pakistan. The current jihadi movement did not originate in the late 1980s, as many might presume. Rather the six decade-long conflict has been a steady low-intensity conflict, which has been amply aided by the active support of the Pakistani military and its intelligence arm, the Inter-Service Intelligence (ISI). Similarly, supporting the anti-Castro Cubans has long been a part of US foreign policy, which led to the disastrous Bay of Pigs invasion in 1961.[109] Similarly, the US government has in many parts of the world covertly supported many dissident groups which can be called terrorist organizations.

Beside ideological and foreign-policy rationale, governments may also support terrorist groups in order to save their own societies from being their target. This is a sort of "protection money" that Palast claims prompted the Saudis and the Gulf states to secretly supply al-Qaeda with large sums of money.[110] Since nearly every nation considers supporting dissident movements as part of their active foreign policy or out of some other domestic political concern, the United Nations has been unable to pass a legislation defining— and thereby banning its support by the signatories—"terrorism."

Dissident organizations also become involved in legitimate business ventures from banking in Riyadh to running taxicabs in Belfast. The economic system in the orthodox Islamic world attempts to straddle a delicate divide between what is acceptable in the Islamic tradition and the needs of a modern economy.[111] Thus, the theocratic Islamic economy must operate within a system that does not allow income taxes or interest on loans, and must treat voluntary charitable donations as outside the accounting process. As a result, Islamic banks from the Pakistani Bank of Credit and Commerce (BCCI)[112] to Saudi Dar al-Maal al-Islami (DMI) and Dallah al-Baraka (DAB) have raised suspicion and accusations of supporting all kinds of violent activities from financing terrorism to supporting the Pakistani nuclear proliferator A.Q. Khan's illicit operations. Even the US State Department has charged that Osama bin Laden had controlling interest on the DMI.[113]

Beside these legitimate business ventures, terrorist organizations engage in every kind of illegal activity from kidnapping and hostage taking for ransom, bank robbing, human trafficking, drug trading, gun running, smuggling, and even running prostitution rings. All of these operations carry the risk of alien-ating the support base, if the group loses its moral message. However, not every society is the same when it comes to the cultural acceptance of the various means of getting involved in these activities. Therefore, they pose a dilemma for the terrorist groups between seeking political legitimacy and raising money for their operations. I will discuss this issue in greater depth in Chapter 7.

Although I presented the case of terrorist groups engaging in legitimate and illegitimate business activities, not all of their activities can be classified along this binary classification. In the immigrant communities from the vari-ous lesser-developed nations strewn around in the Western world, sending money home is a matter of utmost priority. Since the cumbersome, expensive, and often non-existent corresponding banking system in their own countries makes it difficult to transfer money through the formal channel, they send money home through a time-honored system called the *Hawala*, which was, perhaps, created sometime in the dim past of the early medieval era to meet the similar needs then. Under this system the sender contacts a *Howaladar* (the one that operates the system) and gives him a certain amount of money. The *Howaladar* in London, Paris, or New York, in turn, contacts his counterpart, from whom the intended collects the corresponding amount in local currency. The entire system works on trust and through a network of traditional con-tacts, without keeping much of a paper trail. This system, which is controlled mostly by Indians and Pakistanis, helps millions of Asians and Africans to transfer funds internationally. This not only ensures safety, but it also evades detection by the authorities. A joint World Bank and International Monetary Fund study concluded that:

> The anonymous transfer of funds through the [*Hawala*] systems has also attracted concerns about their potential use as a conduit for terrorist funds. Because there is no requirement for identification documents or source of funds, a [*Hawala*] dealer can initiate or facilitate a multiplicity of transfers, which conceal the ultimate origin of the funds through their network in different jurisdictions. The recipient of funds can use the funds to conduct a terrorist act. Once the transaction is completed, all customer identification documents, codes, or references are most likely destroyed, except, perhaps, those required for settlement purposes.[114]

Dynamics of terrorist movements

The interaction between a dissident group and the state authorities shapes the dynamics of their mutual destiny. We can show the process with the help of Figure 4.10. In this figure, the dynamic interaction is shown with the help of two forces: the terrorism increasing force (TIF) and the terrorism attenuating force (TAF). We should note that at each point in the history of a conflict the

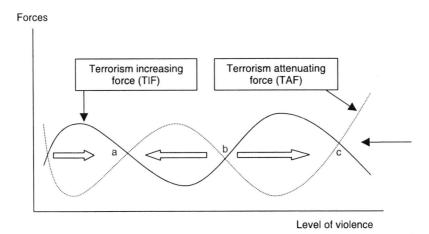

Figure 4.10 Dynamic interactions and growth and decline of violence.

two forces exist side by side and their relative strength determines the outcome of the violent movement.

The dynamic interactions between the government and a violent dissident group are depicted in Figure 4.10. In this diagram, the vertical axis measures the relative strength of the two forces. If at any point the increasing force is greater than the attenuating force, the level of violence (shown on the horizontal axis) spirals out. However, since it cannot increase indefinitely, a society generates from within the forces that reduce the level of violence. During the course of a violent campaign, the society often settles for a long-standing standoff of low-intensity conflict, where the two forces seem to achieve a point of stable equilibrium. At this point, each side knows its limits and does not want to transgress the threshold. Take, for instance, the conflict between Hizbullah in Lebanon and the Israeli Defense Force. For several years, the Israelis became used to the Hizbullah sending short-range missiles across its borders and Hizbullah became accustomed to low-level Israeli retaliation. These tit-for-tat responses can keep the two adversaries on a more or less stable level of violence. In the stylized depiction of this dynamic relationship in Figure 4.10, point "a" shows a stable equilibrium. To the left of this point, the terrorism increasing forces (TIF) will gain the upper hand. This may happen due to the inner politics of the dissident groups, wanting to increase pressure on the government, or the government, seeking to satisfy public's demand to punish the members of the opposition group. If by any chance one of the parties takes a bolder action and the level of violence increases to the right of the point "a," the desire not to escalate the violence to an unacceptable level makes the reaction muted from the aggrieved party. As a result, the society becomes bogged down in a steady cycle of conflict. Situations like these are usually characterized by low-intensity violence, since a high level of violence produces its own dynamics, which takes it up to an even higher level of escalation, or countervailing forces generate conditions to reduce the intensity of fighting. This situation is also one of military stalemate, with neither side having the punch to knock the other out.

This equilibrium of the two forces can be severely shaken for a number of reasons. For instance, if any one party takes a move that is considered to be way outside the realms of a proportionate response, violence escalates to a new height. This sudden move, causing a shift of the curves (not shown in the diagram), can come as a deliberate action by the government of the terrorist organization, often due to a change in leadership, a gross miscalculation by either side or as a result of some historical accident. The combatants may wish to push the level of conflict to a different level with the hope of achieving a total victory over the other or it may be the outcome of a misunderstanding.

Richard English quotes Tom Maguire, one of the IRA men to whom the events of the Easter Rising, following a brutal crackdown by the British forces in 1916, was a "life-transforming event."[115] The British policy of using utmost force only helped forge Irish nationalism. McGuire writes: "The Easter insurrection came to me like a bolt from the blue. That is why the rise of charismatic leaders and abrupt points of escalation and dissipation punctuate the chronicles of all movements, I will never forget my exhilaration, it was a turning point in my life."[116] Another IRA activist Tom Barry pointed out: "through the blood sacrifices of the men of 1916, had one Irish youth of eighteen been awakened to Irish nationality. Let it be recorded that those sacrifices were equally necessary to awaken the minds of ninety percent of the Irish people."[117] Such deliberate policy missteps by the authorities are always exploited by rebel leaders and others in society to keep the flames of hatred glowing for generations to come.

A radical shift in the stable equilibrium point can also be the result of a miscalculation by the leadership. The crisis across the Israeli–Lebanese border, which escalated into a full-scale war in the summer of 2006, is widely seen as an outcome of miscalculation on both sides.[118] Thus, *The Economist* writes:

> In launching his raid Nasrallah [the leader of Hizbullah] was in fact doing nothing new. In recent years, Hizbullah has mounted several similar raids into Israel. It got away with them, even when Israel was led by Ehud Barak and Ariel Sharon, tough prime ministers, who had been war heroes too. Their reactions were astonishingly mild.[119]

However, when the Hizbullah fighters sneaked across the border and, in a raid, killed several Israeli soldiers and abducted two others, the response was swift and overwhelming. From all indications, *The Economist* is right in stating that this time Nasrallah had miscalculated. In fact, after the war, which many Israelis saw as a humiliating defeat for Israel, Nasrallah admitted the miscalculation. In terms of our diagram, this brazen act by the Hizbullah pushed the dynamic relationship to a point where violence spiraled out of control. At this point the overwhelming forces of TIF would escalate violence to a very high level, resulting in many deaths and billions of dollars worth of damage to the economies of Israel and Lebanon.[120]

During the course of a conflict, there are moments when the future hangs in the balance. In my stylized rendering, this is the unstable equilibrium "b," where a small push can send the society to the path of a peaceful resolution of hostilities, or can set it up for huge escalation of violence. For instance, in the waning days of the Clinton Administration, as a last ditch effort, Yasser Arafat and Israeli Prime Minister Ehud Barak were brought to Camp David. As the world waited for a solution to the most intractable problem of all, all hopes were dashed when it ended without any agreement. This officially brought the Oslo peace process to an end. Within days, the entire region experienced the most violent spates of suicide attacks by the Palestinians and the Israeli retaliated with matching ferocity.

Historical accidents, outside the realm of the leaders of the dissident group and its adversary the target government, can also throw a society experiencing prolonged low-intensity conflict into the path of radical escalation of violence. In 1994, an American-born Jewish extremist Baruch Goldstein opened fire on a group of Muslims praying at the Cave of the Patriarchs in the city of Hebron, killing 29 Arabs and wounding nearly 150. This act of violence inflamed passion among the Palestinians and the violence escalated to a new high. The history of every mass movement provides examples of events causing huge escalations of violence. The impacts of TIF and TAF over time are shown in Figure 4.11, where a continuation of a low-intensity conflict is suddenly shaken up by rapid escalation of violence. This quickly takes the society to an extremely high level of violence. Since this level of violence is unsustainable over a long period of time, the terrorism attenuating forces swell up to force a return to the old status quo, a negotiated compromise, or a victory of one side over the other.

The death of a movement

The death of a movement comes from three different, often interconnected, reasons. First, a movement dies when its political goals become no longer relevant in the face of a changed political reality, or the support base becomes disillusioned or gets tired of violence. It can be argued that the growing affluence of the Republic of Ireland and the general apathy of the British public to the cause of the Protestants in Northern Ireland laid the foundation to a peaceful outcome of the longest-standing conflict, where the oldest organized dissident group in the world, the IRA, was forced to accept the reality of a divided Ireland.

Second, a dissident group, particularly one that is organized in a strict hierarchical structure around a charismatic leader, can suffer military defeat in the hands of far superior government forces. With the leaders killed or behind bars, the group disintegrates and disappears from the pages of history.

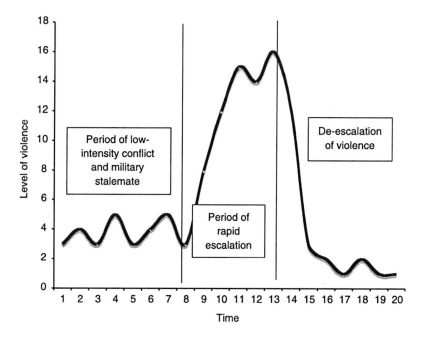

Figure 4.11 Hypothetical impact of TIF and TAF over time.

This fate is particularly applicable to relatively small groups, with little or no connection to the larger community. Many European groups, such as the Greek Revolutionary Organization 17 November[121] and the Symbionese Liberation Army[122] in America, suffered such a fate.

A radical movement ends when the leadership accepts an offer to join the democratic processes of a nation. With the leadership eschewing violence and deciding to contest the elections, violence subsides. The decision by Daniel Ortega of the Sandinista movement to contest in the Salvadoran election in 1990 essentially brought the violent conflict to an end.[123] This is usually the outcome of a negotiated agreement.

Finally, a group can achieve its military and political goals. Once these goals are reached, the need to fight on also disappears. Thus, the recent Communist rebellion in Nepal is on its way toward establishing a constitutional monarchy and joining hands with other political parties to form a democratic regime.[124]

In sum

Figure 4.12 sums up my arguments offered in this chapter. The top part of the figure shows the factors of individual motivations for joining a dissident group to achieve a set of public goods for the entire community. Rational individuals overcome the free-rider problems through a combination of incentives

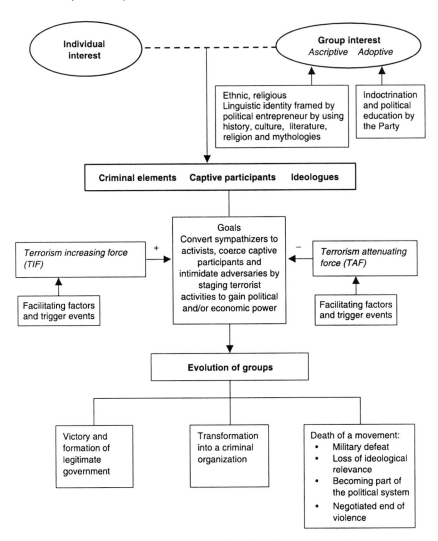

Figure 4.12 Individual and group: a static view of evolution of terrorist organizations.

that appeal to their selfish interest as well as ascriptive or adoptive group welfare. A dissident group is composed of the ideologues, the mercenaries, and the captive participants.

A group gains or loses strength through its support bases (the easy riders and the sympathizers). The policies of the governments and the strategies adopted by the group leadership create the relative strength of the terrorism increasing force (TIF) and terrorism attenuating force (TAF). When the terrorism increasing forces overwhelm the attenuating forces, violence increases. The level of violence reduces when the reverse takes place. These two forces are influenced by the trigger events and other external factors.

With time, a group evolves. A few become victorious and become part of the legitimate government in the newly formed government, such as in Israel, Algeria, and Kenya. Some groups turn toward the economically lucrative side of the movement, and resemble more of an organized crime syndicate than a political movement. As we have noted, most groups die out. Their death comes when they suffer a military defeat. Their leaders are captured or killed, most group members scatter, leaving the organization voluntarily or are imprisoned. The Italian Red Brigade, the Black Panther movement, and the Naxalites in Bengal in the early 1970s provide good examples of military defeat. A violent dissident group may also disappear from the pages of history when their ideology becomes increasingly irrelevant in a changing world. As a result, they begin to lose vital public support among their bases. Perhaps the Basque separatist group ETA makes a good example of this. Finally, a terrorist group may become mainstream as a result of a negotiated settlement. If the current peace process is maintained in Northern Ireland, the IRA as an organization may indeed be relegated to the pages of history.

Terrorism does not happen in a vacuum. This chapter discusses its origin through the interaction between a dissident group, the target state authorities, and the trigger events and other exogenous factors. This dynamic interaction shapes the ebb and flow of sociopolitical violence, including terrorism. In the process, apart from escalation and deceleration, there can also be prolonged periods of low-level tit-for-tat conflict.

5 Faith, nationalism, and class warfare

The birth of a movement

What can my enemies possibly do to me? My paradise is in my heart; wherever I go it goes with me, inseparable from me. For me, prison is a place of [religious] retreat; execution is my opportunity for martyrdom; and exile from my town is but a chance to travel.

Ibn Taymiyya (c. 1300)[1]

Your democratically elected governments continuously perpetuate atrocities against my people all over the world . . . Until we feel security, you will be our targets. And until you—you stop the bombing, gassing, imprisonment and torture of my people we will not stop this fight.

Muhammad Sidique Khan (2006)[2]

Fanatics have their dreams, wherewith they weave a paradise for a sect.

John Keats, *The Fall of Hyperion*

Every movement starts with an idea: an idea of a group of people being wrongfully treated by another. Sometimes the offending group consists of "those" who have deviated from the "true path" of a common religious faith; sometimes "they" are accused of being interlopers with no claim to the land; and sometimes the "others" are seen as the source of economic exploitation. And most often these ideas shadow a long history of enmity with the odious "others." No mass movement can, therefore, be studied as a single event.[3] The narration of any mass movement, therefore, must begin from an arbitrary cut-off date. When we carefully examine the history of these mass movements we find the presence of a set of long-standing grievances based on separate group identities, punctuated by the rise of important political entrepreneurs who shape these movement through time. The combined effort of these leaders, built on collectively felt frustration, shapes the evolution of a movement. The ideologies of the collective—religious, nationalistic, or socialistic—mix freely with people's selfish interest and, in the process, produce violent movements worldwide. Once spawned, some movements experience rapid growth while most others quickly dissipate.

Previously I argued that belonging to a group is part of biological makeup and serves as a strong source of human motivation. In this chapter, I will closely examine the birth of the ideas that propelled three specific movements: the Islamic violence that is currently vexing the West, the Middle East and parts of Asia and Africa; the Irish Catholic rebellion by the IRA; and the Communist-led insurgency in India, loosely called the Naxalites. Through my narratives, I would like to show that, in the final analysis, religion, nationalism, and socialism only serve as the basis of shared identity. Although religious zealotry, hyper-nationalism, and Godless Communism may appear to be distinct ideologies, at their root all three of these speak to the fundamental human need to belong to a larger community. As a result, religious and national identities follow the contours of the dividing lines of economic class. The aim of the Islamists is often to uproot the current highly unequal economic structure and replace it with an egalitarian vision that would evoke the image of Lenin and Mao. Similarly, the ultranationalists nearly always embrace a certain religion and promise an equitable society. In a revealing statement, Ayman al-Zawahiri even characterized Osama bin Laden as the "new Che Guevara."[4] In most discussion on terrorism and political violence a neat classification is made among nationalistic, religious, and economic class-based groups.[5] The MIPT electronic databank, for example, presents information along this line of broad classification.[6] The question of nationalism has created deep ideological rifts in the Islamic world and within Communism; however, at the core, all of these often become indistinguishable and the group ideologies fall on a continuum along three-dimensional axes rather than on the basis of a strict separation. My discussion of Islamic rebellion, the Irish nationalism, and the Naxalite movement will demonstrate this point.

Islam: from theology to arms

Religion, which is the source of peace and solace to many, also provides its followers with a ready identity, complete with the images of good and evil, heroes and villains, "us" and "them." With powerful symbols it defines in no uncertain terms the boundaries of its binary worldview. The taciturn God's words are open to interpretation by the religious leaders. In blind religious obedience, faith trumps our need to question and to reason. In their interpretation, the priests, the rabbis, the monks, and the mullahs demand unquestioned adherence from their followers. As a result, every religion has been at once a source of spiritual comfort and an instrument of indiscriminate carnage.

Among the great religious faiths in the world, the history of Islam is no different. However, what is perhaps unique about Islam is that Prophet Muhammad, unlike Jesus or Buddha, was also a king. He led his troops to the battlefields, had a worldly family life, and left behind an established penal code, which prescribed in great detail the punishment for every transgression. Islam, therefore, perhaps more than any other religion, encompasses every aspect of life: spiritual, social, economic, and political. In Islam, every worldly action is judged from the interpretation of the Koran, the *Hadith* (the Prophet's life story and tradition recorded by people who knew him), and the *Sha'ria*.[7] Since the Holy books were written well before our lives became complicated with the advent of myriad technologies, the proper path for a modern Muslim requires their interpretation. Apart from the Koran, the Sha'ria and the Hadith, Islamic tradition also recognizes the analogies to the Prophet's life and his words to judge situations not encountered in the Koran or the Hadith. Furthermore, the mainstream Islamic tradition also recognizes the consensus by the leading religious scholars.

The attraction of Islam through ages has been its simplicity as well as its message of equality among its believers. However, perhaps the most significant message of Islam is the concept of Ummah, or the community. Anyone who accepts Allah as the one and only true God and Muhammad as His messenger is included in the global Islamic family of Ummah. Once included, even the lowliest of the low is accorded equal status during religious observance. The Koran forbids the spilling of the blood of fellow Muslims and protects the rights of women to own property. Because of the existence of the Sha'ria, Islam not only specifies the rewards and punishments of the afterlife, it also clearly establishes the path to righteous living and the penalties for secular transgressions, often in minute detail.[8] This extreme specificity, absent in all other religions, has been a source of strength as well the fountainhead of conflict among its many factions. The unequivocal message of right and wrong has attracted many seeking surety in an otherwise uncertain world; at the same time, it has lent itself to the forces of utmost literalism to the words of the scripture. Consequently, Islamic revivals have trodden an all-too-familiar path: a religious scholar, being dismayed by the failings of the social order, in general, and its rulers, in particular, preaches their violent overthrow in the name of God. His radical messages attract the attention of the authorities, which put him in prison, torture him, and in many cases put him to death. The path of political Islam has thus been paved by the torn bodies of the martyrs, their sacrifices inspiring the multitude to the path of radicalism for ages to come.

Division within Islam started immediately after the death of Muhammad in the year 632. The nascent community was divided into those who supported the direct bloodline of the Prophet to succeed him and those who supported his trusted friend and father-in-law Abu Bakr. The Sunnis supported the claims of Abu Bakr, but the Shias favored keeping the leadership of the Caliphate within the House of the Prophet (*ahl al bayt*—"people of the House") by supporting his cousin and son-in-law Ali. This struggle for succession erupted in an extremely violent civil war, where Muslims were shedding the blood of other Muslims and, in the process, created the deep chasm between the two branches of Islam. The resulting anarchy, called *fitna*, holds a special place in Islam's collective memory of the horrors of fratricidal frenzy.

Mass violence followed Islam almost from its inception for another reason.

Islam has a strong ascetic core, whose simplicity in living has clashed with the more materialistic parts of its adherents throughout its history. The first such uprising occurred within a short time after Muhammad's death. A group of Islamic fanatics called the Kharijites, which literally means the "rejectionists," took up arms against the *Caliph*. Arguing that Islam's rulers had already become corrupted by worldly concerns, the Kharijites preached jihad against fellow Muslims, breeding violence in their path. One of them assassinated Imam Ali as he was leading a prayer in 661. Although the Kharijites disappeared as a group from the pages of history after nearly two hundred years, their puritanical version of Islam has resonated with a large number of people and created violence and upheaval all through its history.

In 1257, after a relentless expansion of the Islamic Empire lasting over six hundred years, which saw nearly two-thirds of the known world under its domination, Islam faced the first real challenge to its existence: Hulagu Khan the Mongol ruler sacked Baghdad, the primary seat of Muslim civilization, with a cruelty that paled even the legendary ruthlessness of Attila the Hun. The sight of impotency in the face of such unimaginable atrocities shocked an ascetic Islamic scholar, Ibn Taymiyya (1263–1328). Taymiyya fled the devastated Baghdad and took refuge in Cairo, then the second most important base of the Islamic Empire under the Mamluk regime. His radical messages upset the seats of power. Taymiyya was imprisoned and was brutally tortured. Undeterred, Taymiyya called for jihad against the non-believers.[9]

The ascetic ideology of Islam received a significant boost when in the mid-eighteenth century a village sheik, Ibn Abdul al-Wahhab, began preaching in the Arabian Peninsula. Wahhab's ideological orientation was along the lines of Taymiyya's. Similar to Taymiyya, Wahhab intended to purify Islam to its old glory days by cleansing its practices of what he called innovation and idolatry. Wahhab considered the spread of Sufism, a mystical form of Islam that permeated Arabian society at that time, as a threat to the true faith. He also rejected the personal worship of Prophet Muhammad.[10] Some of his followers even destroyed Muhammad's grave in order to prevent it from becoming an idol-worshipping shrine. In his teachings Wahhab rejected the analogies and consensus by the scholars and based his faith solely on the literal understanding of the Koran and the Hadith. As he drew an ever-larger flock of followers, he struck a deal with Muhammad Ibn Saud, a local chieftain. Their joint enterprise—*mithaq*, a binding agreement to be honored till eternity by their successors—suited both men well. It allowed the radical preacher to preach his version of Islam without the fate of his hero, Ibn Taymiyya. A grateful al-Wahhab declared the rulers of Mecca and Medina as apostate, which allowed Ibn Saud to conquer the holiest shrines from fellow Muslim rulers and become the primary guardian of Islamic faith, the keeper of the key. As Tariq Ali points out: "Ibn Wahhab provided theological justification for almost anything Ibn Saud wanted to achieve: a permanent jihad that involved looting other Muslim settlements and cities, ignoring the Caloph, imposing the tough discipline on his own people and, ultimately, asserting his own rule over neigbouring tribes in an attempt to unite the Peninsula."[11] Their agreement recognized Ibn Saud and his house as the chief of political administration, and Ibn Abdul al-Wahhab and his house, the sole authority on Islamic interpretation.[12] Together, the two men laid the foundation of Saudi Arabia, the only nation on earth today which bears the name of a family. With Wahhabism being the state religion, it became inseparable from the Saudi political life.

Jihad and its justification

Jihad, by which a Muslim feels justified in joining a battle, has been a complicated concept in Islam. The literal translation of the term is not "holy war" but "struggle." Jihad to a Muslim implies struggle for the path of righteousness. The jihad is also divided into greater jihad and lesser jihad. The greater jihad is fought in hearts and minds, where an individual strives to live by the code of Islam: faith in Allah (*shahada*), five times of prayer (three times for the Shi'as), fasting during the month of Ramadan, charitable contributions to the poor and to Islamic causes (zakat), and pilgrimage to Mecca (*hajj*). Together they constitute the five pillars of Islam. Against the constant struggle of worldly temptations, pious Muslims wage their jihad.

The lesser jihad is directed against a threat to the *Dar-al–Islam*, or the land of Islam from the *Dar-al-kufr*, the land of non-believers. When *Dar-al–Islam* is attacked, as Taymiyya insisted, it is the religious duty of every Muslim to join the forces of jihad. This is the defensive jihad. Islam, being a proselytizing religion, requires each believer to strive to spread the words of God through religious conversion. It is explicitly forbidden to convert people by force, as the Koran states, "There is no compulsion in religion." However, as a part of the offensive jihad, it is the obligation of each Muslim to propagate Islam through voluntary contributions, prayer, and by defeating the forces of "falsehood" in the battlefields.

The need to call for jihad in defense of the religion is widely recognized in Islam. What is not clear, however, is who has the authority to issue a *fatwa* (religious edict) to declare war, particularly under Sunni Islam where, similar to Protestantism in Christianity, there is no central hierarchy of authority. This lack of a religious chain of command has caused confusion among the faithful and has given rise to heated debates among religious scholars. Among many authorities of Islamic jurisprudence,[13] the authority to declare jihad comes from the Koranic verse: "O ye who believe! Obey Allah, and obey the Messenger, and those charged with authority among you" (4:59).[14] Under normal circumstances, only the head (the Caliph) of the Islamic state has the authority to call for a jihad, because the laws of Islam were designed with the idea of a unified Ummah, one collective nation with a Caliph at its head speaking with moral authority to call to arms. If the Caliph delegated the duty to a head of military operations, it could, in theory, be issued by him as long as the express consent is there, in which case he would be speaking in the name of the Caliph. There has never been a difference of opinion on this. The Qur'an tells Muslims to obey the prophet and to obey those in charge of their affairs.

The situation is slightly different for the more hierarchical Shi'a clergy. In Shi'ite Iran, under Khomeini's "authority of the jurist" rule, the head of the Islamic state can call for jihad. In that case, for instance, if the Majlis passes a fatwa, the President can declare it, with, of course, the acquiescence of the Ayatollah. In a formal set-up, the procedure to call for jihad is analogous to the functioning of the British parliamentary system.

After Islamic leaders started fighting amongst themselves, they each declared themselves the head of state, resulting in confusion. In today's nation states, the largely secular type leadership has seen the rise of respected people of religion who have arrogated to themselves this right. As a result, the Sunni Mullahs in many countries have issued *fatwas* urging the faithful to join the jihad.

From frustration to fatwa: the spread of global jihad

The Islamic Empire spread like lightning soon after the Prophet's death and, for nearly a thousand years, remained the predominant force in the "known world." They not only conquered a vast territory but had achieved a level of science, literature, and arts unseen in human history at that time. Inheriting the great traditions of Persia and Arabia, Muslim scholars translated the works of Aristotle, Ptolemy, Euclid, and Galen, which at that time had been lost to the Europeans, mired in the prejudice and conflict of the "Dark Ages." To this, the Arabs brought two of the biggest innovations of the ancient world: paper technology from China and the concept of zero from India. It is indeed difficult to imagine the world today without the contributions of the Arab/Muslim world.

Yet, like all other civilizations of the past, the Islamic civilization began its steep path to decline. In 1492, King Ferdinand and Queen Isabella routed the Moors from the plains of Andalusia. For the first time, being free of fighting, the coffers of Spanish king were full enough to take chances on an eccentric Italian man with a business plan that was rejected by the Spanish Academy of Sciences several times—Christopher Columbus had severely underestimated the circumference of the earth. The victory over the Moors allowed Ferdinand and Isabella to provide Columbus with financial backing, which paid off in unimaginable riches from the New World.

For the next five hundred years the Islamic Empires saw a steady stream of defeats. The most significant of these reversals took place in the waning years of the seventeenth century. In the late summer of 1697, a combined Christian force decisively defeated the Ottoman Sultan, Mustafa II, at the Battle of Zenta. For the first time in their memory a Muslim ruler had to enter into a treaty with a Christian Prince addressing him as an equal partner.[15] The signing of the Treaty of Carlowitz (26 January 1699) was a source of utter humiliation for the Ottoman Emperor, since such a language was totally unfamiliar to the mighty ruler.

Since then, the defeats of the Islamic nations cascaded down on them, until in 1918 the last standing Empire in Istanbul was vanquished by the victorious Allied forces during World War I. Historian Bernard Lewis gives a number of reasons for the steady decline of the Ottoman Empire vis-à-vis the European forces.[16] He argues that the primary reason for its demise was its shutting out and losing interest in the non-Muslim world, particularly in Western Europe. Lewis points out that since Europe did not have any Islamic shrine nor was it particularly wealthy compared with the territories of the East, the Ottomans had little knowledge of the Europeans. They did not know, nor did they care, about the inventions of Leonardo da Vinci, Copernicus, Galileo, or Newton. The discovery of the Americas held little interest for the Ottomans. Yet, with the discoveries of the far-away continents, two important events took place. The need to travel by sea gave birth to improved technologies in naval warfare, from sturdier ships, sails, and canons, to navigational instruments. As a result, all the subsequent colonization—from Francisco Pizarro to Commodore Perry—came on the back of superior European naval power. Furthermore, the opening up of the sea routes to the Orient cut out the Arab middlemen for overland trade, causing economic hardship in many parts of the Arab/Muslim world. Second, the colonies in the new and the old world quickly made many Western European nations wealthy. With wealth came the leisure time to devote to science and technology. In the meantime, the Reformation had unshackled the pursuit of science, which manifested in every area of human endeavor from medicine to military. The Islamic world, deeply turned inward, could not compete with the West.

Starting with the late 1800s, as the demise of the glory days was becoming evident to everyone in the Islamic world, a series of nationalistic uprisings started taking shape, inspired by the prospect of a religious revival. The strain of literalism that was imbedded from the inception slowly emerged as a precursor to the global jihadism. Although most of these movements failed to achieve their goals, the life and work of those who willingly gave up their lives became enshrined in the Islamic history and mythology to inspire others to rise up against perceived injustice to follow their examples.

First, armed resistance against the colonial Europeans and their collaborators came from Muhammad al-Mahdi. Known as the "*Mujaddid*" (the renewer of the faith), Mahdi declared war against an "apostate" Egyptian regime, which, in collaboration with the Ottoman Turks, was ruling the Sudan. His rag-tag army—empowered by religious zeal and the promise of paradise—routed a much larger joint force in a series of battles. Mahdi's claim of a direct lineage from the Prophet added to his charismatic appeal. Being emboldened by his early successes Mahdi began promoting pan-Islamism with himself at the head.[17] In 1885, a triumphant Mahdi entered the gates of Khartoum. Within a matter of a few months, he was dead. Soon the Egyptians struck back, this time in partnership with the British, and re-conquered the Sudan from Khalifa Abdullah Muhammad.[18] Although Mahdi did not live long enough to enjoy the fruits of his military success, his legacy is still shaping the history of Sudan and has left an indelible influence in the development of pan-Islamic radicalism. Through Islam, Mahdi gave expression to the northern Sudanese nationalism, which sees itself as a part of the Arab Middle East that extends from the "Gulf" nations to North Africa, instead of the continent of Africa. This identity lies at the core of the current crisis of the Darfur region.[19] Furthermore, the mystique of another warrior prophet helped develop Islamic revivalism in the neighboring Egypt, through the establishment of Muslim Brotherhood.[20]

The stirrings of Islamic identity in the aftermath of the destruction of the Islamic Empire came in the Indian subcontinent among some of the best-educated intellectuals. Among them, the most significant contribution was made by the poet Muhammad Iqbal (1877–1934). A Cambridge-educated scholar and a barrister at Lincoln's Inn, Iqbal wrote in Farsi and in Urdu. Although he was more prolific in Farsi, his revolutionary poem *Shikwa* ("Complaint"), first recited in Lahore in 1908, created an immediate sensation among the Muslim intellectuals. In a most eloquent way, Iqbal, after apologizing for the audacity of addressing Allah, passionately protested that it was the Muslims who recognized His greatness and spread His words at the cost of their blood. Yet at the end it is them who are at the bottom. Iqbal pointed out that Muslims have fought the enemies of God without any selfish desire and had even stopped in the middle of the fiercest battles to pray. It was through their true and single-minded devotion they were able to establish the kingdom of the true God on earth. Then why are the non-believing Christians and even the idolatrous Hindus dominating over the Muslims? Iqbal's passionate plea did not end there. Five years later, he wrote another poem, *Jawab-i-Shikhwa*, "The Answer to the Plaint." The answer from God reflected the mainstream ideas, known as salafism (the "righteous" or "pious" ancestors): the Muslims are at the bottom of the social rung because they strayed from the glorious path that was shown by the Prophet and his companions. Islam can regain its glory days only by going back to the ideals set by the first three generations of Muslims.[21]

The poet's laments did not fall on deaf ears. On the political front, his writings are considered to be the inspiration for the establishment of the Islamic state of Pakistan. However, around 1900, Iqbal was not the only one seeking answer to the causes of the retreat of the Islamic world. A strong movement of salafism was afoot in several parts of the Islamic world.

Although the adherents of salafism would claim that it began with Muhammad, as a modern movement it started in Egypt in the mid-nineteenth century among intellectuals at al-Azhar University, the preeminent center of Islamic learning, located in Cairo. Islamic scholars, such as Muhammad Abduh (1849–1905), Jamal al-Din al-Afghani (1839–1897), and Rashid Rida (1865–1935), began what some call the second *Ijtihad*, or the period of intense questioning.[22] Their conclusions by and large followed what was expressed in the poems of Muhammad Iqbal.

The wave of Islamic revivalism, which preached political Islam, reached the shores of the subcontinent. The Muslim seminary founded in Deoband, India became the focal point of a conservative stream of thought, which along with the piety of salafism also preached active jihad against all evils. The teachings of Wahhabism in Saudi Arabia found a kindred soul in the Deobandi movement. Together, they gave birth to a short-lived movement in India called the *Khilafat*, which aimed to help the ailing Caliphate in Turkey. One of the early followers of this religious fundamentalist movement was an Indian Islamic scholar of great reputation, Sayyid Abul A'la Maududi. In Islamic terminology, the world was mired in ignorance, *jahiliyyah*, which was lifted only when Muhammad showed the true path. In his powerful denunciation of the prevailing state of the Islamic world, Maududi called his contemporary society *jahili* or ignorant of the true path. His contributions became enshrined in the constitution of the newly founded Pakistan, which was "Islamic in both letter and in spirit."[23] Maududi's writings were to serve as the cornerstone of much revolutionary Islamic thought today, including the Taliban, who claim their philosophical mooring in his teachings, along with those from the Deobandi school.

The winds of salafism turned more political. In Egypt it produced another significant step toward the latter-day global jihadism when Hasan-al-Banna (1906–1949) established the Muslim Brotherhood (*Ikhwan al-Muslimun*). Al-Banna preached that the powerlessness of the Egyptian government was a direct result of its emulating the Western ways. In 1924, when Kemal Pasha replaced the last vestige of the Islamic Caliphate in Istanbul with a regime that was openly hostile to traditional Islam, al-Banna, similar to the Khilaphat movement in India, began Islamic revivalism in Egypt. His blistering criticisms were aimed at the Egyptian authorities as well as the spineless al-Azhar university for failing to give the much-needed moral leadership.[24] He argued that the only way Egypt, and all other Islamic nations, can get back to their days of glory was by the strict adherence to Islam.[25] His Muslim Brotherhood boldly declared: "God is our purpose, the Prophet our leader, the Koran our constitution, Jihad our way and dying for God's cause our supreme objective."[26] Although al-Banna failed in his attempt to violently overthrow the authoritarian regime in Egypt and was assassinated in 1949 by the agents of the state, he casts a towering shadow of influence over the global jihadi movement that was to come half a century later.

In the evolution of the concept of modern-day jihad, which sees violent politics as a means of achieving religious objectives, no one is more important than another Egyptian, a disciple of al-Banna, Sayyid Qutb. However, before we delve into Qutb's contributions to the jihadi movement, it is important to take a moment and understand him in the context of his time. The history of post-World War II Egypt was entangled in its conflict with the newly founded state of Israel, and the Cold War pitted the West against the Communist regimes to the East. During this time the division between nationalism and pan-Islamism, which started with the establishment of a secular regime in Turkey, became sharpened. To the strict Islamists, it presented a Hobson's choice, where the decadence of the Western lifestyle was an affront to the traditional culture and faith and, on the other side, the "godless" Communists were even more abominable. In this struggle, the Egyptian nationalist Gamal Abdel Nasser rejected the forces of the former colonialists, Britain, France, the US, and their lackeys the Israelis. A secular Nasser embraced nationalism, fueling the wrath of the Muslim fundamentalists. From the beginning the Muslim Brotherhood was much more hostile to the enemies inside, whom they declared traitors and apostate, than to those outside of the religion. To the followers of al-Banna and Qutb, Nasser was the enemy number one.

After graduating from a teachers' training college, Sayyid Qutb (1906–1966) worked for the Egyptian Ministry of Education. In 1948, he was sent to the US for higher education. Although Qutb was impressed by the technological advances he saw in the country, he was deeply affected by the racism at the time. However, what alienated him even more was, for him, the moral degradation of the West.[27] The prevalence of free mixing between men and women deeply offended him. From his first-hand experience, Qutb penned his book *Milestones*, which is regarded as the manifesto of the modern jihadi movement. We cannot possibly understand the movement without carefully examining Qutb's arguments.

Similar to all other "political entrepreneurs" in history, Qutb alleged the West had a millennium-long "enmity toward Islam" and had followed a "well-thought-out scheme . . . to demolish the structure of Muslim society."[28] Qutb married the ideas of jahilia offered by Maududi to characterize the current Islamic society with Ibn Taymiyya's call for a duty of all Muslims to wage jihad against apostates and, thereby, extended Ibn al-Wahhab's ideas of a just society to its fullest extent. He asserted:

> . . . the Muslim community has long ago vanished from existence . . . we can say that the Muslim community has been extinct for a few centuries, for this Muslim community does not denote the name of a land in which Islam resides, nor is it a people whose forefathers lived under the Islamic system at some earlier time. It is the name of a group of people whose manners, ideas and concepts, rules and regulations, values and criteria, are all derived from the Islamic source. The Muslim community with these characteristics vanished at the moment the laws of God became suspended on earth.[29]

Apostasy is a serious crime in Islam, punishable by death. Through such a radical claim Qutb at once declared the entire Muslim society *takfir* (declaring a Muslim to be an infidel) and opened up the gates of an uncompromising struggle. Qutb firmly rejected the idea of a peaceful coexistence by stating: "Islam cannot accept or agree to a situation which is half-Islam and half-Jahiliyyah ... The mixing and co-existence of the truth and falsehood is impossible."[30]

Specifically, Qutb's ideas can be summarized as follows. First, the only Muslims that are worthy of emulation are the first generations of Islam, since they alone followed the true teachings of the Koran. The rest of the world has always been mired in Jahiliyyah or ignorance. This is the cornerstone of the salafism.

Second, Qutb steadfastly rejects nationalism. He points out that if Muhammad wanted to only unite the tribes of Arabia, he could have done it. Instead, he established his rule in the name of Allah. Therefore, nationalism has no place in Islam and anyone from any corner of the world can be part of the Ummah.

Third, in his lifetime, Muhammad did not start a social movement simply to redistribute wealth from the rich to the poor. He could have done it to bring the poor on his side during the trying days of fighting with the other tribes of Arabia. Thus, by denouncing the central premises of nationalism and socialism, he claimed that true social justice could come only after a society had been established on the principles of the Koran.[31]

Finally, Qutb argued that given the fact that Islam is being threatened by the *Takfiri* regimes of the Islamic world, it is the duty of every Muslim to join the jihad. It is interesting to note that since he denounced primarily the Muslim rulers, the Egyptian government arrested him on the charges of conspiring with the Western agents against the Nasser government. He was imprisoned, brutally tortured, and, after going through a secret trial by a military court, was executed in 1966. His death only added to his aura as a Shahid or a martyr and his writings have formed the foundation on which modern Islamic terrorism has built its global edifice.

In the following chapter, I will discuss the course by which the salafi movement gained strength and rose to challenge the West through the formation of al-Qaeda and other nationalistic Islamic groups, such as Hamas and the Palestinian Islamic Jihad.

The IRA and the "Troubles" of Northern Ireland

> If you are not confused about the Irish issue, then you just don't understand.
> A common aphorism in Northern Ireland

Hate and the baby's bib: keeping alive the fire of hatred

12 July is a day of celebration in Northern Ireland. A most strange kind of celebration this is. The Orange Order parades mark the victory of the Protestant Prince William of Orange over the Catholic King James II at the Battle of the Boyne in 1690. To the revelers and those who revile them, it

makes little difference knowing the facts of the murky seventeenth-century politics that brought a Dutch mercenary prince into combat with an English king with a questionable claim to the throne.[32] To the enthusiasts, historical facts are minor annoyances, to be conveniently ignored.

For weeks (and perhaps months), the Protestants plan for this day. Homes get fresh coats of paint, the street sides are festooned with decorative items that loudly proclaim their allegiance to various groups, each neighborhood tries to outdo the others in its naked demonstration of hate and macho jingoism. Elaborate floats get ready to display various battle scenes, muscular men brandish swords and puncture the air in front, enacting the stabbing to death of their enemies. In the parade the sublime mixes freely with the macabre. Men and women don their finest, the children wave flags, and huge posters depicting of the virtues of temperance carried by inebriated men draw loud hoots of cheer from the assembled crowd. In anticipation of that day the Catholics also plan ahead: the meek leave town on vacation, while the brave prepare for restoring the honor of their faith. The night before the parades, every Protestant neighborhood constructs elaborate structures, so high that some place beacons to ward off low-flying aircrafts. They are made of piles of wood, cardboard, old furniture or anything that is flammable, and are decorated with all the symbols that are dear to the Catholics. The tri-colored flags of the Republic to the south flutter nervously in the air atop the strange structures in anticipation of being set on fire at midnight. In the age-old battle, symbols of division are restricted not only to the Republican flag, they spill over every kind of political beliefs and affiliations. The IRA defines itself as a progressive civil rights movement. Therefore, it claims its ideological affiliation to the other "oppressed" people from many parts of the world. Since the Catholics sympathize with the Palestinian and the civil rights movement in the US, the sides of the streets leading to the bonfire proudly display the Israeli and the Confederate flags.

In the mean streets of Belfast and Londonderry, everything is seen through the prism of the religious divides. The high fence that separates the two working-class neighborhoods transcends into the hearts and minds of many. In this binary world, children from a very early age are taught to differentiate between a "Catholic look" and a "Protestant look."

Most businesses close down for the 12 July revelries. The fear of renewed mayhem hangs heavily over the entire town. Bed and breakfasts stop booking for the week; even large hotels, in a fashion reminiscent of the Battle of Britain, switch off all lights, as if anticipating air raids.

Like clockwork, the streets of Belfast and other cities of Northern Ireland erupt in violence. Young men (and women) get shot, beaten up with serious injuries, and some get killed. In the midst of the mayhem, while seeking the heart of the "Troubles" on Shankill Road, which meanders westward from central Belfast through a working-class "loyalist" enclave, I came upon a shop selling festive articles, knickknacks, and small mementos. From the shop display I picked up an infant's bib showing a clenched fist with inscriptions boldly claiming, "Ulster, We Shall Never Surrender!" I saw a cherubic face adorned with the fighting words; the baby chortled and gave me a broad smile as our eyes met. In this part of the world, as in many others, hatred comes with mother's milk; it is bred in the bone. In these parts, loathing is a learned behavior, passed on from one generation to the next. Around the world, where ancient conflicts flourish, innocence is inextricably intertwined with the vile.

A brief history of continuing enmity

Depending on the motivation of the researcher, the history of sectarian violence in Ireland can begin in the late twelfth century when the forces of the English Crown invaded the island, or in 1690,[33] when the Protestant king laid the foundation of the English domination, or in 1916 when the watershed events of the Easter Rising took place,[34] or in 1972 when the events of Bloody Sunday re-energized the moribund IRA and the "Troubles" started anew.[35]

Since the IRA is the longest living dissident organization and it involves Great Britain, Ireland, and the US, perhaps more has been written on this conflict by academics, journalists, security experts, and fiction writers than all other conflicts in the world put together. Therefore, in this narrative, I will briefly discuss the sources of mutual fear of the Catholics and Protestants in Northern Ireland, which has kept this conflict alive for centuries.

The struggle for the control of the Emerald Isle began around 1155 when a Papal Bull allowed King Henry II of England to invade a divided land consisting of feuding warlords. As the winds of Reformation swept Europe in the fifteenth century, Ireland remained staunchly Catholic. Facing a threat from the occupied indigenous population, the Protestant English king actively encouraged settlement of coreligionists from Britain, particularly in the northern part of Ireland. The battle for control of the island came to a head when the Protestant William of Orange vanquished Catholic James II and unified Ireland under English rule. The migration of the Scots and the English and their economic and political dominance over a vast population of natives speaking Gaelic and practicing Catholicism paved the way for a conflict based on a mixture of ethno-nationalism, religious identity, and even economic class struggle.

The history of Irish resistance to the British colonial rule can be safely narrated from the mid-nineteenth century, when James Stephens established a secret society dedicated to change the servile attitude of his fellow countrymen. The Fenian Society, as it came to be known, also aimed at creating "Home Rule" for Ireland, whereby the British would grant them the autonomy to establish a democratic republic, albeit under the British Crown. Such a change in the political arrangement would have enhanced the political and economic power of the Catholics. Fearing their loss of privileged status, the Protestant minority in the northern region organized and armed its own secret organization, the Ulster Volunteer Force (UVF) in 1912. Their goal was to scuttle the Home Rule Bill that was being debated in the British Parliament at that time. The Bill was passed in 1914 but was delayed in its implementation because of the British involvement in World War I.

It is interesting to note that the history of the IRA deeply intertwines with the formation and development of the UVF. Over time the two protagonists have not only fought each other, but also when it appeared that a compromised solution could be reached, the fear and apprehension of one would rekindle violence and, in the process, reenergize its protagonist. This is because, in this world drawn only by the broadest strokes and Catholic–Protestant rivalry, the game was always seen as zero-sum—one party's gain was necessarily viewed at the other's loss. In Ireland, bullets and ballots have often been used interchangeably. The formation of the militant and illegal IRA coincided with the establishment of its political twin the Sinn Fein (meaning "ourselves," or "self-help").

The Protestant opposition sunk the possibilities of Home Rule and, in 1916, the violent uprising and the consequent savage retaliation by the British forces marked the beginning of the struggle for Irish independence. To the impatient Catholics, the Rising was seen as a strategic move to compel their colonial rulers to concede when it was most vulnerable due to its engagement in World War I. To the loyal Protestants, such timing seemed as if it were the ultimate treachery.

As the conflict deepened, by 1919 the war of Irish independence began in earnest. By 1921 the British recognized the war was in a stalemate, which neither could win outright. As a result, London recognized the need to reach some kind of deal. For the British the dilemma was that they recognized the practical needs of granting sovereignty to Ireland, but feared its profound implications for the Empire. Public opinion in Great Britain had been, to some degree, turned against the Irish war because of some of the highly publicized violence by British soldiers in the Easter Rising. But the main impetus for a deal came from a widespread perception of the futility of ongoing conflict since neither side was nearing victory. In that sense, it is a precursor to the events that took place in the north of Ireland a couple of generations later—although in the latter case, this recognition took several decades.[36] And, in both cases, a weary British public was far more willing to accede to the demands of the Catholic south than were the Protestants in the Ulster region.

After nearly three years of bloody conflict, a compromise on the conflicting demands was reached. Ireland achieved some measure of independence, while six counties of Northern Ireland, where the Protestants were in majority, succeeded in remaining within the political boundaries of the United Kingdom. This "half-empty" arrangement may have satisfied the majority on all sides, but only reinforced the resolve of the extremists on either side of the divide for a complete victory.

This new arrangement created a confusing situation. The Catholics were in an absolute majority in the Irish Republic, whereas they were in a minority in Northern Ireland. To the Irish nationalists, the presence of the British Crown in any part of the island smacked of colonialism. In contrast, the Protestants in the North remained in constant fear of drowning in the sea of Irish Catholics. As a psychological defense mechanism, the Protestants became much more loyal to the government in London and the Catholics embraced their Gaelic and religious identities with gusto. With a long history going back nearly seven hundred years, each side had plenty of opportunity to spin their own version of history and create images of good and evil, allies and enemies, heroes and villains.

The Naxalites and the Communist movements in India

The transformation of India, widely acclaimed as one of the most remarkable events in the history of the past couple of decades, is often likened to teaching an elephant to dance. The lumbering beast long languishing in the near-stagnant "Hindu rate of growth" of annual GDP per capita during much of her post-Independence era suddenly broke out into a breakneck speed of 8 percent rate of growth, among the highest sustained rates in the world. As the world focusses on this astonishing achievement,[37] a new menace to the country's security is emerging largely outside the public's gaze. This is coming from a resurgent Maoist group operating within the country. Although the attacks on the urban centers and the areas of symbolic importance, such as the train bombings in Mumbai or the attack on the Parliament, get most of the media attention, the new Marxist movement poses a significant danger to India's long-term future.

By some estimates, nearly 20 percent of the land is currently under the dominating influence of Maoist rebels, loosely known as the "Naxalites."[38] The affected areas extend from the border with Nepal to the north to Andhra Pradesh in the south. According to a recent report by the Ministry of Home Affairs, the Naxalites are active in more than one hundred districts, some of which are so inaccessible and remote that they form the only parts of India that are yet to be properly surveyed.[39] The number of deaths from Naxalite violence is also on a steep rise.[40] The fact that these well-armed cadres have been able to carve out "compact revolutionary zones" in 13 states is a case for deep concern.

To be sure, India faces a plethora of insurgencies from a wide variety of groups, spread all over the vast country. However, until lately while the groups fighting in Kashmir and those in the North East received most of the attention, the insurgency from the Maoists remained largely unnoticed even within India. As the seriousness of the situation becomes apparent, Manmohan Singh, the Prime Minister of India, in 2006 called it the "biggest internal security threat."[41] In this chapter, let us examine the history of its birth till 1967, when rebellion spread widely throughout the north-eastern state of West Bengal and particularly affected the metropolitan city of Calcutta.

The Naxalite movement

The Naxalite movement began with a relatively insignificant attack by the largely landless peasants in Bengal, in the foothills of the Himalayas, known as the "Terai region." It happened in a village called Naxalbari. In March 1967, police came to investigate reports of looting of food grains and guns from the homes of the village landlords. As the former Police Commissioner narrates the story, a large number of police were sent there, primarily as a show of force.[42] They marched into the village of Naxalbari and saw a group of surly "tribals."[43] When the police inspector who was leading the posse approached the villagers they shot arrows, killing him. When reinforcements arrived, the police demanded the surrender of those guilty of shooting. The reply came with more volleys of arrows. Thus began what Peking Radio would later call the "Spring thunder in Terai."

I have argued that no mass movement can be studied as a single event. The story of the Naxalite movement is no exception. The movement by the Maoists in the north-eastern Indian state of West Bengal that started in the late 1960s carried the seeds planted by the endless peasant rebellions in colonial India. In fact, no less than 110 violent peasant uprisings have been recorded between 1783 and 1900.[44] Similarly, in nearly half a century of the subsequent colonial rule in the twentieth century, there were numerous peasant uprisings. The colonial exploitation of the Indian peasantry was of epic proportions. The first rebellion started a hundred years before the Naxalite movement. With the high price for indigo as a dye for fabric manufactured in Europe, the British colonialists started forcing the peasantry in Bengal to plant the inedible cash crop instead of traditional food grains.[45] This inevitably brought widespread hunger in the rural areas and led to the first rebellion in the 1860s.[46] The dreadful stories of their exploitation inspired the publication of a number of important novels and plays, which helped create the first stirring of nationalism in India.[47] Although the exploitation of peasants in India has been exceptionally brutal, despite this shameful past, none of these uprisings could be considered spontaneous.[48] They were all parts of some other larger movements or were orchestrated by the village leaderships. In these rebellions, Bengal always took the lead. So much so that around 1915 an exasperated King George V asked a new governor of the province, "What is *wrong* with Bengal?"[49]

The tradition of rebellion continued in Bengal. India gained her independence at the stroke of midnight on 15 August 1947, with a promise from the Prime Minister, Jawaharlal Nehru, to keep its "tryst with destiny." Yet almost exactly two decades later, in the middle of 1967, trouble started among the tribal people in North Bengal. Under the leadership of a faction of the Communist Party, particularly from an urban romantic named Kanu Sanyal, and a long-time Party activist and theoretician, Charu Mazumdar, groups of landless peasants, drawn mostly from the ranks of the tribal people of India, started looting food grains and firearms from the homes of the landlords. At the heart of this rebellion, as has been in the past, was the question of ownership and distribution of land.

Land tenancy in India draws its tradition from the colonial needs of the British East India Company. This early privatized version of imperialism conducted its business on the backs of the peasants, supported by a group of indigenous landlords. In the late seventeenth century the British Corporation granted these landlords, known as *Zamindars*, the ownership of land in return for their collection of tax revenue.[50] The landlords, in turn, subleased their holding among landless peasantry, typically for half their yield.[51] In the case of North Bengal, these sharecroppers were mostly drawn from the tribal people of the neighboring states to the east, many of whom had lived in the area for generations.[52]

The legacy of the colonial land tenancy system continued to spawn extreme inequity in the distribution of arable land. For instance, based on the 1971 census, in Naxalbari, a minuscule portion (4 percent of the population) of rich landlords owned the bulk of the land.[53] Nearly 60 percent of the population was without any landholding. Most of these rural poor ended up becoming sharecroppers, working for the landlords without any tenancy rights. The situation was typical of other neighboring areas where the Maoist movement found its firm footing.

Communist movement in India: the historical context

The history of Communist-led peasant uprising in India started in a district called Telengana in the southern state of Andhra Pradesh and in several north and central districts of Bengal. Around the time of independence, under the active leadership of the Communist cadres, a group of peasants attacked and killed a number of landlords in Telengana.[54] In Bengal, a new movement, *Tebhaga*, challenged the established rules of land tenancy. Traditionally, the landlords used to get 50 percent of the crops, which the tenants would produce with their own investment of seeds, fertilizer, water, and, of course, labor. The term "tebhaga," which roughly means "one third," was what the peasants offered the landlords.

The Communist movement in India has always kept its umbilical chord firmly attached to the leadership of foreign countries. As a result, the fortunes of the movement often waxed and waned with the paths taken in Moscow or Beijing. Bengal had an intimate relationship with the early Bolshevik movement. A Bengali nationalist named M.N. Roy, fighting the British colonial rulers with a number of terrorist organizations, went into exile in around 1915, first to the US and then to Mexico. In Mexico City, he met Mikhail Borodin, an exiled Russian Bolshevik, and was converted to Marxism. With Borodin's help, Roy attended the Third Congress of the Third International in Moscow.[55] The Communist Party of India (CPI) soon after its birth suffered a great setback in prestige and credibility when, having opposed the Nazi regime in Germany and forcefully denounced Hitler,[56] the supplicant Communists in India suddenly opposed the British war effort in 1939 after Stalin signed a Non-aggression Pact with Hitler.

The second blow to the prestige of the CPI came shortly after independence. In 1951, a delegation from India went to Moscow and met Stalin. Although there is no written report of the exact conversation, the delegates were taken aback when Stalin, perhaps eager to establish a relationship with the newly independent nation to the south, instructed them to abandon violent revolution and to take advantage of the wonderful system of parliamentary democracy.[57] Suddenly, to the chagrin of a small number of more extremist supporters, to whom it appeared to be a betrayal of the rural poor, the CPI left the peasants to their own devices and called off the movement.[58]

The frustration of the aborted movement in Telengana spawned another rebellion in the northern part of the restive state of Andhra Pradesh, the Srikakulam district. A small group of disgruntled revolutionaries of the Communist Party started working among the hill tribes by forming *Girijan Sangham* (Hill People's Association). The intense exploitation of these tribal people proved to be yet another fertile ground for peasant uprising. Mehra points out the major causes for this uprising.[59] First, the tribal people started feeling the demographic and economic pressure from the rest of the nation as they started getting pushed out of their traditional holdings. The better-educated plains people began moving in, sensing their vulnerability. Quite often they were offered a minimal price for their land or were offered easy credit at exorbitant rates, which, when they defaulted, caused them not only to lose their meager possessions, but also relegated them and their families to *de facto* enslavement. In response to this growing discontent, in 1956 the Andhra government set up a state-run credit-finance department specifically for the tribal people. Unfortunately, greed and extreme corruption by the state officials only made the situation worse.[60] Finally, under the leadership of the Communist activists, the hill tribes in Srikakulam were mobilized to go on the warpath. In these remote forested areas, the rebels declared their "liberated zones," began an annihilation policy of the local landlords and money lenders, started collecting "taxes," and set up "revolutionary courts" to mete out brutal justice against "class enemies" and the "enemies of the revolution." With matching brutality by the state police and military forces the Srikakulam movement was broken in the mid-1970s.

Marxism and violent rebellion: an ideological perspective

In order to place the discussion of the Communist movement in India in context, we must take a brief detour into the ideological confusion within Marxism and the global Marxist movement, which has repeatedly caused its splintering. The origin of this fundamental conundrum can be traced to the writings of Karl Marx and other early writers. Although Marx himself had little doubt about the ending of the capitalist era, the later practitioners were less certain about it. From the earliest Marxist literature, there has always been some confusion whether the transition from capitalism to socialism would come as part of an inevitable manifest destiny of the intrinsically flawed system just the same way as feudalism gave way to capitalism in Europe and elsewhere or as a result of deliberate activities of a revolutionary party. Marx argued that the capitalists' insatiable acquisitiveness would lead to concentration of income in the hands of an ever fewer group of people. Being overloaded with goods and services that cannot find their price, there will be an inevitable process where profits would fall, causing a spiraling effect of increased unemployment and an even lower rates of profit.[61] In order to save themselves from their fate, the capitalist nations must always seek out new markets. For them, it would come in the form of colonial expansion.[62] However, this too would be temporary, as the inevitable limits to market expansion would start creating havoc within the capitalist system. The ensuing economic crisis would ultimately implode the capitalist system, as the alienated working class, being aware of their true class interest, would bring about an end to the existing socioeconomic and political structure. This would introduce a new era of the dictatorship of the proletariat headed by the Communist Party. In fact, Marx even predicted this end game as follows: "when the class struggle nears the decisive hour . . . a small section of the ruling class cuts itself adrift, and joins the revolutionary class."[63] However, the question still remained as to the role of the Communist Party in ushering in this revolutionary change. Reflecting this confusion, Lenin, in his seminal work *What Is To Be Done?*, praised another important Marxist writer, Karl Kautsky, for his insight, but took him to task for being a revisionist; Kautsky assumed that the revolution would come about through spontaneous outbursts of rebellion by the working class without the leadership of the Communist Party.[64]

This confusion regarding the role of the Communist Party became much more acute when the democratic nations allowed communist parties to participate in the political processes after the end of World War II.[65] In this debate, Stalin and the Soviet Communist Party, perhaps being secured within their own borders, opted to play along with the rules of the game in the democratic nations. This emphasis on the electoral system to bring about a social change was stressed at the 19th Party Congress, when Gregory Malenkov, the Secretary of the Soviet Communist Party, proclaimed that "We have not the least intention of forcing our ideology or our economic system upon anybody. The export of revolution is nonsense. Every country will make it if it wants to and if it does not, there will be no revolution, says Comrade Stalin."[66]

The eschewing of revolutionary movements, the replacement of bullets with ballots, of course, did not sit well with the more radical factions. This contradiction was not simply in rhetoric but also reflected a deep chasm within the global Communist movement, which quickly reached the shores of India.[67] The question was simply, whether the transition to the next stage of Marxist evolution was going to take place peacefully, through the

Communist Party working within the law and gathering power gradually through constitutional means, or whether the existing sociopolitical and economic system could be uprooted through a violent revolution.

Propaganda by deed

At this point, it is important to note the third point of disagreement among the revolutionaries. Collective movements require the presence of collective identity, which defines the group and the community and, at the same time, identifies the enemy.[68] For most of us, identities based on race, religion, or language come naturally, often from birth. How about the Marxist class identity? Identity is a psychological construct. While the other forms of irredentist identities may come with mother's milk,[69] Lenin,[70] Mao,[71] and Ho Chi Minh[72] were emphatic in their assertion that class identity must be painstakingly taught to the peasants and the workers.

However, while Lenin, Mao, and Ho Chi Minh, realizing the difficulty in inculcating the notion of a collective identity based on economic class, advocated a long process of indoctrination of the proletariat, by contrast, other revolutionaries, particularly in Latin America, such as Che Guevara[73] and Carlos Marighela,[74] assumed that class identity was present in the minds of the exploited workers and peasants. It was bubbling just under the surface and could be quickly ignited through propaganda by deed. Thanks to the countless generations of egregious exploitation, the ground was already fertile for revolutionary fervor. All that was required for its deliverance was a fitting action. The appropriate metaphor was the single spark that would start a prairie fire. After working with the landless peasants for years, Charu Mazumdar and Kanu Sanyal were convinced that the "objective condition" in India was ripe for a massive uprising against an oppressive social and political system.[75] The spark that was to ignite the "class hatred" was going to be the grisly killings of the *jotdars* or the village landlords and the rapacious moneylenders. The argument was that as soon as the peasants were shown that they could redress their grievances by killing the sources of their oppression, their natural "class hatred" would well out in cascades and flood the plains of Bengal. Mazumdar and his youthful followers took the connection between the killings and the revolutionary fervor as an act of faith.

Mazumdar, therefore, despite his professed allegiance to Mao and Lenin, was, in fact, following the lines of Guevara. He argued that in their attempt to seize political power under the prevailing conditions:

1) Building of a mass organization was unnecessary, since the country was ready for a revolution.[76] All that was needed was a spark.[77]
2) The class enemy can and should be annihilated through terrorist tactics, rather than be overwhelmed through electoral politics.
3) Any economic agenda for the rural poor must wait until the revolutionary seizure of power.[78]

At Mazumdar's urging, violent actions started and soon engulfed the entire state of West Bengal and parts of the neighboring state of Bihar. Although nearly every city and small town was affected, Calcutta suffered the most. We will examine the implications of these ideas on the development and demise of the Naxalite movement in India in the following chapters.

In sum

In this chapter I have traced the birth of violent political movements. First, by comparing the history of the four disparate groups—the IRA, Hamas, al-Qaeda, and the Naxalites—we can see that all of them are drawn out remnants of past conflicts. While the contours of the group identities have evolved over time, the enmity among the combatants has been kept alive by a long list of political entrepreneurs framing the current issues of grievance, thereby shaping the collective identity of the community. For survival, apart from the ideological message, a group also needs to develop roots in the community and dispense essential public goods that the government is unable or unwilling to provide. I have also shown that in the final analysis religion, nationalism, or Communist ideology are simply the vehicles through which a group's identity is channeled. A closer examination reveals that all three overlap in their messages: the religious identity of Islam is often defined along the lines of certain ethnicity accompanied by a strong message of economic equality. Similarly, nationalism is frequently combined with a specific religion. Communist movements, despite their professed avoidance of ethnicity, mobilize people along ethnic lines.

6 Growth of a movement

Accounting for rapid escalation of violence

Most terrorist organizations—similar to small businesses—die on the vine. According to one study conducted in the early 1990s, 90 percent of these organizations ceased their operation or were totally defeated within the first year of the conflict.[1] Only a small fraction of the groups (about 10 percent) survive. And among those which do, many continue their fight for a long time, sometime spanning many decades and even a century. Take, for instance, the IRA, which has survived as a recognizable entity around the aspirations of Irish nationalism for nearly one hundred years. The various groups of the PLO have been around for nearly fifty years and many of them are still extremely active. In contrast, al-Qaeda was established less than a quarter century ago, and it has already left an indelible mark on world history. In the previous chapter, I discussed the birth of a movement by tracing the path of the ideas that helped create an organization; in this chapter, in the light of my previous discussion, I will analyze reasons for a group to experience rapid growth.

What determines a group's longevity? First, it seems reasonable to argue that a group that enjoys a wide base of popular support for its ideological goals has a much better chance of survival than those which are relatively insulated from the general public. How does a newly formed group develop a mass base of support? History shows that for some groups, the prevailing political condition provides a ready platform from which to launch its actions. The colonies of the European powers were prime examples of this. It is no surprise that a vast population, being ruled by a small number of ethnically, linguistically, culturally, and even religiously different people from a distant land, would provide a fertile ground for groups intent on gaining sovereignty through violent actions. However, the notion of a single nation and nationalism does not appear automatically even under these ideal circumstances. It evolves slowly through the work of political entrepreneurs as well as leaders in the field of art and literature to portray the unifying image of a single community spanning a geographic space. However, when the concept of nationalism sweeps across the land with the interlopers clearly identified, a group is likely to find widespread support for its activities.

Many of the successful groups do not arrive on the scene as political organizations. They first appear as charitable association of dedicated volunteers intent on providing much-needed public services that the government is unable or unwilling to offer. The involvement in providing public goods accords these groups much-needed political legitimacy and public acceptance.

Another way a group can ensure its survival is by tying it ideologically to a prevailing global movement. This area of a group's evolution has not been sufficiently explored in the scholarly literature. For instance, by hitching itself to a larger ideology, a group can suddenly reenergize itself to carry out a local fight. Thus, the Abu Sayyaf group in the Philippines was essentially made up of loosely organized Muslim gangs of bandits entrenched in the jungles of the isolated southern islands of Basilian and Jolo. The history of this conflict goes back to 1566, when Spanish forces descended on these islands with a long memory of fighting Muslims in their own country. When they encountered the local Muslim population, they were bent on continuing their European war with equal ferocity.[2] The resulting cruelty and violence left an indelible mark on the archipelagos when it was passed on to the Christian Filipinos. The ethno-religious tension mounted in the 1970s when the government sponsored Christian migration into these islands. The Cold War and the newly acquired oil wealth by Muslim nations such as Libya and Saudi Arabia forced Ferdinand Marcos to negotiate a truce with the newly formed Moro National Liberation Front (MNLF) in 1976. As Rogers reports, the truce only made the situation worse, as the national government's attention was shifted away from the southern provinces, creating a power vacuum, which was quickly filled by various local warlords.[3] The rebel group took on more of a religious character when in 1978 a cleric named Hashim Salamat formed the Moro Islamic Liberation Front (MILF). The group, still composed of a local rag-tag bunch of brigands, took a step toward global prominence in 1990 when a MILF militant Abdurajak Janjalani established contact with Osama bin Laden's brother-in-law, Muhammad al-Khalifa. Their meeting led to the formation of yet another jihadi organization, the Abu Sayyaf group. Rogers points out:

> The new group proclaimed a radical Islamic ideology and gained early notoriety with grenade attacks on Christian targets. Before long, however, it had diverted its energies to ransom-driven kidnapping. Soon, members of the criminal underground had emerged in key leadership positions, and the group's Islamic identity was subordinated to the quest for profit. After Janjalani's death the Abu Sayyaf deteriorated into a loose federation of bandit chiefs bound mainly by convenience.[4]

Finally, realizing its true nature, the al-Qaeda disavowed its link with the Abu Sayyaf organization.[5]

Jessica Stern argues that a successful group must be protean in its ideology and be able to change with altered political realities.[6] This adaptability, according to Stern, allowed the Islamic Movement of Uzbekistan (IMU), for example, to have a longer life than expected. After the demise of the Soviet Union a number of former Soviet high-level officials took over the reins of power in the central Asian republics. Among them, the regime of Islam Karimov was one of the most corrupt and repressive. The IMU was originally established as an opposition to Karimov. However, they allied themselves with Mullah Omar and the Talibans in Afghanistan, which increased their power and position.

Running a charitable organization, much less a rebel force, requires monetary resources. Groups that do not have a well-thought-out plan for raising money would inevitably be wiped out.[7] The groups that begin by offering services are usually supported externally. For radical Islamic groups support came from the oil-rich Arab nations and Iran. The formal creation of the Organization of the Petroleum Exporting Countries (OPEC) in 1965 accorded a huge economic power to the cartel. By holding tough on the prices of its product, the cartel was instrumental in making its members hugely rich. Although its unity and politics will have always been open to question, there is no doubt about the fact that the 1973 oil embargo and the resulting price hike added to the vast coffers of OPEC member nations. The second significant event took place in 1979 when the ousting of the Shah of Iran created a global shortage of petroleum products. As the Saudis boosted their oil production to make up for the temporary loss of Iranian oil, the sky-high prices—still the highest in inflation-adjusted dollars—significantly enhanced their economic might. Having the world's largest reserves of crude oil, Saudi Arabia, which accounts for over a third of the total OPEC production, was flushed with money.

With their newfound wealth, both Saudi Arabia and Iran pursued their own politics, which are inextricably intertwined with their goals of establishing religious hegemony. It is not only that the governments of the oil-rich Islamic nations would sponsor groups of their own liking, but huge sums of money began flowing through various charitable organizations. Napoleoni points out:

> In Saudi Arabia, for example, there is no tax system or internal revenue service, consequently no one is able to audit the accounts and keep track of monetary inflows and outflows. Although companies regularly pay zakat,[8] the donation is not an official tax, but a voluntary payment for which no records are required. The structure of Islamic banking system is of no help either. Most transactions are in cash. . . . Although oil has brought immense wealth to countries like Saudi Arabia, the kingdom is still a tribal society, with a strong cash culture.[9]

Islamic banks also apply zakat to every transaction or contract.[10] They deduct the equivalent of 2 percent of personal wealth and transfer them to charitable organizations. With the 6,000 member Saudi royal family alone, it was estimated that the yearly zakat was around \$12 billion in 2002.[11] Financial power of such magnitude played a crucial role in spreading radical Islam in many parts of the world. Islam being an aggressively proselytizing religion, and trying to spread the Koran to non-believers being part of every Muslim's religious duty, supporting these radical groups posed little moral dilemma in the Arab world.

In many countries around the world—wherever there were sizeable Muslim populations—money flowed in. As the first visible sign, the local mosques might be repainted and/or rebuilt or new mosques would be constructed. Soon these mosques would be staffed by preachers with the strictest interpretation of the Koran along the Wahhabi line. Many of these firebrand preachers, particularly in the poorer countries, would find sympathetic audiences. The religious schools—the Madrassas—funded by the Arab/Muslim nations attracted large numbers of children from poor families. In these Madrassas the children are taught to read and write and, most importantly, are given food. Both of these are attractive to parents desiring to help their children escape the vicious cycle of poverty. Unfortunately, the curriculum in these Madrassas had little relevance to worldly scholarship. They seldom taught students math or science. Neither did they provide any training for a job of any kind. The outcome of this religious indoctrination—often involving long hours of rote learning of verses in an unfamiliar language with biased interpretation by the teachers—was the radicalization of disaffected young men and women into political Islam, which help spread the influence of the jihadi groups, such as al-Qaeda and others fighting in many parts of the world.[12]

Compared with the Arab nations, Iranian support was much more specific during this period. They provided funds and arranged training for Hizbullah in Lebanon. And, despite Hamas being a Sunni group, the Iranians helped them with training in explosives and provided other material support.

Apart from the help in developing ideology, the longevity of many dissident groups was helped by a number of external factors, which included the counter-terrorism policies of the government. Let us now examine briefly the history of the IRA, Hamas, al-Qaeda, and the Naxalites to understand the reasons for their longevity and periods of rapid growth.

Sectarian conflict in Northern Ireland: the IRA

"In 1968, the Irish Republican Army (IRA) was a moribund, shriveled and irrelevant organization. Its membership was tiny and in long decline, its bantam resources diminished further with each year, and its political front, Sinn Fein, was an irrelevance boasting little electoral mandate."[13] Thus, Andrew Silke, reflecting the common wisdom, saw the IRA before it suddenly exploded with a renewed burst of energy. In face of increased hostility from the Protestant gangs, the IRA was being outmanned and outmaneuvered. In its feeble state it was unable to protect its people and, in the minds of many, the IRA meant "I Ran Away."

Richard English, however, somewhat disputes this accepted version of history and finds seeds of discontent beginning in the early 1960s that would later explode in open violence claiming many lives.[14] In any case, the decade-long history of the IRA fifty years after the Easter Rising offers an object lesson in the rapid growth of a mass movement. Therefore, in this section, I will discuss the process of escalation of violence and the establishment of the much more violent and politically active Provisional IRA, spanning the period from 1962 to 1981.

In the 1960s the Catholics in Northern Ireland lived a decidedly restricted life. The Protestant majority kept them out of the civil service, the judiciary, and even managerial positions in the flourishing private sector. The schools were segregated along the lines of religious affiliation. The more prestigious institutions of higher education's student body did not reflect the percentage of the Catholics in the population. Another big source of frustration for the Catholics living in the large northern cities was housing. The Protestants were clearly favored in the allocation of council housing. The democratic process was of little help, since the Protestant politicians would successfully gerrymander and draw up the boundaries of the voting districts in a way that would minimize the influence of the Catholic votes.[15]

By looking at the plot of the number of people killed due to sectarian bloodshed in Northern Ireland (Figure 6.1) we see that violence escalated from 1969. From this plot we can visually distinguish four segments. The first segment between 1968 and 1976 shows a huge increase in violence with about 92 people killed per year. The next 11 years show an almost steady level of

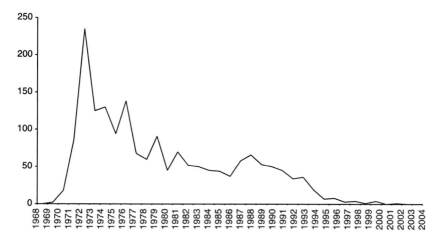

Figure 6.1 Number of people killed by the IRA.

Source: I am grateful to Ignatio Sanchez Cuenca for the data on the IRA. See also McKittrick (2000).

violence, with the number of average yearly fatality cut nearly by half to 57. The third segment, spanning 1988 to the present, shows a steady decline to the level of near zero killings. The average number of deaths attributed to the IRA was about 20 per year, while in the last five years the average has declined to about 2. Let us now draw a thumbnail picture of the "Troubles" of Northern Ireland and examine the reasons for the rapid growth of the IRA and the group's ability to maintain a strong violent presence. Therefore, my narrative will cover the 20-year period from 1968 through 1987.

For more than 200 years, the marching season in the summer months has been a focal point of conflict between the Protestant and Catholic communities in Northern Ireland. The Protestants of the Orange Order who arranged most of these parades claim that they are part of their cultural heritage, commemorating key historical events. The Catholics, on the other hand, take these triumphalist marches as an affront to them since they all celebrate the Protestant victory over Catholic forces. Trouble inevitably begins when the parade goes through the Catholic neighborhoods.

August 1969 was no different. The Apprentice Boys Parade through the city streets marks the relief of the siege of Derry in 1689, after the city gates were locked against King James' forces by apprentice boys vowing "No Surrender." However, this time, the riots became more intense. They began in Derry and quickly spread to Belfast. As the Royal Ulster Constabulary (RUC) sprung into action, primarily against the stone-throwing Catholics, pitched battles erupted between the Catholics and the police force. The broadcast pictures of police beatings and gun battles drew worldwide condemnation. What irritated the Protestants in Northern Ireland and their protector, the British government, was a veiled threat from the Irish Republic of an armed invasion of the north to protect the interest of the Catholic minority.[16] This provocation prompted Protestant mobs engaging in operations akin to "ethnic cleansing" in Yugoslavia, where 3,000 Catholic families were driven out of their homes and neighborhoods. In retaliation, nearly 500 Protestant families were also uprooted from heavily Catholic areas of the two cities.[17] Since the minority Catholics suffered disproportionately in the tit-for-tat atrocities, a new and much more aggressive group emerged out of the old IRA: the Provisional IRA (PIRA). As the government failed to meet the security needs of the Catholics in Northern Ireland, the immediate task of this new militant group was to protect the Catholic neighborhoods against attacks from the Protestant gangs.

Fearing for the safety of the Catholic population, 10,000 British troops were sent to Northern Ireland, despite loud protests from the Protestants. The soldiers quickly brought the explosive situation under control. The British government imposed a substantial reform on the recalcitrant majority. These reforms met nearly all the demands put forward by a growing civil rights movement, which shortly disbanded having achieved its goals.

Unfortunately, it is impossible to secure peace and implement democratic reform at the barrel of a gun. Similar to the experience of other foreign troops sent to keep peace in the middle of a civil war, the British troops soon found themselves fighting the very population they were sent to protect.[18] The PIRA was growing in strength and actively acquiring more funds, guns, and volunteers. The emerging power of such a violent group caused concern and the British troops stepped up on their search and seizure operation, which brought it directly into confrontation with the much more self-assertive Catholic group.

These operations were carried out with brutality. Lee reports that in 1971 more than 17,000 Catholic homes were searched.[19] As the troops rummaged through homes for weapons or fugitives, they would leave them nearly totally destroyed and occupants thoroughly humiliated. Yet most often these searches yielded very few weapons or incriminating evidence to suggest an active involvement in the PIRA.[20] The growing indignation of the Catholics only helped the PIRA. Taking full advantage of the situation the PIRA stepped up on its acts of provoking the troops into further alienating the Catholics.

If the defining moment in the nationalist struggle came during the Easter Rising when the picture of the British soldiers firing at unarmed Dubliners in April 1916 galvanized the Irish resistance movement, fifty years later on Sunday 30 January 1972, another such atrocity proved to be a watershed event in the violent history of Northern Ireland. Known as "Bloody Sunday," the British Paratroopers in Derry opened fire on a crowd of Catholics and killed 13 people. The powerful tales of the abuses of the security forces further increased the influence of the PIRA. Thus, Silke notes, "Strong local support, ample manpower, and newly acquired funds and weapons allowed the PIRA to conduct an unprecedented campaign of violence against the RUC, judiciary and army."[21]

The level of violence in Northern Ireland continue to spiral out of control. Exhausted and demoralized, within eight weeks of Bloody Sunday the British government dissolved the Protestant-dominated Stormont regime, deposing the unionist Prime Minister Brian Faukner. The power to rule was taken away from the elected Northern Ireland Parliament and was transferred to a British cabinet minister. The next two decades marked desperate attempts by the British government to walk the fine line between the Protestant fear and the Catholic aspirations.[22] However, in the meantime, the suspension of the Stormont government added to the anxiety of the Loyalists. This added to the tension as sectarian violence continued to claim many lives.

Fearing a power vacuum created by the suspension of democracy, London tried a forced power-sharing between the two groups in January 1974. Unfortunately, this forced effort at conflict resolution satisfied neither side. The PIRA violence continued unabated and in May the Ulster Workers Council, a Protestant group with strong ties to the paramilitary groups, called a general strike to force a new election. Given the Protestant majority, the outcome of the election was a foregone conclusion and the British government refused to give in. At the same time, fearing a Protestant backlash, the army was unwilling to break the crippling strike. In the end, Westminster gave in and declared its willingness to reinstall democracy by calling a new constitutional convention.[23] The Catholics summarily rejected the call for democracy. With the battle lines clearly drawn and very well understood, neither side wanted to give in. Killings continued to escalate.

Having failed a top-down solution, the British for a while tried the tactic of "chatting up the gunmen." The purpose was to win the goodwill of the fighting men through direct conversation. In order to appease the extremists on both sides, the authorities in London in 1974, despite vocal opposition from the moderates, recognized the legal status of the Protestant paramilitary group, the Ulster Volunteer Force, and the political arm of the IRA, Sinn Fein. The appeasement worked for a while as a ceasefire was called. However, soon the truce broke, and the number of killings started rising again in 1975. The following year, a constitutional convention became hopelessly deadlocked, and the British became resigned to the long-term prospect of a non-democratic direct rule of Northern Ireland.

Violence subsided in the second phase in 1977. One of the primary reasons for this decline in violence was due to the return of the police instead of the soldiers. O'leary points out that "The return to 'police primacy' in 1977 was associated with a reduced level of killings. Armed police are more restrained than soldiers trained to kill in combat."[24] Soon the region settled down to a lower level of killings by the rival groups.

Direct rule was acceptable to the Protestants since it reaffirmed the British ties to the province. The Catholics rejected it. In 1981 in a change of tactic, the IRA organized a hunger strike of its prisoners. The strategic self-immolation of Bobby Sands and nine others galvanized support for the IRA to an unprecedented level.[25] Over time, the politics of polarization continued, where talking and killing went on simultaneously. Each time there was a ray of hope, it was dashed by the incommutable logic of a zero-sum game of sectarian violence. In 1986, a bomb exploded in a Berlin nightclub frequented by off-duty US soldiers. Intelligence reports indicated the culpability of Libya and its revolutionary leader Muammar Qaddafi. In a retaliatory move, the Reagan Administration bombed Tripoli and the port city Benghazi. Libya claimed that the raids killed 37 people including an infant adopted daughter of the Libyan strongman. Two of his sons were seriously injured. This strong-armed response to terrorism was extremely popular in the US. And this bold retaliatory move is often cited as an example of a successful counter-terrorism effort.[26] However, later analyses showed that the long-term effect of this bombing only helped solidify Libyan resolve to support anti-Western forces all over the world, including in Northern Ireland.[27] The supply of a huge cache of weapons by Libya in 1989 once again boosted the level of violence in Northern Ireland for years to come.[28]

With this thumbnail sketch of the history of violence in Northern Ireland, let us discuss the reasons for the success of the IRA in gaining strength and remaining a viable military and political power against one of the strongest security forces in the world. O'Leary correctly observes that "[o]perating mostly within a territory with just over a million and a half people, and for most of that time within a support base of a minority of the minority cultural Catholic population of approximately 650,000, the IRA's organizational endurance was impressive. It survived the efforts of five UK prime ministers to crush it—Harold Wilson, Edward Heath, James Callaghan, Margaret Thatcher, and John Major."[29]

I argue that during the 20-year period beginning 1968, for a number of different reasons, the ideology propagated by the IRA could remain strong within a significant segment of the Catholic population in Northern Ireland and in the Republic of Ireland. The dissident group's effort was further facilitated by its ability to raise sufficient funds[30] through various illegal means[31] as well as receiving financial help from the Catholic Diaspora, particularly in the US.[32] Also, having a sympathetic regime—the Republic of Ireland—as a neighbor, the IRA benefited from having moral and political support across the border. They also used the Republic as a sanctuary.

Furthermore, the IRA has been innovative in its tactics as well as its organizational structure. When one tactic failed (e.g. "proxy bombing") it quickly abandoned it and moved on to other more effective methods. Along with attacks on the adversaries, the IRA also kept a strict hold on its political base through recrimination and vigilantism, where defections and other acts of disloyalty were punished severely. The need for keeping the followers in line increased as the ideological struggle weakened over time.[33] The IRA was also quick to adapt to changing situations in its organizational structure. After 1977, when the British placed a greater emphasis on policing instead of trying to crush the movement with the use of troops, the IRA responded by changing the way it was organized. Until then the IRA was organized along a strict hierarchy mirroring the British army, "complete with officers, staff and line, and territorial brigades, battalions, and companies."[34] However, it reorganized into smaller cells of "active service units" (ASUs). By strict division of labor, each ASU was given specialized tasks, such as bombing, sniping, execution, vigilante attacks, and robberies.[35] This change in the organizational structure minimized the risks of both detection by the police and defection from its political base.

The collective identity of a community defining its enemies and allies can be kept alive indefinitely in the face of evident injustice. The Protestant majority, by imposing a system based on discrimination of the Catholic minority, made sure that the enmity would prevail. The jingoistic marches, observed with ritualistic fervor, kept the mutual hatred alive.[36] Under these circumstances it is not difficult to see why the IRA would have a sympathetic base on both sides of the Irish border.

However, the question is why did violence flare up in 1969? As English points out, in 1962, Cathal Goulding took over as the IRA's Chief of Staff. "Goulding in 1962 inherited an IRA that was in a weak condition. Funding had dried up, they were short of weapons and there were not enough volunteers coming through to replace those who had been imprisoned or killed."[37] Goulding introduced a new thinking in the strategic approach of the IRA. First, it developed a preliminary plan for another military campaign. However, more importantly, Goulding changed the ideological orientation and embraced Marxist new-left ideology that was sweeping Europe at that time. English makes this important ideological transition crystal clear:

> There was less emphasis during the 1960s on military training, and more on a leftist definition of republic struggle: 1967 saw the IRA Army Council alter Sinn Fein's constitution in favour of a socialist republican objective, and, in Cathal Goulding's own words, "Republicanism stands for the liberation of people. We have been accused of being to the left, but if that means seeking an end to the partition, to the exploitation of our people and placing them in the position of masters of their destiny rather than slaves of a capitalist economy, then we are to the left."[38]

With rhetoric like this, Goulding and his fellow radicals, through intense ideological discourse in the discussion groups, the Wolfe Tone Societies, carried out a complete makeover of the movement.[39] This was a profound change for the IRA, since the original IRA drew its membership mostly from the Catholic population of Ireland[40] and the leadership of the original IRA was profoundly steeped in Catholic ideology and religion.[41] Another important innovation took place when the tired retrogressive movement was given the shape of a civil rights movement. By making it into a struggle for justice and equality for the minority in Northern Ireland, the IRA elevated their struggle from a narrow nationalistic aspiration to seeking justice for the oppressed people all over the world.

The possibility of a renewed military campaign along with a civil rights movement wrapped in Marxist rhetoric was sure to unsettle the Protestant leaders in Northern Ireland. The success of Martin Luther King, Jr. in forcing the entrenched White power in the American South to end discrimination must have created a deep impression in the minds of the Protestants. Given their profound apprehension, it is not surprising that the civil rights movement would meet with extreme violence from the Loyalist groups. Their overreaction, which culminated in the Bloody Sunday massacre, made sure of the IRA's viability as a formidable force for the next two decades. In fact, Silke observes: "The IRA themselves worked to provoke harsh measures from the unfortunate security forces, knowing fully well the benefits it would reap in terms of support and recruits."[42] In fact, the large flow of volunteers after the 1969 confrontation were known as "the sixty-niners."[43] The IRA has also been remarkably nimble in its strategic adjustment. They changed their targets as well as modes of attack to suit the changing needs of the time. In their struggle, the IRA had clearly identifiable enemies: the British soldiers, the Protestant paramilitaries, and the Royal Ulster Constabulary, which was nearly 100 percent Protestant.[44] Finally, in solving the puzzle of the IRA's long life, we cannot overstate the importance of the Catholic diaspora, particularly in the US, in providing the necessary funds to continue their struggle.

Thunder from the Islamic world

Nationalism versus religious fundamentalism in the Palestinian conflict

The previous chapter examined the evolution of the religious notion of jihad and the birth of the global salafi movement. This section will analyze how this essentially religious concept was translated into violent political action.

The end of World War II saw the birth of two nations on the opposite ends of the divide based on religious identity: Pakistan and Israel. Since then no new country has been formed on the basis of religion alone.[45] To the Muslims around the world, the birth of the former was a source of pride and comfort, while the latter, a wellspring of resentment and anger. The establishment of a Jewish state with claims to half of Jerusalem, the third most revered shrine in Islam, was like a dagger through the heart to many.

In reaction to Israel, a rift developed in the Arab world. Islam does not recognize separate political entities of nationhood and instead promotes the idea of the community, Ummah. Analogous to Marxism, where nationalism is seen as an epiphenomenon, the idea of a separate nation is simply alien to Islam. Yet the draw of nationalism is so strong that since the end of World War II every successful revolution, including the one carried out by Ayatollah Khomeini in Iran, has defined itself in national terms; the newly formed nations have been named the Islamic Republic of Iran, or the People's Republic of China, and so forth. By naming themselves in terms of a specific nationality, in contrast to the Union of Soviet Socialist Republics, all of these countries have defined themselves "firmly in a territorial and social space inherited from (their) pre-Revolutionary past."[46] Eric Hobsbawm, therefore, is correct in pointing out that despite the best efforts of the Marxist theorists in trying to wipe out nationalism, the Communist rulers utterly failed in preventing these nations from assuming nationalist character "not only in form but also in substance,"[47] as was evident after the violent dissolution of the USSR[48] and Yugoslavia.[49]

A similar pattern has emerged in the Islamic world, where the nationalist fervor has faced a constant struggle with the millenarian zeal of those who have rejected separate political entity based on ethnicity, geography, language or a common culture. Whenever religion has been tested against nationalism as a bond, nationalism has gained the upper hand. It did not work to unify the Arab world under one banner: Pakistan split apart from Bangladesh through a bloody uprising, and after the overthrow of Saddam Hussain, Iraq quickly descended into a bloody civil war along the lines of sectarian and ethnic divisions.

It is indeed ironic that while in the 1950s and 1960s it was nationalism in the Islamic world which was seen as the biggest threat to the West and the US, the rise of al-Qaeda and pan-Islamism has taken its place in the past decade and a half. In the earlier period, the nationalist rebel leaders often targeted the religious fundamentalists, accusing them of actively colluding with the enemies of the land. The tables have turned. In the recent conflict, the millen-arians are accusing the nationalists of collaborating with the Western powers. Similarly, the US is currently trying to hunt down the likes of Osama bin-Laden and promoting Hosni Mubarak in Egypt and Musharraf in Pakistan.

The first confrontation with the Western economic and military interests based on nationalism in the Islamic world started in Iran. In 1953, a demo-cratically elected Muhammad Mosaddeq was determined to reduce the power of multinational oil companies, which he believed were dictating terms that were against the interest of his country. Masaddeq nationalized the Iranian oil industry, which had been under British control through the Anglo-Iranian Oil Company (today known as British Petroleum or BP). This brought about a constitutional crisis, when some pro-Western members in his cabinet con-sidered such a move as unconstitutional. Finding an opportunity, the British and the US governments orchestrated a coup, known as Operation Ajax, to oust Mosaddeq and to reinstitute the monarchy of Reza Pahlavi.[50] Three years later in Egypt when Gamal Abdel Nasser nationalized the Suez Canal, the British and the French, in secret collusion with Israel, attacked Egypt.[51] During and after the ensuing Suez Crisis, Nasser accused the religious fundamentalists of treasonous acts of making contacts with the US and British intelligence services. These accusations led to many of the leaders' incarceration, torture, and execution by the Egyptian security forces.

By most accounts, the history of Palestinian nationalism began with the rise of the Palestine Liberation Organization (PLO) in the mid-1960s as a distinct-ive nationalistic movement.[52] The early Palestinian struggle was subsumed within the broader Arab identity promoted by Gamal Abdel Nasser and the secular Baath Party of Syria. However, the devastating war of 1967, along with the success of a small band of fighters in inflicting heavy damage to a column of Israeli armed forces in the village of Karameh, created an intense feeling of Palestinian pride separate from the wounded Arab identity. As a result of the ensuing political dynamics, a number of groups, such as the Fatah, the Syrian-sponsored Saiqa, the Popular Front for the Liberation of Palestine (PFLP), and its offshoot the Popular Democratic Front for the Liberation of Palestine (PDFLP), with diverse ideological orientation, merged under the umbrella of the PLO.[53]

Among the various groups under the PLO, the Fatah is the largest. Although the PLO is largely secular, the Fatah's cultural ethos is distinctly Sunni Islamic. Fatah also carries the largest number of cadres and resources and, until his death in 2004, was dominated by Yasser Arafat and his group of Palestinians who lived in exile before 1994 and then located in the Gaza strip and the West Bank regions.[54] The Fatah's ideology being highly nation-alistic, it quickly charted a course that is distinct from the interests of other

Arab nations. Thus, the Fatah considers itself as the most mainstream Palestinian organization and, as such, is entitled to "speak for the Palestinian question."[55]

The Popular Front for the Liberation of Palestinian (PFLP) is a Marxist-Leninist group founded in 1967 by George Habash. In its ideology, the PFLP sees itself as the representative of the working-class Palestinians and aims at liberating all of Palestine and establishing a democratic socialist state.[56] Although the PFLP was one of the original members of the PLO, it withdrew itself from the umbrella organization in 1993 in protest at Yasser Arafat's peace accord with Israel and joined the Alliance of Palestinian Force to oppose the Oslo Agreement. However, this alliance proved to be short lived. In 1996 the PFLP split from the Alliance and its ideological brethren, the Democratic Front for the Liberation of Palestine (DFLP).[57] After the breakdown of the Oslo peace process and Arafat taking a more radical approach toward Israel, the recent years have seen a closer cooperation between the PFLP and the PLO.

The Palestinian national identity—similar to that of most other Islamic nations—collides and yet often comfortably coexists with the other overarching identity of Islamic Ummah. While the PLO was following a mostly secular path and was rising in popularity, the prospect of a peaceful settlement with the Jewish state brought about violent disagreements within the Palestinian community. It pitted the largely secular and increasingly accommodating PLO against those holding a strong Islamic identity along with the ideology of not acceding even a "thimbleful" of Palestinian sand to Israel. Hence, challenges to the PLO, in general, and Arafat, in particular, came primarily from two groups, Hamas and the Islamic Jihad. In January 1988 the PLO and the leadership of the *intifada* movement issued a 14-point declaration calling for a Palestinian state to coexist with Israel. A month later Hamas was officially founded.[58]

The name Hamas is an abbreviation of *Harakat al-Muqawama al-Islamiyya* (Islamic resistance movement). It emerged as an Islamic alternative to the PLO during the first intifada uprising in the Gaza Strip and the West Bank. In its ideology, Hamas is opposed to the secular character of the PLO[59] and its program of creating a separate Palestinian state in the Gaza Strip and the West Bank.[60] By placing the issue in the religious Islamic context, meaning, and imagery, Hamas has been able to successfully put together a mass political movement that directly challenges the power and authority of the Palestinian Authority (PA). The rise of Hamas is further attributed to the frustration of the Palestinian populace regarding the inability of the PA to deliver a transparent, democratic, and efficient administration. Furthermore, since the peace process began in 1993, the PA emerged to the world as the sole representative of the Palestinian people. As the successive Israeli governments negotiated with the PA, Hamas saw itself being increasingly marginalized. Therefore, Hamas maintained a delicate balance among its professed political radicalism, its myriad social-service delivery programs, and its opposition to the PA through a shrewd use of controlled violence that not only confronts the Israeli government but also challenges the PA's dominance among the Palestinians. In the process, inspired perhaps by the success of Hizbullah in Lebanon, the tactic of suicide bombing emerged as a strategic weapon of choice for the group. As well as being spontaneous expressions of frustration, Hamas learned to use them to further its own political agendas. Mishal and Sela, having undertaken a comprehensive study of Hamas and its ideology, point out that "Hamas's decision-making processes have been markedly balanced, combining realistic considerations with traditional beliefs and arguments, emphasizing visionary goals but also immediate needs".[61] The Hamas leaders orchestrated the sacrifices of their young followers through preaching in the mosques, published leaflets and directives, and through the socializing influence, which permeates nearly every aspect of life in the oppressive Gaza Strip and the West Bank.[62]

Political ideology through the fundamentalist interpretation of Islam, however, is not a monopoly of Hamas. In fact, its professed nationalism is in direct conflict with the pan-Islamic transnational identity professed in the Koran.[63] Hence, it comes as no surprise to know that Hamas's mixture of the two identities (Palestinian and Islamic) would be in conflict with an even stricter interpretation of Islam. This came from the group the Palestine Islamic Jihad (PIJ).

Although a number of small radical Islamic Palestinian groups have been active under the general title of the PIJ (*Harkat al-Jihad al-Islami al-Filastini*), among them the Fathi Shaqaqi faction is the most prominent. Dismayed by the lack of radicalism of the Islamic Brotherhood, specifically toward Israel, Fathi Abd al-Aziz Shaqaqi, a Palestinian born in the Gaza Strip and an Egyptian-trained physician, along with Abd al-Aziz Odah and Bashir Musa established their own jihadi umbrella organization around 1979. The group was particularly inspired by the revolutionary success of Ayatollah Khomeini in Iran. Even though adherence to a single Imam is inimical to the Sunni tradition, Shaqaqi penned an admiring tract profiling the Ayatollah, which prompted his expulsion from Egypt. Because of the PIJ's emphasis on Pan Islamic ideology, the group maintained a close contact with the radical groups in Israel as well in Syria, Lebanon, and Iran. Over the years, the PIJ has developed its base among intellectuals and students, primarily in the Gaza Strip. The assassination of Shaqaqi in October 1995 in Malta[64] robbed the PIJ of its charismatic leader and, after Hamas switched to suicide attacks, the two groups started cooperating closely with each other.[65] Although the PIJ is much smaller than Hamas, and has little or no street presence, it offered the like-minded Palestinians and other Arabs sympathetic to their plight another avenue to direct their anger and frustration.

Although both Hamas and the PIJ trace their origin to the Muslim Brotherhood movement in Egypt, there is a clear distinction in the order of priorities set forth by the two groups, particularly regarding the question of Jihad. The Muslim Brotherhood, like many other fundamentalist Islamic movements, saw Jihad as a general duty of all Muslims and proposed that first "proper Islam" should be established throughout the Muslim world. Only after this primary goal is achieved should violent jihad be directed against Israel. In contrast, the irredentist Hamas movement switched the two priorities. It maintained that, first, jihad should be directed at liberating all of Palestine and then, the Muslims should direct their attention to the goal of restoring the "true faith" to the rest of the Islamic world. However, both groups absolutely reject any political arrangement that would result in the relinquishment of any part of Palestine to the non-believers.

The byproduct of the Oslo Peace Agreement was the strengthening of the PLO as the sole representative of the Palestinian people, a prospect that threatened its ideological rivals. In response, Hamas and the PIJ stepped up their violent campaign against the Israeli government. In particular, they discovered the power of suicide attacks. These attacks succeeded in inflicting deep damage not only on Israeli politics[66] but also, for the first time, the cruel equation of relative losses, measured in terms of lives lost, turned against the Israelis.[67] Facing this unprecedented level of violence, Israel reacted sharply by imposing new punitive measures based on collective punishment, which further alienated and radicalized a large segment of the Palestinian population, to whom any peaceful coexistence with the Jewish state lost its appeal. This process of disenchantment was also aided by the corruption and ineptitude of the Palestinian Authority to set up an efficient government. Finally, its inability to secure an independent Palestinian state from the increasingly recalcitrant Labor Party government of Ehud Barak exposed the futility of the cooperative strategy of the PA and the fundamental weaknesses of the Oslo peace process.[68] Heightened tension created by the symbolic incursion of Sharon to the al-Aqsa Mosque and the consequent spate of attacks by the radical Palestinian groups dealt the final death knell to the peace process. Ehud Barak's defeat and the election of Ariel Sharon saw the formal end of the process of a negotiated peace. Seeing the prospect of losing the global recognition of being the sole representative of the Palestinian people as well as losing political clout among its constituents, a number of factions within the PLO umbrella organization (e.g., the Martyrs of al-Aqsa, the Fatah-Tanzim, and the PFLP) started following the path drawn by Hamas and the PIJ and decided to carry out the most successful of the violent strategies, suicide bombings.[69]

Al-Qaeda

The war in Afghanistan against the Soviet invaders was one of those watershed events that have shaped the history of the Islamic violent movement that is still plaguing the world today. The Afghan War drew volunteer Mujahideen from all over the Arab/Islamic world. The process was reminiscent of another war and another call to action to a very different time, place, and cause: the way idealistic volunteers from many Western nations, including the US, joined the Spanish Civil War (1936–39).[70]

Unlike regular military fighting with government support, the young men combating the Soviet forces in a far-away land had no support system. There was no way the families back home could get news about their loved ones nor could they send care packages to them. In order to fill this pressing need, a young Saudi businessman from one of the wealthiest families in the world, Osama bin Laden, started an organization called al-Qaeda (the base). During the war, al-Qaeda won widespread admiration and support for its work in allowing the fighters to keep in touch with their families.

One of the first Mujahideen to join the fray in Afghanistan and to put the struggle against the Soviets in a religious context was Sheik Abdullah Azzam, an Islamic scholar and an adherent of the founders of the modern jihadi movement, Sayyid Qutb and his disciple Muhammad Abd al-Salam Faraj. Like his intellectual predecessors, Azzam believed in the violent resistance against all non-believers.[71] Azzam worked tirelessly to combine all the Islamic forces to fight against the Soviets. Soon, he was joined by Osama bin Laden and Ayman al-Zawahiri. In their combined effort, al-Qaeda transformed itself from a charitable organization to an active fighting force.[72]

Problems, however, soon erupted within the jihadi family. Azzam was particularly ecumenical and rejected the internecine fights among Muslims as *fitna*, or chaos, that followed soon after the Prophet's death, which split asunder the Ummah into Shi'a and Sunni. He supported strikes against the non-Muslim countries, but firmly rejected the notion of the takfir (declaring the unfriendly rulers of the Islamic world as "apostate") and calling for a jihad against the "near enemy." The aftermath of the expulsion of the Soviet military from Afghanistan brought about a fierce debate, much like the followers of Stalin and Trotsky in the post-war Soviet Union, within the group regarding future direction of the jihadi movement.[73] Hardened by his treatment in the hands of the Egyptian government, al-Zawahiri was not willing to lose sight of the Muslim authorities who would collaborate with the West. In his *Knights Under the Prophet's Banner*, al-Zawahiri defined the goals of the global war against the Western powers and Russia by clearly identifying the enemies: 1) the United Nations, a rubber-stamp organization for the US; 2) the rulers of the Muslim world friendly to the US and the Western nations; 3) the multinational corporations; 4) the international communications and data-exchange system; 5) the international media, newspaper, television, etc.; 6) the international relief agencies which are in reality the fronts for the Western interests.[74]

In this debate, bin Laden at first sided with Azzam and rejected the idea of takfir. However, in 1989, Azzam and his two sons were assassinated in the Pakistani city of Peshawar.[75] Although nobody claimed responsibility for it, suspicion fell on the faction of the group that wanted to target the takfiri regimes of the Arab world, friendly to the West.[76]

The global jihadi movement and al-Qaeda might have been relegated to the dusty pages of history had it not been for the start of yet another Western invasion in the Arab/Muslim world, the Gulf War of 1990–91. The invasion against Saddam Hussain's Iraq demonstrated clearly to the adherents of the movement the continuing incursion of the Western (and Christian) world on Arab land and the control of its oil wealth. To add salt to the open wound, the holy lands of the Saudi Arabia were, for the first time, opened up for use by the military forces of the infidel nations, where none was allowed to set foot before. Fearing the worst for Islam and his homeland, Osama bin Laden pleaded with the Saudi King not to allow the coalition forces to establish bases within Saudi Arabia. To many fundamentalist Muslims, Saddam Hussain was a takfir, whose secular Baath Party was a thorn in their sight. Bin Laden wanted to fight the invaders in Kuwait with his army of Mujahideen. However, facing an imminent danger from a much more powerful neighbor amassing troops across the border, the King rejected bin Laden's proposal and instead invited the UN forces into the heart of the Arab land.

In the meantime, another set of events in the al-Qaeda movement were playing out. Every prolonged violent conflict creates its own dynamics. Often this involves the large number of young men who get involved and, at the end of the hostilities, find themselves without a job, necessary education, or even a real purpose in life. The only training they would have received was in fighting and in other areas of guns, ammunitions, and explosives. The same was true for the Mujahideen. Known as the "Afghan Arabs," the core fighting group of al-Qaeda was restless and ready for action. Nearly every country in the region was apprehensive of these battle-hardened men returning home and stirring up trouble. Many of these men became involved in the chaos of the Afghan Civil War that followed the Soviet withdrawal, particularly on the side of the fundamentalist warlords, such as Gulbuddin Hekmatyar. Later, they would develop a strong alliance with the Taliban, who would be victorious with the covert and overt help of Pakistan and its intelligence agency, the ISI.

In order to accommodate the battle-hungry rank and file, the leaders of al-Qaeda decided to move to Sudan. Sudan proved to be an ideal place for them since its reign of power had just been taken over by a sympathetic Islamist government headed by Muhammad Turabi. Around October 1990, the headquarters of al-Qaeda moved to Khartoum. Soon after the Gulf War began, tired of lobbying the Saudi royal family against the deployment of foreign troops on its soil (and with the Saudis becoming increasingly irritated by this upstart zealot), bin Laden cut his final ties to his homeland and went into exile to the Sudan.

With time, new provocations and opportunities arrived when the wars in Bosnia and Chechnya started. The tale of atrocities against the Muslims swelled the ranks of the volunteers. A series of spectacularly successful attacks against the US military (in Somalia in 1993 and in Yemen against the USS *Cole* in 1999), its embassies (in Nairobi and Dar-es-Salaam in 1998), and the 9/11 attacks in 2001 added to the mystique of Osama bin Laden and al-Qaeda. Finally, there was a possibility that in the immediate aftermath of the 9/11 attacks when world opinion was squarely against al-Qaeda and their Afghan protectors, the Taliban, the radical Islamic group would have suffered a huge military defeat. However, the focus of the US and its allies became distracted by the war in Iraq. Once again, as has happened many times in history, an unwise policy in the pursuit of the so-called "global war on terrorism" gave life to the retreating radical group. The war in Iraq not only exposed the weakness of a conventional force in asymmetric and unconventional warfare, it also provided a fertile ground for future terrorism. This is because of three primary factors. First, another war against another Islamic country, particularly where the *raison d'être* for the invasion, the claims of the existence of weapons of mass destruction, turned out to be false, deepened the worst doubts about the "true motives" of the US and Western powers. Second, the pictures of the tortured prisoners in Abu Ghraib and stories of mistreatment and indefinite incarceration of large number of Muslims in Guantanamo prison not only damaged the US image around the world, they also inspired many to seek revenge through terrorist attacks. Many young men started to flock to Iraq to join the jihad much the same way as their predecessors had gone to Afghanistan. Finally, the wide-spread sectarian violence and the civil war that broke out in the aftermath of the destruction of a fragile nation, cobbled together in a haste after World War I, turned Iraq into a failed state.[77] Like all other failed states it quickly become a breeding ground for all sorts of illegal activities, including terrorism.

Having discussed the evolution of al-Qaeda—not only as a group, but also as a movement—the question can now be asked: why did it become such a force so quickly?

There are several reasons for it. First and foremost, the innovation of the global salafi movement that gave it quick success was due largely to its ability to define its goals clearly and with the language and imageries of the Islamic tradition. After generations of shared humiliation, the intellectual leaders from Hassan al-Banna to Sayyid Qutb to Osama bin Laden could articulate the feeling that were deep inside many in the Muslim world. Together, they were able to frame the battle in individual terms. As Sageman puts it: "This was a battle that every Muslim must face to defend his creed, society, values, honor, dignity, wealth, and power. To mobilize, the masses needed a leader-ship that they could trust, understand and follow; a clear enemy to strike at; and removal of the shackles of fear and weakness in their soul."[78]

The world events played an important role in the spread of the Islamic movement. On the one hand, they created a situation of increasing frustra-tion as well as creating hope for an Islamic revolution. The creation of Israel with the claim of half of Jerusalem was like a bolt of thunder to the Muslim world, where generations had grown up learning about glories in the distant past and humiliating defeats since then. The wounded pride created a condi-tion of fraternal deprivation, where some turned to nationalism and some to their Islamic identity. A number of political and religious leaders gave a shape to this generalized condition of hopelessness and anger. A long litany of grievances, along with disappointing economic performance, particularly of the Arab countries, added fuel to the fire. The final blow to Arab/Muslim pride came with the invasion of Afghanistan and Iraq. These attacks only made it possible for the radicals to spread their message.

Revolutionary fervor is not only the product of frustration but also of hope. The cause of the revolutionary optimism was aided by number important world events. The success of Indian Muslims in carving out a separate nation for the Muslims in Pakistan created widespread elation in the Islamic world. However, the first real cause for celebration for many in the Islamic World came in 1979 when the Shah of Iran was ousted in a successful revolution led by the theocratic forces of Ayatollah Khomeini. The articulation of a clear message identifying the enemy and proposing a utopian society based on the time-honored tradition of Islam was evident to the adherents. The extremist groups were able to attract many to their cause. When the mighty Soviet military withdrew from Afghanistan under relentless attacks by the various Afghan and Mujahideen groups, the Islamic fundamentalists took all the credit for defeating the superpower, ignoring the role played by the other Arab/Muslim regimes, most notably Saudi Arabia. The final round of "victory" for the literalist jihadis came with the sight of the most incredible attack at the heart of the US on 9/11. Together the militant leaders were able to portray an image of strength of al-Qaeda and the jihadis far beyond what could be attributed to these groups.

The failed state of Afghanistan after the withdrawal of the Soviet forces provided an ideal sanctuary for the radicals. These men were also greatly aided by Pakistan and the ISI. Having a strong base of operation, they could develop a resolute chain of command linking groups in many parts of the world, committed to violence.

Finally, the economic power of the oil-rich Arab nations, in pursuit of religious hegemony, allowed their radical messages to be heard. Through an existing network of mosques and mullahs the groups were able to become a formidable adversary to the Western powers.

The Indian context: the shaping of the Naxalite movement

The confrontation between the two mainstream Communist ideologies became obvious to the rest of the world as the decade of the 1960s came along. The ideological rift that had grown between the Soviet Union and China in the post-war period affected the Communist parties in India. The problem for them deepened even further in 1962 when India and China became embroiled in a border dispute, which escalated into a military conflict between the two Asian giants.[79] The Soviet Union, a natural ideological ally of China, remained largely neutral in the dispute. The direct confrontation with a Communist country put the Communists in India in a quandary. Those who would not take the patriotic position of defending India would be quickly labeled as traitors. Once again, the international situation, as in 1939, sowed confusion and dissent among the Indian Communists. Furthermore, the Communist movement in India was badly shaken up in the early 1960s, when it was discovered that one of the most respected members of the CPI, S. A. Dange, had made secret deals with the government to cooperate in exchange for his release from jail. The situation was exacerbated even further when the simmering conflict between China and the Soviet Union broke out into an open military confrontation along their Siberian border in 1964. This was the straw that broke the proverbial camel's back in the party unity within the Indian Communist movement. The older members of the CPI remained loyal to the Soviet Union and the brasher, younger members formed a new party, the Communist Party India, (Marxist) or the CPI-M. A group of the CPI-M cadres continued to work with the landless peasants in North Bengal.

This split, however, did not please everybody within the more radical pro-Chinese Party, the CPI-M. Although we can look at this split and hypothesize about cynical power-grab and personality conflicts among the top leadership, it would be a mistake to understate the importance of moral, ideological issues that caused this rupture.[80] The issue of violent revolution, one of the most vexing ideological problems within Marxism, reared its head once again. To those who believed in the violent uprising of the working classes, the older members of the CPI were nothing short of betrayers to the cause, particularly since they had already sold out the peasants in 1951 during the Telengana uprising.[81] Therefore, when the CPI-M decided to join the electoral politics, it alienated a number of its cadres, particularly those who were already involved in organizing peasants in West Bengal.

The mid-1960s was a time of great change, both internally and externally, that was affecting the nascent nation in a profound way. The early promises of comprehensive land reform, which would allow the Fanon-esque wretched of the earth living wages, remained exactly that, promises. In the meantime, the so-called "Green Revolution" founded on the cultivation of hybrid, high-yielding Mexican rice and corn, which would transform a perennially hungry nation into a net exporter of food, was taking root, causing a steadily rising level of income disparity in the rural areas.[82] In the midst of those rising expectations, the local newspapers started carrying inconspicuous reports of desperate peasants, unable to feed their families, committing suicide.[83]

In the state of West Bengal, where the tradition of revolutionary fervor dates back at least a century, a new leader emerged, named Charu Mazumdar. If all mass movements start with the birth of an idea, the Naxalite movement came into being with a set of nine essays that Mazumdar penned while serving time in jail around 1965.[84] Born in 1911 to the family of a small landlord, Mazumdar had risen to a middle-level party official in the CPI-M. In these essays, he asked the question: why did the Communist movement not succeed in India? To him, the answer was simple. The Chinese Communist Party under the leadership of Mao Zedong had shown the correct path to a proletarian revolution. However, Mazumdar argued that along the way the followers of the revisionists in Moscow and their followers in India betrayed the

Indian movement. The second important thesis for Mazumdar was that revolution in India must come, not from the urban centers, but from its heartland, from the peasants in the villages.

In the previous chapter I mentioned the fundamental disagreement that has split the global Communist movement from its inception—whether revolution was to come spontaneously or as a part of a deliberate military action by the Communist Party. Soon another tactical question emerged among the revolutionaries: should the movement start from the villages or be based at the urban centers? While the origins of the Russian Revolution had a distinct urban/industrial workers flavor,[85] the Chinese Communist movement, in contrast, was primarily rural based.[86] This distinction fueled excited debate, in which Charu Mazmumdar and Kanu Sanyal came down on the side of a rural movement. They argued that India was primarily a "semi-feudal, semi-colonial" society and, mimicking Mao, raised the slogan "encircle the cities from the villages."[87]

The year 1965 proved to be a tumultuous year in the history of India. On 1 September, a full-scale war broke out between India and Pakistan that lasted over two weeks. With the nation convulsed with patriotic fervor, the Chinese government, by calling itself an "all-weather friend" to Pakistan, sided with India's arch enemy. Once again, the loyalty of the Communist Party members to the nation was put to test. However, by now, the pro-Chinese CPI-M, already seriously considering being a part of the Indian political system, was quick to condemn China for its alliance with Pakistan. Once again, for the likes of Charu Mazumdar, such an admonition of Chinese policies proved to be too much. The path was being paved for a further split in the CPI-M.

The ideological rift between the CPI-M and its more radical members became wider when the former decided to join the democratic process and compete in the elections. The opportunity came quite unexpectedly. The Indian National Congress, the party credited with the independence of India had become unpopular in West Bengal. The year 1966–67 also brought acute food shortages along with high inflation. The lack of monsoon rain caused India to turn to the US for assistance for wheat and rice. In the midst of this growing discontent and fears of yet another famine, the opposition parties to the ruling Congress formed an alliance, United Front, and won the state election. The Indian Congress Party, which had ruled India since her independence as a practically undisputed leader, faced its first electoral defeat in West Bengal.[88] As a part of the winning coalition, the CPM was given two of the most important cabinet positions. The Party leader Jyoti Basu was given the Home Ministry, responsible for internal security, and H. P. Konar the Ministry of Land Revenue, which was in charge of, among others, the thorny issue of land reform.[89] The electoral victory brought out the division within the Party even more sharply. Now in power, the CPM, the ultimate outsider, suddenly became "part of the establishment." As the Home Minister, the Party boss was in charge of maintaining law and order in the state, while the other stalwart was entrusted with the task of redistributing land. Being faithful to the Indian Constitution and yet remaining faithful to revolutionary goals was an impossible balance that CPI-M was unable to perform. The younger members had grave doubts about the democratic system to deliver the revolutionary goals and were ready to form their own party.[90]

Soon, Calcutta and much of West Bengal were plunged into chaos due to widespread violence. The police and military operations made everyday lives nearly impossible. The Naxalites had quickly secured their place in history.

If we closely examine the reasons for the rapid rise of the movement, we will see the following factors. First, Bengal had a long history of violent resistance. Even when the rest of the nation heeded to the call of non-violence by Mahatma Gandhi against the British Raj, the Bengalis were always skeptical. In fact, the real opposition to Gandhi came from one of his Bengali followers, Subhash Chandra Bose, who fled India and, with the help of Nazi Germany and Imperial Japan, formed an exile army from the captured Indian soldiers in the occupied southeast Asia.[91] Along this line, Bengal was no stranger to peasant rebellion and had a rich tradition of violent resistance going far back in history. The tales from the Telengana movement from faraway Andhra Pradesh inspired many in West Bengal. However, it also had the memory of its own peasant rebellion, the Tebhaga movement.

Second, the plight of the poor, particularly in the rural areas, where the much-touted land reform had but little impact. Periodic droughts and lack of opportunities made the situation untenable for a large number of peasants relegated to subsistence living. Under these dire circumstances, the peasants in Bengal were receptive to the revolutionary way out of their misery.

Third, the decades of socialist planning, which emphasized capital-intensive heavy industries at the expense of job creation in the more labor-intensive service and consumer-goods sector, created unemployment, especially among college educated youth.[92] These young men, uncertain about their economic future, supplied the primary impetus for the revolution. The wave of the new-left movement that was sweeping the Western nations had created a condition where the Marxist rhetoric was an easy sell to the urban intellectuals.

Fourth, the prevalence of Cultural Revolution in China provided ideological justification as well as a blueprint for starting a Maoist rebellion in Calcutta. The translation of Mao's ideas to suit the conditions in India was done by Mazumdar, which quickly found a receptive audience among the college students and other dedicated members of the CPI (M).

Finally, the birth of the Naxalite movement in Calcutta coincided with the formation of the first leftist government in Bengal. The CPI (M), being part of the government, was unsure about moving against their ideological brethren. This initial hesitancy, which included sparingly using the police force against the insurgents, added to the power of the group.[93]

In sum

The narratives of the evolution of groups that have experienced rapid growth show a similar pattern. All of these successful groups are formed around a set of longstanding historical grievances. In all cases there is a sense of overall failure of the existing government and the prevailing socioeconomic system to redress these grievances. The history of a long-surviving movement or a group is punctuated by the rise of charismatic leaders, who gave a political shape to the grievances by putting them in a larger theoretical concept of religious vision, nationalism, or class struggle. The leaders' explanations not only contained a conceptual explanation of the prevailing conditions, they also identified in the clearest of terms the enemies of the people. Since the objective conditions change with time, the political entrepreneurs need to be adaptable in their strategic use of theory as well as tactics. Since the strength of a group is directly linked to the support of the base, many successful groups in history start out as charitable organizations working to make available the basic needs of life that the government is unable or unwilling to provide. Once established, a group requires ways to communicate with the masses. Those with a ready supply network, either through the mosques or other means of communication, can experience a rapid growth. However, the biggest help in promoting a radical group comes directly from the target government. When the authorities engage in activities that are seen as grossly unjust, disproportionate, or immoral, they only provoke further violence by the groups. These are the trigger events in history or acts of political provocation, which only help propel a group to a higher level of visibility and acceptance by its support base. Finally, waging war against an organized government requires a lot of resources. A group gets a huge boost when they can develop a steady source of money and weapons. This support can come through a number of legal and illegal means, including support from another government.

7 A marriage made in hell?

Terrorism and organized crime[1]

[The criminal] wants his crime to be seen as an accident, while the terrorist wants even an accident to seem designed.

Diego Gambetta[2]

There will always be a gap between those who take the political goals seriously and those who are drawn to the cause because it offers glamour, violence, money, and power.

Michael Ignatieff[3]

Bin Laden does not mind trafficking in drugs, even though it's against the teaching of Islam, because it's being used to kill Westerners.

Unnamed US Department of Defense official[4]

Introduction

To many, the two secretive organizations, terrorist groups and organized crime, are the conjoint twins of our modern-day scourge. The media often reinforces this perception by painting the two as one and the same with ominous outcomes resulting from their collaboration. In fact, a quick search of "terrorism" and "organized crime" in newspaper databases would convince anyone of the close link between the two.[5] As threats posed by new developments in terrorism have grown in recent years, many intelligence and national security agencies have became concerned about the prospect of a convergence of terrorism and organized crime. Such concerns found their expression in 2001, merely two weeks after the attacks of 9/11, when the Security Council of the United Nations adopted a resolution noting "with concern the close connection between international terrorism and transnational organized crime, illicit drugs, money-laundering, illegal arms trafficking, and illegal movement of nuclear, chemical, biological and other potentially deadly materials."[6] A more recent *US News and World Report* story states that the Drug Enforcement Agency (US DEA) claims that nearly half of the 41 groups on the US government's list of terrorist organizations are tied to drug trafficking.[7] Although there is speculation aplenty regarding the nefarious nuptial, several painstaking studies paint quite a complex connection between the two.[8]

The problem with conducting research on the actual functioning of criminal organizations is their secretive nature. The difficulty is compounded when we attempt to examine politically motivated secretive terrorist groups. When the two are combined, the confusion escalates nearly exponentially. While the terrorists want to portray a clean image, every government attempts to discredit dissident movements by dismissing them as a criminal bunch. Since the political leaders carry a much louder voice, in popular imagination, the nexus between terrorist groups and transnational organized crime is often taken for granted.

In this chapter I would like to put this emerging literature within a behavioral framework and then evaluate the hypotheses in light of the extant evidence. Toward this goal, the chapter is divided into four sections. The first section will draw a conceptual distinction between the two organizations. The second will define the nature of collaboration between them. In the third section, I will present the arguments for a behavioral model for explaining their relationship within a theoretical context. In order not to impede the flow of discussion I have placed the outline of a formal microeconomic model in Appendix B.

Separating terrorism and organized crime

At first blush, terrorism and organized crime seem to be cut from the same cloth. Both operate outside the legal framework of society, both are secretive, and both use violence to terrorize others. Therefore, if we need to make a distinction between the two, it will not be on the basis of their acts but their motivations. Hoffman, thus, correctly argues: "the terrorist is fundamentally an altruist: he believes he is serving a 'good' cause designed to achieve a greater good for a wider constituency ... The criminal, by comparison, serves no cause at all, just his own personal aggrandizement and material satiation."[9]

The salience of Hoffman's argument is evident when we place the US State Department's definition of terrorism side by side with the US Federal Bureau of Investigation's (FBI) definition of organized crime. The US State Department defines terrorism as: "*politically motivated violence* perpetrated against non-combatant targets by sub-national groups or clandestine agents, usually intended to influence an audience" (emphasis mine).[10] In contrast, the FBI succinctly defines organized crime as "continuing and self-perpetuating criminal conspiracy, having an organized structure, fed by fear and corruption, and *motivated by greed*" (emphasis mine).[11] Given an apparent fundamental difference in motivation between altruism and greed, Jamieson notes that:

> Organized crime and terrorism are correctly viewed as quite distinct phenomena. Essentially, the terrorist is a revolutionary, with clear political

objectives involving the overthrow of a government or status quo, and a set of articulated strategies to achieve them. Organized crime actors are inherently conservative: they tend to resist political upheaval and seek conditions of order and stability, those more conducive to their business activities.[12]

Let us develop this issue further. From a behavioral standpoint, a terrorist group attempts to achieve public goods, the benefits of which must be *shared with the entire community that the group claims to represent irrespective of an individual's participation in the endeavor to procure it.* In contrast, a criminal gang does not operate out of any apparent "higher calling." Their predominant motivation is the provision of private and/or quasi-public goods, *which are shared only among the immediate members of that group.*[13]

The importance of this fundamental distinction between the two groups becomes even clearer when we consider their respective strategies of action. A terrorist group undertakes violent activities to communicate with its base, its adversaries, and ultimately, its "clients" and other significant parties.[14] As a result, many of these acts mix violence with drama. Through "propaganda by deed," politically motivated dissident groups claim responsibility for activities that are designed to shock a community and thereby gain political prominence. Since an effective terrorist group must retain support from its political base, it has to be ever mindful of the potential damage from being too closely associated with a criminal organization or being perceived as becoming one. In contrast, a criminal group is necessarily secretive and will typically aspire to function completely under the radar of the state apparatus; to gain public attention is not part of its motivation. As a result, while a terrorist group would normally strive to upset the political status quo, inviting anarchy and chaos in the process, a sophisticated organized crime group would only want to work within the political system through bribery, and violence directed selectively against certain segments of the society. Therefore, criminal organizations, like any other commercial venture, are conservative and would want to preserve the status quo. The reason organized crime groups loathe to be too closely associated with a politically minded dissident group is, as Dishman notes, "not because of higher moral values—but because it [is] bad for business."[15] In sum, from their very nature, each group develops strategic reasons not to cooperate with the other in a prolonged manner and maintain a strict separation between them.

Defining collaboration and the behavioral precepts

In order to understand the essence of their relationship it is important to distinguish between *collaboration* and *transformation.* I have presented four areas below, the first two of which are areas of collaboration and the following two are matters of transformation or metamorphosis:

1   A terrorist group collaborates episodically or on a sustained basis with organized crime groups in order to purchase or transport weapons (including weapons of mass destruction) and/or other resources (e.g., false passports and other documentation) as well as operatives.

2   A terrorist group collaborates episodically or on a sustained basis with an organized crime group in order to engage in criminal activities to raise money to carry out its political agenda.

3   A terrorist group develops "in-house capabilities" to engage in non-political criminal activities, such as bank robbery, gun running, human trafficking, drug dealing, money laundering, for the purpose of sustaining its political goals. In the extreme case, a terrorist group, in effect, abandons its political agenda and becomes a criminal organization.

4   And finally, when a criminal group collaborates on a sustained basis with terrorist groups in order to engage in acts of political violence and terrorism and, in effect, transforms into a politically oriented group.

Let us discuss the four possibilities, first on the basis of a theoretical perspective and then evaluate them with empirical evidence. I would like to demonstrate that the occurrence of the first two are going to be relatively rare, the third, a more probable outcome, and the fourth almost improbable.

Methods of raising money

A number of investigative journalists and academic scholars have shown that in order to sustain itself, every terrorist organization must develop a sideline of both legal and illegal activities to raise money.[16] An effective terrorist group, not unlike a business, must have division of labor, and specialization of function or task. Within its structure, even the most ideological group must include members whose primary function is to raise money.[17]

There are several avenues for raising money. For some political groups, the primary source of funding is through voluntary contributions by their political base, wealthy benefactors, or interested foreign governments. They also raise funds through coercive means of extraction from businesses or the general population, money laundering, arms and human smuggling, and sales of narcotics (or at least extortion of drug dealers if investment in narcotics is unviable when weighed against the potential political fallout from doing so), and through various financial scams. With each of these methods of raising money comes a price tag to a terrorist group's reputation and political legitimacy among its constituents.

A number of Islamic charitable organizations, such as the Benevolence International Foundation (BIF), the Holy Land Foundation (HLF), and the al-Haramain Islamic Foundation (AIF), were raising money in the US for years and were accused of diverting at least part of it to fund various groups, including Hamas, Hizbullah, and al-Qaeda.[18] They escaped government detection, particularly until the 9/11 attacks.[19] The BIF was founded in 1992 as a non-profit organization in Illinois and was affiliated with a group of wealthy donors, particularly from the Persian Gulf countries, who financed the Mujahideens in Afghanistan fighting the Soviet military. During its trial, it was revealed that it had transferred over $300,000 to various jihadi groups in Bosnia and Chechnya. The HLF was established in 1998, originally under a more provocative name, "Occupied Land Fund," and immediately started sending money to Hamas. Over the years, it sent over $12 million dollars to the radical group. The AIF was founded in Saudi Arabia in 1992 and became one of the most important centers of conduit of money for the Wahhabi charities and had an annual budget of $30–$80 million, with offices located in over 50 countries.[20]

Based on a priori arguments, we can conjecture that voluntary donations carry the least amount of cost from the perspective of the support base, since it is done without coercion and, in the case of the Islamic group, as a part of religious duty. Since every terrorist group is inspired by the promises of procuring public goods, we can surmise that in order to maintain an image of "non-criminality" and ideological purity, a terrorist group would prefer to raise money through what is perceived to be a "legitimate" source.[21] Thus, contributions by the diaspora in North America and elsewhere in the world for the Provisional IRA and the LTTE would fall into this category.

The same is true with support received from foreign governments. These activities do not tarnish the image of a dissident group. Hizbullah receives contributions from its patron states, Iran and Syria, while various Kashmiri groups are reportedly assisted by the Pakistani intelligence agency, the ISI.

Beside these voluntary methods, terrorist organizations get involved in every kind of illicit activities. These involve drug trafficking, gun running, people smuggling, and identity theft, along with demands of protection money from businesses and property owners.

It is often the case that until the target states wake up to the dangers associated with such financial flows the fund-raising activities of these groups are left alone. After the 9/11 attacks, however, the attitude of many governments underwent a radical transformation. The publication of the US State Department's expanded list of terrorist organizations made it more difficult for many of these groups, even those engaged in nationalist causes and not targeting the US, to openly collect contributions.

However, costs to the group start to rise as fundraising activity becomes coercive. Along with the possibilities of retribution from the authorities, such activities can quickly generate resentment and loss of popular support among the client base of a dissident organization.

In Chapter 4, I arranged terrorist groups across a continuum of "highly ideological" and "close to criminal behavior" in three broad clusters—ideological, professional, and anomic terrorists—according to their revealed preference for choice of activities. My empirical results suggest that among the groups in this study, al-Qaeda, Hamas, and the Palestinian Islamic Jihad fall into the category of "highly ideological." This is because many of their characteristic tactics involve suicide attacks, requiring the ultimate sacrifice from their members. The second category of groups includes the Provisional IRA and the Basque ETA. The groups in this category combine ideological intensity with a great deal of circumspection for the personal safety of their operators. The third category (near criminal groups) comprises groups such as Abu Sayyaf of the Philippines, the Colombian FARC, and the Peruvian Sendero Luminoso (Shining Path), which are much more tilted to the money-making criminal activities.[22] Although there is no accurate data on the relative importance of the various sources of funding for these groups, by considering the nature of finance sources (see Table 7.1), we can see that their revealed preference for raising money corresponds closely to my findings based on the groups' activities. The groups that are more ideological get their funding in greater proportion from voluntary contributions or state patronage, while those which are more criminally inclined fund their activities through the narcotics trade, hostage taking, and racketeering.

Behavioral assumptions

A plethora of case studies have advanced our knowledge in this area. In order to put this emerging debate on a theoretical perspective, I propose a model based on two simple behavioral precepts. I hypothesize that a group can choose any combination of "terrorist" and "criminal" activities. The nature of collaboration between the two groups will be based on the relative strength of ideological commitment (relative preference for public good over quasi-public good) and the cost differential for engaging in two kinds of extra-legal activities.[23] The leadership of a dissident organization determines the strength of ideological preference, while the target authorities and the political base of the group impose the costs.

Given a group's ideological orientation, it must evaluate the relative costs of getting involved in the two kinds of activities. It seems safe to assume that the state (the target authority) is likely to be asymmetrical in its response to the activities of terrorism and ordinary crime. Terrorism poses a political as well as more diffuse security threat to the entire nation. In contrast, organized crime activities target only certain sections, often considered to be on the fringes of the society. Given this important tactical distinction, it is safe to assume that, for the most part, the state would react more sharply to the threat of terrorism than to acts of organized crime.

As an extremist group collects money to fund its violent activities, it attracts the attention of the target authorities, with the possibility of legal sanctions and even military retribution. Apart from the legal sanctions by the state, the cost of raising money through illegal means carries another kind of a cost. Every politically motivated dissident group must be careful about its reputation to its support base, which is its true "oxygen."[24] Any coercive method of raising money, such as protection payment or "taxes," can increase resentment. Even those activities that do not impose direct hardship on the community can still be unpopular if the group gets too close to criminality in its behavior or violates the fundamental cultural norms.

Collaboration between terrorist groups and criminal organizations

In light of the above discussion, I present three broad hypotheses regarding collaboration between terrorist groups and organized crime syndicates. First, fighting with an organized government is an expensive proposition. Yet to be seen as being intimately involved with known organized crime syndicates is harmful to the reputation of a political organization. Facing this dilemma most terrorist groups would rather develop "in-house" capabilities for raising money through various extra-legal ways than developing long-standing collaborative arrangements with criminal gangs.[25] If such a relationship is established, it will be episodic rather than sustained. Thus, in 2002, a study commissioned by the United Nations Centre for International Crime Prevention (CICP) asked world governments to indicate whether there was evidence of collaboration between the two kinds of group.[26] Results from 40 responding governments indicate that only 22 percent of the groups engaged in sustained levels of collaboration both internally and externally. Furthermore, 30 percent of the groups showed no link whatsoever (see Figure 7.1). Based on this evidence, the study noted that, "The nature of the links between the two types of groups seemed to be primarily logistical and financial, denoting the presence of alliances of convenience. It tended to be operational, in those relatively rare instances where there were also some ideological and political links between the two groups."[27] Other studies, including a report by the Manhattan Institute's Center for Policing Terrorism, while discussing the connection between terrorism and organized crime, only mention terrorist organizations' involvement in various illegal activities and not their establishing working relationship with crime syndicates.[28] Given the cost of cooperation for both the groups, we can assume that a marriage between the two is highly unlikely. Thus, Dishman concludes that "little evidence

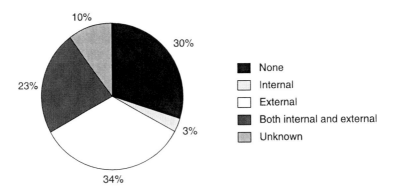

Figure 7.1 Cooperation between terrorist and organized-crime groups.

suggests that Mafia groups and terrorists are interested in pursuing collaborative arrangements with each other to traffic contraband or commit other crimes."[29]

Second, I hypothesize that a group's choice of fundraising activities would reflect its ideological orientation and the sensibilities of its support base. Although information on the financing is extremely meager, particularly when it comes to a comparative analysis among various groups, MIPT RAND database does provide the composition of financing. I have presented the information in Table 7.1, which shows that the percentage of money coming from charitable donation is higher for the highly ideological groups, such as the original al-Qaeda or Hamas. It is also an important source of financing for the IRA. However, the anomic groups, such as FARC in Colombia, Sendero Luminoso in Peru, and Abu Sayyaf in the Philippines, are dependent mostly on kidnapping and extortion. The choice of these methods of fund raising also reflects the cultural tradition within which a

Table 7.1 Terrorist organizations and methods of funding.

Dissident group	Method of funding
Ideological	
al-Qaeda (original)	Bin Laden's personal fortune and a variety of his investments and business partnerships throughout the years have contributed to the pool of al-Qaeda funds. Additionally, al-Qaeda receives funding from charities from all parts of the Arab/Muslim world
Hamas	Iran (state-sponsored); donations (especially through Islamic charities); remittances from Arab expatriates; commercial enterprises (sewing and weaving centers and cattle farms)
Palestine Islamic Jihad	Iran provides an estimated $2 million of state-sponsored funding to PIJ annually
Hizbullah	Iran and Syria; world-wide fundraising operation
Professional	
ETA	Kidnapping, extortion, robbery
IRA	Extortion (from Northern Irish Catholics); bank robberies; donations from Catholic-Irish descendants outside of Ireland (substantial amounts come from the US)
Anomic	
Abu Sayyaf	Largely self-financed through ransom and extortion; suspected to receive support from Islamic extremists in the Middle East and South Asia
FARC	Cocaine trafficking and production; extortion; kidnapping; hijacking
Sendero Luminoso	Cocaine trafficking

Source: Compiled from information presented in the MIPT Rand web site: http://www.tkb.org/Home.jsp

group is operating. Drugs are strictly forbidden in Islam and are particularly so in the brand of Islam that al-Qaeda promotes. Yet US drug-enforcement agencies continue to accuse the puritanical group of dealing in drugs.[30] I have seen absolutely no credible evidence of al-Qaeda's dependence on drug money during the early years of its operation. However, it will perhaps not be unreasonable to conjecture that as the group moved to the lawless Afghanistan, where harvesting of poppies is widespread, from Sudan, its prohibition against accepting money from the production sales of narcotics began to wane. This dependence may have increased reflecting the post-9/11 realities when the central command was restricted to the failed state of Afghanistan, and Saudi Arabia and the other Gulf nations were somewhat more vigilant in their effort at stopping the money spigot from zakat donations.

Third, the allure of easy money is tremendous. In order to maintain a group's ideological purity the leadership must be vigilant at all times to maintain its reputation. The allegations of less ideologically oriented recruits getting involved in criminal activities have come from many sources. Thus, writing on the situation of the Northern Ireland conflict, Ignatieff comments: "The IRA bears as much relation to the Mafia as it does to an insurrectionary cell or a radical political party and the motivations that draw young people into the movement are often as criminal as they are political."[31] Strongly disputing this claim of the IRA developing a Mafia-type characteristic, O'Leary points out that based on interviews with the IRA activists,[32] evidence from autobiographies,[33] as well as evidence of actual recruitment, contradict this often repeated assertion about many dissident groups. O'Leary points out that unlike the Mafia leadership, neither the ordinary IRA foot soldiers nor their leadership lived in luxury. Some leaders, such as Gerry Adams, have become comparatively wealthy, primarily from his writings and lectures and not by skimming off the top of the funds raised for political purposes. In fact, the recruitment for the group went up only when there were political provocations, including threats from paramilitary attacks and not for greater "rent seeking" opportunities. These accounts also make it clear that when a member is found to have taken money from the IRA fund, he is either ostracized or faces vigilante justice.[34]

O'Leary is unequivocal in stating that while individual members may not always reflect the "austere virtues" of the IRA, as an enforced official policy, it "does not do drugs."[35] For instance, the Provisional IRA was deeply involved in acquiring money through contraband cigarettes and alcohol, and through extortion, but was keen on trying to portray a "clean image" by avoiding being directly involved in drug dealing.[36] This policy of ideological puritanism created tension within the ranks of the IRA. Initially separated along ideological lines, when a small faction, the INLA, began dealing with drugs, the IRA began to fear for its reputation. Sensing the danger of losing political legitimacy within its own base, the IRA simply killed off the small band of rogue members during what is known as the "night of long rifles."[37]

In contrast, the leaders of Sendero Luminoso in Peru, facing no such cultural constraints, delved into drug trading.[38]

It is entirely possible to assume that the two groups would develop a stronger tie of collaboration when they face a common enemy. Mincheva and Gurr, through a narrative of Islamic resistance in Bosnia and Kosovo, argue that network connections, which often include known criminals, are made through a common ethno-religious identity at times of war.[39] This interesting case study, however, points to extraordinary periods in the history of a group: at times of an all-out civil war. This collaboration not only reflects the impact of a common ideology but also of taking the opportunity of a condition of lawlessness, as I will discuss later on in this chapter.

Transformation of groups

After discussing the issues of collaboration, let us now turn our attention to the question of transformation. Based on my simple behavioral assumption, I hypothesize that while it is possible for a terrorist organization to turn primarily to criminality, it will be extremely unusual for a criminal organization to turn into a political movement.

Since political organizations have a natural tendency to lose their ideological compass, in order to preserve their orientation, the leadership must exercise strict control. This is possible when the movement is structured along a hierarchical chain of command. When a group adopts a more flexible non-hierarchical pattern, the risk of some of its units getting involved in unacceptable behavior increases. For instance, when the central command of al-Qaeda was portraying a picture of a rigid Islamic code of conduct, the independent Madrid cell financed its operation by selling hashish.[40] If unchecked, there is a possibility that in time such activities would draw those whose only interest is making easy money through drug trafficking.

In contrast, I argue that even when a criminal group starts out with some goals of attaining public goods, it will quickly revert to becoming an almost entirely criminal enterprise. That being said, a criminal group can sometime engage in limited altruistic behavior. The Medellin Cartel, headed by Pablo Escobar, made efforts to improve the lives of the poor people living in the area, perhaps in some ways not unlike the fabled Robin Hood. However, Escobar's devotion toward providing public goods was short-lived at best and his generosity was closer to bribery than true benevolence.[41]

The case of the Italian Cosa Nostra provides another example in support of this hypothesis. After the invasion of Sicily by the Allied forces during the World War II, the help of the Mafia was clearly recognized. As a reward for their support, some members of the Mafia were not only allowed to carry weapons but were installed as mayors and law-enforcement officials throughout western Sicily. This process of political legitimization helped their expansion in the immediate aftermath of the war not only in Italy but also in the US.[42] However, this opportunity to become part of the legitimate political process was soon abandoned in favor of making money. The Cosa Nostra demonstrates the clearest case where a criminal group was given an unprecedented opportunity to become a legitimate political force but essentially reverted back to its familiar ways.

Are there cases where a criminal group may want to upset the status quo and attempt to terrorize an entire society in the same manner of a terrorism campaign? In those rare cases where a criminal group might wish to target an entire society, its goals would still remain confined to the attainment of quasi-public good without upsetting the status quo. A criminal group would choose such an option only as a last resort, and almost always when faced with a decisive move by the government to eliminate it. However, in those cases where a group might target an entire society (and using terrorist tactics), its goals would *still* remain the attainment of quasi-public good without upsetting the status quo. For instance, the Italian Mafia started its campaign of car bombing in 1993, where it targeted a television personality, bombed a train, and planted bombs that damaged, among other cultural icons, the Uffizi Gallery in Florence. Yet, these acts, while superficially similar to other acts of terrorism, differed in one important area: the aim of this campaign was devoid of any political aim. It did not purport to change the Italian society but simply wanted to frighten the government into ceasing its law-enforcement activities. Therefore, given this important distinction, these attacks cannot be classified as terrorism. When a criminal gang uses violence, it is generally to disrupt an investigation or an interdiction. Through the selective use of violence, it will try to dissuade the authorities from pursuing the group.[43]

The dynamics of relationship

My static model, based on the factors of behavioral motivation and relative costs, offers insight into the process by which a group chooses its optimal mix of terrorist and criminal activities. However, in reality groups evolve due to the dynamic interactions of perceived benefits and costs, shaping their choice of optimal mix. In this section, I will examine the conditions under which groups are likely to alter their strategic behavior.

Shift in ideology

A dissident group's ideological orientation may change as a result of a change in the attitude of the leadership, the altered composition of its followers, or a weakening of its ideological position due to an altered sociopolitical condition. Let us examine these three conditions of change.

When a group is strictly hierarchical, its leadership may decide to develop the group's involvement involved in criminal activities to raise funds in the fight against the forces of an organized government. In such situations, the leadership must decide precisely to what extent (and in what ways) it ought to become involved in criminal activities. A variety of challenges await terrorist leaders when this pathway is taken. Through various incentive structures, including a sense of planning (however informal) around rewards, punishments and managed expectations, the leadership faces a constant challenge of keeping its rank and file focused on the central mission of the group.[44]

Given the omnipresent temptation of easy money, a dissident group is likely to drift into the gray area of ideological confusion when the leaders are themselves attracted by money and power and allow the organization to be much more closely aligned with criminal activities. The loss of ideological compulsion can also happen when there is the loss of a strong leader due to death or capture. Perhaps the case of Abu Sayyaf provides one of the clearest examples of this. In 1990, after decades long struggle, a young ideological radical named Abdurajak Janjalani and Osama bin Laden's brother-in-law Mohammed al-Khalifa founded the Muslim separatist group. At first the ideological purity espoused by al-Khalifa and Janjalani led to the jihadi character of Abu Sayyaf and bin Laden rewarded them with a $3 million contribution.[45] However, soon it became involved in kidnapping and ransom taking. As Rogers points out, "members of the criminal underground had emerged in key leadership positions, and the group's Islamic identity was subordinated to the quest for profit."[46] After Janjalani's death in 1998 the group transformed itself into a "loose federation of bandit chiefs bound mainly by convenience."[47] Sageman reports that as soon as Osama bin Laden came to know of the true nature of the erstwhile Islamic group, he cut ties with the group.[48] In general, when terrorist organizations cease to have a clear political orientation and ideology, if the group retains its organizational structure, it usually drifts toward hooliganism or criminal activities.[49] Thus the IRA vigilantism became more savage toward its own people after a ceasefire was called.[50]

The groups that are linked primarily through "inspiration" are formed along small bands of isolated cells. The development of a group based on cells can happen when a counter-terrorism campaign deprives the group leadership of maintaining a strict hierarchical structure. Fear of detection will heavily influence a group to choose between either a network of centralized cells or forming independent, isolated cells. The example of a network-based cell structure can be found in the Hamburg-based al-Qaeda operation that was central to the 9/11 attacks. In this case, the cell operated independently and depended upon the al-Qaeda core (*Sura Majlish*) to funnel money and other logistical support. In contrast, the attacks by the Madrid and the London cells that carried out the train bombings, having come after the beginning of an intense counter-terrorism campaign, had to rely more on its own wits, without any direct involvement by the al-Qaeda leadership. Additionally, the attempted bombing by the groups in Casablanca in 2003 was largely bungled because of lack of central coordination and training.

There are some violent social movements that start not with any ideological aspiration, but because of competition over natural resources. For instance many civil wars, especially in the West African countries, are fought with very little ideological inspiration. In these cases, as Collier and Heffler point out, greed wins over grievances and the distinction between a political organization and a criminal group is largely lost.[51]

Finally, a group can lose its ideological compass when the primary reason for its existence becomes obsolete, while it retains its organizational structure. Thus, the Provisional IRA, the longest running dissident movement in the world, may have come to a dead end for its ideological position long before developments in the current peace process. The politics of the two Irelands started taking their own course almost as soon as the political boundaries demarcating the two were drawn. After Sinn Fein joined the parliamentary politics in the North, its military wing started becoming less relevant from a purely ideological position. Yet its strict hierarchical structure, in order to maintain that position, began to become turned inward. The number of victims from the PIRA violence became predominantly Catholic, as a part of vigilantism[52] and extensive criminal activities.[53] The ideological situation has become increasingly difficult and complex in Northern Ireland, with the primary goal of uniting the entire island under one flag taking a backseat in the Republic of Ireland, due to its own economic prosperity and a clear ambivalence towards the Troubles. Furthermore, while Europe is thinking about a continental unity, irredentist movements proposed by the IRA and ETA[54] may be seen as anachronistic by a significant majority of their own bases. In such a case, the possibility of these two organizations' contact with criminal elements will only increase.

Changes in relative costs

From my arguments, it is clear that cost considerations enter into the calculus of a dissident group in two forms. When a group engages in questionable activities, its leaders attempt to minimize the costs of alienating its base by justifying these actions. For instance, the Madrid cell that financed its operations through drug trafficking claimed that the illicit activity was "for Islam."[55]

The second cost factor is a part of the explicit imposition of punitive measures imposed by the target authorities. When it comes to this aspect of the costs, we may consider two extreme cases, where the difference in costs of engaging in the two activities is severe, and where the cost differential is negligible. A society that imposes an extremely stiff price for engaging in terrorist activities may exhibit a situation similar to those prevailing in the totalitarian Communist states, where political dissidence was nearly non-existent, while there was a flourishing underground economy. In contrast, a failed state with a very weak government will have little ability to differentiate between the two and/or impose punishment for violation of the rules. I argue that such a situation is currently prevailing in Afghanistan and Iraq. In such a situation, the distinction between the two groups will likely be blurred.

A significant transformation in a terrorist group's orientation can also take place when an existing cost differential between the two types of activities is altered. The relative costs of engaging in acts of terrorism versus criminal activities can increase or decrease. For instance, the relative cost of terrorism increases when the authorities develop "get tough" policies by enacting new laws or starting extensive police and military campaigns against dissident groups. In contrast, however, the cost differential decreases when the government is weakened and starts drifting toward a condition of being a failed state. In this weakened condition, the state loses its capability to impose stiff penalties for both terrorist and criminal activities.

Dishman argues that as an ideological group gets decentralized, perhaps as a result of increasingly effective counter-terrorism activities, there will be an increasing chance of some cells developing connections with criminal groups.[56] As discussed above, the unintended consequence of a successful operation can set in a process of decentralization, which can weaken the ideological strength of a dissident group and push them toward criminality.

Finally, when the state loses its ability to impose sanctions we can see that the distinction between the two types of groups begins to fade. This is because, under a condition of anarchy, the costs of collaboration will go down for both groups. Since a crime group is interested in making money, if the price for doing business with a politically motivated group is no different than being engaged in other criminal activities, there will be no disincentive for the criminals to establish linkages with terrorist organizations. Although data on this is understandably sparse, we can conjecture that the current conditions in Iraq, Afghanistan, Somalia, etc. point to the fact that as the hold of the existing social organizations disappears, the moral and behavioral restrictions that build a wall of separation between terrorist groups and organized crime will also tend to disappear.

The relationship between terrorism and organized crime is indeed complex. In order to develop a proper perspective on terrorism and organized crime, we must develop an analytical framework and not approach it from a prejudiced perception. Thus, Schmid clearly warns: "terrorism—that peculiar mix of violence, politics, and propaganda—should not be confused with mainly profit-driven organized crime. The vague narco-terrorism formula with its implicit call to fuse the 'war on drugs' and the 'war on terror' might offer a misleading intellectual roadmap to address the problem of terrorism."[57]

In sum

The relationship between terrorism and organized crime has often been shrouded in mystery, misconception, and speculation. These misconceptions arise because of several reasons. When faced with political challenges from groups that use extra-legal methods of protest, every government attempts to portray the members of dissident groups as common criminals. Such accusations aim at undermining the political legitimacy of these groups. Since it takes money to combat the forces of an organized government, all dissident groups engage in activities of various measures of illegality. Given the natural allure of money and criminal activities, it is not surprising that a dissident group may transform into a criminal organization, particularly when its political goals become fuzzy, organizational structure weakened, or the leaders themselves are more interested in making money for themselves. Similarly, when there is the possibility of external support, some criminal groups attempt to drape themselves in the cloak of political idealism as a cover for their illicit activities.

In the end, however, the two organizations are entirely different animals. Each faces a certain cost for cooperating and developing a sustained relationship with the other. Given the differences in motivations and costs, any marriage, other than one of convenience, is highly unlikely. On the other hand, it is highly likely for a terrorist organization without a strong religious or cultural prohibition, a steady source of non-coercive method of raising fund, and a strong leadership enforcing discipline and constantly reinforcing the political ideas, to veer off toward criminality. In contrast, a criminal group, despite the occasional similarity in tactics, will remain strictly non-political.

8 Demise of dissent

The endgame of terrorism

The intensity of terrorism, even from the well-entrenched groups, subsides. No group is able to continue violence at a very high rate for a sustained period of time. As killings rise and violence from all side escalates, over time the *terrorism attenuating force* begins to gather strength. In Figure 4.12 (on p. 100), I have shown the end of dissent with three possible outcomes: a) the absolute victory for the group; b) its transformation into a largely criminal organization; or c) a military and political defeat. Although the diagram presents the alternatives as clear-cut outcomes, in reality there can be a number of combinations of these three endings of protracted conflicts. A group may win a partial victory and decide to join the democratic political process. As a group becomes mainstream it loses its reason for being a revolutionary force. If parts of its organizational structure remain intact, it can transform itself from an essentially vigilante group, trying to keep the fledgling flock together within the confines of an ever-loosening ideological imperative, into a criminal gang. Or a group may be obliterated through intense police and military actions, but if the cause, which gave birth to the dissent, remains strong, another group may pick up the ideas and start their fight all over again. The cases of the IRA and the Naxalites reflect this ambiguity of outcomes. In the first case, the IRA has come to a truce to fully join the peace process and, in the other, after a burst of activity in the 1970s, the Naxalites in India were defeated in West Bengal but the movement has resurfaced in a much more entrenched way in other parts of the country.

However, before delving deep into the experience of the two groups, we must remember that participation (and disengagement) in terrorism takes place at two intimately interconnected levels. At the individual level volunteers and activists decide to sever their involvement with the party. At the group level, the leaders decide to end their rebellion voluntarily through negotiations or involuntarily by succumbing to the counterterrorism efforts by the target government.

Individual activists leave terrorism for the same reasons they join. As I have argued, groups offer a powerful source of motivation. They fulfill the fundamental human need of belonging to a community of like-minded people. It also accords rectitude and respect from family, friends, and the community.

Moreover, the macho image of a gun-toting rebel may attract attention from the opposite sex. The group may also provide a means of support for the participants by offering monetary rewards for services. In other words, joining a group fulfills many of the basic needs of self and group utilities. When such utilities are no longer there, or the cost of perpetuating it outstrips the benefits, the erstwhile terrorists leave their rebellious lifestyle.

In a series of detailed publications Horgan has analyzed and documented the reasons for individual decisions for leaving terrorism behind.[1] His study clearly indicates that when people decide to leave the life of a terrorist, they do not make such decisions at a moment of epiphany. Rather, for most of them, similar to the decision to join a group, it comes slowly over time, often blurring the distinction between a terrorist and a non-combatant civilian. Reflecting Horgan's findings, I argue that the pursuit of self and group utilities is not a binary—"either/or"—decision but a matter of trade-off in everyday lives. Horgan argues that the process of disengagement follows two lines: psychological and physical. He points out that: "The psychological disengagement manifests through disillusionment with some aspect of the group, at least resulting from in a change of attitude, beliefs or identity."[2] This may transpire as the ideological grip on the followers slackens or the factors of private utilities (matters of personal life, such as employment, love, and family responsibilities) become more important than achieving ideological goals, or the cost imposed by the society on the rebel life becomes unbearable.

The ideological hold on the followers can loosen for many reasons. For instance, an operative may experiences a moral dissonance witnessing the suffering of those whom he had dismissed as "enemies." Such a psychological conflict may also present itself when he begins to question the basic premises of the ideological struggle. A follower may become disillusioned by the conduct of the leader or may have severe disagreement with a particular policy decision taken by the leadership. Every movement, large or small, starts with an idea offered by a leader, which inspires a multitude. However, when staying in power is the only idea that inspires the leadership, the movement faces an imminent danger of defection by its rank and file members.

The physical disengagement takes place either voluntarily or involuntarily. Voluntary physical disengagement is the result of psychological disenchantment. Involuntary disengagement happens when they are ejected from the movement by the leadership for violating the group's code of conduct, or are apprehended by the security forces.

In contrast to the followers the decision to voluntarily give up the path of violent resistance by the leaders may come relatively suddenly. When a rebel group gives up arms through a negotiated settlement after a protracted war, they either go into some sort of a direct power-sharing arrangement or become part of a democratic political process. For either of these to happen, the leaders must be sure of their personal safety when they lay down their arms, be confident about maintaining its popular base of support and, in the case of a decision to take part in a democratic process, the country must have a democratic tradition.

Until now, I did not delve into the question of how leaders take their momentous decisions. While the importance of leadership is recognized in the terrorism literature, few have closely examined the way the leaders make important choices. However, recent advancements in decision theory have advanced a *polyheuristic* perspective, significantly adding to our understanding of the complex process by which leaders make up their minds.[3] The rational-choice theory assumes that an actor faces an unlimited choice of possible actions.[4] The actor evaluates each action against its expected outcome and chooses the one that gives her the greatest benefits compared to the cost. The problem with this approach is that nobody can consider an infinite set of possible actions. Nor can we conduct an elaborate evaluation of the uncertain outcomes. The polyheuristic approach is the combination of a diverse work by economists, political scientists, social psychologists, and cognitive scientists.[5]

In the 1970s and 1980s, Nobel Laureate economist Herbert Simon argued that human beings do not have an infinite brain capacity nor the time to evaluate each action to arrive at the point of maximum utility.[6] Instead, we are "cognitive misers" and look for ways to achieve a "*satisficing*" solution, which would simply be *sufficient* to *satisfy* our needs, given the constraints of time, resources, and cognition. However, others, including Kahneman and Tversky, have shown through numerous experimental designs that rational people do not complete analyses of most outcomes and, instead, depend on shortcuts or "heuristics" to arrive at a solution. These heuristics can be based on personal experience, religious beliefs, or ideology. By combining many of these diverse research approaches Mintz explains poliheuristics as a two-step process where in the first step the menu of choices is significantly narrowed by the decision-makers based on a "non-compensatory" method.[7] That is, some of the options, regardless of compensation or apparent "rationality," will not be acceptable due to their political and ideological implications. After the elimination of the unacceptable options, in the second stage of the process, the remaining ones are evaluated for optimality solution in the traditional economic sense.

Thus, others will have to understand why a leader has chosen a dangerous path of confrontation when another avenue for a negotiated settlement was open, which was summarily rejected out of hand. For instance, in July 2007, a group of extremists under the leadership of some radical mullahs developed a base in the famous Red Mosque, a landmark in the Pakistani capital city of Islamabad. The mullahs were running a madrassa, which was attended mostly by students from poor families in the tribal north-west frontier provinces of the country. From this base, the students would fan out and enforce their Taliban style of strict Islamic laws. They would close down music stores, firebomb stores selling alcohol, and would "arrest" and punish women, accusing them of prostitution. They also stockpiled huge amounts of arms and ammunitions. Finally, after trying to appease them for several months, Parvez Musharraf decided to lay a siege of the large mosque compound. After a bloody exchange of fire, the Pakistani military gave an offer of peaceful surrender to the leader, Abdul Rashid Ghazi, which he rejected immediately. The siege ended with the death of scores of people, including many young students in their early teens along with their leader.[8] The question is, how do we explain the decision-making process that led to the death of Ghazi and his charges?

Mintz identifies a number of non-compensatory political and personal-loss factors, the presence of which will prevent a leader from accepting a compromise, regardless of the amount of the expectation of reward.[9] These non-compensatory loss-aversion variables are:

- Threat to a leader's survival
- Significant drop in public support for a policy
- Significant drop in popularity
- The prospect of an electoral defeat
- Domestic opposition
- Threat to regime survival
- Intra-party rivalry and competition
- Potential collapse of the coalition, government, or regime
- Internal or external challenge to the regime
- Threat to political power, dignity, honor, or legitimacy of a leader
- Demonstrations, riots, and so forth
- The existence of veto players (e.g., pivotal parties in parliamentary government)

However, we should remember that the weights that are placed on these factors would vary according to the ideological orientation, which is missing from Mintz's explanation. For instance, in the explanation of the siege of the Red Mosque in Islamabad, the aspect of the leader's personal safety, which is likely to feature prominently in the minds of most leaders, was secondary to other considerations of religious ideology. Therefore, for Ghazi, the choice set did not include an unconditional surrender as a viable option. In any case, the understanding of this two-step process provides us with a very useful set of tools to analyze the decision-making path and the outcomes of many world events, including the ones we are discussing. In light of this above discussion let us examine the voluntary demise of IRA violence in Northern Ireland and the involuntary defeat and subsequent resurgence of the Naxalite movement in India.

The IRA: ballot box versus Armalite

Despite occasional flare-ups, violence in Northern Ireland began its downward trend during the past two decades. From 1988 violence dropped to nearly zero during the middle of 2000 through a labyrinthine process of negotiations that started with the Clinton Administration taking an active interest in the Irish peace process.[10] For our purpose, it is not important to discuss the details of the process that brought about the latest agreement. Rather, I will concentrate on the reasons for the IRA leaders' decision to trade their Armalites, as guns are known in that part of the world, for the ballot box.

How do we account for this change in strategy by the IRA? In a thoughtful analysis, Brendan O'Leary[11] and Richard English[12] have given several reasons for the IRA leadership's decision to agree to a political solution. On the basis of this analysis, I would like to offer an explanation of the reduction of violence by the IRA.

The rise in IRA violence was primarily in response to an unjust social, political, and economic situation in Northern Ireland. To the IRA, the struggle in the late 1960s was not about sectarian differences, but essentially a nationalistic uprising[13] with a strong socialist ideological bend. However, as the civil rights movement took roots, primarily among the Catholics in Northern Ireland, the Protestant majority, recalling a long history of sectarian conflict and continuing animosity, reacted with extreme suspicion, which quickly translated into violence by the paramilitary forces. The Royal Ulster Constabulary, a Protestant police force, did not act as a neutral arm of the law and, instead, on some occasions worked closely with Protestant extremists. Even the British troops who came to protect the beleaguered minority soon found themselves fighting off the IRA terrorists after their heavy-handed methods alarmed the very people they were sent to protect. The cycle of violence was broken when the civil rights movement was largely able to achieve its political goals.

The impetus for a negotiated settlement gains momentum when the leadership understands the futility of pursuing an armed struggle. For the IRA, it came as Gerry Adams, in particular, took the initiative to back a political solution to a situation of a military stalemate.[14]

During the earlier peace proposals for democratic reform in Northern Ireland, the Catholic minority was a reluctant partner, since due to the composition of the population in the province, a majoritarian form of government meant an automatic secondary position for them. However, a profound demographic transformation was taking place in the region that made the IRA much more confident about its future with a parliamentary system. Table 8.1 presents the composition of religious affiliation in Northern Ireland. This table clearly demonstrates the increasing strength of the Catholic community, but, perhaps more importantly, the percentage of those who belong to other Protestant denominations, or are non-Christians or refuse religious identification has undergone a dramatic surge. In face of this changing reality, it was a prudent move on the part of the IRA to renounce violence. In fact, as O'Leary points out, "The IRA's decision to cease fire in 1994, and later renew it, had one primary beneficiary: Sinn Fein."[15]

Table 8.1 Religious composition of population in Northern Ireland (percent).

Year	1961	1991	2001
Catholic	34.9	38.4	40.3
Protestant (Presbyterian and Church of Ireland)	53.2	49.1	34.0
Other (Other Protestant denominations, non-Christians, non-stated, and none)	11.9	12.5	25.7

Source: Northern Ireland Statistics and Research Agency. Based on the UK Census figures.

Another important factor is the economic prosperity of the Republic of Ireland and the United Kingdom in the past two decades. The history of Ireland is one of perennial poverty, punctuated by periods of famine and extreme food shortage. The difference between the industrialized Northern Ireland and its prosperous Protestant majority and the rural poverty and backwardness in the south made the conflict a quintessential struggle of modernization. Even Great Britain in the 1970s was falling behind its European neighbors. However, the economic turnaround, particularly in Ireland, has been nothing short of spectacular. Between 1995 and 2006, the real per capita GDP has risen at a steady clip of 6 percent per year, making Ireland's figure 40 percent higher than the four big European economies and the second highest in the European Union behind tiny Luxembourg. In its newfound strength Dublin has been less interested in the question of the unification of the island under a single Irish flag. A changed economic and political scene has also made the IRA's central ideological position anachronistic in the eyes of both the UK and the Irish Republic. In 2006, the UK was Ireland's biggest trading partner. Even in the politics of the EU, the two English-speaking nations have often taken a joint stance, thereby solidifying the mutual relationship. In such a situation, the conflict in Ireland on a sectarian plain is difficult to maintain.

Just as a government can take unwise policies that exacerbate a situation of violent confrontation, a dissident group can also do serious damages to its power and prestige through missteps and bungled actions, which can undermine a group's image and hasten disengagement by the volunteers. For the IRA these mistakes came in two forms.

First, it is extremely difficult to keep up the intensity of an ideological struggle when the revolutionary party also attempts a peaceful solution. Thus Gerry Adams was frank when he admitted that: "When the struggle was limited to armed struggle, the prolongation of truce meant that there was no struggle at all. There was nothing but confusion, frustration, and demoralization, arising directly from what I call 'spectator politics.' "[16] During these prolonged periods, the IRA became far more involved in brutal vigilante operations than attacking the rival paramilitary groups.[17] These attacks had a clear effect on the IRA support base, although it was never fully articulated for fear of reprisals. The *New York Times* reporter Lizette Alvarez describes the situation as: "In the Catholic neighborhoods of Belfast, the Irish Republican Army has long served as judge, jury and, in some cases, executioner, meting out its own brand of vigilante justice. Catholics who defy the IRA's dictates end up with broken kneecaps. Those who betray the IRA wind up dead."[18] On 30 January 2005 a young Catholic man, Robert McCartney, was attacked in a crowded Belfast bar. He was dragged outside, beaten with iron pipes, his throat slit and torso slashed open. He was left to die, while his attackers coolly went back, wiped off the blood from the bar, warned everyone against talking to the police about the murder, and had a drink afterwards. This would not have been an uncommon occurrence, except for his five sisters, who took up his case to the world and tried to punish the killers. This unprecedented act of bravery on the part of the McCartney sisters clearly articulated the frustration of the community tired of vigilant-ism, shakedown for protection money, and other forms of heavy-handed activity. Although acts of vigilantism can have a significant impact on the base of support of a dissident group, it remains one of the least researched areas of terrorism study.[19]

The second areas of IRA violence that eroded its support within its base were directed at their enemies. However, the 1990s campaign of "proxy bombing" turned many people off its tactics of violence. During the funeral service of Patsy Gillespie, the victim of the forced "suicide" attack, Roman Catholic Bishop Edward Daley openly condemned the IRA and its sup-porters by calling the IRA and its supporters "followers of Satan."[20] This action, Moloney points out, significantly discredited the IRA to the national-ist community.[21] Similarly, in 1998, a car bomb exploded in a crowded market place in Omagh, Co. Tyrone in Northern Ireland, killing 20 people, including a pregnant woman. The news shocked the public. Although it was probably carried our by the Real IRA, who were against the peace process, regardless who actually carried out the attack, acts of violence such as these only strengthen the hands of those in the Republican camp working to a negotiated settlement.[22]

Finally, although it is not fully appreciated in Northern Ireland, the impact of globalization and the joining of the EU must have a long-term effect on the psychology that had defined the conflict in terms of ancient hatred. When the whole of Europe is forging closer links and the streets of Dublin and Belfast are teeming with new immigrants, it is difficult to predict how long this conflict will last.

The Naxalites

The spark and the prairie fire

In 1967, on the very day the Communist Party India, Marxist (CPI-M) took office as a full partner in the United Front government, the first incident of violence from Naxalbari was reported in the newspapers.[23] As the news of the peasant revolt became known, it immediately placed the CPI-M, now a part of the state apparatus, in an awkward situation. Being part of the ruling coalition government, it had sworn to protect law and order. Yet to move against the revolutionaries could be ideological suicide. Confused, the leftist government in Calcutta sent several fruitless delegations to the region. Eventually in early 1968, the government turned to its police force for maintenance of law and order. Finally, as the former Police Commissioner Ranjit Gupta writes, "In less than a week's time peace was restored. 'Spring thunder in Terai', as Beijing called it, vanished without a trace."[24]

Later that year Mazumdar left the rural North Bengal and went to Calcutta. By this time, he and his ideology were well known among the left-leaning intellectuals and Communist activists in the metropolitan city. On a sweltering May Day in 1969 in front of the Calcutta landmark, the former icon of the colonial rule the Octarloney Monument,[25] by this time renamed *Shaid Minar* (Monument of the Martyrs), the Naxalites formed their own Party by adding another letter to the name, CPI (Marxist Leninist) or CPI-ML. Although touted during the inauguration speeches as a spontaneous response to the treachery of the ruling CPI-M, the new CPI-ML emerged with a full slate of party hierarchy. Having previously launched its own Bengali and English-language newspapers, it instantly staked its claim as the sole revolutionary face of the Communist movement in India.

In the meantime, crisis deepened as violence spread from the urban centers of Calcutta to many parts of rural West Bengal.[26] The call for action by the radical Maoists resonated with the youth in Calcutta, especially those attending the best colleges, particularly the city's most noted institution of higher education, the Presidency College. These were the scions of the privileged. Fed on the generations of leftist literature, inspired by theatres and movies demonstrating clearly the accumulated social injustice, these intellectuals bought into the philosophy offered by Mazumdar. The wave of anti-establishment rhetoric created a global movement, where Jean-Paul Sartre mixed freely with Herbert Marcuse and Karl Marx. It created an atmosphere where young people, much the same way as the youth in the Islamic world today, could feel a global affinity with oppressed people everywhere.

To Mazumdar and his followers, the conditions in India resembled a tinder box, where all that was needed was a spark. This, they believed, would come from a campaign of killing the landlords, the money lenders, and all other agents of imperialism. The targets of the villages were easily marked, but in the cities the Naxalites started targeting beat police officers and other ordinary folks for whatever reason. For some reason, as the Police Commissioner points out, the Naxalites never targeted the high-ranking police officers. Nor did they target the judges and other prominent members of the community.[27]

Apart from the annihilation campaign in the villages, the Naxalite movement aimed at bringing about a cultural revolution in India. First, they boldly proclaimed "China's Chairman is our Chairman. Chinese path is our path."

Second, they started attacking some of the most cherished cultural icons from art and literature as purveyors of "reactionary" ideology.[28] Realizing that the backbone of their movement was the youth, they targeted the education system by disrupting classes and, in some cases, were able to close down institutions of higher education for weeks at a time. Heeding the calls of Mazumdar, believing that the "revolution" was just around the corner, some of the best and brightest students from Calcutta went to the villages to organize the peasants against the landlords and moneylenders.

It is interesting to note at this point the patterns of participation in the movement. Like all other mass movements, the Naxalite movement was launched on the backs of the youth. Based on intelligence reports we note that 78 percent of the participants were below 30 years of age.[29] However, despite the efforts of the party to portray this as a movement of the poor, tribal people, and people belonging to scheduled caste, the vast majority of them (65.33 percent), in fact, came from the upper-caste Hindu families. Also, 39 percent of them had post-secondary education (college students or graduates), and over 41 percent had high-school education. Less than 20 percent were illiterate. Considering the fact that over 70 percent of the country was illiterate in the 1960s, the participant profile clearly did not match that of the country at large, much less the rural areas where the movement was taking place. The Naxalite movement, in fact, despite its birth in rural North Bengal and its spread in other parts of the state, was essentially a movement powered by the educated, urban youth from middle- and upper-middle-class families.

A quick death . . . and reincarnation

As the CPI-M Party and its allies in the newly formed government started feeling uncomfortable with the revolutionary fervor of their more radical brethrens, it opened up a new window of possibility for the Congress government in New Delhi. They could claim a situation of anarchy prevailing in the eastern state and, under the Indian Constitution, could declare a "state of emergency." Under this sweeping declaration, they would suspend the freshly elected state government and impose from the center a "President's Rule" in March 1970. This emergency measure would also allow the central government to suspend all rights and impose a government by fiat from Delhi.

Under the new rule there was no ambivalence toward the Naxalites, exhibited previously by the United Front government with its Communist allies. In April a joint campaign was launched by the Indian military (Eastern Frontier Rifles), the Central Reserve Police.[30] They coordinated their efforts with the local police.[31] At the same time, on 2 April 1970, Radio Peking in a broadcast announced that: "At present, the flames of the peasants' armed struggle have spread to West Bengal, Bihar, Utter Pradesh, Punjab, Himachal, Orissa, Assam, and Tripura, and particularly Andhra Pradesh."[32] With the memories of a military defeat fresh in the minds of an anxious nation, highly exaggerated proclamations from across a hostile border only added to the apprehension and fear and gave the forces of the government a total hand in suppressing the rebellion. The arms of the Indian government took full advantage of this and, with limitless power accorded to the police, it proceeded to destroy the Naxalite movement.[33]

However, the world changed once more for the Communist radicals in India. Once again, it worked against the Maoists. Trouble was brewing on the eastern border with Pakistan. Pakistan was curved out in two wings, separated by 1,000 miles of Indian territory. It was going to be the homeland of the Muslims in the subcontinent. Religion was going to be the glue that would keep together the disparate people, who were of different ethnic origin, spoke different languages, and had completely different cultural traditions. Islam was thought to be the source of identity for the nascent nation. It did not happen. West Pakistan, dominated by the Punjabis, became embroiled in a struggle with the Bengali Muslims in East Pakistan. Their tortured history ended up producing a near genocidal pogrom carried out by the West Pakistani military in the east, when in 1971 India, taking advantage of the chaos, came to the aid of the East Pakistanis. Indian troops, together with the Bengali *Muktibahini* (freedom fighters), routed the Pakistanis.[34] Waves of patriotic pride swept the entire country. The tales of atrocities carried out by the Pakistani military were so gruesome that world opinion quickly turned against Pakistan. Once again, China proclaimed its support for her "all-weather friend" Pakistan. By this time the CPI-M was completely free of any ideological tie with China. Only the Naxalites (CPI-ML), being caught on the wrong side of history, once again dealt themselves a self-inflicted wound by going against the tide; they came down on the side of China and, by default, Pakistan.

The Naxalites and the CPI-ML never much cared for popular support. They assumed that everybody was waiting for the revolution to begin and would join in from every direction as soon as the conditions became right. Their miscalculations and immaturity simply caught up with them. In 1971, at the height of Naxalite troubles, when fear in the city was paramount, elections were held. Riding at the crest of her popularity, Indira Gandhi and her coalition became victorious in West Bengal. The tide had turned against the Maoists in the state.

The Naxalite movement reached its pinnacle, in terms of violence, around 1970–1972; after that it was quickly suppressed by the police and military action in West Bengal. By 1975, the last embers of violent revolution were stamped out of the state of West Bengal and adjoining areas.

Understanding the demise of the movement and the birth of the people's war group

The Naxalite movement in West Bengal was doomed to fail for a number of different reasons. In the context of my proposed behavioral model I can state that the early Naxalites did not realize the difficulty of generating an adoptive identity of economic class. The party's unshakable faith in Mazumdar's characterization of the contemporary Indian condition resembling a tinder box, and all that it needed was a spark, was totally misplaced. This mechanistic view of human motivation caused the Naxalites to ignore the need to create a mass base through a long process of indoctrination. In fact, Mazumdar was more interested in fitting the Chinese line of Cultural Revolution to India, without much idea of the context in which the movement was launched and its effect on Chinese society. His inability to appreciate basic human nature was amply demonstrated when he began the slogan "China's Chairman, Our Chairman." A nation, freshly at war with its neighbor, could never have accepted such a position. Furthermore, the attacks against some of the most cherished cultural and historical icons of Bengal created resentment among the populace, which was summarily dismissed as "bourgeoisie sentiment." Although there was no survey of popular sentiments at that time, when the police crackdown began, despite much hardship, the general public—with the exception of the sympathizers of the Naxalite movement—accepted the excesses of the police force.[35]

While the ideological stance of the party did not endear it to the urban centers, in the rural areas, even among the tribal population, it lost its allure when Mazumdar won an ideological contest against Sanyal and declared that the movement was not for the economic gains of the poor sharecroppers but for its ultimate aim of gaining political power. Such nebulous goals made little impression on the hungry and the impoverished. Thus, in the end, the Naxalite movement was deprived of a mass base both in the urban and in rural areas.

In the meantime, the ruling Communist Party in West Bengal, the CPI-M, embarked on a rural development project. Starting in 1970–1971 alongside the federal government in New Delhi, the state government increased its budget for the support of the rural poor.[36] The CPI-M also took aim at the iniquitous land-tenure system and undertook limited but significant land redistribution. These steps allowed the CPI-M to develop an exceptionally strong rural base. The development of this political base not only enabled it to effectively deal with political radicalism but also solidify its dominant position in West Bengal politics for the subsequent three decades.

Organizationally, the CPI-ML was weak. As the movement shifted from its rural base to the urban centers, it depended primarily on young college students from middle- and upper-middle-class families. By heeding Mazumdar's call, many of them went off to the villages to organize the peasants. However, in the traditional rural setting they were not the "fish in the water," as Mao has imagined the revolutionaries to be, they were merely *fish out of water*. These urban dreamers were aliens in an alien land. As they proceeded to annihilate the class enemies, they often found themselves on the wrong side of the villagers' wrath. For, in a village, the relationship between two individuals, even the most unequal ones, is not based solely on economic grounds. A moneylender is tied by many social and traditional links to his customers. As a result, the policy of annihilation of class enemies often identified the revolutionaries as the enemies of the people.

The leadership being on the run nearly from the beginning, in the urban areas, the party quickly became a haven for those who had little ideological commitment to the cause.[37] These neighborhood thugs by taking advantage of the chaos took over the operational control and became the public face of the Naxalites. Their actions eroded the base of support even further.

Tactically, the government played its card correctly. The police force was built up; between 1961 and 1971 expenditure on police increased fivefold.[38] However, in dealing with the Naxalites, the local police developed its low-level intelligence gathering.[39] Many of the same local thugs who were claiming to be the Naxalites were recruited in a government paramilitary force called the Home Guard, as were paid informants. When the military was deployed, it did not spearhead the operation and, instead, played only a supporting role to the local police.[40]

Finally, the international condition proved to be less than helpful for the Naxalites. Most successful guerrilla groups in history are aided by forces across the national borders. This help comes in the form of offering safe sanctuaries or providing arms and ammunition. In the early stages of the movement it looked as though China would provide such help. However, apart from effervescent reporting of the creation of "liberated zones" by Radio China, it offered very little material support or safe haven to the Naxalites.[41] Furthermore, at the height of the movement, the destruction of East Pakistan and the birth of Bangladesh created an Indian client state across the border from West Bengal. As a result, the revolutionary movement was deprived of support which many others around the world have found to be invaluable.

The people's war group and the latter-day Naxalites

In July 1972, Charu Mazumdar was arrested and died in police custody in Calcutta amid widespread allegation of torture and maltreatment. His death threw the Naxalite movement in West Bengal into a state of chaos. The divisions within the ranks deepened further when in the 10th Party Congress in China, Lin Biao, the quintessential firebrand revolutionary and heir apparent to Mao, was denounced as a "traitor" and a "counterrevolutionary." Many in the Naxalite movement followed Lin Biao and were inspired by his famous quote that guerrilla warfare was the "only way to mobilize and apply the whole strength of the people against the enemy." The internecine conflict within the Chinese Communist Party fractured the Naxalite movement into pro- and anti-Lin Biao factions and was quickly suppressed in West Bengal.[42]

The following three decades, while India slowly threw away its old practices of government control of the economy and embraced a free market and China became a nation of hyper-capitalism, the Communist movement in

India moved away from the glare of public view and quietly migrated from the urban centers to the more remote "tribal" areas. Currently, there are nearly 40 different groups that are active, which are loosely called the Naxalites or the Maoists. Of these, two groups are most significant, the People's War Group (PWG) and the Maoist Communist Center (MCC). The former is dominant in the southern states of Andhra Pradesh, Orissa Chhattisgarh, Karnataka, Maharashtra, and Tamil Nadu, while the latter is most active in the northern part of India in Bihar, Jharkhand, Uttar Pradesh, Uttaranchal, West Bengal, and Madhya Pradesh (Figure 8.1).

The miserable exploitation of the tribal people in India gave a strong base

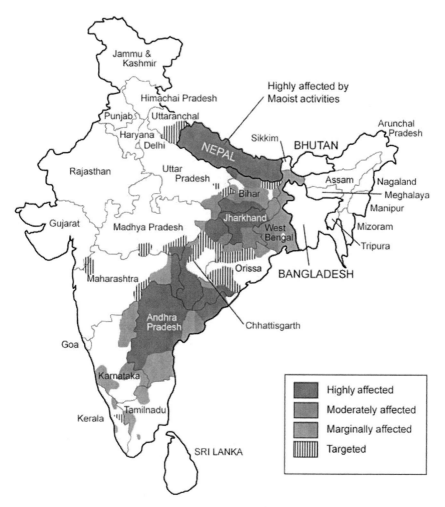

Figure 8.1 Naxalite-affected areas in India (2005–2006).

Source: adapted from the Institute of Conflict Management.

for the Communist activists.[43] Their efforts launched a fresh wave of the movement that is currently gripping India (see Figure 8.2 and Table 8.2). And, by some accounts, the Maoists have carved out a corridor from Nepal's border with India to Andhra Pradesh and are currently controlling 15–20 percent of the country. In 2006, the number of active members of Maoist guerrillas had swelled to 20,000, according to an estimate by an Indian intelligence official.[44] However, Mehra estimates the number at a much higher 55,000.[45] These numbers clearly indicate that the new movement is getting more and more entrenched. In September 2004, the PWG and the MCC came together to form a new party, the Communist Party of India,

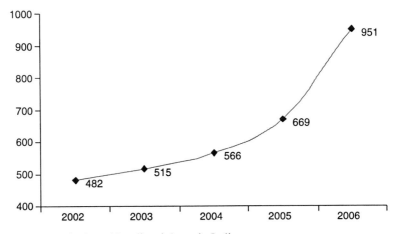

Figure 8.2 Deaths from Naxalite violence in India.

Source: Ministry of Home Affairs, Government of India. Data for 2006 is estimated.

Table 8.2 Deaths from left-wing extremism.

	2006*	2005	2004	2003	2002	Total
Andhra Pradesh	95	206	74	140	96	611
Bihar	36	94	171	128	117	546
Chhattisgarh	296	165	83	74	55	673
Jharkhand	64	118	169	117	157	625
Madhya Pradesh	0	3	4	1	3	11
Maharashtra	34	53	15	31	29	162
Orissa	18	14	8	15	11	66
Uttar Pradesh	1	1	26	8	9	45
West Bengal	11	7	15	1	7	41
Other States	0	8	1	0	1	10
Total	555	669	566	515	485	2,787

Source: Ministry of Home Affairs, Government of India.

*Compiled from newspapers by Institute for Conflict Management, New Delhi. The data for 2006 is only for the first seven months of the year.

Maoist.[46] This merger was designed to strengthen the insurgency and increase the levels of violence in the affected regions of India. A BBC wire-service report quoted a high-ranking official of the Indian government, who observed under condition of anonymity: "To say that Naxalites are running a parallel government in Bihar would not be incorrect."[47]

It will, however, be a mistake to think of the 40 or 80 groups that make up the movement as one coherent force. For instance, in Andhra Pradesh, the movement is much more in line with traditional Marxist/Maoist ideology, whereas in the more backward Bihar class warfare is often confounded with caste.[48] Also, being less ideological, the movement in Bihar is closer to a criminal organization than in other parts of the country. As a result, the leadership of the Andhra-based PWG is quite clear about its strategies and political goals. For instance, Vara Vara Rao, one of the primary ideologues of the PWG, explained that the Maoists' armed struggle has two goals. Its immediate goal is to redistribute land to the peasants. However, in the long run, it aims at capturing political power through armed struggle and to establish a Communist regime in line with Maoist principles.[49]

Furthermore, the picture of the corridor stretching from the Nepalese border to the tip of the Indian peninsula in the south (Figure 8.1) can also be misleading, since it may overrepresent the Maoists' strength. Instead of thinking of the Maoist insurgency as a growing cancer, the alternate view may be one of isolated pockets surrounded by an unaffected nation. History will tell which version of the story is more reflective of reality on the ground.

A dangerous precedence: Salwa Judum

Facing the resilience of the movement, the authorities have attempted to fight the growing influence of the Naxalite movement by organizing the tribal people into a paramilitary force, under the title of *Salwa Judum*, meaning "peace initiative" in one of the tribal languages. A local politician, of the opposition Congress Party in the newly created state Chhattisgarh, initiated this counterrevolutionary movement, which is also enthusiastically supported by the current Hindu nationalist BJP Chief Minister of the state, Raman Singh. Salwa Judum was originally touted as a grass-roots movement, spontaneously cropping up in response to the excess of the Maoists. Soon the state started to supply them with weapons, from bows and arrows to guns. Although in the beginning the novel movement was hailed in the press as a fitting counterterrorism move,[50] it is now drawing a much more alarming response from those journalists and human rights activists who have visited these largely inaccessible regions. From their reports a far less flattering picture is emerging.[51]

In Chhattisgarh, one of the poorest states, where the caste Hindus constitute an insignificant minority yet firmly control state politics, this broad-based support at the very top of the political echelon may ultimately signify a disconnection with the tribal majority.[52] Many observers note that Salwa Judum, far from being spontaneous, is the result of a deliberate policy by the government, which in effect is outsourcing its law and order responsibilities. As a part of their campaign against the Maoists, the pro-government militia of Salwa Judum is often compelling entire villages to join them or face violent retribution.[53] Consequently, violence has increased vastly in these areas, largely unnoticed by the country. In fact, a broadening war of tribe against tribe has created a virtual civil war in parts of the country.[54]

The apparent success of Salwa Judum in the early years prompted other state governments to emulate the Jharkahndi "innovation." The Andhra government, similarly, established a special tribal battalion of about 12,000 men called the "Girijan Greyhound."[55] Although the "Girijan Greyhound" is reported to be better trained and disciplined than its counterpart in Chhattisgarh,[56] many are rightfully apprehensive of their impact on the overall rule of law in the affected areas.[57]

The endgame for the Naxalites

The Communist movements in India were born under the Communist Party of India (CPI), which gave the historical grievances of the peasants a political context. However, the Telengana movement in the South fizzled out when the CPI abandoned it. The failure of this early movement gave birth to the new Communist Party India, Marxist (CPI-M).[58] The members of this new party a decade later sowed the seeds of the Naxalite movement in West Bengal. However, when the CPI-M also deserted the revolutionary cause to be a part of the Indian political system, yet another party, the Communist Party of India, Marxist-Leninist (CPI-ML), was born to carry the revolutionary banner. The Naxalite movement in West Bengal was defeated because it neglected to maintain its political base, both in the urban centers and in the rural areas as a result of a series of strategic mistakes by the leadership.

After the demise of the Soviet Union, Francis Fukuyama confidently predicted the victory of free-market democracies over the forces of the totalitarian Communist system.[59] When the Soviet Union imploded from within and, in an act of amazing transformation, Mao Zedong's China reinvented itself as a one-party capitalist nation, many, along with Fukuyama, imagined the end of Communism. It did not happen that way. The current spread of Maoist ideology in Nepal and in India has clearly proven that the news of the death of Communist idealism is highly exaggerated.[60]

The economic plight of the isolated tribal people in India has once again created conditions where Maoist movements can flourish. The high rate of overall economic growth did not touch the rural poor, particularly those living in the most economically and socially marginalized tribal areas of the country. A recent *Frontline* report states that between 1997 and 2005 nearly 25,000 farmers committed suicide by ingesting pesticide and other chemicals.

The lowering of the prices of agricultural products due to technological innovation through the introduction of commercial farming has exacerbated the terms of trade with the industrial sector and has widened the income gap even within the rural areas.[61]

This problem is particularly acute in the southern and the western states, such as Andhra Pradesh, where the Naxalites have found their strongest base. Among the tribal people in the pristine hills and forests the economic woes are further compounded by the fact that they have no property rights to the land. The move toward land reform in India stalled with the switch from socialism to market liberalism. Consequently, these hapless people found themselves increasingly on the wrong end of the globalization process. As Mehra points out, the much-touted food-for-work program, the National Rural Employment Guarantee Scheme, and other anti-poverty programs never addressed the basic problems facing the rural poor, particularly those living in the tribal areas.[62] To add to the misery, the commercial interests clashed with the traditional lifestyle of the tribal people as the outsiders moved in for the lucrative resources that the forests had to offer. The mining, logging, and agricultural interests collided squarely with the interests of the tribal people and the latter lost. The power-hungry nation, looking for cheap and non-polluting hydroelectric power, developed plans for large dams, displacing and consequently further alienating these already marginalized communities.

The presence of a strong political base has made the current insurgency much more difficult to manage than the Naxalite movement in West Bengal in the 1970s. There are several other reasons for this.

First, the current Naxalite leaders have taken the time to develop a true mass base. Although they come from the urban intelligentsia, many of them have spent the past 20 years with the indigenous people. As a result, unlike the city-based police force, many of these leaders have developed deep roots within the community through marriage and the necessary language skills. Having such deep differences in language, history, culture, and religious practices, the "class consciousness" for the most part has taken the form of ascriptive identity for the tribal population separating them from the rest of the country. In view of such a chasm, the police force, comprising the "outsiders," is seen as an alien force of oppression.

Second, a large part of the affected terrain being remote and without easy access, the insurgency has found conditions similar to those in western Nepal where the Maoists, having taken advantage of the poverty and inaccessibility, could develop a strong enough base for the insurgency to force King Gyandendra to relinquish control over his country.[63]

In contrast, the villages of West Bengal were parts of the existing transportation and communication network, which aided rapid and effective deployment of the security forces. Furthermore, while the movement in Nepal could bring in a large part of the secular movement, the popularity of the Maoists in India has remained confined within the tribal population.[64]

Third, dissident organizations are constructed on a strict hierarchical basis or on the basis of inspiration, a shared ideology with small cells and groups.[65] The old Naxalite movement in West Bengal, despite its early claims of being non-hierarchical, became strictly so with Mazumdar being accepted as the unquestioned leader of the movement.[66] It was, therefore, easier to suppress the movement with his arrest and his subsequent death. As soon as Mazumdar was gone from the scene, the movement collapsed. In contrast, the current movement is much more grounded on shared ideology. The groups are much less hierarchical to the extent that even the leaders are sometimes unknown outside a limited circle.

Fourth, the presence of unruly and untrained, yet heavily armed, paramilitary forces such as the Salwa Judum and the "Girijan Greyhound" can infinitely complicate the situation. A history of paramilitary forces shows that most often these forces get out of control and create genocide and human rights disasters.[67]

Fifth, the Naxalite movement in West Bengal was internationally isolated, without the opportunity for the insurgents to take refuge in a friendly base across the border. The current situation is shaping up quite differently. With the Maoists firmly in control in neighboring Nepal, and the corridor running straight through to the southern states of Andhra Pradesh and Tamilnadu, the PWG members have reportedly been able to establish contact with the LTTE in Sri Lanka, and have vastly improved their knowledge of explosives through the Sri Lankan rebel group.[68] According to one police report, the leadership of the Communist Party Maoist in Nepal, including Prachanda and Baburam Bhattari, were trained in the forests of Jharkhand.[69] It is safe to assume that the favor is now being returned as the Maoists are likely to be a major player in Nepalese politics in the future. Similarly, the current Bangladesh government is far less amicable to India and there are allegations on the Indian side of its helping the radical groups across the border. Historically, such international linkages have always made insurgencies much harder to manage.

Finally, it is safe to say that if the legitimate concerns of the poorest people in India are not addressed, it can only help those who offer alternate solutions outside the democratic system. The history of violent insurgency in West Bengal has shown that such movements die out only when the government begins to redress some of the major grievances of the oppressed communities.

It is of course true that the Maoist rebellion has not reached the urban centers of India. Unlike in Nepal, where support for the Maoists is strong even in Kathmandu, Maoists in India currently hold little or no base in the urban areas, which are enjoying the fruits of rapid economic growth. Therefore, the threat to the Indian government may seem remote. However, the fact that the more dedicated groups, particularly the CPI-Maoists in Andhra Pradesh, have developed contacts with groups such as the Sri Lankan LTTE and their co-ideologists in Nepal, could be the source of a much greater challenge to the nation's security. Although geographically the region of Maoist insurgency seems remote, it contains large deposits of iron ore, coal, and many other materials that a nation on a steep growth curve desperately needs. Most importantly, a permanent region of instability at the heart of the country would spell disaster for the free flow of trade and commerce in the nation.

India is located in one of the most volatile neighborhoods in the world. All the neighboring countries are featured among the top 25 of the failed state index constructed by *Foreign Policy*.[70] The weakening of central control at India's borders cannot be good news for its own political and economic stability.

In the ultimate analysis, however, the strength of India rests within its democratic system. The political legitimacy of the democratic process has been internalized by even the poorest of the people, which filters down to them through the elected body of the village council (*Panchayat*) that governs the social, political, and cultural lives of every villager.[71] This bottom-up democratic process ultimately provides the glue that has kept the diverse country together for 60 years, while all her neighbors have become embroiled in ethnic and religious conflicts. Despite all the promises, India is still one of the poorest nations in the world, with all the accompanying growing pains. As the elephant learns to dance, unless it watches its steps, a slip may spell disaster not only for its own wellbeing but also, in an increasingly intertwined world, its implications can indeed be far reaching.

In sum

Rebellion is as old as authority itself. Although violent uprisings have been part and parcel of human social existence from its very beginning, individual extremist groups and movements die. And most of them wither on the vine. Even the most established ones face threats to their existence for three primary reasons: a) having achieved their political objectives they become part of the government; b) they are defeated through police and military operations; and c) the groups lose their ideological orientation and turn into criminal organizations. Reality, however, is much more complex and the demise of dissent may come as a combination of the three. A dissident group's political goal may become irrelevant in a changing world and, as a result, it may lose its support base. The support base may also be lost due to the actions of the groups themselves, which include overstepping of the cultural norms, involvement with criminal elements, oppressive vigilantism, etc. As a result of a push from its leadership, the IRA, for instance, began to shift toward participation in the political process by increasingly eschewing violent actions against its Protestant adversaries and the state. The altered political and demographic landscape on both side of the divided island contributed heavily to the hopes for a peaceful solution to the longest-standing conflict in the world. Yet, during the time when peace negotiations are continuing, unless the leadership can keep strict control over its restive revolutionaries, an extremist party can turn toward vigilantism and criminality. The Naxalites in West Bengal suffered a military defeat due to a number of similar reasons. First, the Naxalites did not attempt to develop a mass base, as they believed that the country was ripe for a revolution. Second, their aspirations of a "cultural revolution" often undermined the cultural and political norms of the society. World events also stood in the way of their gaining a strong foothold in the state, particularly in the urban areas. However, after their defeat in West Bengal, the Naxalites began concentrating on the remote tribal areas of the country. By not repeating the same mistakes of the past, they are currently emerging as a force in India and are increasingly challenging the authorities in a wide swathe of the land.

9   Terrorism's trap

A winnable war?

Addiction to failure

Facing the prospect of being targeted for violence by a small group of extremists, particularly from another country, every society has felt angry, insecure, and utterly confused about what to do. A CBS/*New York Times* poll conducted from 18 to 23 May 2007 found dwindling support for the embattled President. By a 10 percent margin, the majority (52 percent) of Americans disapproved of the way George W. Bush was handling the campaign against terrorism.[1] A few months earlier an SRBI survey published in *Time* found that 56 percent of Americans believed that US policies in the Middle East were hurting the war on terrorism, with only 29 percent believing that they helped.[2] Despite a widely unpopular president pursuing a disastrous policy of preemptive intervention in Iraq, another CBS/*Wall Street Journal* poll asked: "If the federal government has evidence of groups or countries that are preparing to commit terrorist attacks on the US, should US policy be to attack these groups or countries, or not to attack them until they actually commit a terrorist act?" Quite amazingly 40 percent of the respondents backed the idea of a preemptive attack. Only 39 percent thought that the US should wait for an actual attack to take place.[3] This is a far cry from the days before the invasion when President Bush enjoyed nearly 90 percent of public support for invading Iraq, an unprecedented popularity at any time for any particular public policy. As the US forces became bogged down in the quagmire of an ensuing civil war and the death toll of the troops crossed 3,500 in mid-2007, the polls indicated a reversal of public opinion. Yet, as we can see, even at this point, most of the public thought it would be prudent to have a preemptive military strike if there was "evidence of groups or countries" preparing for an attack.

This conundrum often plagues the debate on what to do when terrorism strikes. The sight of innocent, unsuspecting people being killed or injured gives all of us a collective sense of insecurity. Some have called the post-terror attack psychology a product of "cognitive narrowing," where the society in unison puts on a blinder. Our need for quick and decisive revenge overwhelms the evidence of history.[4] Indeed, revenge is a primal sentiment, fulfilling many of our psychological needs including righting the perceived injustice[5] and/or making sure that such atrocities do not happen again in the future.[6] Even among primates the drive to correct the past acts of injustice is similarly strong. In fact, a number of studies as well as experiments in social psychology have established the sad fact that people often prefer a position akin to the proverbial cutting off of one's own nose to spite others; they would accept less desirable outcomes just to take revenge on those who had offended them.[7]

In our anger, when we dispense with calm calculation and the choice of effective countermeasures, we only create conditions under which the fires of hatred can be kept burning for generations to come. In their haste, throughout history, governments have overstepped their bounds and have fallen into the trap laid by the terrorists. It is as if we are addicted to failed policies of the past.

Since that defining fall day in 2001, an avalanche of scholarly contributions has enriched our knowledge base on the various issues regarding terrorism. In this volume I have attempted to provide a structure to these myriad contributions by offering a theory of individual motivation, which includes both self-interest and group-interest. On the basis of this theoretical perspective I have explored reasons for the birth, growth, transformation, and demise of organizations that engage in strategic violence to achieve some political objective.

I have argued that "terrorism" is simply a label of convenience and, by defining it broadly, I have discussed it simply as a strategy taken by a mass movement. Facing a huge asymmetry of power a dissident group adopts shock tactics to achieve certain short- and long-term goals. In the short run, through these atrocities a terrorist group announces its existence and signals its commitment to its political goal to it adversaries, support base, and to the world, which it sees largely as ignorant or apathetic to its cause. An extremist group's immediate objective includes two broad goals. It aims at increasing the "market share" of public support among its base. And it attempts to change some government policies, including an unacceptable peace process, which ignores their demands. In the latter role, they may act as "spoilers" to disrupt what the majority wants and, in the process, radicalize the entire society on both sides of a conflict. However, these are only the short-term objectives. Most often terrorist groups try to bring about a fundamental change in society by gaining political sovereignty for their own people along the lines of ethnicity, language, religion, or economic class.

When we face a clear and present danger, we often exaggerate the threat. In order to evaluate the nature of the threat posed by terrorism, in this concluding chapter I will first address the questions: How successful are the terrorist organizations in achieving their goals? Under what conditions do they become successful? In the following section, I would like to present some empirical evidence to the extent that terrorism threatens us globally. The data clearly demonstrates that there is hardly any congruence between the actual danger of terrorism and the public anxiety that it produces. The menace is often vastly overstated. The question then is: why do we fall into the trap set by small groups of extremists and give in to the impulse of overreacting? We know that when a government reacts in a way that is seen unfair and draconian by a large segment of a community it only strengthens the hands of the extremists. Yet most often governments seem to be addicted to the failed policies of the past. Some noted cognitive scientists have offered an explanation of this strange addiction, which we will examine. On the basis of these discussions, I will propose the outlines of public policy to manage the risks of terrorism. Finally, similar to any other commodity, national security comes at a price. In the aftermath of a devastating attack against unarmed civilians and cherished national symbols there is a pronounced tendency to assume "any cost" to prevent such future attacks. In the final section, I will discuss the price for our collective security.

Does terrorism succeed?

The title of Harvard law professor Alan Dershowitz's book *Why Terrorism Works* presumes that the terrorists are destined to win since the international community repeatedly rewards these groups with appeasement and legitimization, refusing to take the necessary steps to curtail attacks.[8] In contrast, others have argued that terrorism and insurgencies rarely win.[9] Let us examine this question in a bit more detail. As we have noted, the infant mortality rate of terrorist organizations is extremely high; nearly 90 percent of them disappear from the pages of history within a few years of their birth. Those that survive can live for a very long time, some for nearly a century. Sometimes a group may change its name along the way or even alter its ideological orientation while others may migrate from the country of their origin to other parts of the world.

The goals of a dissident organization can be divided into short-term strategic objectives and long-term aspirations. Those movements, which target ordinary citizens and objects of national symbolic importance, do so with three primary short-term objectives. As we will see below, through their acts of violence, the terrorist organizations are frequently able to attain their short-term objectives.

Short-term objectives

"We exist"

Any organization, legal or illegal, that depends on mass participation must engage in an advertising campaign. A private firm does this through traditional mass marketing while the terrorist groups do it through acts of spectacular violence. Therefore, the first objective of a newly formed group is to announce to their support base and their adversaries their existence. After an act of violence, a group trying to gain notoriety claims responsibility for it. In fact, when a particular act is successful in getting world attention, it is not unusual for several rival groups to take credit for it. That is why, in places like Iraq, Afghanistan, or in Palestine, when a person of "high value" is kidnapped the responsible group releases video messages clearly showing its group emblem. The ability of a group to quickly gain world attention through acts of extreme violence is well documented in history. For instance, the concept of Palestinian nationalism and a newly created group the Popular Front for the Liberation of Palestine (PFLP) entered into the global consciousness when in 1969 its members hijacked a US jet and blew it up in front of television cameras. Within three months the United Nations General Assembly recognized the "inalienable rights of the Palestinian people."[10] Similarly, 18 months after staging the kidnapping and murder of 11 Israeli athletes during the Munich Olympics, Yasser Arafat was invited to address the UN General Assembly.[11]

However, there are limits to these "advertisements." As a group comes into prominence, it risks attracting attention from the target government. Unless a group can develop a strong mass base, such unwelcome attention can prove to be the cause of their undoing.

Market share

Terrorist organizations that are rooted in a community, rather than being financed and operated from outside, play for the hearts and minds of their support bases. Their operations are carefully selected to adhere to the local customs and traditions, where each action may be choreographed for a larger audience. Thus, when an Islamic group beheads a kidnap victim with a sword, the images are laden with symbolic significances. The sword occupies an important religious and political place in the Islamic tradition. When pushed into a corner and faced with the prospect of annihilation of his nascent community, Prophet Muhammad picked up the sword of justice, with which he protected his followers and punished the perpetrators of aggression. That is why the flag of Saudi Arabia is adorned with the picture of a sword; Saddam Hussain with the same imagery in mind sculpted a gate with two enormous swords in Baghdad. Hence, beheading with a sword carried a message for the community which would have been lost if they were shown as being shot to death. In contrast, the PIRA in Ireland would rather use the gun as a tool for sending violent messages.[12]

These acts, deliberately chosen in conformity with the community standard and sensibility, are designed to increase the market share of public opinion of a dissident group. Hamas challenged the Fatah group and the PLO for the Palestinian support. Through a deliberate campaign of suicide attacks it demonstrated its commitment to the people, tired of Israeli occupation, corrupt rule by the Palestinian Authority and lack of progress in forming a sovereign Palestinian state in the West Bank and the Gaza Strip. The message of equating the death tolls with the Israelis struck a sympathetic chord with many within the Arab population, hungry for revenge.[13]

At times, as we have seen, imprudent acts may overstep the bounds of what is culturally acceptable and may cost a group support among its own base. History is full of examples where a violent group has overstepped its bounds and has paid dearly in terms of public support. In the long history of the IRA, we have seen several such examples. For instance, on 24 October 1990 the IRA took an entire family hostage in the city of Derry and forced Patsy Gillespie to drive a car loaded with a bomb through a British Army checkpoint, where it was blown up by remote control, killing five soldiers as well as the "human bomb," Gillespie. In the violent parlance of the "Troubles," it was known as "proxy bombing." This method of striking at the enemy was gaining popularity among the IRA operatives, when the organization realized that the Republican support base was firmly rejecting such tactics. Quickly, the IRA stopped the proxy bombing.[14] Similarly, the Irish National Liberation Army (INLA), an offshoot of the Catholic movement against the British rule in Northern Ireland, became increasingly isolated as a result of its violent attacks and engagement in all kinds of criminal activities.[15] The Naxalite movement in West Bengal competed for market share of the left-leaning segment of the population with the more establishment-oriented CPI-M by engaging in revolutionary acts of violence. However, after making significant progress in attracting young recruits, they started losing popular support due to their emphasis on meaningless violence and the inclusion of street thugs in their ranks, particularly in Calcutta. They further lost support as they initiated a Maoist styled "Cultural Revolution" and attacked some of the most revered cultural icons of Bengal.[16]

Inducing overreaction by the opponents

Built in 944, the al-Askari mosque is among the holiest shrines of Shi'a Islam. The beautiful mosque with its golden dome has absolutely no military significance. Yet in February 2006 a small group of armed men walked inside, tied up the guards and set off explosive charges, destroying the dome and causing severe structural damage to the place of worship. Even in the tortured reasoning of sectarian violence such an act is hard to fathom. Yet the goals of the perpetrators were crystal clear: they were inviting a revenge attack from the radical Shi'ite militias. The forces of the firebrand preacher Moqtada al-Sadr were all too obliging. The resulting bloodbath, which was designed to destroy the middle ground of sanity and reinforced the worst suspicion among the combatants about their respective enemies, strengthen the hands of those who are at the extreme ends of the sectarian divide. Another similar attack on a mosque took place a year and a half later. Predictably, a leader of the black-bearded, black-shirted Shi'ite militia, the Mahdi Army, told a Western reporter, "The Sunnis made the explosion in Samara. Now we have only one road. If we don't destroy the Sunnis, they will destroy us." The radical Sunnis had achieved their strategic goal![17]

It is the same reasoning that prompted the 9/11 attacks on US soil, and the train bombings in London, Madrid, and Bombay. In the perverted logic of the extremist, politics inviting carnage of their own community in order to increase their support base makes perfect sense. The terrorist groups are most often successful in achieving this strategic objective. In the following section I will discuss why the organized societies most often fall into this terrorists' trap.

Particular policy change/spoiler

Terrorist groups are also sometimes successful in achieving their short-run goals of compelling their opposition to alter the course of certain policies. As we have seen, many of the suicide attacks by Hamas were timed to spoil the middle ground of a compromised settlement. Unfortunately, the hawks within the Israeli government, being less interested in giving up land for peace than the professed rhetoric of their leaders, won the internal debate. The general public, following the extremists in and out of the government, refused to distinguish between Hamas and the Palestinian Authority. Without exploiting the division between the two and supporting the PA, they were far more interested in viewing the entire Palestinian community as a single entity. The myriad punishments meted out to the Palestinians, from destruction of the homes of the suicide bombers to closing of the borders with Israel, imposed severe costs on everybody regardless of political orientation. This polarization allowed Hamas and the PIJ to achieve their intermediate policy objectives. By playing into the hands of the extremists, the Israeli authorities fell into the trap and let Hamas succeed as spoilers of the peace accord.

Long-term goals

The long-term goals of the radical resistance groups involve a fundamental change in the power relationship within a society: the nationalists want independent states; the Communists, the end of the capitalist system; and the religious fundamentalists, a society built around their own interpretation of the scripture. Scholars, journalists, and politicians alike have often downgraded the abilities of terrorist organizations to achieve their long-term political goals. Thus, Schelling points out, they often accomplish their "intermediate means toward political objectives . . . but with a few exceptions it is hard to see that the attention and publicity have been of much value except as ends in themselves."[18] Let us now examine the history of mass movements and terrorism to see how many of them have been successful in achieving their goals.

History, of course, does not speak with one voice and is always open to interpretation. By looking back we are often not sure exactly which forces caused a certain event in the past. However, if we carefully examine the most popular interpretations of history, a certain pattern emerges. If we scrutinize the four waves of modern terrorism[19] we see that the anarchists did not succeed in transforming society by making it non-hierarchical and non-authoritarian. Their philosophy, which precluded the formation of hierarchical party organizations, did not allow them to achieve their ultimate goals of socioeconomic equality. The second wave of terrorism was remarkably successful. The Stern and the Irgun gangs were among the significant forces in driving out the British and creating the sovereign nation of Israel. Through a campaign of bombing, they were able to create an atmosphere of terror among the British administration and the war-weary armed forces stationed in the region.[20] Similarly, the largely peasant movement, the Mau Mau guerrillas, were able to successfully attack the European colonialists and the plantation owners to pave the road for Kenyan independence.[21] After World War II, the French attempted to crush the Algerian independence movement by extreme force.[22] As Moran points out, "Algeria's National Liberation Front (FLN) rarely possessed the means to conduct sustained operation of any scale. They succeeded despite their limited resources because their adversaries were repeatedly reduced to fighting fire with fire, a disastrous tendency that finally ruined them."[23] The more draconian a position that the French military and the associated paramilitary forces took, the stiffer the Algerian resistance became. The cycle of violence was spiraling out of control with the claims of over a million dead and the tales of torture reaching mythical proportion,[24] when a tired French government of Charles de Gaulle granted Algeria independence in 1962.

A similar success story for a terrorist organization can be found in the history of Cyprus, which remained under British domination after the end of World War II. The EOKA was a Greek Cypriot nationalist organization that fought for the expulsion of British troops from the island and its political unification with Greece. The group received surreptitious support from successive Greek governments in the form of arms, money, and propaganda on radio stations broadcast from Athens. The EOKA began its terrorist campaign in 1955, targeting the British military and their Cypriot supporters, including the Turkish minority, who opposed the Greeks and, instead, sought unification with Turkey. The bombing campaign brought about an inevitable cycle of violence. However, EOKA's political aims were partially successful when Cyprus gained its independence in 1960, but, because of the opposition of its Turkish minority and their benefactor, the government in Turkey, the island could not become a part of Greece.[25]

The wave of anti-colonial terrorism waned as most of the European colonies gained their independence in the 1960s, with the last armed resistance achieving its political goal in Angola. The UNITA (National Union for Total Independence of Angola) and their rivals the National Front for the Liberation of Angola (FNLA) were able to exhaust the Portuguese colonialists and gained independence in 1975.[26]

By that time, the third wave of terrorism was well under way. The leftist movements created a worldwide surge of violence. Unlike the anarchists, the new left movement, learning from the success of Communist Parties of Russia, China, and their client states, began their campaign by forming organized party structures. As the Cold War heated up, the Communist giants, particularly the USSR, were also eager to support dissident movements in the West and in the countries of the Western allies. As a countermeasure, the US and its NATO allies helped the reactionary and pro-establishment forces in the third world nations. Groups sprung up in North America, Europe, Asia, Africa, and Latin America that challenged the existing political and economic establishments. These terrorist groups and insurgencies, unlike the anti-colonial waves, however, met mostly with failure. The IRA, after nearly a century of fighting, failed to unify Ireland. The French Canadian group the *Front de Libération du Québec* (Québec Liberation Front), commonly known as the FLQ, could not carve a separate French nation out of Canada.[27] The Weathermen, the Symbionese Liberation Army, and the Black Panthers all failed miserably to achieve their political goals. In Latin America, the radical groups from the Shining Path to the Tupamaros, despite creating large-scale mayhem, could not change their societies and establish Communist regimes. The Sandinistas in Nicaragua, after a long and inconclusive war, joined the democratic political process.[28] The FARC in Colombia has been able to hold on to territories under its control in Colombia.[29] In the Middle East, leftist groups such the PLO, after decades of fighting, were able to achieve some success in returning to the West Bank and the Gaza Strip, but were unable to drive the Israelis to the sea, or even get a separate state for the Palestinians. In India, the Naxalite movement had little discernible impact on the social and economic structure of the nation. The irredentist Sikh extremist group the Khalistani Movement, despite creating a huge cycle of violence, disappeared from the scene without achieving any of its political or territorial goals.[30] Neither could the Kashmiri insurgents achieve their political goals after six decades of constant fighting.[31]

The achievements of long-term goals of the current wave of religious warfare are equally meager. With the help of the leftists and a broad coalition of the anti-Shah opposition, the forces of Ayatolllah Khomeini were able to establish a Shi'ite theocratic state. In the neighboring Afghanistan—thanks to the assistance of Pakistan and its benefactor, the US—the Taliban were able to expel the mighty USSR military and, after a bitter civil war, were able to form a government in the image of their own Sunni Islamic ideals. However, the rest of the jihadi movements, from Indonesia to Kashmir, from Chechnya to Israel, often after decades of fighting, have little to show for it.

In order to understand the circumstances under which a group achieves its ultimate objectives, I have presented information on the dissident groups that are still active or have been active in the recent past in Table 9.1. When we combine the list of successful groups from Table 9.1 with the previous generation of groups that were able to achieve their goals, we see an emerging

Table 9.1 Recent extremist groups, goals, and outcomes.

	Long-term goals
Successful groups	
Communist Party of Nepal-Maoist (CPN-M) (1996)	Establishment of a Marxist state and abolition of monarchy in Nepal. Largely successful in becoming part of the political process
Hizbullah (1982)	Expulsion of Israeli Army from Lebanon
Taliban (1994)	Drive out the invading Soviet forces and establish an Islamic state in Afghanistan
UNITA (1966)	Angolan independence from Portugal. Successful in driving out the Portuguese
Partially successful groups	
Liberation Tigers of Tamil Eelam (LTTE) (1974)	Creating a separate state for Sri Lanka's ethnic Tamil people
Revolutionary Armed Forces of Colombia (FARC) (1964)	Overthrow the current democratic government of Colombia and replace it with a Communist government
United Self-Defense Forces of Colombia (1980s)	Combat leftist terrorist organizations operating in Colombia, primarily the FARC and ELN
Unsuccessful or ongoing	
Abu Hafs al-Masri Brigade, (2003)	Global jihadism in line with al-Qaeda in Europe
Abu Nidal Organization (1974)	Destruction of Israel
Abu Sayyaf Group (ASG) (1991)	Creation of an independent Islamic state encompassing parts of Southern Thailand, the island of Borneo, the Sulu Archipelago, and Mindanao areas of the Philippines
al-Fatah (late 1950s)	Original goal: destruction of Israel and establishment of a secular Palestinian state
al-Qaeda (late 1980s)	Establishment of an Islamic Caliphate in the world
al-Qaeda Organization in the Land of the Two Rivers (2004)	Expulsion of coalition forces and establishment of an Islamic state based on Sharīah in Iraq
Ansar al-Sunnah Army (2003)	Expulsion of coalition forces and establishment of an Islamic state based on Sharīah in Iraq
Armed Islamic Group (1992)	Overthrow the secular Algerian regime and replace it with an Islamic state
Communist Party of India-Maoist (2004)	Establishment of a Marxist state in India
Dagestan Liberation Army (1999)	Creating Islamic Republic of Dagestan
Front for the Liberation of Lebanon from Foreigners (FLLF)	Destruction of the PLO, Syria, and its Lebanese allies. Right-wing Lebanese Christian Phalange Party
Hamas (1987)	Destruction of Israel
Irish Republican Army (1922)	Unification of Ireland
Jemaah Islamiya (1993)	Creation of an Islamic state in Indonesia

(*Continued overleaf*)

Table 9.1 (Continued)

	Long-term goals
Khalistan Movement	Creation of an independent Sikh nation
Lashkar-e-Taiba (1989)	Restoration of Islamic rule over all parts of India based on Wahhabism
Lord's Resistance Army (1992)	Idiosyncratic—overthrow the government of Uganda
Mujahideen Shura Council (2005)	Removal of coalition forces from Iraq
Palestinian Islamic Jihad (late 1970s)	Destruction of Israel
Popular Front for the Liberation of Palestine (1967)	Destruction of Israel and other conservative Arab regimes, replacing them with Marxist-Leninist states
Riyad us-Saliheyn Martyrs' Brigade (early 2000)	The creation of an independent Islamic republic in Chechnya (and other primarily Muslim parts of Russia such as Dagestan, Kabardino-Balkaria, Ingushetia, Ossetia, and Tataria)

Note: the year of the birth of extremist groups is within parentheses.

pattern. The most successful wave of terrorism included those groups which aimed at expelling foreign occupiers from their lands. From the anti-colonial movements in the 1940s, 1950s, and 1960s, the current crop of successful groups have fought an enemy that came across its political boundaries. The Taliban gained victories against the Soviet military, Hizbullah in Lebanon were successful against the Israelis, just like the Algerian FLN won against the French, the Mau Mau in Kenya, the EOKA in Cyprus, and the Jewish gangs in Palestine were able to drive out the British forces. After Indonesia invaded and occupied the tiny island called Portuguese Timore in 1975 under the pretext of fighting Communism, the East Timorians fought a brutal fight and were able to expel the ruthless Indonesian army in 1999 to form their own nation. It is extremely important to recognize that in each case the occupying force lost its will and did not consider the benefits of holding onto power to be worth the cost in lost lives, popular support, and international reputation. This is true not only for violent terrorist groups but also for non-violent movements, such as that led by Mahatma Gandhi in India. Thus, after a careful study of the history of the Indian anti-colonial movement, French is absolutely correct in pointing out:

> The British decision to quit [the Indian subcontinent] had been based on neither altruism not strategic planning. It was not the logical culmination of a policy of benign imperial stewardship, like a kindly parent allowing a child to ride its bicycle unassisted from the moment it learned to pedal.

Nor was it the inevitable consequence of unquenchable socio-political forces, with the people of India rising up as one to drive the invaders into the sea. For many Indians, especially in the south, the deal was sewn up by English-speakers in New Delhi who in the 1940s were of distant importance.

Rather, the British left India because *they lost control over the crucial areas of administration, and lacked the will and the financial or military ability to recover that control.*[32]

(Emphasis mine)

This is perhaps the Vietnam syndrome, which at the end makes terrorism and insurgencies victorious. In contrast, where a more powerful government (and the people it represents) considers the fight central to its national identity and does not lose its political will, a decades- or even century-old struggle by dissident groups, however bloody, fails to achieve its political goal. The IRA could not unite the entire island, because if it were up to the British government, they would have left their northern enclave long time ago. It was the threat that the Protestant majority felt in being absorbed into Catholic Ireland that kept the struggle going.[33] Similarly, despite sixty years of insurgency and violence, the Islamic militant groups based in Pakistan could not loosen the grip of Indian government in Kashmir.[34] The Indians, in general, accepted the costs of the fight and refused to give in. The Tamil Tigers in Sri Lanka can maintain a hugely expensive—both in terms of human lives and in terms of lost income—civil war, but they have not so far been able to carve out an independent nation in the north.[35]

The lesson that we can draw from this discussion is that while terrorist organizations are most often able to achieve their short-term strategic objectives, very few can reach their long-term goals. They can do so only when the protagonist government loses its will to fight, which happens only when it does not consider the prospect of their loss vital to their own political integrity. This insight may predict a dismal outcome for the current US occupation of Iraq. In contrast, despite the possibility of many lost lives, history is against bin Laden and the jihadis in achieving their cherished goals of a global Islamic Caliphate.

Assessing the global threats of terrorism

In the current climate of overheated and oversimplified political rhetoric and round-the-clock media coverage it is easy to lose perspective on terrorism. President George W. Bush's war on global terrorism conjures up images of armies of terrorists stretching from one end of the globe to the other. Yet when we look at the facts there often seems to be an utter disconnection between actual threats of terrorism and the state response.[36] In terms of cold numbers, the comparison between the probabilities of death from international terrorism, where the attackers come from outside of the country, with other real dangers, seems almost absurd. In the past 38 years, the MIPT RAND Corporation database records on average 375 deaths from terrorism per year worldwide. This compares with roughly the same number of people who drown in bathtubs in the US alone (about 320).[37] Even when we add the total fatalities during the past ten years resulting from both international and domestic terrorism, the number rises to nearly 32,700, which is less than the automobile-related deaths for a single year in the US. By comparing the number of deaths from terrorism with those from natural disasters like the recent tsunami in South Asia and earthquake deaths in Pakistan, the national obsession with the threat may indeed seem Kafka-esque.

Terrorism's threat does not always come from the outside. The deaths of more than 200 people in the Oklahoma City bombing should serve as a stern reminder. The war in Iraq and Afghanistan and instability and sectarian fights in countries such as Pakistan and India should warn us against making this artificial distinction between domestic and international terrorism. However, because the MIPT database contains information on both types only since 1998 (it used to collect data only on international terrorism between 1968 and 1997), we are limited in our global information on terrorism by a decade. I have plotted the time-series data on the number of fatalities for the past decade to examine the existence of a trend (Figure 9.1). As we can see, although the figure for total fatality from terrorism in the world is showing an

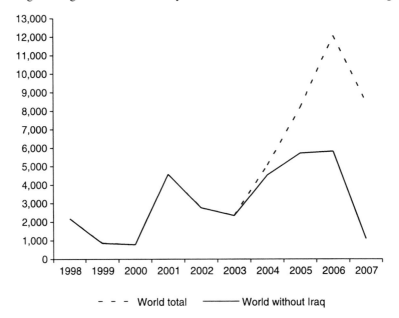

Figure 9.1 Deaths from domestic and international terrorism: global trend 1998–2007.

Source: MIPT RAND database.

Note: 2007 data estimated by projecting the figure for the first 6 months.

upward trend, there is no such trend of ever increasing violence if we exclude the data from a single country: Iraq. In fact, between 2004 and 2007, Iraq contributed nearly half (49.26 percent) of the total fatalities in the world.[38]

How about the composition of ideology? The data reveals that since 1998, 52.8 percent deaths and injuries from terrorist attacks are caused by religious groups, 37 percent by nationalist groups and 10.2 percent by Communists, leftists, anti-globalization, and radical environmental groups. Although, true to Rapoport's (2004) claim, there is a preponderance of violence from those groups which are inspired by religious vision, there is hardly a trend to suggest that the composition has changed over the past decade (see Figure 9.2). Furthermore, as I have argued, in the matters of constructed identity many of these differences, which are presented as clear-cut categories,[39] seem to have considerable overlap.

Looking at the future

Given this past we may speculate on the future trend of global terrorism. In an insightful work, Lia has explored the structural factors that will influence

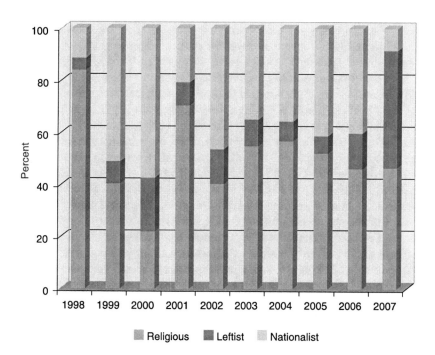

Figure 9.2 Composition of deaths and injuries from domestic and international terrorism: global trend 1998–2007.

Source: MIPT RAND database.

Note: 2007 data is for the first 5 months.

the future trend.[40] Terrorism is spawned within an ecology consisting of forces of politics, economics, technology, demography, and psychology. "Prediction is a hazardous job, particularly when it comes to the future," goes the popular wisdom told in a jest. Yet, following Lia, we may venture at this perilous undertaking by examining the trends of these factors.

Samuel Huntington described the current global political system as uni-/multi-polar, where a strong hegemon (the US) is surrounded by a growing number of regional powers.[41] The regional rivalries and the influence of the only superpower are creating a mix within which the forces of conflict are often strengthening. During the Cold War period, the predominant force was the tug-of-war between the US and the USSR. However, in the new era of a uni/multi-polar world, many of the forces of conflict kept in check during the Cold War have been unleashed. The changing winds are fanning the fires of ancient hatred. This overall trend is being further complicated by the proliferation of weapons of mass destruction, the creation of new nation-states, and increasing ranks of failed states. The conflicts generated by these changing political realities are driving the need for intervention by the hegemonic and other regional powers. These interventions, through military might or through peacekeeping operations, are creating their own dynamics for the resurgence of terrorist threats. Within this bubbling cauldron of conflicting forces, the non-governmental organizations are playing an ever-important role. While many of these non-governmental organizations are working for peace and understanding, many others, through the guise of charity work, are in fact fomenting hostility and mutual suspicion.

The economic structural factors influencing the global outcome of terrorism consist of economic inequities (both among and within nations), the conflict and collusion between the business interests of transnational corporations and the political impotency of national governments, the influence of organized crime (providing an ominous nexus with terrorist organizations), and the dependence on the oil flow from some of the most volatile regions of the world.[42] The trend toward a greater income inequality within nations is being exacerbated by the influx of new immigrants, legal and illegal, from less developed to more developed parts of the world. This massive migration does not only include the developed Western world, where the new immigrants are often forced to live in segregated urban ghettos; it impacts on other parts of the world as well. Economic refugees from Bangladesh, for instance, have poured into the border states of India, creating or deepening the existing hostility among the population. The same is true in Africa, where transnational as well as intra-national displacement and migration are at the heart of many violent conflicts.

Rapid population growth is putting demographic pressure on most of the lesser-developed nations. Rapid growth rates of population are accompanied by a pyramidal distribution with a very large proportion of young men and women. This emerging cohort represents not only an insatiable demand on resources, particularly in the poorer parts of the world and among the migrant minority population in the affluent West, but also supplies the bulk of the foot soldiers of political radicalism. As a result, migration is proving to be another incendiary factor affecting the future trends of terrorism.

The impact of changing technology on the future global trends in terrorism is also becoming increasingly apparent. The technologies of communication and transportation, as well as the creation of new weapons, are making the prospect of peace more precarious. The Internet has truly revolutionized the world of terrorism by providing an incredible weapon for the spread of ideas across the globe. It has also opened up and is opening up ever-new areas of concern.[43]

The mainstream economic theories of economic growth and development do not take into account the political and institutional environment within which a nation must achieve its economic goals. As a result, the standard neoclassical economics predicts that all boats would rise when the tide comes in.[44] As conflicts engulf the developing nations,[45] they get mired in a retrogressive process of economic growth. This process, if unchecked, can drag a nation to the dreaded condition of a failed state with all its accompanying problems, for itself, its immediate neighbors, and the entire global community.

Accounting for addiction to failure

Through their egregious acts of violence terrorists provoke an organized society to overstate the danger, over-generalize the adversaries to include every member of a community as terrorists or their sympathizers, and over-react with indiscriminate countermeasures that only deepens the crisis. At times, by listening to the political rhetoric on both sides, it seems that they are repeating the same mantra about each other. On both sides the leaders claim that the only language that the others understand is one of force. On both sides of the violent divide the leaders see a singularity of purpose to harm them by their adversaries. And the leaders most confidently promise victory. Thus, Sean MacStiofain, the Provisional IRA's Chief of Staff, puts it most aptly: "It has been said that most revolutions are not caused by revolutionaries in the first place, but by the stupidity and brutality of governments."[46] Witnessing this repeated cycle in history, where the mere show of force has failed to deliver on the promises of peace, security, and justice, we may ask ourselves: why are we addicted to failure?

Cognitive scientists Kahneman and Renshon argue that the reason we often seem to be addicted to failure is perhaps rooted in the way we process information.[47] They observe that on the national scene:

> As the hawks and doves thrust and parry, one hopes that the decision makers will hear their arguments on the merits and weigh them judiciously before choosing a course of action. Don't count on it. Modern psychology suggests that policymakers come to the debate predisposed to believe their hawkish advisors more than the doves. There are numerous reasons for the

burden of persuasion that doves carry, and some of them have nothing to do with politics or strategy. In fact, a bias in favor of hawkish beliefs and preferences is built into the fabric or the human mind.

Kahneman and Tversky and their associates have carried out extensive research, which revealed a series of important biases in perception that guide human understanding of uncertain outcomes.[48] Based on these much-celebrated findings, Kahneman and Renshon argue that political leaders' proclivity to be swayed by the hawks is rooted in three fundamental errors.[49] These fundamental facts about human decision-making are equally applicable to the side of the dissidents.

In a conflict, people are prone to commit the *fundamental attribution error*, where they fail to understand the context and constraints within which their adversaries must operate. As a result, we cannot understand the behavior of our adversaries and are apt to attribute the worst possible motives for their moves. At the same time, we have difficulty in seeing how our enemies may not understand our own motivations. Thus, in a conflict situation the political leaders of the target government are likely to trust those who would anticipate the worst possible actions by a violent dissident group. Similarly, the leaders of a radical group are apt to misunderstand the moves of the heads of the target government.

Psychological experiments reveal that people are *overtly optimistic* about their own abilities. Most of us think of ourselves as smarter, more attractive, more understanding, etc. than we actually are. As a result, we suffer from an illusion of control, where we consistently exaggerate our ability to manage a situation even when the actual outcomes are random or are the products of forces beyond our control.[50]

Finally, human beings are *poor statisticians* when it comes to the understanding of uncertainty.[51] The precept of probability theory tells us that a rational individual would view probability on an even plain. However, in actuality we do not know how to process the information properly. In a card game, if we are losing we are likely to ignore the fact that each successive hand is independent of the other and, instead, bet more money ("double or nothing") by reasoning that since we have had a string of bad luck, it is bound to change in the next round. In the area of public policy to deal with the threats of terrorism, the political leaders would embrace the failed policies of the past in spite of evidence of their failure for the same set of reasons.

As a result of these psychological forces, the leadership on both sides become prisoners of their rhetorical excesses, from which it becomes nearly impossible to extricate. Passions are inflamed and the media plays a very important role. In a conflict media biases on all sides quickly drown the calls for compromise. Syndicated columnist Georgie Anne Geyer provided a graphic account of the creation of mass hysteria by the clever use of images by the media in the Yugoslav civil war in 1989. She writes:

The most terrifying indicator of what was to come was the television in my hotel room in the Inter-Continental [in Belgrade]. There, on that little screen—part of the new technology that so many thought would unite the world—one saw hours of Serb propaganda. Serb cemeteries from battles lost 800 years ago vied with Serbian women crying at the grave— the Serbs as eternal victims.[52]

Anyone familiar with the media presentations all over the world, including in the West, can understand its role in creating a condition of frenzy. The media, being afraid of being labeled as disloyal, presents stories that paint the darkest possible pictures of the protagonists. Even the Internet, while provid- ing contrary information from many sides, fails to bring about a balanced discussion. Most of us seek our own zones of comfort when it comes to polit- ical news.[53] As a result, we see, read or listen to news reports and discussions that fit our particular political orientation. Not having the same reference points, people tend to talk past one another. This tendency is most pro- nounced when it comes to highly charged emotional issues, such as terrorism and national security. Under such a polarizing atmosphere every politician would take the safest course of action, promising to be the hardest against the threats of terrorism. Similarly, within the dissident community, most often the most firebrand orators gather the largest followings. Given our natural ten- dency to repeat the mistakes of the past, it is incumbent upon the leaders to help create an atmosphere where prudent policies can be discussed and debated.

Outlines of long-term policies

An understanding of the human motivations that propel a society to the path of violence can lend itself to the development of the outlines of policy prescriptions. Once again, if we understand the factors that influence the terrorism increasing and attenuating forces—ideological factors, factors of self-interest, the cost of participation and the external factors—we can sketch out the broad policy parameters, which might help bring the levels of social violence down.

Addressing the questions of the ideology of hate

Recognizing the power of ideology. Since it is impossible to overcome problems of collective action without the presence of ideology, we must realize the power of radical political discourse. It is indeed painful for Western democra- cies, established on the foundation of freedom of expression, to deal effect- ively with speech that incites people to resort to violence to redress injustice. Therefore, more than punishing the flame-throwers, the society must encour- age the moderate middle by promoting an open dialog. It is not an easy task since ideologies are rooted in strong moral convictions. For many in Pakistan the support of Mujahidins fighting the forces of India across its border is a moral issue. Similarly, in the Muslim community, many would support the basic premises of spreading Islam and living by its strict rules of conduct. In such a situation, the promotion of the middle ground must come from within. The Islamic tradition of *ijtihad* (interpretation and reasoning based on the sacred text) provides an avenue where such disputes can be resolved through dialog and interpretation by the legal scholars. Unfortunately, the tradition of *ijtihad* was abandoned nearly 500 years ago, though some have seen its revival as one way of bridging the gap.[54]

Addressing the grievances of the community. Violent conflicts arise when a community feels collectively aggrieved; when it believes that its members have been treated unfairly for no reason other than being born in a particular race, religion, linguistic group, or nationality. Such perceptions must be addressed. This would require meaningful actions addressing some of the most vexing hot-button issues that inflame passion among many in the Islamic world. For instance, it would certainly help the cause of peace if solutions could be found in the conflicts that are plaguing Palestine, Iraq, Afghanistan, Kashmir, and Chechnya. It is important to note, however, that no solution to these intractable problems will ever eliminate violence, since there are no universally acceptable solutions to these long-festering battles based on zero-sum claims, where one group's gain must come only at the expense of some other's. However, although the final outcome may not be universally accepted, if the process by which these issues are addressed is seen as fair by a significant majority of the population, peaceful resolutions may yet evolve.

Refraining from playing with fire—people's extreme emotions. It is indeed ironic that many extremist groups around the world were, at times, promoted by national governments as a strategic deterrent to some other force. For instance, the US found it expedient to befriend the religious zealots and to channel their fury against the Soviet occupiers of Afghanistan. Indira Gandhi found Sikh religious extremists to be a good ally against a moderate political party that was about to defeat the Indian Congress Party in a state election. Successive Pakistani governments have supported Islamic militants waging war in India and in Afghanistan. The Saudis have actively promoted religious fanatics as a part of their state policy of exporting Wahhabism. There is evidence to suggest that the Israeli government initially saw Hamas as a counterweight to Arafat and the PLO. In each case, the monster turned against Dr Frankenstein; the Mujahideens and their fanatical allies in Afghanistan turned their guns against the US and the West, Gandhi was assassinated by her Sikh bodyguards, the Saudis are waging an ongoing battle against terrorism from their erstwhile foot soldiers of religious hegemony, and Hamas is the biggest threat to Israeli security. Governments all over the world, therefore, must resist the temptation for such quick solutions, particularly when it comes to supporting groups based on religious fundamentalism.

Dangers of overreacting. Target governments all over the world must understand the aims of the extremists. The causes of the extremist groups are best served when the society becomes polarized. For instance, Hamas routinely stages suicide bombings and other acts designed to create outrage among the Israelis at critical points of the peace process and national elections. In such a situation, the governments and their leaders must resist the temptation to dig into the national anger and mete out collective punishments to the community from which the terrorists have emerged.

Distinguishing among ideologies. I have argued that not all terrorist groups are based on the same ideological fervor, nor do they espouse the same ideological goals. A blanket term such as the "global war on terror" only confuses the issue by seeking "one-size-fits-all" policies. The goals of the nationalistic groups are different from those of the millenarian groups. In the nationalistic struggles, such as in the cases of Israel, Sri Lanka, or India, it may be possible to find a territorial or power-sharing compromise. However, no such solution can be sought while dealing with the millenarian groups such as al-Qaeda. A successful strategy to deal with these groups must come through a much more subtle understanding of their ideologies and finding appropriate responses to counter their appeal among their potential recruits. Similarly, there are groups which are very close to being criminal organizations. Governments must find ways to distinguish among these groups and find appropriate policies to confront them.

From adversaries to stakeholders: promoting self-interest

Since people are not inspired by ideology alone, one of the primary deterrents rests with government's ability to convince its citizens of its ability to provide the best opportunity for their own personal welfare. This can be done in many ways.

Reduction of poverty and income inequality. The forces of globalization are increasingly concentrating income in the hands of the few. Research shows that the middle class acts like the pillar that keeps the integrity of the social structure. The societies that do not enlarge the size of the middle class are destined to experience increased levels of political instability.[55]

Demonstration of ability to provide public goods. Our social contract with our rulers requires that they provide us with public goods, health, education, provision of security, and a rule of law, among others. When a government is unable to provide these, people look to others for these goods. Every successful dissident organization has been able to find firm footing among its support bases by providing public goods. Hamas and Hizbullah began as charitable organizations providing basic healthcare, childcare, education, etc. The volunteers in troubled tribal areas of India promoting Maoism have been able to develop deep political roots by being integrated in the oppressed communities and providing some of the much-needed social services. The reason the paramilitary armies in Iraq became popular among many is because they provided security when the Iraqi military and the occupying US forces failed to do so. The Taliban in Afghanistan similarly enjoyed wide-ranging public support, as they were able to bring back a modicum of law and order after a hugely destructive civil war. Even the most unpopular US government was able to shed a lot of its negative perception among the Pakistani people after its quick humanitarian response following the devastating earthquake in 2005.[56] According to a poll in the immediate aftermath of the delivery of humanitarian assistance, the percentage of Pakistanis with a favorable opinion of the US doubled from 23 percent in May 2005 to more than 46 percent in less than six months. Support for Bin Laden over the same period dropped from 51 percent to just 33 percent. In fact, 78 percent of those surveyed said that American assistance had made them feel more favorably disposed toward the US; even an astonishing 79 percent of those with confidence in bin Laden had a more favorable view of the US because of American earthquake aid. These results provide clear evidence of turning the tides of the toughest public opinion with the demonstration of goodwill.

Reaching political accommodation whenever possible. Violent conflicts with non-state actors are always framed in moral terms. Each side, particularly the governments, proudly proclaims that it does not negotiate. Yet history tells the opposite story. In nearly all cases, where conflict grinds on, both sides are pushed to sit down at the negotiating table. In this test of will it is important to remember one important lesson: there are limits to power when it comes to coercion, particularly in a constitutional democracy. Being based on rules of law, democracies cannot hope to bring order through police and military action alone. Hence, whenever possible, it is best to come to a political compromise with the dissident groups, particularly when there is a broad-based popular support for the groups' stated goals. Conflict in Nicaragua came to an end when the Sandinistas decided to join the democratic process. Similar examples can be found in many parts of the world, including Nepal and India.

Costs of participation

Using law enforcement rather than the military. In fighting terrorism it is most tempting and politically most expedient to look for a quick military victory. During my research for this book, I conducted extensive interviews with terrorism experts, law-enforcement officials, and military and civil intelligence officials from many affected countries. If there was one area where I found a dose of unanimity, it was in their unequivocal support for using the police instead of the military. As one of the experts told me, "after all, at the end of the day, the police officers go back to their homes in the community while the military personnel after an operation go back to their isolated barracks." Terrorism being largely a social problem, the relative effectiveness of the two is never in doubt. Reflecting the same sentiments, Diego Gambetta points out:

When the Italians and the Germans were confronted, respectively, by their Red Brigades and Red Army Faction (Baader Meinhof), they did not lose their nerve, or round up half of the working class, or imprison scores of intellectuals, or suspend civil liberties and democracy. They hit the terrorists hard with better *policing* and effective legal tools.[57]

The military can be effective when it plays a secondary supportive role to police and intelligence services. The use of the military alone in fighting a social phenomenon such as terrorism can indeed be counterproductive.[58] On the other hand, the Indian experience in combating Sikh extremism in Punjab and the Maoists in West Bengal clearly demonstrates the efficacy of using military in a secondary role. In fact, whenever the military has taken the lead, such as in the "Operation Blue Star,"[59] where the Indian Armed Forces forcibly entered the holiest religious site of Sikhism, it only made matters worse by fueling further rebellion.[60]

Using more human intelligence than scientific surveillance. Terrorists wage people-oriented war. From the earliest writings on terrorism and guerrilla warfare, it has been recognized that the terrorists use their ability to melt into the general populace. Therefore its suppression requires infiltration and other forms of surveillance based on human assets.

Torture

Until recently the tyrants had it easy. Ghengis Khan could kill and rape every single person in the conquered land without worrying about its moral implications. Even the colonial British rulers were largely unaccountable for their behavior. In today's world, however, the center of gravity of public morality has shifted. The wanton disregard of codes of ethical conduct often catches up with the perpetrators. The Western world prides itself as nations of rule of law. When stories of the grossest violation of human rights accompany graphic pictures, they assault our sensibilities. These not only shame us but also serve as the biggest recruiting tools for the next generations of young volunteers ready to avenge the past. In an excellent study, Hafez describes the importance of the Abu Ghraib prison scandal and others tales of torture and humiliation as the motivation for suicide bombers in Iraq.[61]

Yet, considering the gravity, the public debate on torture in the US has largely been muted. Perhaps this ambivalence can be understood when faced with the so-called "ticking bomb" question.[62] That is, if we knew that a captured terrorist knows where a weapon of mass destruction is hidden and is going to go off shortly killing untold number of people, would we not want to beat it out of him? When asked, very few of us are willing to remain faithful to the strictest codes of conduct. Yet, this "ultimate" question has a series of imbedded assumptions, which are rarely to be encountered outside a Hollywood studio.

The first assumption is that there is a weapon of mass destruction, which is ready to go off at any moment. Second, that the prisoner is fully aware of its location (and perhaps even the knowledge of how to diffuse it). Third, the captors are absolutely certain of the captive's intentions and his knowledge. Fourth, the only effective way to get at the required information is through torture. When we disentangle the obvious question it demonstrates its improbability. However, acts of terrorism do not have to involve mass killings; it may be about saving a single life of a hostage. Even in such a situation, we need an act of faith to assume that the captured terrorist has all the knowledge to assist us in our attempt to save life. Now, even after we are absolutely certain that all the four conditions are met, the critical question remains: how effective is torture as a tool for getting information?

During my interviews with intelligence officials—including some whose names are often closely associated with torture—I was struck by their near unanimous assertion that torture is an effective tool for gaining critical confessions. I was repeatedly told that when tortured, some become even more obstinate, while others confess and fabricate stories that they think the interrogators want to know. In either case, the value of such responses is in doubt. Yet torture is a part of everyday prison life in many parts of the world, particularly at times of crisis. How then do we account for torture when so many of the experienced officers are skeptical of its worth? Apart from the chance of gaining important information, the answer may once again be found in psychology. In the 1960s psychologist Phillip Zimbardo shocked the world with his series of experiments, known as "prisoners and prison guards."[63] These experiments clearly demonstrated the importance of group thinking, by which randomly selected college students took on the most sadistic persona of the prison guards in charge of their "prisoners." Without a clear leadership from the top, it is perhaps natural for those entrusted with extracting information to engage in the most brutal behavior.[64] Regardless of the psychology, however, there is no doubt that as a countermeasure against terrorism, the tales of torture are perhaps far more injurious to a nation's effort at suppressing terrorism than they are effective.

Facilitating factors

Other than the factors that directly affect the motivations of people to get involved in the politics of mass violence, there are a number of other components of public policy that are important in managing the threats of terrorism. They are as follows:

Multinational approach. Andrew Silke, in discussing counterterrorism policies, brings up an apt analogy from Greek mythology of Hercules fighting the multi-headed serpent monster Hydra.[65] Apart from having many heads, Hydra had one extraordinary power—when one of its heads was struck off two more would spring up. In his adventure, Hercules was accompanied by his nephew Iolaus. As the battle went on, Hercules was on the verge of being defeated. Seeing his uncle in distress, his much weaker nephew grabbed a torch and, every time Hercules cut off one of the heads, Iolaus would sear it with his burning torch and prevent the monster from growing back its heads. Although Hercules was credited with slaying Hydra, he could not have done it without the help of his nephew. This story appropriately serves as a metaphor for US foreign policy. In 1998, an influential blue-ribbon panel on international terrorism was assembled with bipartisan support from Clinton and the Republican Congress. After a year of painstaking work, the US Commission on National Security, 21st Century came to a prophetic conclusion: "America's military superiority will not protect it from hostile attacks on our homeland. Americans will likely die on American soil, possibly in large numbers."[66] Countering threats of international terrorism requires international cooperation. Since in an increasingly interconnected world the effects of instability and violence are not going to be restricted to where they originate, the global community must address some of the broader issues of combating terrorism and present a united front. This must be done not only through covert operations but also by publicly taking a stance against indiscriminate violence, wherever it may take place.

Constricting the life-blood of the terrorist groups by restricting money. Money is the life-blood of any organization, including the ones waging clandestine wars. These funds come from both illegitimate and legitimate sources. Study of terrorist group funding reveals a consistent pattern of fund raising. Some of the funds come from trafficking in drugs, cigarettes, alcohol, etc. Others are raised through small contributions by the domestic constituents as well as the diaspora. Also, it is not unusual for a dissident group to acquire a few extremely wealthy financiers. Laundering money and investing it in legitimate businesses can also raise the necessary resources for terrorist organizations. Finally, many terrorist groups are funded by state sponsorship. Any policy of deterrence of international terrorism must develop a global consensus to stop the flow of funds to the extremist organizations.

Being realistic in expectation. We must know that terrorism cannot be totally prevented, but with time, its attractions may wane. There are many terrorist movements that posed great threats to the global community but that have ultimately become spent forces. As scholars, we must devote much greater effort in understanding the dynamics of their demise. With the advent of technological advances in the areas of communication, transportation, and the ability to enhance the destructive power of the weapons, the ability of future terrorist groups to bring death and destruction is going to increase exponentially. Furthermore, my study indicates that terrorist groups are able to achieve their political goals only when the larger community finds the cost of confronting them to be unacceptably high. This is typically the case when a nation goes over its border in order to colonize another nation or in order to extend its political and military hegemony. Powerful nations would do well to keep this important lesson in mind.

In sum: the price of fighting terrorism

Terrorism is spawned by the tension between individual freedom and collect-ive obligation, between private initiative and public purpose, and between our brightest hopes and darkest fears. In the final analysis terrorism reflects the fundamental conflict that defines us as social beings. As a part of our social lives, we can never eradicate the threat of terrorism, but similar to all other threats, from the spread of pandemic to earthquake and tsunami, we can manage its worst menace.

Terrorism, by its very nature, is a mixture of violence and theater. It accomplishes its immediate goal by setting a time-honored trap. This trap is for an organized society to overreact. The government of the target state responds predictably, particularly when it comes to international terrorism. Facing unexpected death and destruction perpetrated by foreign nationals—however small compared to other calamities of life—nations all over the world experience something akin to a collective post-traumatic stress syn-drome. The made-for-television violence, magnified by the media, deepens our collective sense of insecurity. In this condition of national paranoia, politicians vie for being the most hawkish against the threat. In the face of such a threat no price seems high enough. Although the cost of counter-terrorism varies from the moral consideration of killing innocent civilians as a part of collateral damage to the suspension of some of the most cherished rights of the individual, even the financial costs of overreaction from a strictly economic perspective seem overwhelming.

Facing an external threat, nations have always behaved in predictable ways. The assassination of the Austrian Archduke by a Serbian terrorist plunged the entire world into a catastrophic war just the same way as the attacks of 9/11 have created a global crisis, when the US invaded Iraq as a part of a broader "war on terror." Similarly, responding to the kidnapping of two of its soldiers by Hizbullah, Israel's war in Lebanon, for a while, seemed to spiral uncontrollably. The long-term implications of these actions are yet to be fully realized or even understood.

Any action to counter the threat of terrorism often carries a huge price tag. In the aftermath of the 9/11 attacks the sole superpower quickly decided to invade Afghanistan and Iraq, attempting to punish the guilty and protect the American public from future attacks. In the process the costs of these and other counterterrorist endeavors have piled up to an unprecedented level. According to the Congressional Research Service (2007), the war effort itself has had a price tag of $510 billion so far. The money has been approved by Congress for military operations, base security, reconstruction, foreign aid, embassy costs, and veterans' healthcare for the three operations initiated since the 9/11 attacks.[67]

To this astronomical sum, we must add the costs of homeland security undertaken not only by the federal government but also by various state governments and even local governments. For instance, New York City, the prime target of the attacks, has developed its own security force at a cost of millions of dollars.

However, these costs are just the beginning. The heightened sense of insecurity in the US is spilling over on its borders on both sides of the country. Increased restrictions at the borders are costing billions in trade with Mexico and Canada, the biggest trade partner of the US. The fear of illegal immigrants is currently sweeping the country. Alarmists are claiming that a totally sealed border is essential as a safeguard against international terrorism, despite the fact there are few reported cases in North America or Europe where illegal immigrants have taken part in terrorist attacks. Yet this fear is propelling the US to embark on the construction of a wall sealing its border with Mexico. When asked about the price of this monumental project, an influential lawmaker commented, "Whatever it costs." As extremism is producing extremism, xenophobia is on the rise all over the world.

If increased poverty and indignation make a volatile mix, our overreaction all over the world can only make us less secure in the long run. Indeed the cost of overreaction is adding up to much more than is commonly understood. The possibility of disruption in oil supply is contributing to its rise in price. It is not only impacting those who can afford it the least, but by transferring money to the most volatile regions of the world, where much of the oil is produced, it is propping up corrupt dictators, demagogues, and some of the most ardent benefactors of international terrorism.

These costs, however arduous, are not one-time expenditures. As governments attempt to punish the perpetrators they bring death and misery to the population; these, in turn, spawn more acts of terrorism. This is not to say that the threats of terrorism to global security are not real. The problem is that, facing horrific acts of violence, we often lose our perspective and become eager to assume any cost, any consequence of our impulsive actions.

The price of fighting terrorism includes compromise of some of our most cherished values. The pictures of tortured prisoners in the prisons of Abu Ghraib and Guantanamo Bay have done more damage to the image of the US around the globe than anything the terrorists could have inflicted. Facing the unknown threats of another devastating attack, the US public was all too eager to dispense with many of their fundamental rights, which had defined the country to the outside world. The costs of these losses are impossible to measure in monetary terms.

In this book I have argued that the roots of most conflicts can be traced to the distant past. However, that does not mean that longstanding conflicts cannot be ended. It is often fashionable to talk about ancient hatred, yet there is no reason to believe that we are destined to keep the fire of enmity alive forever. Walking around in war-ravaged Europe sixty years ago, a blink of an eye in the millennia-long history of continuing acrimony, could anyone have predicted the formation of the European Union? Standing in front of the burning White House in 1812, how many would have anticipated the cross-Atlantic love-fest that has characterized for the most part the

Anglo-American relationship at least since the beginning of the Lend-Lease program? In fact, there is nothing eternal about ancient hatred. Humans have always drawn boundaries to define who they are and who their enemies are. These boundaries have never remained etched in stone. Up until the medieval times, societies centered around small geographic spaces along the lines of tribes, clans, and families. As we come closer to each other through improved technologies of transportation and communication, it is likely that the borders of our imaginary communities are expanding, often transgressing political borders of nation states. Some of these expanded identities are uniting us like nothing before, while others are polarizing with unequal ferocity.

I began this book with a personal narrative. Therefore, it may not be inappropriate to end it on a similar note. In 2003 I had the honor of being invited to a panel discussion hosted by Nobel Peace Prize winner Eli Wiesel. The title of the panel was "Fighting Terrorism for Humanity."[68] Wiesel challenged the panelists by asking if it was possible to fight terrorism *with* humanity. At first blush, the simple question raised by the sagacious gentleman of peace may appear to be too dreamy, the musing of an impractical peacenik. However, a closer look at the intellectual gauntlet thrown down by Wiesel reveals its profound nature. In the final analysis, the struggle against terrorism is a contest for the hearts and minds of the people. In this contest, if the West is going to prevail, it cannot do so by dispensing with its most cherished values of tolerance, individual freedom, and adherence to the rule of law. In our quest for victory it seems important for us to know what we are fighting against, but it is even more important to keep in mind what we are fighting for.

Appendix A

Trade-off between interests of the individual and the collective: an expanded assumption of rationality

My theoretical arguments can be presented with the help of the standard methodological tools of microeconomics. I have argued that belonging to a group and acting on its welfare is just as fundamental to human rationality as the pursuit of self-interest. By combining these two motivations, I posit that an individual's actions are not only the outcomes of an actor's self-interest—as argued by the proponents of neoclassical economics and the public-choice school of social science—but are also derived from a distinct utility obtained from furthering the welfare of the group in which the individual actor claims his/her membership. Within this framework, therefore, a rational actor is not a single-dimensional self-utility maximizer but also one who seeks a balance between the conflicting demands of individual interest and community wellbeing.

For this model, let us hypothesize that private goods are produced by individual effort, while collective goods are produced as a result of joint effort through collective movements. The individual efforts reflect an actor's self-utility, whereas joint actions are functions of the actor's strength of collective identity. This trade-off is depicted in Figure A.1, where the vertical axis measures the utility goods derived from private goods, such as personal income, power, and rectitude. The horizontal axis measures the amount of utility that an actor derives by contributing to the procurement of collective goods (e.g., end of discrimination, gaining of national independence, establish of a society based on a specific religious vision). The indifference curves measure the relative utilities obtained by an actor by engaging in the two kinds of activities. Budget line (I) measures the constraint of time that an individual must allocate between the two endeavors. In this diagram, an individual, *ceteris paribus*, attains the point of equilibrium—the ideal mix between the pursuit of self-interest producing goods and collective-utility producing goods—by spending S1 amount of time toward attainment of private goods and C1 amount of time for collective goods.

The budget line depicts the combination of time devoted to the two kinds of activities. Thus, a totally self-absorbed person might devote the entire day (100 percent of the time, shown as the point of intersection between the

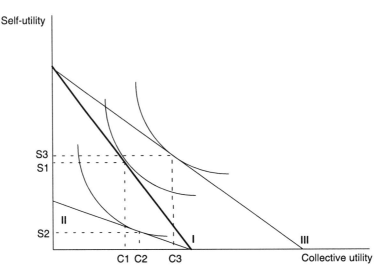

Figure A.1 Self-utility and collective utility: effects of changes in political environment.

budget line and the vertical axis) in the pursuit of private goods, whereas another person, being totally devoted to the group, would pursue its welfare every waking hour of the day.[1]

The slope of the budget line shows the amount of the two goods an actor can produce by working the total available working hours. The conditions which may alter this slope depend on the following factors:

Changes in economic opportunities. The budget line measures the "opportunity cost" of time. That is, it shows how much an individual can expect to produce one good by giving up another. However, this budget constraint is not fixed over time and can have shifts based on changed sociopolitical and economic conditions. That is, it will move according to the relative "cost" of procuring the two goods. For instance, if, due to better economic conditions, an actor is able to generate more private goods by devoting the same amount of time as before (the cost of private goods going down), the budget curve will register an upward shift along the vertical axis. If, on the other hand, economic conditions deteriorate or the actor faces unemployment, the amount of private goods than an actor can achieve will be truncated. This situation is being depicted in Figure A.1, where the budget line dips down along the vertical axis. I have shown this shift with budget line (II). As a result of this changed economic condition, even though the opportunities for producing collective goods do not go up (the government maintains strict law and order), the reduced economic opportunity cost will produce a higher level of political protests and other forms of collective action to the changed level of C2. Thus, if the nation experiences an economic decline the truncated economic opportunities will allow people to devote more time in the pursuit of collective goods. This greater engagement in collective action may show up as increased political protest or terrorism.

In contrast, if economic opportunities improve, an individual will be able to make more goods, which create private (self-interest) goods. Therefore, the opportunity cost of resources to divert to the pursuit of collective goods will go up. This will cause an actor to devote more time to the production of private goods. In order to keep the diagram simple, this changed budget line is not shown. However, by following the same logic, this shift will cause the actor to neglect the pursuit of collective goods and, instead, to strive harder to achieve private goods. In these cases, citizens might accept lack of individual freedom, corruption and even gross violations of human rights as they trade those collective goods for personal economic wellbeing.

Changes in political opportunities. Changes in political opportunities can also alter people's perception of their ability to achieve a proper mix of the two goods. For instance, if the central government weakens from war or some other natural or man-made catastrophe, the lessening of the government's coercive capabilities may cause a bandwagon effect. When the fear of retribution goes down, people feel free to express their disaffection for an established political system. In Figure A.1, this changed attitude causes the budget line (I) to shift to the right to (III). This shift will be reflected in a rapid increase in participation in collective actions by the actor.

Political opportunities can also be determined by the government's attitude toward repression of views of its political opponents. For instance, if the government decides to crack down on the dissidents, it can truly truncate the budget line, thereby causing the prospective participants to significantly scale back their involvement, and drive a wedge between their public pronouncements and private views. Once again, in order to keep the diagram clean, I have not shown it in Figure A.1.

Shift in the relative preference. The relative weight that an actor imputes between the two competing time-consuming efforts determines the direction of the indifference maps. In a standard economic argument this relative weight is treated as given. It is based on an actor's individual taste and preference. However, I argue that the relative preference is based on the strength of an actor's collective identity, which is contextual and shaped by the political leaders and the external environment. The emergence of a new leader may increase an individual's preference for collective goods. For instance, the rise of Osama bin Laden has inspired many to join violent Islamic organizations from many parts of the Islamic world.

The relative preferences may also change as a result of an external event. For instance, the sight of the 9/11 attacks caused many in the US to sign up for military duty despite the increased possibility of death and injury in the battlefield. In such situations, an actor would prefer a different mix of the two goods, which will be shown as a change in direction of the vector of the

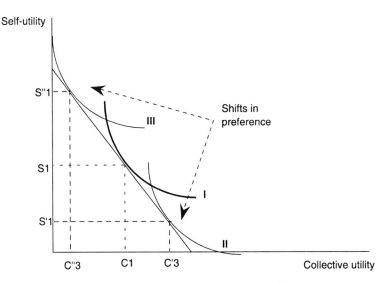

Figure A.2 Self-utility and collective utility: effects of leadership.

indifference maps. Figure A.2 depicts this situation. As can be seen in Figure A.2, a change in the relative preference for collective goods would cause the indifference map to shift to the right (II); people place more emphasis on the pursuit of collective goods by becoming political activist of all sorts, from freedom riders to urban guerrillas.

Appendix B

Terrorism and organized crime: a formal model

At first blush, terrorist groups and organized crime seem very much alike. However, despite their many similarities the fundamental distinction between the two rests with their motivations. A terrorist organization's primary objective is political, such as a change in the government, independence for a part of a country, or the establishment of a new social order based on a certain political or religious view. By nature, these are public goods. If these goals are attained, the benefits emanating from them flow to every member of a community regardless of participation. In contrast, a criminal gang is not interested in attaining political goods. Instead, they aim for quasi-public goods (or "common pooled resources"), which benefit only the members of the organization. This is an important distinction and, for this reason, Dishman correctly points out that "drug barons and revolutionary leaders do not walk the same path to success."[1]

We hypothesize that similar to an individual actor, discussed in Appendix A, any group can participate in two kinds of activities. The first aims at procuring public goods, benefiting the entire community and the second, quasi-public goods, promoting the welfare of only the members of the group. We further assume that public goods are achieved through altruistic acts of terrorism, whereas the quasi-public goods are acquired by taking part in criminal activities.

$$\text{Max } U = \pi_p(P) + \pi_q(Q) \tag{1}$$

Where U = Utility derived by a group by engaging in the two types of activities

P = Public goods (benefits to the entire community regardless of participation)

Q = Quasi-public goods (benefits to the group members and its leadership)

π_p = Relative weight placed by the organization in achieving public goods (P)

π_q = Relative weight placed by the organization in achieving quasi-public goods (Q)

Since a group can engage in procuring either a public or a quasi-public good, we write: $\pi_p + \pi_q = 1$

The relative preference ($\tilde{\omega}$) for the two goods determines the ideological orientation of the group:

$$\tilde{\omega} = \frac{\mu_p}{\mu_q}$$

Since the two kinds of organizations are distinguished by their relative need to procure public goods, we can see that for a politically motivated dissident organization, $\pi_p > \pi_q > .5$. Similarly, for a criminal organization, the preferences are reversed, $\mu_q > \mu_p > .5$. As we have seen in Chapter 4, not all terrorist organizations are the same in the putative relative importance they place on ideological goals. While groups like al-Qaeda and Hamas operate from a strong ideological position, others, such as the Abu Sayyaf in the Philippines, tend to be much more interested in making money for their core membership. Thus, those rare groups that are purely ideological will have weights of $\pi_p = 1; \pi_q = 0$. However, for primarily criminal groups $\pi_p < \pi_q$ and those which are purely criminal, $\pi_p = 0; \pi_q = 1$. And for those groups that operate from mixed motives the relative weights for the two are greater than 0. Since it is impossible to be a pure altruist,[2] we can conjecture that while terrorist organizations would operate from a mixed motive ($1 > \pi_p > .5$), for most criminal groups such confusion of objectives are rarely present. The relative strength of this ideological position of a terrorist group reflects the importance it places on its activities. Thus, while engaging in criminal activities may be less risky and more remunerative (especially for the core group members), in choosing the appropriate mix, the leadership must weigh in the risks of loss of political legitimacy as a result of their close association with criminal activities.

When a group engages in extra-legal activities, it risks being apprehended and punished (C). The parameters of this cost function are externally given to the terrorist groups as a result of deliberate public policies adopted by the governmental authorities and implemented by the law-enforcement agencies and the military. I further assume that a group has the capability ($\bar{C}$) to absorb a finite amount of cost incurred as a result of their extra-legal activities.[3] This cost figure incorporates the negative sanctions imposed by the state authorities.

Thus, for the two activities, a group faces the total absorbable cost (TC) of:

$$TC = c_p P + c_q Q = \bar{C} \tag{2}$$

Based on the previous discussion, we can write the maximand as:

$$\text{Max } U = \pi_p P + \pi_q Q + \lambda(\bar{C} - c_p P - c_q Q)$$

The first order condition shows preference for the two activities:

$$\frac{\delta U}{\delta P} = \pi_p - \lambda c_p = 0 \tag{3}$$

and,

$$\frac{\delta U}{\delta Q} = \pi_q - \lambda C_q = 0 \tag{4}$$

This model yields the familiar maximization principle of marginal utility from an activity being equal to its marginal cost. However, this simple formulation allows us to develop a number of important hypotheses, which can help us understand the complex findings of various case studies discussed in Chapter 7.

The geometric version of the model is shown in Figure B.1. In this diagram, the vertical axis measures the utility that a group derives from obtaining public goods, while the horizontal axis indicates the utility of quasi-public goods. The 45-degree line shows an equal preference (.5) for the two goods. Any position above this line implies that a group derives a greater utility from achieving a unit of public goods than from a unit of quasi-public good, while the positions below show the opposite. We may recall that we assume that a group obtains public goods through terrorist activities and quasi-public goods by being

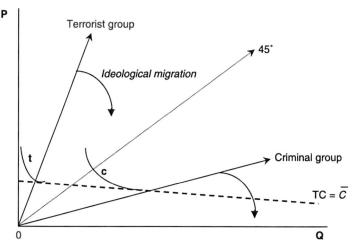

Figure B.1 Transformation of groups.

engaged in criminal endeavors. Thus, a hypothetical terrorist group will typically demonstrate a position shown by the indifference map (t). In contrast, a criminal organization will choose its optimal mix along the indifference map (c).

The dashed line TC is analogous to a budget constraint, within which a group must choose a combination of the two activities in order to maximize its utility. We may note that the slope of the cost curve presupposes a higher cost imposed by the state for engaging in terrorist activities.

Based on the presented model, we can conclude that for a terrorist organization the preference for collective good over quasi-public good gets weaker as $\tilde{\omega} \to .5$. If it becomes lower than .5, then it is no longer a political organization. We can assume that this ratio is the outcome of a decision taken by the leadership of the organization.

From the structure of the model it is clear that since the cost of participation in a terrorist activity is higher than that of engaging in ordinary criminal activity, given the financial need of a organization to sustain its enterprise, it must recruit those who are deft at criminal activities. Therefore, a terrorist organization will always have the tendency to veer off toward criminality for its own sake. Only a strong leadership within the organization can prevent it from its metamorphosis.

In contrast, a criminal organization having a lower value of $\tilde{\omega}$, and a higher price tag for getting involved in political activity will be much more reluctant to cooperate with a known terrorist organization. Therefore, if the two develop any cooperative arrangement, it will be episodic rather than sustained.

Given the differences in their relative preferences, a terrorist organization will be far more likely to develop in-house capabilities for raising money through illegal means than working in close cooperation with an organized crime group.

These calculations may change if the central government becomes weak and, in extreme cases, becomes a failed state or, within a relatively strong political, military, and law-enforcement capability, develops "brown spots" of lawless areas. In such cases, the cost differential between the two kinds of activities would disappear and, unless the dissident leaders can enforce discipline, the distinction between the two groups is likely to disappear.

Notes

Preface

1 Setting a long family tradition to follow this former terrorist, Nagen Sengupta went to England for higher studies after a mistrial, where a British judge acquitted him due to police misconduct. He returned home to join the "establishment" and became the director of one of the country's best-known research institutes. In a twist of fate, he was befriended by Lord Lytton, Governor of Bengal. After their meeting, in 1925 Lytton announced sweeping legislation and arrested over 150 leaders of the various anarchist and other terrorist groups. Suddenly, in the eyes of many of his countrymen, the hero became a traitor, as the Bengali newspapers dubbed Sengupta "Lytton's buddy."

1 Introduction

1 For evidence of shifting emphasis on terrorism as a part of the traditional international relations (IR) curriculum within the discipline of political science, see Maliniak *et al.* (2007).
2 Eckstein (1964: 1).
3 It should be noted that this impressive number of publications is but a fraction of what has been written on the subject of terrorism, since I have searched specifically with a single term "terrorism." If the search was expanded to include "terror," "insurgency" or any number of other terms, the total number would balloon. Moreover, this list only includes the published books and does not consider articles written in scholarly journals, newspapers, and magazines.
4 Although I am calling it "new," I have proposed this expanded assumption of human rationality in a number of books and articles. See, for instance, Gupta (1990, 2001a).
5 As we will see below, the goals of the original IRA were much more religious in nature and evolved over time.
6 Rapoport (2006).
7 Ibid.: 16.
8 See Begin (1951).
9 Horgan (2005: 86, emphasis in original).
10 Rapoport (2006: 16).
11 Schama (1989).
12 Schama (1989).
13 Schmid and Jongman (1988).
14 Ibid.
15 See Naylor (1997: 6; 2002: 14–18) and Reuter (1983: 75).
16 Ruby (2002: 10).

17 See Rummel (1994).
18 See Gambetta (1993); Stanley (1996); Varese (2001); Volkov (2000, 2002); Jamieson (2005).
19 The concept of public goods was introduced by Samuelson (1965) and public goods are generally defined with two important attributes: *excludability* and *exhaustibility*. Public goods are for the enjoyment of every member of the community, regardless of their level of involvement in the effort at procuring these goods. Thus, if tax dollars pay for clean air, a destitute person who does not pay any taxes is free to enjoy the benefits of a clean environment. Second, the benefits of public goods do not get exhausted with the increase in the number of users. Therefore, when a new child is born, nobody will worry about her share of the clean air (for further information, see Baumol and Blinder, 1985: 543–544).
20 See Hutt (2004: 6–7).
21 See Whelpton (2005).
22 Tilly (2004: 1, emphases in original).

2 Theories of the origins of movements

1 See Atran (2003).
2 A quick Google search by "9/11" and "conspiracy" yields 2.7 million hits.
3 Maleckova (2005).
4 Jai (2001).
5 Tyson (2001).
6 Bammel and Moule (1984). It is interesting to note at this point that many books on terrorism make obligatory references to the Sicarii as examples of ancient terrorists. Along with the Sicarii and the Jewish zealots, following the influential work by Rapoport (1984), the authors also mention the "Thugs" in India and the "Assassins" in the Middle East. While the Sicarii and the Assassins (Lewis, 1968) may be considered as "terrorists," since they were motivated by causing political changes, the Thugs were distinctly non-political and engaged in simple banditry as a result of pervasive poverty in eighteenth-century India (Dash 2005; van Woerkens 2002).
7 See, for example, Richard Cohen (2002).
8 Juergensmeyer (2000).
9 Hadith Al-Tirmidhi in the Book of Sunah volume IV, chapters on The Features of Paradise as described by the Messenger of Allah, chapter 21, About the Smallest Reward for the People of Paradise. The same Hadith is also quoted by Ibn Kathir in his Koranic commentary (Tafsir) of Surah Al-Rahman: "The Prophet Muhammad was heard saying: 'The smallest reward for the people of paradise is an abode where there are 80,000 servants and 72 wives, over which stands a dome decorated with pearls, aquamarine, and ruby, as wide as the distance from Al-Jabiyah [a Damascus suburb] to Sanaʿ [Yemen].' "
10 See Konet (2001); Morgan (2002).
11 The reflex reaction to characterize acts of politically motivated violence as insane cuts across culture and geography. After the 2002 bombings of nightclubs in Bali, Indonesia, which killed over 200 people, the local Chief of Police General Made Pastika's instant reaction was "these must be crazy people" (BBC, "Third World War: Al Qaeda," broadcast on 24 February 2004, quoted in Horgan 2005: 47).
12 See Post (2005); Merari (2005); Horgan (2005).
13 See Hafez (2006); Gunning (2007).
14 See Bloom (2005); Narayan Swami (1994); O'Duffy (2007).
15 See Ergil (2007).
16 See Sen (1999a).
17 See Sen (1999b).

18 See Woodward (2002, 2006).
19 See Zakaria (2003).
20 See Rapoport (1977, 1984).
21 See Sandler *et al.* (1983) and Sandler and Lapan (1988).
22 See Crenshaw (1981, 1985, 1986).
23 The Internet database JSTOR records only a total of 16 articles in the top political science, sociology, and economic journals between 1940 and 1980 with "terrorism" in their title.
24 See, for example, Weinberg *et al.* (2004); Victoroff (2005); Bjorgo (2005).
25 Laqueur (1977).
26 Skocpol (1979).
27 Rapoport (1977, 1984, 2005).
28 Wilkinson (1971, 1974, 1977, 1981).
29 Jenkins (1975).
30 Schmid and de Graaf (1982).
31 Hoffman (1998).
32 Gunaratna (2002).
33 Stern (1999, 2003a).
34 See, for example, Miller (1996); Napoleoni (2003, 2005); Hassan (2001); Harris (2007).
35 Clarke (2004, 2007).
36 For an excellent elucidation of the difference between a historian's use of a rule and a scientist's use of paradigms, see Kuhn (1970: 43–51).
37 Freud (1930).
38 The term "dynamics" was borrowed from nineteenth-century physics, "in which the flow of mental and libidinal energy is deterministically expressed, repressed, or discharged" Victoroff (2005: 22). For an excellent discussion of the various psychological theories and evaluation of their analyses, see Horgan (2005).
39 Taylor (1988: 140).
40 See Taylor (1988).
41 See Ferracuti and Bruno (1981); Kent and Nicholls (1977); Olsson (1988); Pearlstein (1991); Turco (1987); Kellen (1979).
42 Post (1993); Robins and Post (1997); Post (2005); Post (2006); see also Wolfenstein (1967); Feuer (1969).
43 Hacker (1976); Cooper (1977).
44 The most famous case of mental insanity defense was the 1981 assassination attempt on President Ronald Reagan by John Hinckley, Jr.
45 See Victoroff (2005: 12–13).
46 Crenshaw (1981); Ferracuti (1982); Reich (1998); Silke (1998); Merari (1998); Horgan (2003, 2005).
47 Post (1995); Schneider and Post (2003).
48 Russell and Miller (1983); Clark (1983); Weinberg and Eubank (1987); Strenz (1988); Handler (1990); Post (1997); Robins and Post (1997); Hassan (2001); Pedahzur *et al.* (2003); Horgan (2003); Sageman (2004).
49 See Kohut (1972, 1978).
50 Pearlstein (1991).
51 Akhtar (1999); Crayton (1983); Shaw (1986); Wallerstein (1995).
52 Victoroff (2005: 23); see also Lazek (1995).
53 See Sarraj (2002).
54 Sears *et al.* (1998: 1).
55 Aristole (1962).
56 See Dollard *et al.* (1939).
57 Adorno *et al.* (1950).
58 Erikson (1956).

59 See Sherif (1935, 1966).
60 Sherif and Hovland (1961).
61 See Tajfel (1970, 1981, 1982).
62 Post (1997, 1998, 2004); Robins and Post (1997). See also Volkan (1988, 2004a, 2004b).
63 See for example Volkan (1988, 2004a).
64 See Bandura (1973, 1998).
65 Stern (2000).
66 Damasio (1994).
67 Damasio (1994: 51).
68 In the area of political decision-making, see Marcus *et al.* (2000). For an example of more direct understanding of the brain in economic decisions, see Underhill (2000).
69 The Marxist concept of alienation has given birth to an extremely rich literarure. See for instance Seeman (1959); Dean (1961); Regin (1969); Schacht (1970); Schwartz (1973); Guthrie and Tanco (1980).
70 Mao (1961).
71 Lenin (1969).
72 Loveman and Davies (1985).
73 Marighela (1985).
74 Banerjee (1980); Ray (2002).
75 For an excellent discussion of Max Weber's contribution toward the constructivist theory, see Jim Stone (1995: 396).
76 See, for example, Epstein (1958); Furnivall (1944); Geertz (1963); Gordon (1964); Isaacs (1974); Naroll (1964); Mitchell (1956).
77 Rex (1995).
78 Kuper (1969).
79 Barth (1970); Glazer and Moynihan (1975).
80 Lake and Rothchild (1998).
81 Jackson and Penrose (1993); Wendt (2004).
82 Durkheim (1933).
83 Newman (1991: 454).
84 See Lemert (2007) for one of the latest evaluations of Durkheim's theory of how the process of modernization creates conflict in a society.
85 Barber (1995).
86 Deutsch (1953).
87 Smelser (1963).
88 Lipset (1963).
89 See Huntington (1965).
90 Davies (1962).
91 Feierabend and Feierabend (1966, 1972).
92 Gurr (1970).
93 Dollard *et al.* (1939).
94 Banks and Textor (1963); Banks (1971); Feierabend *et al.* (1969); Taylor and Hudson (1973); Taylor and Jodice (1982).
95 Russell and Miller (1978); Horgan (2005); Post (2003).
96 Sageman (2004).
97 Berrebi (2003); Sageman (2004).
98 Hibbs (1973); Gupta (1990); Krueger and Maleckova (2003); Sandler and Enders (2004); Arce and Sandler (2005).
99 Kaplan (1994); Homer-Dixon (1999); Collier and Sambanis (2005).
100 Fearon and Laitin (2003).
101 O'Leary and Tirman (2007: 11).
102 Farber (1968); Shneidman (1985, 1999); Merari (1990); Sageman (2004).

103 Sarraj (2002).
104 Hibbs (1973), Venieris and Gupta (1983), and Muller (1985) attempted to correlate political violence with inequality in income. See also Russett (1964); Paige (1970); Paranzino (1972); Midlarsky (1982); Midlarsky and Roberts (1985); Seligson (1966).
105 Gupta (1990).
106 Tilly (1978, 1993); Tarrow (1994); McAdam (1982); McAdam *et al.* (1997).
107 Varshney (2002).
108 The seminal work in this area is found in Max Weber's analysis of Protestant work ethics.
109 For a more detailed discussion of this process, see Gupta (2001a).
110 Edgeworth (1881: 16).
111 It would, of course, be a colossal mistake to portray Adam Smith as being oblivious to the cultural, historical, and moral aspects of human nature. His much less studied book *The Theory of Moral Sentiments*, written nearly a decade prior to *The Wealth of Nations*, proposes a fuller set of motivations. For a brilliant discussion of Adam Smith's work, see Sen (1977).
112 Redman (1993) argues that the link between the two is mostly superficial.
113 See Hetherington (1983). Hetherington also points out that Newton himself became involved with economics and in 1717 established the first monetary rating for gold, set at approximately 85 shillings per ounce. The establishment of such a benchmark greatly aided the later development of the measures of inflation.
114 It is interesting to note that while Adam Smith offered his famously reductionistic view of human nature, in *The Theories of Moral Sentiments* he expresses a much wider view. In it Smith argued that human behavior was determined by what he called the "passions" (e.g., sex, hunger, fear, and anger) and the "impartial spectator." This impartial spectator (a "moral hector looking over the shoulder of the economic man": Grampp 1948: 317) helps people get over their short-term impulses. This impartial spectator includes, among others, "self-denial": Smith, (1759 [1976]: 26). For an excellent discussion of the complex view of the economic man, see Ashraf *et al.* (2005) and Evensky (2005).
115 Stigler and Becker (1977).
116 Popper (1960).
117 See Downs (1957). And for a simple explanation, see Shepsley and Bonchek (1997) in political science. See Oberschall (1973) for an example of early use of rational-choice theory in sociology.
118 Stigler and Becker (1977: 89).
119 For an excellent early discussion of this hegemonic influence of neoclassical economics, see Hirschleifer (1985). For one of the latest, see Ruttan (2002).
120 Downs (1957)
121 Lichbach (1995).
122 Chong (1991); Kydd and Walter (2002).
123 The literature on the use of "rational actor" model to political rebellion is voluminous. I am mentioning only a few representative ones. See, for instance, Stohl (2003). See Morrow (1997) on international conflict.
124 For one of the best explanations of game theory, see Dixit and Nalebuff (1991). For a much more working explanation of game theory and decision-making under uncertain condition, see Gupta (2001b), Shepsley and Bonchek (1997).

3 Selfish altruist: modeling the mind of a terrorist

1 Sen (2006: 17).
2 Kellen (1984: 10), quoted in Hoffman (1998: 43).
3 Foucault (1970: xi).
4 Ibid.: xxiii.
5 See Durant (1950).
6 See Smith (1995).
7 C.B. Macpherson (1962: 3). Macpherson calls this "possessive individualism."
8 Dawkins (1979).
9 See Gould (1990, 1994) for an excellent account of this misunderstanding of the Darwinian theory of evolution.
10 Spencer (1879).
11 For a historical explanation of Social Darwinism in the US, see Hofstader (1944). And for its development in Europe, see Jones (1980).
12 See, for example, Lichbach (1995).
13 See, for example, Chong (1991); Kydd and Walter (2002).
14 See, for example, Stohl (2005).
15 The list of well-known economists offering blistering criticism of their own discipline, in general, and its underlying assumption, in particular, is indeed long. See, for example, Robinson (1962); Hahn (1970); Gordon (1971); Johnson (1971); Kornai (1971, 1985); Phelps-Brown (1972); Ward (1972); Heller (1975); Latsis (1976); Schelling (1978); Elster (1979a, 1979b, 1983); Georgescu-Roegan (1979); Hahn and Hollis (1979); Simon (1979); Blaug (1980); Bell and Kristol (1981); Dyke (1981); Pitt (1981); Nelson and Winter (1982); Hicks (1983); Akerlof (1984); Matthews (1984); Das Gupta (1985); Helm (1984, 1985); McClosky (1985); Solow (1986); Steedman and Kraus (1986); Woo (1986); Bowles (1998).
16 Dahl (1961: 763).
17 Sen (1987: 16).
18 Marcuse (1964).
19 Olson (1968).
20 Samuelson (1954).
21 The characteristic "exhaustibility" is also frequently called non-rivalrous.
22 See Baumol and Blinder (1985: 543–544).
23 Mueller (1979: 146).
24 Ostrom (1998: 1).
25 Hirschman (1971: 5).
26 Tullock (1971).
27 Lichbach (1998).
28 *New Webster's Dictionary of the English Language*, Deluxe Encyclopedic Edition, 1981, p. 31.
29 Andreoni (1989, 1990).
30 Rose-Ackerman (1996).
31 See, for example, Rose-Ackerman (1996).
32 Schuessler (2000: 4).
33 Olson (1968: 161–162). Notice that Olson calls this behavior "nonrational or irrational," which is in the strict sense of the narrow definition of economic rationality.
34 Fiorina (1990: 334).
35 Ostrom (1998: 9).
36 Hirschleifer (1985).
37 Becker (1976). See also, for instance, Grossbard-Schtman (1993). See also Grossbard-Schtman and Clague (2002).

38 Friedman (1953: 3).
39 Friedman's bold assertions helped create a lively debate in epistemology, known as the "F-Twisted theory" (F—after Friedman). For an excellent perspective, see Blaug (1980) and Musgrave (1981).
40 Lichbach (1997: 95).
41 Ostrom (1998: 9).
42 Rose-Ackerman (1996: 701).
43 Ostrom (1998).
44 Becker (1996: 7).
45 Becker and Stigler (1977).
46 See Satz and Ferejon (1994).
47 Lichbach (1997: 95).
48 Gupta (1987; 1990; 2001a; 2002; 2005); Gupta and Singh (1992); Gupta *et al.* (1997); Bandyopadhyay and Gupta (2002).
49 Kuhn (1970: 10) defines "normal science" as "research firmly based upon one or more past scientific achievements, achievements that some particular scientific community acknowledges for a time as supplying the foundation for its further practice."
50 Becker (1996).
51 Wade (2007).
52 Goodall (1986, 1990).
53 de Waal (2006).
54 de Waal (1996); Fehr and Fishbacher (2003); Camerer and Fehr (2006).
55 Wilson (1975).
56 Hauser (2006).
57 Quoted in Hafez (2006: 43).
58 During one of my trips to India, I met a father whose activist son went to a violence-filled tribal area and was killed. The father told me that when he warned his son of the dangers, he replied: "I know the risks. But tell me father, if you don't let me go, and you think it is important that we do something about these problems, whose son would you send in my place?"
59 Darwin (1859: 166).
60 See Sober and Wilson (1998: 26).
61 Darwin (1859: 166).
62 Wyne-Edwards (1962: 20).
63 Maslow (1968).
64 Tajfel (1970, 1978, 1981, 1982).
65 Kahneman (1973); Kahneman *et al.* (1982); Kahneman and Tversky (1984).
66 Bandura (1973, 1998).
67 It is interesting to note that National Public Radio's solicitations for donations stress the fact that "paying for something you like is the *right thing to do.*" The call to fulfill social obligation seem to work effectively for the organization, dependent on voluntary contributions.
68 An incomplete list of this burgeoning field would include Sweetser and Fauconnier (1996) in cognitive science; Entman (1993), Lakoff (1996), and Capella and Jamieson (1997) in communications studies; Emerson (1972) in psychology; MacCaffery *et al.* (1995) in law; Chong (1996) and Druckman (1999) in political science; Snow and Benford (1992) in mass movements; Gamson and Modigliani (1987) and Ekeh (1974) in sociology.
69 London (1970); Baron (1995, 1996); Carroll and Fernandez (2007).
70 Monroe (1996).
71 Avalos (2005).
72 Konet (2001); Morgan (2002).
73 Popper (1960: 16–17).

74 Gupta *et al.* (1997). Also, Gupta (1990) used the index of ethnolinguistic factionalism (Taylor and Jodice 1982) as a surrogate for the strength of collective identity.
75 Gupta (2001a).
76 See cultural anthropologist Clifford Geertz (1963). See also Isaacs (1974).
77 See Smith (1983). See also Rex (1995), Nagata (1981).
78 Mack (1984).
79 See Robins and Post (1997); Post (2003).
80 Also see Volkan (2004a, 2004b).
81 Anderson (2003).
82 For this reason, unlike ascriptive groups, people join adoptive groups later in their lives. However, sometimes, even seemingly "adoptive" group identity can be pinned on people from birth. For instance, in Colombia, the period of "violencia" in the 1950s and 1960s pitted "liberals" against "conservatives." With time, these labels came with parents' affiliation or even simply by the place of birth (Chernick, 2007). During this period of extreme atrocity there are pictures of young women raped and killed, with flags planted in their vaginas, stating that "this womb will never produce another conservative" (or "liberal"). See Campos (1968). I am grateful to Brian Loveman for his help.
83 Ibid. (2003: 7).
84 Atran (2002).
85 This is known as "signaling" in game-theory parlance.
86 Dawkins (2006).
87 Juergensmeyer (2003).
88 Avalos (2005), Benjamin and Simon (2002).
89 Holmes (2005: 151–152).
90 Are human beings hard-wired for God? Neurologists d'Aquili and Newberg (1999), Newberg *et al.* (2001), and Newberg and Waldman (2006) claim that our brain structure is designed to believe in the supernatural. As a result, regardless of culture, religious experiences appear to be remarkably similar; people experience similar kinds of exuberance after a religious experience. Neurologically, these responses are produced by certain regions of the brains. Scans show that during meditation certain parts "light up," producing a universal sense of pleasure and exaltation. Atran (2002), however, does not attribute much significance to the neurological claims, and emphasizes the evolutionary need for religion in producing group solidarity.
91 Lewis (2002).
92 Selbourne (2005).
93 Rushdie (2001).
94 For an open indictment of the mainstream Islam as a source of violence, see Hamid (2007).
95 Avalos (2005).
96 Pape (2005).
97 Juergensmeyer (2003: 141).
98 Although the police departments across the nation have reported a surge in domestic abuse following football games in the US, a number of studies have disputed such claims. See, for example, White *et al.* (1992), Sachs and Chu (2000). I am grateful to Brian Spitzberg for making this point.
99 For a very interesting description of fan behavior among English soccer hooligans, see Buford (1992).
100 Hobsbawm (1964).
101 Anderson (2003: 5).
102 Seton-Watson (1977: 5).
103 O'Brien (1988: 80).

104 See Anderson (2003: 2).
105 Schumpeter (1939).
106 For a more structured discussion of the political entrepreneur, see Shepsle and Bonchek (1997: 241–250).
107 See, for example, Simon *et al.* (2001).
108 Frohlich and Oppenheimer (1978) introduced the concept of an entrepreneur in the context of political mobilization.
109 Milgram (1974).
110 See Kelman and Hamilton (1989).
111 Goldhagen (1996).
112 Gupta (2001a: 169–179); Lalich (2004).
113 Sageman (2004).
114 Zimbardo (2007).
115 Horgan (2006)
116 Ibid.
117 Rapoport (2005).
118 See Gupta (2001).
119 Stern (2005).
120 For an excellent discussion, see Schuessler (2000). See also Bandyopadhyay and Gupta (2002).
121 Maddock and Fulton (1996); Roberts (2004).
122 See Marcus *et al.* (2000).
123 For an interesting discussion of mass communication, see "The Persuaders," *Frontline*, at: http://www.pbs.org/wgbh/pages/frontline/shows/persuaders/

4 The dynamics of dissent: a theoretical perspective

1 Quoted in Tilly (2004: 5).
2 Lawrence (2005: 126).
3 Richardson (2006: 1).
4 Richardson (2006: 1).
5 Krueger and Maleckova (2003).
6 Russell and Miller (1978); Hudson (1999); Horgan (2003); Post *et al.* (2003).
7 Sageman (2004).
8 Pew Research Center (2002). The survey was conducted in Bangladesh, Ghana, Indonesia, Ivory Coast, Jordan, Lebanon, Mali, Nigeria, Pakistan, Senegal, Tanzania, Turkey, Uganda, and Uzbekistan. Although part of the larger survey, Egypt did not allow this question to be asked. This survey was not conducted in Syria, Iran, Iraq, and Saudi Arabia.
9 Bueno de Mesquita (2007b).
10 Bueno de Mesquita (2007b: 12).
11 A simple regression model demonstrates the lack of statistical significance between the two:

$$\text{Ln (fatalities and injuries)} = 2.84 + .014 \text{ percent below poverty}$$

t-ratio	(5.1) ** (0.88)
R-squared	.008
F-statistic	.77 (1,98)

** Significant at 99 percentile level

12 Hibbs (1973); Venieris and Gupta (1983); Gupta (1990); Sandler and Enders (2004).

13 A simple regression results show that while the coefficient for Ln (GDP per capita) is statistically significant, it explains less than 1% of the variance in fatality among nations:

Ln (fatalities and injuries) =2.84 + .014 ln (GDP per capita)
          t-ratio   (4.44) ** (2.84)
          R-squared   .07
          F-statistic   8.07 (1,108)

    ** Significant at 99 percentile level

The figures for per capita GNP were log transformed to reduce their variability.

14 The distinction between egotistical and fraternal deprivation was originally made by sociologist Ralph Dahrendorf (1958).

15 In contrast to the others, Saraj (2002), a noted Palestinian psychologist, has emphasized a feeling of humiliation and shame more than economic deprivation as the root cause of terrorism in Israel and the Palestinian territories.

16 Merari and Friedlander (1985); Berrebi (2003); Sageman (2004).

17 It is important to note that President Bush embraced the idea of spreading democracy as a justification for invading Iraq after a failed search for weapons of mass destruction.

18 Bueno de Mesquita (2007b); see also Li (2005).

19 A quick fitting of a linear relationship corroborates this lack of statistically significant correlation between the dependent and independent variables:

Ln (fatalities and injuries) =3.38 + .049 Democracy index
          t-ratio   (10.85) ** (1.76)
          R-squared   .028
          F-statistic   3.11 (1,107)

    ** Significant at 99 percentile level

20 Pape (2005).
21 See Crenshaw (2007).
22 Fearon and Laitin (2003).
23 Ibid.
24 Rotberg (2004); Debiel and Klein (2002).
25 Rotberg (2002: 90).
26 For one of the best sources of state failure, see the State Failure Taskforce, http://globalpolicy.gmu.edu/pitf/
27 O'Donnell (1998).
28 Napoleoni (2003: 140).
29 http://www.foreignpolicy.com/story/cms.php?story_id=3098&src2=PJA05. These 12 factors include:

    1) Mounting demographic pressures
    2) Massive movement of refugees and IDPs (internally displaced persons)
    3) Legacy of vengeance—seeking group grievance
    4) Chronic and sustained human flight
    5) Uneven economic development along group lines
    6) Sharp and/or severe economic decline
    7) Criminalization or delegitimization of the state
    8) Progressive deterioration of public services

9) Widespread violation of human rights
10) Security apparatus as "state within a state"
11) Rise of factionalized elites
12) Intervention of other states or external actors

30 The variable state failure index alone explains a highly significant 22% of the variance.

Ln (fatalities and injuries) =.73 + .051 State Failure Index
    t-ratio   (.73) (5.3)**
    R-squared   .22
    F-statistic   27.7 (1,98)

** Significant at 99 percentile level

31 Gupta (1990, 2001, 2005).
32 Gupta (1999, 2001).
33 Cleaver and Katsificas (2001).
34 McLlelan and Avery (1977).
35 Lee (2002).
36 O.J. Simpson was a star football player and was married to a white woman. He was accused of the murder of his wife and one of her male friends. The long televized trial clearly demonstrated the wide gap in perception of guilt in the black and white communities. In a very interesting research design, Enomoto (1999) showed that even after controlling for age, gender, income, and education, race provides by far the strongest explanation of sympathy for O.J. Simpson.
37 See, Hacker (1995: 104).
38 See Farley (1997).
39 While most leaders rise through the ranks and work for many years to rise to the top, a few others are the products of accidents of history. Thus, Corazon Aquino was thrust in the forefront of the anti-Marcos movement in the Philippines after her husband Benigno Aquino was assassinated. For an excellent discussion of the birth of leaders, see Post (2004).
40 http://hdr.undp.org.
41 For an excellent discussion of the "Sons of Liberty" movement and its link to the American Revolution, see Rapoport (2006). See also Graham and Gurr (1969).
42 Gupta (2006).
43 Gupta (2007).
44 Sageman (2004).
45 Bueno de Mesquita (2007b); English (2003); Clark (1990); Horne (1978); Bloom (2004).
46 The ICT dataset is by no means perfect. Unfortunately, as I have argued in an article (Gupta 2007), due to the lack of reliable information, we are often held hostage to available data. Currently, we have no other dataset that provides such breakdown of activities of the various terrorist groups.
47 Samuelson (1938).
48 Stern (2005: 112).
49 Olson (1968).
50 Gupta (2001a).
51 Horgan (2005).
52 Horgan and Taylor (2003).
53 See Elster (2005).
54 Hopgood (2005).

55 Benjamin and Simon (2002: 28–29).
56 Schmidt and de Graaf (1983).
57 Combs (2003).
58 Pape (2003, 2005).
59 Mishal and Sela (2000).
60 Bloom (2004, 2005).
61 Gupta and Mundra (2005).
62 de Figueirdo and Weingast (2001); Rosendorff and Sandler (2004).
63 Aronson (1990); Freedman (1991).
64 Ginkel and Smith (1999), DeNardo (1985).
65 Lichbach (1987).
66 Moore (1998).
67 Gupta *et al.* (1993).
68 Kydd and Walter (2002).
69 Bueno de Mesquita (2005b).
70 For an excellent review article, see Crenshaw (2007).
71 Ganor (2002: 141).
72 Elster (2005).
73 Some economists (Berman and Leitin 2007) have defined the objective function of a terrorist organization with the help of "club theory," where the group attempts to maximize the private benefits of their own members. Although such a formulation makes it easy to use standard economic models, the problem with this approach is that it fails to distinguish between a primarily ideology-driven terrorist group and a profit-driven criminal organization.
74 Fair and Shepherd (2006).
75 Pew Research Center (2002).
76 Rapoport (1984); Gupta (2006a, 2006b).
77 Berman (2000).
78 Gupta (1990).
79 Popkin (1978).
80 The importance of holding formal employment is widely recognized in the scholarly literature. Amartya K. Sen (Dreze and Sen 1989) has shown that providing employment during droughts is the best way of preventing mass death. Similarly, Sen (1990) argued that the biggest deterrent for female infanticide is women holding jobs in the formal sector of the economy. Although holding formal employment may be a strong deterrent, it is certainly no guarantee against participation in acts of terrorism. The recent plot to bomb various locations in the UK, hatched by a group of doctors, is ample testimony to this precautionary note.
81 Becker (1976).
82 Gurr (1970).
83 Gupta (1990), Gupta *et al.* (1993), Venieris and Gupta (1983).
84 Guetzkow (1965); Perrucci and Pilisuk (1970); Tichy (1981).
85 Farace *et al.* (1977); Redding (1972).
86 Laupmann and Pappi (1976); Lipnack and Stamp (1986).
87 Sageman (2004); Stohl and Stohl (2007); Robb (2007).
88 Dye and Ziegler (1981).
89 Buchanan (2002); Fulk (2001).
90 Hiro (1989); Munson (1988).
91 Napoleoni (2005: 128–139).
92 For an explanation of the historical and cultural impact on communication, see Oborshall (2004).
93 Sageman (2004: 138).
94 Stohl and Stohl (2007).
95 Thomson *et al.* (2005).

96 Robb (2007).
97 Sageman (2004).
98 Coll and Glasser (2005).
99 Robb (2007).
100 Stern (2003b).
101 BBC (2007).
102 *New York Times* (2007).
103 Wright (2004).
104 Sageman (2004: 140).
105 Gunaratna (2001); Napoleoni (2005).
106 Napoleoni (2005: 120).
107 Pallister and Bowcott (2002). We should be quick to note here that there is no reason to believe that the entire fund was devoted to supporting terrorism. The bulk of the money was used for various religious and social service work.
108 Swami (2007).
109 Schlesinger Jr. (1965).
110 Palast (2002).
111 For an excellent discussion, see Quran (2004), where he describes the dilemma in terms of Islamism and Mammon, the false god of avarice and greed.
112 For a detailed history of BCCI, see Beaty and Gwynne (1993).
113 Napoleoni (2003: 120). See also Daraghai (2001).
114 Quorchi *et al.* (2003: 24).
115 English (2003: 3).
116 Ibid.
117 Ibid.: 4.
118 See *The Economist* (2006), "Madness Reincarnate: The Accidental War." 20 July. http://www.pierretristam.com/Bobst/library/wf-290.htm.
119 Ibid.
120 These types of diagrams have been used extensively in development economics to demonstrate the forces that promote and thwart economic growth. See, for instance, Swan (1962) and Streeten 1967). In psychology, Sidanias and Pratto (1999) use the terms increasing and attenuating forces to explain social dominance.
121 Kassimeris (1999).
122 McLleland and Avery (1977).
123 Walker (2003).
124 Sengupta (2005).

5 Faith, nationalism, and class warfare: the birth of a movement

1 http://en.wikipedia.org/wiki/Ibn_Taymiya#_note-5
2 The leader of the London train bombers in his video statement made prior to his death. See "London Bomber: Text in full." BBC News online, 1 September 2006. http://news.bbc.co.uk/2/hi/uk_news/4206800.stm/
3 For an excellent discussion of the "Sons of Liberty" movement and its link to the American Revolution, see Rapoport (2006). See also Graham and Gurr (1969).
4 Jacquard (2002).
5 See, for instance, Post (005), Schmid (2005).
6 The MIPT database presents groups in ten classes: Anarchists, Ant-globalization, Communist/Socialist, Environmental, Leftist, Nationalist/Separatist, Racist, Religious, Right-Wing Conservative, and Right-Wing Reactionary. See http://www.tkb.org/Category.jsp?catID=2.
7 Esposito (2003).

8 For instance, Berman (2003) points out that Islam specifies:

> dietary regulations, the proper direction to pray, the rules of divorce, the question of when a man may propose marriage to a widow (four months and 10 days after the death of her husband, unless she is pregnant, in which case after delivery), the rules concerning a Muslim man who wishes to marry a Christian or a Jew (very complicated), the obligations of charity, the punishment for crimes and for breaking your word, the prohibition on liquor and intoxicants, the proper clothing to wear, the rules on usury, money lending and a thousand other themes.

9 Although Taymiyya gave the fatwa to wage a jihad against the infidel Mongols, there is no evidence that he actually called for a jihad against the Maluks, whom he did not consider to be the ideals of Islamic piety (Sivan 1985: 90–101).
10 Berkey (2003).
11 Ali (2002: 75).
12 Holden and Jones (1981).
13 Shah (2007).
14 I am grateful to Khaleel Muhammad and Niaz Shah for their help.
15 Lewis (2002: 18–34).
16 Ibid.
17 Husain (2003: 71).
18 Deng (1989: 348, 1995).
19 Flint (2005); Prunier (2005).
20 Voll (1989).
21 For one of the best perspectives on Muhammad Iqbal, see the introduction by Khushwant Singh in Iqbal (1981).
22 Qasim (2002).
23 Husain (2003: 75).
24 Mitchell (1969).
25 Husain (2003: 71–74).
26 Ali (2002: 97).
27 Moussalli (1992); Berman (2003a, 2003b).
28 Qutb (1993: 116).
29 Sageman (2004: 9).
30 Qutb (1993: 130).
31 Ali (2002: 109).
32 Lenihan (2003).
33 See, for instance, Rose (1990).
34 See English (2003).
35 See Silke (2005).
36 I am grateful to Richard English for clarifying this point.
37 For instance, *Time* magazine's issue of 6 June 2006 had the cover story "India, Inc." Almost concurrently, *Foreign Affairs* had a special issue on "The Rise of India." July/August, 2006.
38 This 20 percent figure is widely quoted in many circles in India. For instance, journalist Inder Malhotra mentions this figure in his foreword to Ranjit Gupta's *The Crimson Agenda: Maoist Protest and Terror* (2005). The nature of this domination varies from the "highly affected" areas where the Maoists have set up a virtual parallel government to those areas where state administration is still prevailing, but is under attack from the violent Marxist groups.
39 See Guha (2006a).
40 By using open-source information, the Institute for Conflict Management estimates the number of casualties at nearly double the amount admitted by the

government. See http://www.satp.org/satporgtp/countries/india/database/
fatalitiesnaxal.htm.

41 Sengupta (2006).

42 Gupta (2004: 83).

43 The upper-caste Hindus claim their origin goes back to the fair-skinned Aryans,
who, according to one theory, settled in India in prehistoric times and took over
the land from the indigenous people, many of whom, much like the native Americans in the US, were pushed to the remote forests and other badlands. They are
often the poorest of the poor and are collectively called the "tribals" or the *Adivashis*, which literally translates as the "original inhabitants." According to a
report ("Supporting Indigenous Peoples in the State of the World," 1993. Worldwatch Institute Report on Progress Toward A Sustainable Society, Washington
D.C.), in absolute numbers, India has the largest indigenous tribal population in
the world, although as a percentage they constitute only 7 percent of the
population.

44 Guha (1983: 6).

45 For an excellent discussion of the nature of British colonial exploitation, see Rao
and Rao (1992). This volume also contains an English translation of the famous
play by Dinabandhu Mitra, *Neel Darpan* (The Blue Mirror), which tells the story
of these peasants with such graphic details that it quickly spawned nationalistic
violence in Bengal. See also King (1966).

46 See Bagai (1953). See also Sen (1972).

47 See Chatterjee (1998).

48 Guha (1983).

49 Gordon (1990: 196, emphasis in original).

50 The Zamindari system goes back at least to the Mughal period in the late sixteenth
century. In Persian, the official language of the Mughal Court, *zamin* means
"land" and *dar* means "holder" or "owner." However, land tenure under the
Mughals was not systematic or permanent. The innovation of the British was to
make land ownership permanent and inheritable in return for fixed revenues to the
government.

51 French (1997: 6).

52 Gupta, (2004: 81).

53 Mehra (2000).

54 Pavier (1981).

55 Like Emma Goldman, Roy traveled through many countries and went back to his
home country, disillusioned with both Marxism and capitalism. See Ray (2002).

56 It is interesting to note that prior to 1939, while the Communists in India forcefully
denounced Hitler, a large segment of the population, abiding by the rule "my
enemy's enemy is my friend," remained much more ambivalent about Hitler.
Also, his message of Aryan identity falsely created a sense of affinity in the minds
of many.

57 For a detailed discussion of the meeting of the Indian Communist delegates with
Stalin and its consequent impact on the policies of the CPI, see Banerjee (1980:
86–88). On this, see also Ram (1971: 52).

58 Gupta (2004: 25).

59 Mehra (2000).

60 Calman (1985).

61 See Gilman (1958); Steedman (1977); Sweezy (1981).

62 Avineri (1969).

63 Fernbach (1974: 77).

64 Lenin (1969: 40).

65 Although there is no written record of their conversation, Gupta (2004: 62), quot-
ing some of those who met Stalin in 1951, reconstructed Stalin's direct instruction

as follows: "You [in India] have a very good Constitution. You are not an illegal party any more. You fight the election to parliamentary bodies, and so doing this you can carry the Communist message to people's homes. After capturing parliamentary democracy and after capturing all the fronts of society, you can then promote people's democracy with political power. *You will then have taken over power without violence*" [emphasis mine].

66 Quoted in Gupta (2004: 62).
67 Overstreet and Windmiller (1959).
68 See Gupta (2001a).
69 See Post (2005).
70 Lenin (1964).
71 Mao Tse-Tung (1961).
72 Ho Chi Minh (1961).
73 Loveman and Davies (1985).
74 Marighela (1985).
75 For a comparison between Latin American guerrilla movements and the Naxalite movement, see Singh (2006: 195–197).
76 See Calman (1985: 72–73).
77 See Dasgupta (1975: 9).
78 See Mehra (2000).

6 Growth of a movement: accounting for rapid escalation of violence

1 Rapoport (1992).
2 Rogers (2004)
3 Ibid.
4 Ibid. (2004: 17).
5 Sageman (2004: 151).
6 Stern (2003).
7 See Adams (1987); Anderson (1994).
8 *Zakat* is the charitable contribution that each Muslim must contribute for the betterment of the poor or for the spreading of Islam. It is one of the five pillars of Islam.
9 Napoleoni (2003: 123).
10 Ibid. (2003: 120).
11 Pallister and Bowcott (2002).
12 Swami (2007).
13 Silke (2004: 242); Feeny (2003).
14 English (2003: 81–186).
15 Silke (2004: 242–243).
16 Ibid.
17 Lee (1989: 429).
18 It is interesting to note that the history of military intervention to secure peace has resulted in similar outcomes in many parts of the world. The Indian Peacekeeping Forces were sent to Sri Lanka in 1987 to protect the beleaguered Tamil minority population in the north of the island. Soon, the Indian troops began fighting with the Tamils and, ultimately, in retaliation, in 1991 Indian Prime Minister (then out of office) Rajiv Gandhi was assassinated by a LTTE suicide attacker. Although troops are often sent on "peacekeeping missions," their deployment is often the outcome of a larger geopolitical game played by the rulers of the nation (see Hagerty (1991); Hellmann-Rajanayagam (1989); Pfaffenberger (1988)). For the result of the Indian intervention, see Swami (1994); Karthikeyan (2004).
19 Lee (1989: 433).

20 Lee's data shows a minuscule .27 percent of the ransacked homes had any kind of weapon.
21 Silke (2004: 244).
22 Rose (1990).
23 Fisk (1975).
24 O'Leary (2007: 216).
25 For an excellent discussion of the strategies of self-immolation, see Biggs (2005).
26 Kosnik (2000).
27 See Stohl (1987); Hoffman (1998); Enders *et al.* (1990); Enders and Sandler (1993). See also Silke (2004).
28 Moloney (2002); Coogan (2002).
29 O'Leary (2007: 201).
30 See Horgan and Taylor (2003).
31 See Maguire (1993) for a discussion of extortion, fraud, and other illegal methods of raising money in Northern Ireland by the IRA.
32 Holland (1989).
33 Silke (1999).
34 O'Leary (2007: 203).
35 For instance, recognizing that the former IRA prisoners carried the risk of being easily marked by police or that their loyalty might have been compromised while in prison, they were given jobs in the vigilante units. See Horgan (2005).
36 For a discussion of the Orange Men's claims of cultural tradition to carry out these marches, see Dingley (2002).
37 English (2003: 83).
38 Ibid. (2003: 84–85).
39 The Wolfe Tone Societies were formed to commemorate the bicentenary of the birth of Theobald Wolfe Tone (1763–1798). Wolfe Tone was a leading figure as well as a primary theoretician in the Irish uprising. He is commonly viewed as the Father of Irish Republicanism.
40 Gallagher (1928: 35–36).
41 Brennan (1980: 81).
42 Silke (2005: 244).
43 Bishop and Mallie (1987); McKittrick (2001).
44 I have argued (Gupta, 2001: 184–197) that one of the reasons the revolt of the African-Americans in the 1960s and early 1970s was effectively quelled by the American authorities was due to the fact that following the recommendations of the Kerner Commission (1968), the local police forces were quickly integrated. Having African-Americans in the police department, it did not appear to be an invading force within the community. In Northern Ireland, however, one of the reasons the RUC was not integrated was because of the opposition of the IRA and the Catholic community.
45 It is important to note that while Israel was created as a Jewish state, the early political leaders of the newly formed nation strived to give it more of a secular character. The conflict between the religious and secular Jews was central to their debate over the Constitution and occupies an extremely important role in every aspect of the society. Such debates were much more muted in Pakistan, particularly after the death of Muhammad Ali Jinnah.
46 Anderson (2003: 2).
47 Hobsbawm (1977: 13).
48 Suny (1993).
49 Ramet (1996).
50 Kinzer (2003); Gasiorowski (1991); Elm (1994).
51 Yergin (1991); Kyle (2003); Tal (2001).

52 Al-Shuaibi (1980); Arafat (1982); Nassar (1991); Nofal *et al.* (1998); Sela and Ma'oz (1997).
53 See, for example, Nassar (1991).
54 It is important to note here that I am using the term PLO. After 1994, the organization transformed itself into the Palestinian Authority (PA).
55 Said (1979: 160).
56 Hudson (1972).
57 Although the DFLP was, like the PFLP, a pro-Soviet socialist group, it broke with the latter over its agenda of creating a class struggle among the poor and working class Palestinians.
58 Before this date, Hamas was more of a charitable organization, serving the poor Palestinians primarily in the Gaza Strip.
59 Article 1 of its Charter, mirroring that of the Muslim Brotherhood in Egypt, proudly proclaims, "The basis of the Islamic Resistance Movement is Islam. From Islam it derives its ideas and its fundamental precepts and views of life, the universe, and humanity; and it judges all its actions according to Islam and is inspired by Islam to correct its errors" (Mishal and Sela, 2000: 177). And it adds to the Muslim Brotherhood motto in Article 5, "Allah is its [Hamas's] goal, the Prophet is its model, and the Qur'an is its constitution" (ibid.: 178).
60 Article 11 states: "The Islamic Resistance Movement believes that the land of Palestine is an Islamic *Waqf* [endowed] to all Muslim generations until the day of resurrection. It is not right to give it up or any part of it. Neither a single Arab state nor all Arab states, neither a king nor a president, not all the kings and presidents, nor any organization or all of them—be they Palestinian or Arab—have such authority, because the land of Palestine is an Islamic *Waqf* [endowed] to all Muslim generations until the day of resurrection" (ibid: 181).
61 Mishal and Sela (2000: 3).
62 Stern (2003); Miller (1996).
63 Huband (1998); Kepel (2002).
64 Although the murder of Shqaqi remains unsolved, there is a strong but unproven suspicion that it was the work of the Israeli intelligence agency Mossad.
65 See, http://www.ict.org.il/.
66 Radlauer (2002).
67 In terms of the calculation of cost and benefits, the Jihadi groups all over the world have found suicide attacks to be most cost-effective weapon. Thus Ayman al-Zawahiri, the closest aide to Osama bin Laden, wrote: "The method of martyrdom operations [is] the most successful way of inflicting damage against the opponent and the least costly to the Mujahaidin [organization] in terms of casualties." Quoted in Benjamin and Simon (2002: 28–29).
68 Although the PLO had officially eschewed violence against Israel, the entire time period saw continued armed attacks by the PLO-affiliated groups, although they did not stage any suicide attack, before the peace process came to an end.
69 By this time, an overwhelming portion of the Palestinians was supportive of the suicide attacks against the Jewish state. See Luft (2002).
70 It is indeed interesting to compare the two wars. For an excellent history of the Spanish Civil War, see Beevor (2006) and Thomas (2001).
71 Much of the religious justification of violence against nonbelievers (*Dar ul Kufr*) by the promoters of jihad is based on the Quranic "sword verses." For instance, the Quran (9:5) does say that "When the sacred months have passed, slay the idolaters wherever you find them, and take them, and confine them, and lie in wait for them at every place." However, opponents point out that these verses are said in the context of a desperate defensive war that the forces of Prophet Muhammad were waging at the time. According to this view, in the context of today's world, such a call for violent jihad is inappropriate.

72 See Burke (2003).

73 Associated with this debate was the question of whether to use the funds raised for the jihadi operation against the Egyptian government. See Gunaratna (2002).

74 Al-Zawahiri (2001, part II).

75 Once again, it is impossible not to compare the assassination of Azzam to that of Leon Trotsky. Although there is no hard proof that those favoring Zawahiri carried out the killing, if it is true, it was similar to Stalin's ordering the death of his political and ideological rival.

76 Sageman (2004: 41).

77 For an excellent discussion of the creation of Iraq, see Tripp (2002).

78 Sageman (2004: 23–24).

79 The border region between Tibet and British India was never marked with any kind of precision. Through the snow-covered mountain peaks and valleys, the British Survey of India mapped the boundaries and put up the border markers along what is known as the McMahon line. However, much of the remote and sparsely populated border region fell outside the administrative areas of independent India. The British had claimed that the border drawn up during a joint conference in 1914 was agreed upon by both the Tibetans and the British government. However, Tibet being a vassal state to the Qing Dynasty, China refused to accept the McMahon line. After China annexed Tibet the issue became parmount in the mutual relationship between the two Asian giants. For a discussion of the political significance of the border to the two nations, see Guang (2005).

80 See Franda (1971: 19). See also Ray (2002: 125).

81 Pavier (1981).

82 In the middle of the decade, the former Indian Ambassador Chester Bowles (1969: 83), in an act of unique prescience, warned:

> Landless labourers may accept their wages of two or three rupees a day as long as they know that everyone in their village is poor. However, when they see the landowners' incomes rising rapidly, while their own rising much more slowly, if at all, they become restless and resentful. In other words, the dramatic increases in food output which are occurring—and which should continue to grow in the years ahead—may lead to sharp disparities in income, which in turn, may create an expanding sense of economic and social injustice.

83 Banerjee (1980: 1).

84 For a reproduction of these essays, see Singh (2006).

85 See Trotsky (1959).

86 See, for instance, Swarup (1966).

87 See Mohanty (1977). See also Mukherjee (1979).

88 It should be mentioned that although the Indian Congress Party enjoyed a monopoly of power in Indian politics, as Lijphart (1996) points out, its policies reflected a diverse coalition of interests.

89 See Mehra (2000).

90 Roy (1975).

91 See Gordon (1990).

92 For a discussion of India's central planning model and its implications for the economy, see Rudra (1974).

93 Gupta (2004).

7 A marriage made in hell? terrorism and organized crime

1 This chapter is based on Gupta *et al.* (2007). I thank my co-authors for their help in developing my ideas presented in this chapter.

2 Gambetta (2005: 268).
3 Ignatieff (2003: 122).
4 Quoted in Scarborough (2003).
5 A search using the two terms ("terrorism" and "organized crime") on Pro Quest search engine yields nearly 2000 hits since September 2001, mostly in news-papers and popular magazines. A similar Google search shows over five million entries.
6 US Security Council Resolution # 1373 (9/28/2001).
7 Kaplan (2005).
8 See, for example, Buzan and Waever (2003); Shelley and Picarelli (2002).
9 Hoffman (1998: 43).
10 Ruby (2002: 10). I have generally accepted this definition of terrorism with some qualification of the term "non-combatant."
11 National Security Council, International Crime Threat Assessment web site www.terrorism.com/documents/pub45270/pub45270chap1.html. A more precise definition of organized crime was adopted by the United Nations Convention on Transnational Organized Crime as:

> "Organized criminal group" shall mean a structured group of three or more persons, existing for a period of time and acting in concert with the aim of committing one or more serious crimes or offences established in accordance with this Convention, in order to obtain, directly or indirectly, a financial or other material benefit. "Serious crime" shall mean conduct constituting an offence punishable by maximum deprivation of liberty of at least four years or more serious penalty. "Structured group" shall mean a group that is not randomly formed for the immediate commission of an offence and that does not need to have formally defined roles for its members, continuity of its membership, or a developed structure.
>
> (UN, 2001)

12 Jamieson (2005: 165).
13 The quasi-public goods are also known in the standard economic literature as the "common pooled resources."
14 Schmid and de Graff (1982).
15 Dishman (2006: 367); see also Kenney (2003).
16 See, for instance, Gunaratna (2001); Bergen (2002); Napelioni (2005); Ehrenfeld (2005); Lilly (2006) and Kochan (2006).
17 Sageman (2004) has shown that even a less hierarchical organization, such as al-Qaeda, had a division of labor with a section of the core administrative group devoted solely to raising money for the organization.
18 The United Nations Office on Drugs and Crime defines money laundering as a "three-stage process, which disguises illegal profits without compromising the criminals who wish to benefit from the proceeds. This requires first, moving the funds from direct association with the crime; second, disguising the trail to foil pursuit; and third, making money available to the criminal once again with occu-pational and geographic origin hidden from view" (United Nations Office on Drugs and Crime).
19 See Gartenstein-Ross and Dabruzzi (2007). See also Baker and Nordin (2007).
20 Ibid. (2007: 14).
21 The importance of the support of the client base is well recognized in the litera-ture. For instance Bloom (2004) demonstrates the close association between popu-lar support for suicide bombing among the Palestinian population in West Bank and the Gaza Strip and the staging of suicide bombings by Hamas, the PIJ, and other dissident groups. Similarly, Kalyvas and Sanchez-Cuenca (2005) argue that

how a group must choose its strategies is based on the cultural, religious, and political sensitivities of their base.

22 There are differences even among these groups. Despite the widespread use of drug trafficking and hostage taking to finance their activities, nobody accuses the FARC leadership of living in the lap of luxury (Chernick, 2007).

23 By expanding the standard rational choice hypothesis Gupta (2001) has argued that rational social beings maximize a dual utility function, comprised of self-utility and the utility of the group in which the actors claim their membership. In terrorism research, based on survey research by Muller and Opp (1986), Crenshaw (1998) introduced the idea of "collectively rational" as a source of terrorists' motivation. However, this concept is different from Gupta's since it does not explicitly introduce group identity and, instead, presents the standard rationality hypothesis in a bit different form. The idea of a collective identity has gained ground in terrorism research—see Post (2006).

24 British Prime Minister Margaret Thatcher famously called publicity the oxygen of terrorist groups. In fact, the political legitimacy is the lifeblood of any organization, including terrorists.

25 Dishman (2001); see also Horgan and Taylor (1999, 2003).

26 Dandaurand and Chin (2004).

27 Ibid. (2004: 28).

28 Gartenstein-Ross and Dabruzzi (2007).

29 Dishman (2001: 45).

30 McGirk (2004).

31 Ignatieff (2003: 122).

32 White (1989).

33 Collins and McGovern (1999).

34 McGartland (1997).

35 O'Leary (2007: 207).

36 Because of the needs of the terrorist organizations to keep a "clean" image, Dishman (2006: 374–375) has made an interesting point that when a hierarchical terrorist organization enters into a collaborative arrangement with a crime syndicate, the actual collaboration starts from the middle levels of the two organizations.

37 For a history of INLA, see J. Holland and H. McDonald (1984). See also reports of the Independent Monitoring Commission, at http://www.independentmonitoring commission.org. See also Heskin (1985).

38 For a detailed link between drug trafficking and political activities by Sendero Luminoso, see Palmer, (1995: 278).

39 Mincheva and Gurr (2007).

40 Rotella (2004).

41 There are many instances of brigands taking the role of the legendary Robin Hood to dispense public goods. In the forests of southern India, Veerappan, an elephant poacher and kidnapper, gained notoriety by taking the role of a protector of the remote and repressed village of Gopinathan in the state of Tamil Nadu. He escaped many capture attempts by the forces of Indian government, primarily through the support of the villagers. However, his luck ran out in October 2004, when he was killed in a shootout with the security forces. See *India Today* (2004).

42 Jamieson (2005: 167).

43 Williams and Savona (1995).

44 See Crenshaw (1988) for the importance of leadership in maintaining group adherence to its ideological goals through selective incentive structure.

45 Wells *et al.* (2001).

46 Rogers (2006: 107).

47 Ibid.

48 Sageman (2004: 44).
49 See Debray (1967).
50 Silke (1998); see also Zirakzadeh (2002).
51 See, Collier and Hoeffler (2004).
52 Silke (1998, 1999).
53 Horgan and Taylor (1999, 2003).
54 Alexander *et al.* (2001).
55 Rotella (2004).
56 Dishman (2006).
57 Schmid (2005: 8).

8 Demise of dissent: the endgame of terrorism

1 See Horgan (2006, 2005). See, also Taylor and Quayle (1994).
2 Horgan (2006: 35).
3 A special issue of the *Journal of Conflict Resolution*, 48(1), February 2004 is devoted to the understanding of the poliheuristics of decision-making.
4 Known as "unbounded rationality" in the literature.
5 See Redd (2003).
6 See, for instance, Simon (1987).
7 Mintz (2004). See also Mintz, *et al.* (1997).
8 Khan (2007).
9 Mintz (2004: 9).
10 See Stevenson (1996) and Brams (1998).
11 O'Leary (2007).
12 English (2003).
13 The IRA constitution through several amendments has aimed at creating a social-ist republic, where Gaelic culture and language are well preserved (Moloney 2002).
14 See Moloney (2002).
15 O'Leary (2004: 220).
16 Quoted in Clarke (1987: 29).
17 See Silke (1999).
18 Alvarez (2005).
19 See Silke and Taylor (2000).
20 *New York Times* (1990).
21 Moloney (2002: 347–348).
22 On this, see Moloney (2002).
23 See Ray (1988: 134).
24 Gupta (2004: 83).
25 The towering monument was built in 1848 by Sir David Ochterlony to com-memorate his (and the British) victory in the Nepal War (1814–1816).
26 For an early explanation of the events, see, for instance, Sajal Basu (1974).
27 In the midst of this list of ordinary people, there was one prominent Bengali politician, Hemanta Basu, who was abducted and was killed. Although his killing was widely attributed to the Naxalites, Police Commissioner Ranjit Gupta claimed (2004: 176) that it was an inside political job, undertaken for intra-party political rivalry. Gupta narrates a story of how after the killing, a riotous mob headed by another prominent member of Basu's political party, Forward Block, con-fronted him, demanding an immediate arrest of Basu's assailant. Gupta took him aside and asked, "Will you force me to divulge the intelligence reports about Hemanta Basu's enemies in your party?" It worked like a charm and the leader quietly slipped back into the crowd.
28 Ray (1988: 113).
29 Samanta (1975).

30 Banerjee (1980: 192–193).
31 Gupta (2004).
32 Singh (2006: 89).
33 Banerjee (1980: 196).
34 For a history of the creation of Bangladesh and its impact on the Indian politics, see Mascarenhas (1986). See also Baxter (1997).
35 Gupta (2004).
36 Banerjee (1980: 194).
37 Dishman (2001) points out that when a hierarchical organization, due to a successful counterinsurgency policy, becomes atomized into small independent cells, it exhibits a tendency to veer off toward criminality.
38 Banerjee (1980: 191).
39 Gupta (2004: 140).
40 During the course of my fieldwork, as part of the current project, I met with many law-enforcement and intelligence officials. They almost unanimously maintained that the best way to defeat an insurgency is to depend on ground-level intelligence employed by the local police force. They also held the opinion that the least effective (or even counter-effective) method of combating terrorism and radical political movements is to deploy the military. As one British intelligence officer in Northern Ireland put it, "after a day's work, the military goes back to the barracks, while the policeman on the beat goes back to his home in the community." Therefore, the military, not being able to distinguish between friends and foes, quickly alienates the entire community, which only plays into the hands of the dissidents.
41 Curiously, there is little research that has been done in this area. Therefore, there is no estimate of China's true involvement in providing material support to the Naxalites. However, based on my interviews with the participants in the movement as well as former police and intelligence officers, I have no reason to believe that if China did provide arms, financial support and/or sanctuary, they were of little consequence.
42 See Singh (2006).
43 As Guha (2006a) explains, the allure of the Maoists to the *adivashis* as follows: "Worse off than the *Dalits* (the 'untouchable caste'), and without effective leadership of their own, many *adivasis* saw in the Naxalites an agency some what more welcoming (or at any rate less oppressive) than the state."
44 Sengupta (2006).
45 Mehra (2006).
46 "Maoist Violence Set to Rise." *The Hindustan Times*. New Delhi, 11 April 2006.
47 Kumar (2006: 1).
48 For a historical context of the Maoist movement in Bihar, see Mukherjee and Yadav (1980).
49 Singh (2006: 170).
50 The movement still commands a lot of support from the higher levels of the Indian intelligence establishment. During my many conversations with former officials, I was told that many of the criticisms of Salwa Judum were coming from the political left.
51 For an excellent discussion, see Sundar (2006).
52 According to the National Commission on Women's report (http://ncw.nic.in/pdfreports/Gender%20Profile-Chhattisgarh.pdf), 34 percent of the population of Chhattisgarh is classified as Scheduled Tribes, 12 percent from Scheduled Caste (the so called "untouchables"), and more than 50 percent are classified as Other Backward Classes (OBC). That leaves only less than 4 percent of the population belonging to upper-caste Hindus.
53 See Guha (2006b: 19, 2006c).

54 Reporter Somini Sengupta (2006: 1), who spent time with Gopanna Markam, one of the commanders of People's Liberation Guerrilla Army—one of about 40 different Maosits groups that make up the umbrella organization, People's War Group (PWG)—reports that: "Today the fighting Markam has nurtured for 25 years looks increasingly like a civil war, one claiming more and more lives and hampering the industrial growth of a country hungry for the coal, iron, and other riches buried in these isolated realms bypassed by India's economic boom."

55 "Girijan" means "hill people," which implies the tribal people living in the uplands.

56 Interview with Prakash Singh.

57 See Mohanty (2005).

58 Barry Pavier (1981: 161) was correct, when he points out the cause of failure of the Telengana movement:

> At a time when it is clear that it was possible to build the party on a mass basis throughout Telengana, despite the repression, by relating to the mass struggles, and at the same time building workers' associations which could have been the firm bases for continuing struggle, the most militant elements of the CPI were doing no such thing. They were expending their energies in creating a guerrilla army in the forests and on maintaining a political front with rich peasants and bourgeoisies.

59 Fukuyama (1992).

60 Rapoport (2006) argues that there have been four broad waves of international terrorism, the new left being the third one. It seems that just like the "new left" movement is the intellectual descendant of the older anarchist movement, being spawned by the growing inequality as a part of globalization, a new Communist movement may indeed rise up once again as the fifth wave.

61 http://www.pbs.org/frontlineworld/rough/2005/07/seeds_of_suicid.html, *Frontline*, 6 July 2005. It is interesting to note the parallel between the conditions prevailing in the mid-1960s when, in the midst of rising income in the rural areas due to the "Green Revolution," the plight of the poor peasants caused many to commit suicide. In fact, Banerjee's (1980) description of that period begins with the case of a suicide by a farmer in West Bengal.

62 Mehra (2006).

63 See, for instance, Hutt (2004).

64 See, for example, Yachury (2006).

65 See Stern (2003a: 148, 165). See also Dishman (2006).

66 Mohanty (2006).

67 The impacts of well-armed militias on a nation's human rights abuses are well documented. For instance, see Power (1999). On the subject matter of paramilitary force and genocide, see also Gupta (2001a).

68 Singh (2006: 147).

69 Uttam Sengupta (2006).

70 Pakistan is ranked 9, Afghanistan 10, Bangladesh 19, Nepal 20, and Sri Lanka 25 among the worst failed states. See http://www.fundforpeace.org/programs/fsi/fsindex2006.php.

71 The analogous situation may exist in the US today, where despite the persistent achievement gap, the African-Americans show little signs of political radicalization. See Gupta (1999).

9 Terrorism's trap: a winnable war?

1 http://www.pollingreport.com/terror.htm.
2 *Time*, 30 August 2006. www.angus-reid.com/polls/index.cfm/fuseaction/viewItem/itemID/12966.
3 NBC News/*Wall Street Journal* poll conducted by the polling organizations of Peter Hart (D) and Neil Newhouse (R). 2–5 March 2007. N = approx. 500 adults nationwide.
4 See Gilligan (2000).
5 Kim and Smith (1993).
6 Cota-McKinley *et al.* (2001). Their study points out that men are more driven by revenge than women.
7 Tudge (2002); Tajfel (1981, 1982); Tajfel and Turner (1986).
8 Dershowitz (2003).
9 Abrams (2006); Stoker (2007).
10 Hoffman (1998: 75).
11 Ibid.
12 The spectacle of beheading by the Islamic groups from Pakistan to Iraq sent a shockwave throughout the Western world. Many were quick to equate it with Islam. As a potent symbol of religious fanaticism such acts have just as much to say about Islam as a religion as the burning of the cross by the Ku Klux Klan does about Christianity. See Gupta (2006c: 79).
13 Ahmed (2005).
14 English (2004: 266).
15 English (2004: 177–178).
16 Gupta (2004).
17 Rubin (2007).
18 Schelling (1991: 20).
19 Rapoport (2004).
20 Begin (1972); Heller (1995).
21 Ignatyev (1977); Edgerton (1989); Maloba (1993).
22 Alexander and Keiger (2002); O'Balance (1967).
23 Moran (2001: 110).
24 Horne (1977).
25 Solten (1993).
26 Howe (2004); Henderson (1979).
27 McRae (1990).
28 Kizner (1991); Zimmermann (2001).
29 Roger and Ratliff (1993); Chernick (2007).
30 Oberoi (1987).
31 Bose (2003, 2007).
32 French (1997: xx).
33 Dixon (2006).
34 Swami (2007).
35 Bloom (2005), O'Duffy (2007).
36 Mueller (2005).
37 Stossel (2004: 77).
38 Between the six-year period prior to the invasion (1998–2003), the MIPT database records only 14 deaths from terrorism in Iraq.
39 See, for instance, Post (2005).
40 Lia (2005).
41 Huntington (1999).
42 Rasch (2004).
43 Arquilla and Ronfeldt (2002); Weimann (2006).

44 Yotopoulos and Nugent (1976).
45 Gupta (1990); Alesina and Perotti (1994); Alesina *et al.* (1996); Aron (2000); Barro (2004); see also Lennon (2003).
46 MacStiofain (1975: 115).
47 Kahneman and Renshon (2007: 1).
48 Kahneman and Tversky (1979).
49 See Kahneman and Renshon (2007). Since terrorists aim at achieving public goods for their communities, it is interesting to draw a parallel between the Prospect Theory, proposed by Kahneman and Tversky, and the problems of public finance. For an excellent discussion, see Frank (1997).
50 It is interesting to note while President Bush was proclaiming an easy victory in the global "war on terrorism", Ayman al-Zawahiri, the second in command of al-Qaeda, was predicting that "an end of the West" was imminent. See CNN story "Al-Qaeda No. 2 Says End of West Imminent, Video Shows." (4 July 2007). http://www.cnn.com/2007/WORLD/meast/07/04/zawahiri.video/index.html.
51 On this see the work of another Nobel Lauriate economist, Allais (1952). This anomaly in human assessment of uncertain outcomes is known as the "Allais Paradox."
52 Geyer (1997: E 3).
53 Kernell and Jacobson (2005).
54 Ibrahim (2002).
55 Gupta (1990).
56 Haqqani and Billeen (2005); Brookes (2005).
57 Gambetta (2005: 268).
58 In some countries, particularly in non-democratic nations, the separation between military and police is not very clear cut. In Chile, although there is a formal separation between police and military, the constitutional missions of the military generally include internal order (Loveman, 1993). Furthermore, cases involving police go to military courts, which provide a certain lack of accountability for officers accused of wrongdoing and removes constitutional rights and liberties from civilians in the military courts. It opens up an interesting research agenda regarding the efficacy of police in suppressing terrorism in such societies without resorting to extreme brute force. In any case, we are on safer ground to note that any military or law-enforcement agency that is not grounded in the society that is producing terrorism will be ineffective. The current situation in the northwestern frontier provinces of Pakistan, where the government is increasingly losing its battle against the resurgent Taliban and al-Qaeda, may provide a case in point.
59 Operation Blue Star took place on 3 June 1984, when the Indian military forcibly entered the Harimandir Sahib in Amritsar, Punjab, the holiest shrine of the Sikhs. Although it killed a large number of militants holed in the Golden Temple, it was instrumental in spreading Sikh radicalism throughout the world.
60 See Dhillon (2006); Prakash Singh (2002); Gill (1997); Sarab Jit Singh (2002).
61 Hafez (2007).
62 See Greenberg (2006: 21).
63 Zimbardo (1969).
64 For a most vivid account of the process by which an ordinary person becomes a sadistic prison guard, see Martin (1980).
65 Silke (2005).
66 Kriesher (1999).
67 The cost of a half trillion dollars spent in waging a war on a small group of perpetrators of terrorism may be put in proper perspective with the following example. In the process of tossing out terms such as "billions" and "trillions" it is not difficult to lose sight of the enormous amount of money that is nearly impossible for most of us to comprehend. We know that a million is a very large number.

How about a trillion? If I was asked what I was doing a million seconds ago, I should be able to recall my activities since it was nearly 12 days ago (11.57 days, to be precise). However, to go back to a trillion seconds ago, we must go back nearly 32 thousand years!
68 "Fighting Terrorism for Humanity: A Conference on the Roots of Evil" forum organized by the Norwegian Ministry of Foreign Affairs and International Peace Academy, New York, 22 September 2003.

Appendix A: Trade-off between interests of the individual and the collective: an expanded assumption of rationality

1 In standard economic formulations, the trade-off involving time is shown as between work and leisure. Here, I am holding the demand for leisure as constant.

Appendix B: Terrorism and organized crime: a formal model

1 Dishman (2001: 46).
2 Andreoni (1989, 1990).
3 For a similar assumption, see Enders and Sandler (2005: 36).

Bibliography

Abrams, Max (2006) "Why Terrorism Does Not Work." *International Security*. 31(2): 42–78.

Adams, J. (1986) *The Financing of Terror: How the Groups that are Terrorising the World Get the Money to Do It*. London: New English Library.

Adorno, T. W., E. Frenkel-Brunswick, D. J. Levinson, and R. N. Sanford (1950) *The Authoritarian Personality*. New York: Harper & Row.

Ahmed, Hisham (2005) "Palestinian Resistance and 'Suicide Bombing': Causes and Consequence." In Tore Bjorgo (ed.) *Root Causes of Terrorism: Myths, Reality and Ways Forward*. London: Routledge: 87–102.

Akerlof, George A. (1984) "Loyalty Filters." *American Economic Review*. 73(1): 54–63.

Akhtar, S. (1999) "The Psychodynamic Dimensions of Terrorism." *Psychiatric Anals*. 29: 350–355.

Alesina, Alberto and Roberto Perotti (1994) "The Political Economy of Growth: A Critical Survey of the Recent Literature." *The World Bank Economic Review*. 8(3): 351–371.

Alesina, Alberto, Sule Ozler, Nouriel Roubini, and Phillip Swagel (1996) "Political Instability and Economic Growth." *Journal of Economic Growth*. 1(1) June: 189–211.

Alexander, Martin S. and J. F. V. Keiger (eds.) (2002) *France and the Algerian War, 1954–62: Strategy, Operation, Diplomacy*. London: Frank Cass.

Alexander, Yonah, Michael S. Swetnam, and Herbert M. Levine (2001) *ETA: Profile of a Terrorist Group*. Ardsley, NY: Transnational Press.

Ali, Tariq (2002) *The Clash of Fundamentalism: Crusaders, Jihads and Modernity*. New York: Verso.

Allais, M. (1952 [1979]) "The Foundations of a Positive Theory of Choice Involving Risk, and a Criticism of the Postulates and Axioms of the American School." In M. Allais and O. Hagen (eds.) *Expected Utility Hypotheses and the Allais Paradox: Contemporary Discussions of Decisions Under Uncertainty with Allais' Rejoinder*. Dordrecht, Holland: D. Reidel.

Al-Shuaibi, Issa (1980) "The Development of Palestinian Entity-Consciousness: Part II." *Journal of Palestine Studies*. 9(2): 50–70.

Alvarez, Lizette (2005) "A Killing in Belfast Is Turning Backers Against a Defiant IRA" *New York Times*. 7 March.

Anderson, Benedict (2003) *Imagined Communities: Reflections on the Origin and Spread of Nationalism*. New York: Verso.

Anderson, S. (1994) "Making A Killing." *Harper's Magazine*. 288: February.

Anderson, Thomas S. (2004) "Transnational Organized Terror and Organized Crime: Blurring the Lines." *SAIS Review*. 24(1) Winter: 50–52.

Andreoni, J. (1989) "Giving with Impure Altruism." *Journal of Political Economy*. 97: 1447–1458.

Andreoni, J. (1990). "Impure Altruism and Donations to Public Goods: A Theory of Warm-Glow Giving." *Economic Journal*. 100: 464–477.

Arafat, Yasser (1982) "A Discussion with Yasser Arafat" *Journal of Palestine Studies*. 11(2): 3–15.

Arce, M., Daniel, G. and Todd Sandler (2005) "Counterterrorism: A Game-Theoretic Analysis." *Journal of Conflict Resolution*. 49(2): 183–201.

Aristotle (1962) *Polity*. Trans. T. A. Sinclair. Baltimore: Penguin.

Aron, Jannie (2000) "Growth and Institutions: A Review of the Evidence." *The World Bank Economic Review*. 15(1): 99–135.

Aronson, Geoffrey (1990) *Israel, Palestinians, and the Intifada*. London: Routledge.

Arquilla, John and David F. Ronfeldt (2002) *Networks and Netwars: The Future of Terror, Crime, and Militancy*. Washington DC: RAND Corporation.

Ashraf, Nava, Colin F. Camerer and George Lowenstein (2005) "Adam Smith, Behavioral Economist." *Journal of Economic Perspectives*. 19(3): 131–145.

Atran, Scott (2002) *In Gods We Trust: The Evolutionary Landscape of Religion*. Oxford: Oxford University Press.

Atran, Scott (2003) "Who Wants to Be a Martyr?" *New York Times*. 5 May.

Avalos, Hector (2005) *Fighting Words: The Orgins of Religious Violence*. Amherst, NY: Prometheus Books.

Avineri, Shlomo (1969) *Karl Marx on Colonialism and Modernization*. New York: Doubleday.

Bagai, Jogesh Chandra (1953) *Peasant Rebellion in Bengal*. Calcutta: Subrnarekha Press.

Baker, Ronald W. and Jennifer Nordin (2007) "Dirty Money: What the Underworld Understands that Economists Do Not." The Berkeley Electronic Press.

Bammel, E. and C. F. D. Moule (eds.) (1984) *Jesus and the Politics of His Day*. Cambridge; New York: Cambridge University Press.

Bandura, Albert (1973) *Aggression: A Social Learning Analysis*. New York: Prentice Hall.

Bandura, Albert (1998) "Mechanism for Moral Disengagement." In W. Reich (ed.) *Origins of Terrorism: Psychologies, Ideologies, Theologies, States of Mind*. Washington DC: Woodrow Wilson Center Press: 161–192.

Bandura, Albert (2004) "The Role of Selective Moral Disengagement in Terrorism and Counterterrorism." In F. M. Moghaddam and A. J. Marsella (eds.) *Understanding Terrorism: Psychological Roots, Consequences, and Interventions*. Washington DC: American Psychological Association Press: 121–150.

Bandyopadhyay, Taradas and Dipak K. Gupta (2002) "A Proposal for 'Generalizing Individual Choice Model,' " Public Choice Society Annual Meeting, San Diego.

Banerjee, Sumanta (1980) *In the Wake of Naxalbari: A History of the Naxalite Movement in India*. Calcutta: Subarnarekha.

Banks, Arthur S. (1971) *Cross-Polity Time Series Data*. Cambridge, MA: MIT Press.

Banks, Arthur S. and Robert B. Textor (1963) *A Cross-Polity Survey*. Cambridge: MIT Press.

Barber, Benjamin (1995) *Jihad vs. McWorld: How the Planet is Both Falling Apart and Coming Together and What it Means for Democracy*. New York: Times Books, Random House.

Baron, Lawrence (1995). "The Moral Minority: Psycho-Social Research on the Righteous Gentiles." In Franklin Littell, Alan Berger, and Hubert Locke (eds.) *What Have We Learned? Telling the Story and Teaching the Lessons of the Holocaust. Papers of the 20th Anniversary Scholars' Conference.* Symposium Series. Volume 30. Lewiston: Edwin Mellen Press: 139–159.

Baron, Lawrence (1996) "Religious and Secular Insights into 'Righteous Gentile' " *Shofar.* 14 (Winter): 96–105.

Barro, Robert J. (2000) "Inequality and Growth in a Panel of Countries." *Journal of Economic Growth.* 5(1) March: 1–5.

Barth, Frederick (1970) *Ethnic Groups and Boundaries: The Social Organization of Cultural Difference.* London: Allen & Unwin.

Basu, Sajal (1974) *West Bengal—The Violent Years.* Calcutta: Prachi Publications.

Baumol, William J. and Alan S. Blinder (1985) *Economics: Principles and Policy.* Third edition. San Diego, CA: Harcourt Brace Jovanovich.

Baxter, Craig (1997) *Bangladesh: From a Nation to a State.* Boulder, CO: Westview Press.

BBC (2007) "UK al-Qaeda Cell Members Jailed." 15 June. http://news.bbc.co.uk/2/hi/uk_news/6755797.stm

Beaty, J. S. C. Gwynne (1993). *The Outlaw Bank: A Wild Ride into the Secret Heart of BCCI.* New York: Random House.

Becker, Gary (1976) *Economic Approaches to Human Behavior.* Chicago: University of Chicago Press.

Becker, Gary (1996) *Accounting for Taste.* Cambridge, MA: Harvard University Press.

Beevor, Antony (2006) *The Battle for Spain.* New York: Penguin.

Begin, Menachem (1951) *The Revolt: The Story of the Irgun.* Trans. Shmuel Katz. New York: Simon & Schuster.

Begin, Menachem (1972) *The Revolt.* Los Angeles: Nash Publishers.

Bell, Daniel and Irving Kristol (1981) *The Crisis in Economic Theory.* New York: Basic Books.

Benjamin, Daniel and Steven Simon (2002) *The Age of Sacred Terror.* New York: Random House.

Bergen, Peter (2002) *Holy War, Inc.: Inside the Secret World of Osama bin Laden.* New York: Touchstone.

Berkey, Jonathan P. (2003) *The Formation of Islam: Religion and Society in the Near East, 600–1800.* Cambridge: Cambridge University Press.

Berman, Eli (2003) "Hamas, Taliban and the Jewish Underground: An Economist's View of Radical Religious Militias." NBER Working Paper # 1004. October.

Berman, Eli and David D. Leitin (2007) "Hard Targets: Theory and Evidence on Suicide Attacks." Paper presented at the Institute for Global Conflict and Cooperation conference on Terrorist Organization, University of California, San Diego. 3–5 May.

Berman, Paul (2003a) *Terror and Liberalism.* New York: W. W. Norton.

Berman, Paul (2003b) "The Philosopher of Islamic Terror." *New York Times Magazine.* 3 March; http://members.cox.net/slsturgi3/PhilosopherOfIslamicTerror.htm.

Berrebi, Claude (2003) *Evidence About the Link Between Education, Poverty, and Terrorism Among Palestinians.* www.irs.princeton.edu/pubs/pdfs.477.pdf.

Biggs, Michael (2005) "Dying Without Killing: Self-Immolations, 1963–2002." In Diego Gambetta (ed.) *Making Sense of Suicide Mission.* Oxford: Oxford University Press: 172–208.

Bishop, P. and E. Mallie (1987) *The Provisional IRA*. London: Corgi.

Bjorgo, Tore (2005) *The Root Causes of Terrorism*. London: Routledge.

Blaug, Mark (1968) *Economic Theory in Retrospect*. Rev. ed. Homewood, IL: Richard D. Irwin.

Blaug, Mark (1980) *The Methodology of Economics*. Cambridge: Cambridge University Press.

Bloom, Mia (2005) *Dying to Kill: The Allure of Suicide Terror*. New York: Columbia University Press.

Bose, Sumantra (2003) *Kashmir: Roots of Conflict, Path to Peace*. Cambridge, MA: Harvard University Press.

Bose, Sumantra (2007) "JKLF and JKHM: Jammu and Kashmir Liberation Front and Jammu and Kashmir Hizb-ul Majahideen." In Marianne Heiberg, Brendan O'Leary, and John Tirman (eds.) *Terror, Insurgency, and the State*. Philadelphia: University of Pennsylvania Press: 229–256.

Bowles, Chester (1969) *A View from New Delhi*. Bombay: Allied Publishers.

Bowles, Samuel (1998) "Endogeneous Preferences: The Cultural Consequences of Markets and other Economic Institutions." *Journal of Economic Literature*. 36 (March): 74–111.

Brams, Steven (1998) Cooperation Through Threats: the Northern Ireland Case." *PS: Political Science and Politics*. 31(1): 32–39.

Brennan, M. (1980) *The War in Clair 1911–1921: Personal Memoirs of the Irish War of Independence*. Dublin: Four Courts Press.

Brookes, Peter (2005) "Hearts and Minds" *New York Post*, online edition. http://www.terrorfreetomorrow.org/articlenav.php?id=75

Brookings Institution (2007) "The Hizballah's Staying Power: An Assessment." Washington DC, 10 April.

Buchanan, M. (2002). *Nexus: Small Worlds and the Groundbreaking Science of Networks*. New York: W. W. Norton.

Bueno de Mesquita, Bruce (1981) *The War Trap*. New Haven, CT: Yale University Press.

Bueno de Mesquita, Bruce (1985) "The War Trap Revisited." *American Political Science Review*. 79 (March): 156–177.

Bueno de Mesquita, Ethan (2005a) "The Quality of Terror." *American Journal of Political Science*. 49(3): 515–530.

Bueno de Mesquita, Ethan (2005b) "The Terrorist Endgame: A Model with Moral Hazard and Learning." *Journal of Conflict Resolution*. 49(2): 237–258.

Bueno de Mesquita, Ethan (2007a) "The Propaganda by the Deed: Terrorism, Counterterrorism, and Mobilization." Paper presented at the Institute for Global Conflict and Cooperation conference on Terrorist Organization, University of California, San Diego. 3–5 May.

Bueno de Mesquita, Ethan (2007b) "Correlates of Public Support for Terrorism in the Muslim World." United States Institute of Peace, working paper.

Buford, Bill (1992) *Among the Thugs*. New York: W. W. Norton.

Burke, Jason (2003) *Al-Qaeda: Casting a Shadow of Terror*. London: I. B. Tauris.

Buzan, Barry and Ole Waever (2003) *Regions and Powers: The Structure of International Security*. Cambridge: Cambridge University Press.

Calman, Leslie J. (1985) *Protest in Democratic India: Authority's Response to Challenge*. Boulder, CO: Westview Press.

Camerer, Colin F. and Ernst Fehr (2006) "When Does 'Economic Man' Dominate Social Behavior?" *Science*. 6 January. 311: 47–52.

Campos, German Guzman (1968) *La Violencia en Colombia: Parte Descriptiva.* Cali: Ediciones Progreso.

Capella, Joseph N. and Kathleen H. Jamieson (1997) *Spiral of Cynicism: The Press and the Public Good.* New York: Oxford University Press.

Carroll, Peter N. and James D. Fernandez (eds.) (2007) *Facing Fascism: New York and the Spanish Civil War.* New York: Museum of the City of New York: NYU Press.

Chatterjee, Partha (1998) *The Nation and Its Fragments: Colonial and Post-Colonial Histories.* Princeton: University of Princeton Press.

Chernick, Marc (2007) "FARC-EP: Lasa Fuerzas Armadas Revolutionarias de Colombia-Ejercito del Pueblo." In Marianne Heiberg, Brendan O'Leary, and John Tirman (eds.) *Terror, Insurgency, and the State.* Philadelphia: University of Pennsylvania Press: 51–82.

Chirot, Daniel and Clark McCauley (2006) *Why Not Kill Them All? The Logic and Prevention of Mass Political Murder.* Princeton, NJ: Princeton University Press.

Chong, Dennis (1991) *Collective Action and Civil Rights Movement.* Chicago: University of Chicago Press.

Chong, Dennis (1996) "Creating Common Frames of Reference on Political Issues." In Diana C. Mutz, Paul Sniderman, and Richard A. Brody (eds.) *Political Persuasion and Attitude Change.* Ann Arbor, MI: University of Michigan Press.

Clark, R. (1983) "Patterns in the Lives of ETA Members." *Terrorism*, 6: 423–54.

Clarke, L. (1987) *Broadening the Battlefield: The H-Blocks and the Rise of Sinn Fein.* Dublin: Gill and McMillan.

Cleaver, Kathleen and George N Katsiaficas (eds.) (2001) *Liberation, Imagination and the Black Panther Party: A New Look at the Black Panthers and their Legacy.* London: Routledge.

Cohen, Richard (2002) "Palestinian Suicide Signal Desperation, Irrationality." *Washington Post*: A 14.

Coll, S. and S. Glasser (2005) "Terrorists Turn to Web as Base of Operations." *Washington Post.* 7 August.

Collier, Paul M. and Anke Hoeffler (2004) "Greed and Grievance in Civil War." *Oxford Economic Papers.* 56(4): 563–584.

Collier, Paul and Nicholas Sambanis (2005) *Understanding Civil War: Evidence and Analysis.* Washington DC: World Bank.

Collins, Eamon and Mick McGovern (1999). *Killing Rage.* London: Granta Books.

Congressional Research Service, The Library of Congress: *The Cost of Iraq, Afghanistan, and Other Global War on Terror Operations Since 9/11.* Washington, DC: US Government Publications.

Coogan, Tim Pat (2002) *The IRA.* New York: St. Martin's Press.

Cooper, H. (1977) "What is a Terrorist? A Psychological Perspective." *Legal Medical Quarterly.* 1: 16–32.

Cota-McKinley, A., W. Woody and P. Bell (2001) "Vengeance: Effects of Gender, Age, Religious Background." *Aggressive Behavior.* 27: 343–350.

Crayton, J. W. (1983) "Terrorism and the Psychology of the Self." In L. Z. Freedman and Y. Alexander (eds.) *Perspectives on Terrorism.* Wilmington, DE: Scholarly Resources Inc., 33–41.

Crenshaw, Martha (1981) "The Causes of Terrorism." *Contemporary Politics.* 13: 379–399.

Crenshaw, Martha (1985) "An Organizational Political Approach to the Analysis of Political Terrorism." *Orbis*. 29: 465–489.

Crenshaw, Martha (1986) "The Psychology of Political Terrorism." In Margaret Herman (ed.) *Political Psychology*. San Francisco: Josey-Bass. 379–413.

Crenshaw, Martha (1988) "Theories of Terrorism: Instrumental and Organizational Approaches." In David C. Rapoport (ed.) *Inside Terrorist Organizations*. London: Frank Cass.

Crenshaw, Martha (1998) "The Logic of Terrorism: Terrorist Behavior as a Product of Strategic Choice." In Walter Reich (ed.) *Origins of Terrorism: Psychologies, Ideologies, States of Mind*. Washington DC: Woodrow Wilson Center Press.

Crenshaw, Martha (2007) "Explaining Suicide Terrorism: A Review." *Security Studies*. 16(1): 133–162.

Dahl, Robert (1961) "The Behavioral Approach in Political Science: Epitaph for a Monument to a Successful Protest." *American Political Review*. 55(4): 763–772.

Dahrendorf, Ralph (1958) "Toward A Theory of Conflict." *Journal of Conflict Resolution*. 2: 69–105.

Damasio, Antonio R. (1994) *Descartes' Error: Emotion, Reason, and the Human Brain*. New York: Avon Books.

Dandaurand, Yvvon and Vivienne Chin (2004) *Links Between Terrorism and Other Forms of Crime*. A report submitted to Foreign Affairs, Canada. Vancouver, International Centre for Criminal Law Reform and Criminal Justice Policy, April.

d'Aquili, Eugene and Andrew Newberg (1999) *The Mystical Mind: Probing the Biology of Religious Experience*. Minneapolis, MN: Fortress Press.

Daraghai, Borzou (2001) "Financing Terror." *Time*. November.

Darwin, Charles (1859 [1936]) *The Origin of Species by Means of Natural Selection: or, The Preservation of Favored Races in the Struggle for Life and the Descent of Man and Selection in Relation to Sex*. London: J. Murray. [New York: The Modern Library, Penguin.]

Das Gupta, A.K. (1985) *Epochs of Economic Theory*. Oxford: Basil Blackwell.

Dasgupta, Biplab (1975) *The Naxalite Movement*. New Delhi: Allied Publishers.

Dash, Mike (2005) *Thug: The True Story of India's Murderous Cult*. London: Granta Books.

Davies, James C. (1962) "Toward a Theory of Revolution." *American Sociological Review*. 27: 5–19.

Dawkins, Richard (2006) *The God Delusion*. Boston: Houghton Mifflin.

de Figueiredo, Rui J. P. Jr. and Barry R. Weingast (2001) "Vicious Cycles: Endogenous Political Extremism and Political Violence." Institute of Governmental Studies Working Paper # 2001–99.

De Sousa, Ronald (1991) *The Rationality of Emotion*. Cambridge, MA: MIT Press.

de Waal, Frans (1996) *Good Natured: The Origins of Right and Wrong in Humans and Other Animals*. Cambridge, MA: Harvard University Press.

de Waal, Frans (ed.) (2006) *Primates and Philosophers: How Morality Evolved*. Princeton: Princeton University Press.

Dean, Dwight G. (1961) "Alienation: Its Meaning and Measurement." *American Sociological Review*. 26(5): 753–758.

Debiel, Tobias and Axel Klein (2002) *Fragile Peace: State Failure, Violence and Development in Crisis Regions*. New York: Palgrave.

Debray, R. (1967). *Revolution in the Revolution?* New York: MR Press.

DeNardo, James (1985) *Power in Numbers: The Political Strategy of Protest and Rebellion.* Princeton, NJ: Princeton University Press.

Deng, Francis (1989) "The Identity Factor in the Sudanese Conflict." In Joseph Montville (ed.) *Conflict and Peacemaking in Multiethnic Societies.* Boston: D. C. Heath: 343–362.

Deng, Francis (1995) *War of Visions: Conflict of Identities in the Sudan.* Washington DC: Brookings Institution.

Dershowitz, Alan (2003) *Why Terrorism Works: Understanding the Threat, Responding to the Challenge.* New Haven, CT: Yale University Press.

Deutsch, Karl W. (1953) *Nationalism and Social Communication.* Cambridge, MA: MIT Press.

Dingley, James (2002) "Marching Down the Garvaghy Road: Republican Tactics and State Response to the Orangemen's Claim to March their Traditional Route Home after the Drumcree Church Service." *Terrorism and Political Violence.* 14(3): 42–79.

Dishman, Chris (2001) "Terrorism, Crime, and Transformation." *Studies in Conflict & Terrorism.* 24 (1): 43–59.

Dishman, Chris (2006) "The Leaderless Nexus: When Crime and Terror Converge." In R. D. Howard and R. L. Sawyer (eds.) *Terrorism and Counterterrorism.* Dubuque, IA: McGraw Hill: 367–382.

Dixit, Avinash and Barry Nalebuff (1991) *Thinking Strategically: The Competitive Edge in Business, Politics, and Everyday Life.* New York: W. W. Norton.

Dixon, Paul (2006) *Northern Ireland Peace Process: Choreography and Theatrical Politics.* London: Routledge.

Dollard, John *et al.* (1939) *Frustration and Aggression.* New Haven, CT: Yale University Press.

Downs, Anthony (1957) *An Economic Theory of Democracy.* New York: Harper.

Dreze, Jean and Amartya K. Sen (1989) *Hunger and Public Action.* New York: Oxford University Press.

Druckman, James N. (1999). "Do Party Cues Limit Framing Effects?" Paper presented at the Mental Models in Social Science Conference, University of California, San Diego, 29–31 July.

Durant, Will (1950) *The Age of Faith.* New York: Simon & Schuster.

Durkheim, Emile (1933) *The Division of Labor in Society.* Trans. George Simpson. New York: The Free Press of Glencoe.

Dye, Thomas R. and Harmon Ziegler (1981) *The Irony of Democracy.* Monterey, CA: Brooks/Cole.

Dyke, C. (1981) *Philosophy of Economics.* Englewood Cliffs, NJ: Prentice Hall.

Eckstein, Harry (ed.) (1964) *Internal War: Problems and Approaches.* New York: Free Press.

Edgerton, Robert B. (1989) *Mau Mau: An African Crucible.* New York: Free Press.

Edgeworth, Francis Y. (1881 [1961]) *Mathematical Psychics: An Essay on the Application of Mathematics to the Moral Sciences.* London: Kegan Paul. [New York: A. M. Kelley.]

Ehrenfeld, Rachel (2005) *Funding Evil, Updated: How Terrorism is Financed and How to Stop It.* New York: Bonus Books.

Ekeh, Peter P. (1974) *Social Exchange Theory: The Two Traditions.* Cambridge, MA: Harvard University Press.

El-Maraghi, Mohammed (2001) "Poised in Fear." *Al Ahram Weekly.* 5–11 July.

Elm, Mostafa (1994). *Oil, Power, and Principle: Iran's Oil Nationalization and Its Aftermath*. Syracuse: Syracuse University Press.

Elster, Jon (1979a) "Anomalies of Rationality: Some Unresolved Problems in the Theory of Rational Behavior." In L. Levy-Garboua (ed.) *Sociological Economics*. London: Sage Publications.

Elster, Jon (1979b) *Ulysses and the Sirens: Studies in Rationality and Irrationality*. Cambridge: Cambridge University Press.

Elster, Jon (1983) *Sour Grapes*. Cambridge: Cambridge University Press.

Elster, Jon (2005) "Motivations and Beliefs in Suicide Missions." In Diego Gambetta, (ed.) *Making Sense of Suicide Mission*. Oxford: Oxford University Press: 233–258.

Emerson, Richard (1972) "Exchange Theory: Part I: A Psychological Basis for Social Exchange." In Joseph Berger, Morris Zelditch and Bo Anderen (eds.) *Sociological Theories in Progress*. Vol. 2. Boston: Houghton Mifflin: 38–57.

Enders, Walter and Todd Sandler (1993) "The Effectiveness of Antiterrorism Policies: A Vector-Autoregression-Intervention Analysis." *American Political Science Review*. 8: 829–844.

Enders, Walter and Todd Sandler (2005) *The Political Economy of Terrorism*. New York: Cambridge University Press.

Enders, Walter, Todd Sandler, and J. Cauley (1990) "UN Conventions, Technology, and Retaliation in the Fight Against Terrorism: An Econometric Evaluation." *Terrorism and Political Violence*. 2: 83–105.

English, Richard (2003). *Armed Struggle: The History of the IRA*. Oxford: Oxford University Press.

Enomoto, Carl E. (1999) "Public Sympathy for O. J. Simpson: The Role of Race, Age, Gender, Income and Education." *American Journal of Economics and Sociology*. 58(1): 145–162.

Entman, Robert (1993) "Framing: Toward Clarification of a Fractured Paradigm." *Journal of Communication*. 43: 51–58.

Epstein, A. L. (1958) *Politics in an Urban African Community*. Manchester: Manchester University Press.

Ergil, Dogu (2007) "PKK: Partiya Karkaren Kurdistan." In Marianne Heiberg, Brendan O'Leary, and John Tirman (eds.) *Terror, Insurgency, and the State*. Philadelphia: University of Pennsylvania Press: 323–358.

Esman, Milton (1994) *Ethnic Politics*. Ithaca: Cornell University Press.

Esposito, John (ed.) (2003) *Oxford Dictionary of Islam*. Oxford: Oxford University Press.

Esposito, John and John O. Vold (1996) *Islam and Democracy*. Oxford: Oxford University Press.

Evensky, Jerry (2005) *Adam Smith's Moral Philosophy: A Historical and Contemporary Perspective on Markets, Law, Ethics, and Culture*. New York: Cambridge University Press.

Fair, Christina and Bryan Shepherd (2006) "Who Supports Terrorism? Evidence from Fourteen Muslim Countries." *Studies in Conflict and Terrorism*. 29(1): 51–74.

Farace, R., P. Monge, and H. Russell (1977). *Communicating and Organizing*. Reading, MA: Addison-Wesley.

Farber, M. L. (1968) *Theory of Suicide*. New York: Funk and Wagnalls.

Farley, Christopher J. (1997) "Kids and Race: A New Poll Shows Teenagers, Black and White, Have Moved Beyond Parents." *Time*. 24 November: 88–91.

Fearon, James D. and David D. Laitin (2003) "Ethnicity, Insurgency and Ethnic War." *American Political Science Review*. 97(1): 75–90.

Feeney, Brian (2003) *Sinn Fein: A Hundred Turbulent Years*. Madison, WI: University of Wisconsin Press.

Fehr, Ernst and Urs Fishbacher (2003) "The Nature of Human Altruism." *Nature*. 425 October: 785–791.

Feierabend, Ivo and Rosalind Feierabend (1966) "Aggressive Behavior within Polities, 1948–1962: A Cross-National Study." *Journal of Conflict Resolution*. 10: 249–271.

Feierabend, Ivo and Rosalind Feierabend (1972) "Systemic Conditions of Political Aggression: An Application of Frustration-Aggression Theory." In Ivo Feierabend (ed.) *Anger, Violence, and Politics*. Englewood Cliffs, NJ: Prentice Hall.

Feierabend, Ivo, Rosalind Feierabend, and Betty A. Nesvold (1969) "Social Change and Political Violence: Cross-National Patterns." In Hugh D. Graham and Ted R. Gurr (eds.) *Violence in America: A Report to the National Commission on the Causes and Prevention of Violence*. New York: Signet Books.

Fernbach, D. (ed.) (1974) *Karl Marx: The Revolution of 1848*. New York: Vantage Books.

Ferracuti, F. and F. Bruno (1981) "Psychiatric Aspects of Terrorism in Italy." In I. L. Barak-Glantz and C. R. Huff (eds.) *The Mad, The Bad, and the Different: Essays in Honor of Simon Dinitz*. Lexington, MA: D. C. Heath: 199–213.

Ferracuti, F. (1982) "A Sociopsychiatric Interpretation of Terrorism." *Annals of the American Academy of Political and Social Sciences*. 463: 129–140.

Feuer, L. A. (1969) *The Conflict of Generations*. New York: Basic Books.

Filler, Alfredo (2002) "The Abu Sayyaf Group: A Growing Menace to the Civil Society." *Terrorism and Political Violence*. 14(4): 131–146.

Fiorina, Mossir P. (1990) "Information and Rationality in Elections." In John Ferejohn and James Kuklinski (eds.) *Information and the Democratic Process*. Urbana, IL: University of Illinois Press.

Fisk, Robert (1975) *The Point of No Return: The Strike Which Broke the British in Ulster*. London: Andre Deutsch.

Flint, Julie (2005) *Darfur: A Short History of A Long War*. New York: Palgrave Macmillan.

Foreign Policy. State Failure Index. http://www.foreignpolicy.com/story/cms.php?story_id=3098&src2=PJA05

Foucault, Michele (1970) *The Order of Things: An Archeology of Human Sciences*. New York: Pantheon Books.

Franda, Marcus F. (1971) *Radical Politics in West Bengal*. Cambridge, MA: MIT Press.

Frank, Robert H. (1997) "The Frame of Reference as a Public Good." *The Economic Journal* 107 (November): 1832–1847.

Freedman, Robert O. (ed.) (1991) *The Intifada: Its Impact on Israel, the Arab World, and the Superpowers*. Miami: University of Florida Press.

French, Patrick (1997) *Liberty or Death: India's Journey to Independence and Division*. New York: HarperCollins.

Freud, Sigmund (1930) *Civilization and Its Discontents*. Trans. J. Reviere. London: Hogarth Press.

Friedman, Milton (1953) *Essays in Positive Economics*. Chicago: University of Chicago Press.

Frohlich, Norman and Joe Oppenheimer (1978) *Modern Political Economy*. Englewood Cliffs, NJ: Prentice Hall.

Fukuyama, Francis (1992) *The End of History and the Last Man*. New York: The Free Press.

Fulk, J. (2001) "Global Network Organizations: Emergence and Future Prospects." *Human Relations*. 54: 91–99.

Furnivall, John S. (1944) *Netherlands' India: A Study in Plural Economy*. New York: Macmillan.

Gallagher, F. (1928). *The Days of Fear*. London: John Murray.

Gambetta, Diego (1993) The *Sicilian Mafia: The Business of Private Protection*. Cambridge, MA: Harvard University Press.

Gambetta, Diego (2005) "Can We Make Sense of Suicide Mission?" In Diego Gambetta (ed.) *Making Sense of Suicide Mission*. Oxford: Oxford University Press: 259–300.

Gamson, William A. and Andre Modigliani (1987) "The Changing Culture of Affirmative Action." In Richard D. Braungart (ed.) *Research in Political Sociology*. Vol. 3. Greenwich, CT: JAI Press.

Gartenstein-Ross, Daveed and Kylee Dabruzzi (2007). "The Convergence of Crime and Terror: Law Enforcement Opportunities and Perils." New York: Center for Policing Terrorism. Manhattan Institute (26 March).

Gasiorowski, Mark (1991) *U.S. Foreign Policy and the Shah: Building a Client State in Iran*. Ithaca, NY: Cornell University Press.

Geertz, Clifford (1963) *Old Societies and New States: The Quest for Modernity in Asia and Africa*. Glencoe, IL: Free Press.

Georgescu-Roegan, N. (1979) "Methods in Economic Science." *Journal of Economic Issues*. 13: 317–328.

Geyer, Felix and Walter R. Heinz (eds.) (1996) *Alienation: Society, and the Individual*. New Brunswick, NJ: Transaction Press.

Geyer, Georgie Ann (1997) "Control the Media and Win Bosnia." *San Diego Union Tribune*. 24 November: E4.

Gilman, J. (1958) *The Falling Rate of Profit*. New York: Cameron Associates.

Gilligan, J. (2000). *Violence: Reflections on Our Deadliest Epidemic*. London: Jessica Kingsley.

Ginkel, John and Alastair Smith (1999) "So You Say You Want a Revolution: A Game Theoretic Explanation of Revolution in Repressive Regimes." *Journal of Conflict Resolution*. 43(3): 291–316.

Glazer, Nathan and Daniel P. Moynihan (eds.) (1975) *Ethnicity: Theory and Experience*. Cambridge, MA: Harvard University Press.

Goldhagen, Daniel J. (1996) *Hitler's Willing Executioners: Ordinary Germans and the Holocaust*. New York: Alfred Knopf.

Goodall, Jane (1986) *The Chimpanzees of Gombe: Patterns of Behavior*. Cambridge, MA: Belknap Press of Harvard University Press.

Goodall, Jane (1990) *Through a Window: My Life with the Chimpanzees of Gombe*. Boston: Houghton Mifflin.

Gordon, Leonard (1990) *Brothers Against the Raj: A Biography of Indian Nationalists Sarat and Subhas Chandra Bose*. Princeton, NJ: Princeton University Press.

Gordon, Milton (1964) *Assimilation in American Life: The Role of Race, Religion, and National Origins*. New York: Oxford University Press.

Gordon, Robert (1971) "Rigor and Relevance in a Changing Institutional Setting." *American Economic Review*. 61: 1–7.

Gould, Steven J. (1981) *The Mismeasure of Man*. New York: W. W. Norton.

Gould, Steven J. (1990) *Individual in Darwin's World: The Second Edinburgh Medal Address*. Edinburgh: University of Edinburgh Press.

Gould, Steven J. (1994) *Bully for the Brontosaurus: Reflections in Natural History*. New York: Voyager.

Graham, Hugh D. and Ted R. Gurr (eds.) (1969) *The History of Violence in America: Historical and Comparative Perspectives: A Report Submitted to the National Commission on the Cause and Prevention of Violence*. New York.

Grampp, William (1948) "Adam Smith and the Economic Man." *Journal of Political Economy*. 56(4): 315–336.

Greenberg, Karen J. (ed.) (2006) *The Torture Debate in America*. Cambridge: Cambridge University Press.

Grossbard-Shechtman, Shoshana (1993) *On Economics of Marriage*. Boulder, CO: Westview Press.

Grossbard-Shechtman, Shoshana and Christopher Clague (eds.) (2002) *The Expansion of Economics: Toward a More Inclusive Social Science*. Armonk, NY: M. E. Sharpe.

Guang, Lei (2005) "Realpolitik Nationalism: International Sources of Chinese Nationalism." *Modern China* 31(4): 487–514.

Guetzkow, H. (1965) "Communications in Organizations." In J. March (ed.) *Handbook of Organizations*. Chicago: Rand McNally: 534–573.

Guevara, Che (1985) *Guerrilla Warfare*. Lincoln, NE: University of Nebraska Press.

Guha, Ramchandra (2006a) "The Revolution and Its Children: The Battle for Bastar" *Telegraph Calcutta*. 27 June, p. 19.

Guha, Ramchandra (2006b) "Tribe Against Tribe, Village Against Village: The Battle for Bastar" *Telegraph Calcutta*. 28 June, p. 19.

Guha, Ramchandra (2006c) "Struggle and Strife: The Battle for Bastar" *Telegraph Calcutta*. 29 June, p. 19.

Guha, Ranjit (1983). *Elementary Aspects of Peasant Insurgency in Colonial India*. Delhi: Oxford University Press.

Gunaratna, Rohan (2001) "The Lifeblood of Terrorist Orgnaizations: Evolving Terrorist Financial Strategies." In Alex P. Schmid (ed.) *Countering Terrorism Through International Cooperation*. Milan: ISPAC: 182–185.

Gunaratna, Rohan (2002) *Inside Al-Qaeda: Global Network of Terror*. New York: Columbia University Press.

Gunning, Jeroen (2007) "Hizballah." In Marianne Heiberg, Brendan O'Leary, and John Tirman (eds.) *Terror, Insurgency, and the State*. Philadelphia: University of Pennsylvania Press: 157–188.

Gupta, Dipak K. (1987) "Economic Behavior and the Analysis of Collective Violence." *Journal of Behavioral Economics*. 15(2): 33–44.

Gupta, Dipak K. (1990) *The Economics of Political Violence: The Effects of Political Instability on Economic Growth*. New York: Praeger.

Gupta, Dipak K. (1993) "Le paradoxe de la rébellion: Les relations inter-reciales aux Etats-Unis" *Cultures et Conflict: L'Action Collectives*. Journal of Institut d'Etdes Politique de Paris. December: 9–44.

Gupta, Dipak K. (1998) *Clash of Identities: Albert W. Johnson Lecture*. San Diego, CA: San Diego State University Press.

Gupta, Dipak K. (1999) "Ethnicity and Politics in the US: The Predicament of the African-American Minority." *Ethnic Studies Report*. 15(2) July: 215–254.

Gupta, Dipak K. (2001a) *Path to Collective Madness: A Study in Social Order and Political Pathology*. Westport, CT: Praeger.

Gupta, Dipak K. (2001b) *Analyzing Public Policy: Concepts, Tools, and Techniques*. Washington DC: CQ Press.

Gupta, Dipak K. (2002) "Economics and Collective Identity: Explaining Collective Action." In Shoshana Grossbard-Shechtman and Christopher Clague (eds.) *The Expansion of Economics: Toward a More Inclusive Social Science*. Armonk, NY: M. E. Sharpe.

Gupta, Dipak K. (2005) "Exploring Root Causes of Terrorism." In Tore Bjorgo (ed.) *Root Causes of Terrorism: Myths, Reality and Ways Forward*. London: Routledge: 16–32.

Gupta, Dipak K. (2006a) "International Terrorism and the Costs of Over-reaction." *Public Money and Management*. 26(5) November: 274–277.

Gupta, Dipak K. (2006b) "Tyranny of Data: Going Beyond Theories." In Jeff Victoroff (ed.) *Tangled Roots: Social and Psychological Factors in the Genesis of Terrorism*. Amsterdam: IOS Press.

Gupta, Dipak K. (2006c) *Who Are the Terrorists?* Philadelphia: Chelsea House Publishing.

Gupta, Dipak K. (2007) "The Naxalites and the Maoist Movement in India: Birth, Demise, and Reincarnation." *Democracy and Security*. 3(2): 157–188.

Gupta, Dipak K. and Harinder Singh (1992) "Collective Rebellious Behavior: An Expected Utility Approach of Behavioral Motivations." *Political Psychology*. 13(3): 379–406.

Gupta, Dipak K. and Kusum Mundra (2005) "Suicide Bombing as a Rational Strategy: Hamas and the Islamic Jihad." *Terrorism and Political Violence*. 17(4): 573–598.

Gupta, Dipak K., Richard Hofstetter, and Terry Buss (1997) "Group Utility in the Micro Motivation of Collective Action: The Case of Membership in the AARP." *Journal of Economic Behavior and Organization*. 34. May.

Gupta, Dipak K., Harinder Singh, and Tom Sprague (1993) "Government Coercion of Dissidents: Deterrence or Provocation?" *Journal of Conflict Resolution*. 37(2) June: 301–339.

Gupta, Dipak K., John Horgan and Alex P. Schmid (forthcoming) "A Marriage Made in Hell? Terrorism and Organized Crime." In David Canter (ed.) *Faces of Terrorism*. London: Wiley-Blackwell.

Gupta, Ranjit (2005) *The Crimson Agenda: Maoist Protest and Terror*. Delhi: Wordsmiths.

Gurr, Ted R. (1970) *Why Men Rebel*. Princeton, NJ: Princeton University Press.

Gurr, Ted R. (1993) *Minorities at Risk*. Washington DC: US Institute of Peace.

Guthrie, George M. and Patricia P. Tanco, (1980) "Alienation." In H. C. Triandis and J. G. Draguns (eds.) *Handbook of Cross-Cultural Psychology: Psychopathology*. Boston: Allyn & Bacon. Vol. 6: 9–59.

Hacker, Andrew (1995) *Two Nations: Black and White, Separate, Unequal, Hostile*. New York: Ballantine Books.

Hacker, F. J. (1976) *Crusaders, Criminals, Crazies: Terror and Terrorism in Our Time*. New York: W. W. Norton.,

Hafez, Mohammed (2006) *Manufacturing Human Bombs: The Making of Palestinian Suicide Bombers*. Washington DC: United States Institute of Peace.

Hafez, Mohammed (2007) *Suicide Bombers in Iraq: The Strategy and Ideology of Martyrdom*. Washington DC: United States Institute of Peace.

Hagerty D. T. (1991) "India's Regional Security Doctrine." *Asian Survey*. 31(4): 351–363.

Hahn, F. H. (1970) "Some Adjustment Problems." *Econometrica*. 38: 1–17.

Hahn, F. H. and M. Hollis (eds.) (1979) *Philosophy and Economic Theory*. Oxford: Oxford University Press.

Hamid, Tawfik (2007) "The Trouble with Islam." *Wall Street Journal*. Tuesday, 3 April: A15.

Handler, J. S. (1990) "Socioeconomic Profile of an American Terrorist: 1960s and 1970s." *Terrorism*. 13: 195–213.

Haqqani, Husain and Kenneth Ballen (2005) "Sentiments Shift in the Muslim World." *Wall Street Journal*. 19 December.

Harris, Sam (2007) *The End of Faith: Religion, Terror, and the Future of Reason*. New York: W. W. Norton.

Hassan, Nasra (2001) "An Arsenal of Believers: Talking to the 'Human Bombs.' " *New Yorker*. 77: 36.

Hauser, Marc (2006) *Moral Minds: How Nature Designed our Universal Sense of Right and Wrong*. New York: Ecco.

Heller, Joseph (1995) *The Stern Gang: Ideology, Politics, and Terror, 1940–1949*. Lodon: Frank Cass.

Heller, Walter (1975) "What's Right with Economics?" *American Economic Review*. 65: 1–26.

Hellmann-Rajanayagam, D. (1988–89) "The Tamil Militants—Before the Accord and After." *Pacific Affairs*. 61(4): 603–619.

Helm, D. (1984) "Predictions and Causes: A Comparison of Friedman and Hicks Methods." *Oxford Economic Papers*. 33 (Supplement): 135–151.

Helm, D. (1985) *Enforced Maximization*. Oxford: Clarendon Press.

Henderson, Lawrence W. (1979) *Angola: Five Centuries of Conflict*. Ithaca, NY: Cornell University Press.

Heskin, Ken (1985) "Societal Disintegration in Northern Ireland—A Five Year Update." *Economic and Social Review*. 16(3): 187–199.

Hetherington, Norris S. (1983) "Isaac Newton's Influence on Adam Smith's Natural Laws in Economics." *Journal of History of Ideas*. 44(3): 497–505.

Hibbs, Douglas P. Jr. (1973) *Mass Political Violence: A Cross-National Causal Analysis*. New York: Wiley.

Hicks, John R. (1983) "A Discipline and not a Science." In J. R. Hicks (ed.) *Classics and Moderns*. Oxford: Basil Blackwell.

Hiro, Dilip (1989) *Holy Wars: The Rise of Islamic Fundamentalism*. New York: Routledge.

Hirschleifer, Jack (1985) "The Expanding Domain of Economics." *American Economic Review*. 755: 53–68.

Hirschman, Albert O. (1971) *A Bias for Hope: Essays on Development and Latin America*. New Haven, CT: Yale University Press.

Hobsbawm, Eric (1964) *The Age of Revolution, 1789–1848*. New York: Mentor.

Hobsbawm, Eric (1977) "Some Reflections on the 'Break-up of Britain'." *New Left Review*. 105: 3–24.

Hoffman, Bruce (1998) *Inside Terrorism*. New York: Columbia University Press.

Hofstader, Richard (1944) *Social Darwinism in American Thought: 1860–1915*. Philadelphia: University of Pennsylvania Press.

Holden, David and Richard Jones (1981) *The House of Saud: The Rise and Rule of the Most Powerful Dynasty in the Arab World.* New York: Holt, Rinehart, and Winston.

Holland, J. (1989) *The American Connection: US Guns, Money, and Influence in Northern Ireland.* Dublin: Poolberg Press.

Holland, J. and H. McDonald (1984) *INLA: Deadly Divisions.* Dublin: Torc.

Holmes, Stephen (2005) "Al-Qaeda, 11 September 2001." In Diego Gambetta (ed.) *Making Sense of Suicide Mission.* Oxford: Oxford University Press: 131–172.

Homer-Dixon, Thomas (1999) *Environment, Scarcity, and Violence.* Princeton, NJ: Princeton University Press.

Hopgood, Stephen (2005) "Tamil Tigers, 1987–2002." In Diego Gambetta (ed.) *Making Sense of Suicide Mission.* Oxford: Oxford University Press: 43–76.

Horgan, John (2003) "The Search for Terrorist Personality." In Andrew Silke (ed.) *Terrorists, Victims, and Society.* Chichester, UK: Wiley: 3–27.

Horgan, John (2005b) "The Social and Psychological Factors of Terrorism and Terrorists." In Tore Bjorgo (ed.) *Root Causes of Terrorism: Myths, Reality, and Ways Forward.* London: Routledge: 44–53.

Horgan, John (2005a) *The Psychology of Terrorism.* London: Routledge.

Horgan, John (2006) "Disengaging from Terrorism." *Jane's Intelligence Review.* December: 34–37.

Horgan, John and Max Taylor (2003) "Playing the 'Green Card'—Financing the Provisional IRA: Part 2." *Terrorism and Political Violence.* 15(2) Summer: 1–60.

Horne, Alistair (1977) *A Savage War of Peace: Algeria, 1954–1962.* New York: Viking Press.

Howe, Herbert M. (2004) *Ambiguous Order: Military Forces in African States.* Boulder, CO: Lynne Rainier.

Huband, Mark (1998) *The Liberian Civil War.* London: Frank Cass.

Hudson, Michael C. (1972) "Developments and Setbacks in Palestinian Resistance Movements, 1967–71." *Journal of Palestine Studies.* 1(3): 64–84.

Huntington, Samuel (1965) "Political Development and Political Decay." *World Politics.* 17(3): 386–430.

Huntington, Samuel P. (1968) *Political Order in Changing Societies.* New Haven, CT: Yale University Press.

Huntington, Samuel (1999) "The Lonely Superpower." *Foreign Affairs.* 78(2) March/April: 35–49.

Husain, Mir Zohair (2003) *Global Islamic Politics.* Second edition. New York: Longman.

Hutt, Michael (ed.) (2004) *Himalayan "People's War": Nepal's Maoist Rebellion.* London: C. Hurst & Co.

Ibrahim, Saad Eddin (2002) *Egypt, Islam and Democracy: Critical Essays.* Cairo and New York: The American University in Cairo Press.

Ignatieff, Michael (2003) *The Lesser Evil: Political Ethics in an Age of Terror.* Princeton, NJ: Princeton University Press.

Ignatyev, Oleg (1977) *Secret Weapon in Africa.* Moscow: Progress.

Iqbal, Mohammed (1981) *Shikwa & Jawab-i-Shikwa: Complaint and Answer: Iqbal's Dialogue with Allah.* Trans. Khishwant Singh. Delhi: Oxford University Press.

Isaacs, Harold (1974) "Basic Group Identity: The Idols of the Tribe." *Ethnicity.* 1: 15–42.

Jackson, Peter and Jan Penrose (eds.) (1993) *Constructions of Race, Place, and Nation.* London: UCL Press.

Jacquard, Roland (2002) *In the Name of Osama bin Laden: Global Terrorism and the bin Laden Brotherhood.* Durham, NC: Duke University Press.

Jai, J. J. (2001) "Getting at the Roots of Terrorism." *Christian Science Monitor.* 10 December.

Jamieson, Alison (2005) "The Use of Terrorism by Organized Crime: An Italian Case Study." In Tore Bjorgo (ed.) *Root Causes of Terrorism: Myths, Reality and Ways Forward.* London: Routledge: 164–177.

Jenkins, Brian M. (1975) "International Terrorism: A New Mode of Conflict." In David Carlton and Carlo Schaefer (eds.) *International Terrorism and World Security.* London: Croom Helm.

Johnson, Harry (1971) "Keynesian Revolution and Monetary Counterrevolution." *American Economic Review.* 61: 1–14.

Jones, Greta (1980) *Social Darwinism and English Thought: The Interaction Between Biological and Social Theory.* Brighton, Sussex: Harvester Press.

Juergensmeyer, Mark (2003) *Terror in the Mind of God: The Global Rise of Religious Violence.* Berkeley: University of California Press.

Kagan, Jerome (1989) *Unstable Ideas: Temperament, Cognition, and Self.* Cambridge, MA: Harvard University Press.

Kahneman, Daniel (1973) *Attention and Effort.* Englewood Cliffs, NJ: Prentice Hall.

Kahneman, Daniel and Jonathan Renshon (2007) "Why Hawks Win?" *Foreign Policy.* January/February: 3–17.

Kahneman, Daniel and Amos Tversky (1979) "Prospect Theory: An Analysis of Decision under Risk", *Econometrica*, XLVII: 263–291.

Kahneman, Daniel and Amos Tversky (1984) "Choice, Values, and Frames." *American Psychologist.* 39: 341–350.

Kahneman, Daniel, Paul Slovic, and Amos Tversky (1982) *Judgment Under Uncertainty: Heuristics and Biases.* New York: Cambridge University Press.

Kalyvas, Stathis and Igancio Sanchez-Cuenca (2005) "Killing Without Dying: The Absence of Suicide Missions." In Diego Gambetta (ed.) *Making Sense of Suicide Missions.* Oxford: Oxford University Press: 209–232.

Kaplan, David (2005). "Paying for Terror." *US News and World Report.* 5 December.

Kaplan, Robert (1994) "The Coming Anarchy." *Atlantic Monthly.* February: 44–76.

Kassimeris, George (1999) "17N: Greece's Secret Socialist Spectre." *Jane's Intelligence Review.* 1 November.

Karthikeyan, D. R. (2005) "Root Causes of Terrorism? A Case Study of the Tamil Insurgency and the LTTE." In Tore Bjorgo (ed.) *Root Causes of Terrorism.* London: Routledge: 131–140.

Kellen, Konrad (1979) *Terrorists, What Are They Like? How Some Terrorists Describe Their World and Actions.* Prepared for the Sandia Laboratories. Santa Monica, CA: RAND Corporation.

Kellen, Konrad (1984) *On Terrorists and Terrorism.* N-1942-RC. Santa Monica, CA: RAND Corporation, December.

Kelman, Herbert (1973) "Violence Without Moral Restraints." *Journal of Social Issues.* 29: 29–61.

Kelman, Herbert C. and V. L. Hamilton (1989) *Crimes of Obedience: Toward a Social Psychology of Authority and Responsibility.* New Haven, CT: Yale University Press.

Kenney, Michael (2003) "From Pablo to Osama: Counter-terrorism Lessons from the Wars on Drugs." *Survival.* 45 (3) September: 187–206.

Kent, I. and W. Nicolls (1977) "The Psychodynamics of Terrorism." *Mental Health and Society*. 4: 1–8.

Kepel, Gilles (2002) *Jihad: The Trail of Political Islam*. Trans. A. F. Roberts. Cambridge, MA: Belknap Press of Harvard University Press.

Kernell, Samuel and Gary C. Jacobson (2005) *The Logic of American Politics*. Washington DC: CQ Press. Third edition.

Kerner, Otto (1968) *Report of the National Advisory Commission on Civil Disorders*. Washington DC: Government Printing Office.

Khan, Aamer Ahmed (2007) "Can Musharraf Contain the Militant Threat?" BBC online news. 13 July. http://news.bbc.co.uk/2/hi/south_asia/6897683.stm/.

Kim, S. and R. Smith (1993) "Revenge and Conflict Escalation." *Negotiation Journal*. 9: 37–43.

King, Blair B. (1966) *The Blue Mutiny: The Indigo Disturbances in Bengal 1859–1862*. Philadelphia: University of Pennsylvania Press.

Kinzer, Stephen (1991) *Blood of Brothers: Life and War in Nicaragua*. New York: Putnam Publishing Group.

Kinzer, Stephen (2003) *All the Shah's Men: An American Coup and the Roots of Middle East Terror*. Hoboken, NJ: John Wiley & Sons.

Kochan, Nick (2006) *The Washing Machine: How Money Laundering and Terrorist Financing Soils Us*. New York: Texere.

Kohut, H. (1972) "Thoughts on Narcissism and Narcissistic Rage." *Psychoanalytic Study of the Child*. 27: 360–400.

Konet, Reuven (2001) "Sexual Fantasies of a Suicide Bomber." www.israelinsider.com.

Kornai, J. (1971) *Anti-Equilibrium*. Amsterdam: North Holland.

Kornai, J. (1985) *Contradictions and Dilemmas*. Cambridge: Cambridge University Press.

Kosnik, Mark (2000) "The Military Response to Terrorism." *Naval War College Review*. 53: 13–39.

Krueger, Alan B. and Jitka Maleckova (2003) "Education, Poverty, and Terrorism: Is There a Causal Connection?" *Journal of Economic Perspective*. 17: 119–144.

Kuhn, Thomas (1970) *The Structure of Scientific Revolution*. Second edition, enlarged. Chicago: University of Chicago Press.

Kumar, Pramod (2006) "Maoists 'Strengthening' in India's Bihar – Official." BBC Monitoring South Asia. London: 11 April, 1.

Kuper, Leo "Plural Societies: Perspectives and Problems." In Leo Kuper and M. G. Smith (eds.) *Pluralism in Africa*. Berkeley, CA: University of California Press.

Kuran, Timur (2004) *Islam and Mammon: The Economic Predicaments of Islamism*. Princeton, NJ: Princeton University Press.

Kydd, Andrew and Barbara Walter (2002) "Sabotaging the Peace: The Politics of Extremist Violence." *International Organization*. 56(2): 263–296.

Kyle, Keith. *Suez: Britain's End of Empire in the Middle East*. London: I. B. Tauris & Co. Ltd.

Lake, David A. and Donald Rothchild (eds.) (1998) *The International Spread of Ethnic Conflict: Fear, Diffusion, and Escalation*. Princeton, NJ: Princeton University Press.

Lakoff, George (1996). *Moral Politics: What Conservatives Know that Liberals Don't*. Chicago: University of Chicago Press.

Lalich, Janja (2004) *Bounded Choice: True Believers and Charismatic Cults*. Berkeley, CA: University of California Press.

Laqueur, Walter (1977) *Terrorism*. London: Weidenfeld & Nicolson.

Latsis, S. J. (ed.) (1976) *Methods and Appraisals in Economics*. Cambridge: Cambridge University Press.

Laupmann, E. and F. Pappi (1976) *Networks of Collective Action: A Perspective on Community Influence System*. New York: Academic Press.

Lawrence, Bruce (ed.) *Messages to the World: The Statements of Osama bin Laden*. New York: Verso.

Lee, J. J. (1989) *Ireland 1912–1985: Politics and Society*. Cambridge: Cambridge University Press.

Lee, Jennifer (2002) *Civility in the City: Blacks, Jews and Koreans in Urban America*. Cambridge, MA: Harvard University Press.

Lemert, Charles (2007) *Thinking the Unthinkable: The Riddle of Classical Social Theory*. Boulder: CO: Paradigm Publishers.

Lenihan, Padraig (2003) *1690 Battle of the Boyne*. Gloucestershire, UK: Tempus Publishing.

Lenin, Vladimir I. (1969 [1902]) *What Is To Be Done?* New York: The Free Press.

Lennon, Alexander (2003) *The Battle for Hearts and Minds: Using Soft Power to Undermine Terrorist Networks*. Cambridge, MA: MIT Press.

Lewis, Bernard (1968) *The Assassins: A Radical Sect in Islam*. New York: Basic Books.

Lewis, Bernard (2002) *Middle East: What Went Wrong?* Oxford: Oxford University Press.

Lezak, M. D. (1995) *Neuropsychological Assessment*. Third edition. New York: Oxford University Press.

Li, Quan (2005) "Does Democracy Promote or Reduce Transnational Terrorist Incidents?" *Journal of Conflict Resolution*. 49(2): 278–297.

Lia, Brynjar (2005) *Globalization and the Future of Terrorism: Patterns and Predictions*. London and New York: Routledge.

Lichbach, Mark I. (1987) "Deterrence or Escalation? The Puzzle of Aggregate Studies of Repression and Dissent." *Journal of Conflict Resolution*. 31: 2666–2697.

Lichbach, Mark I. (1995) *The Rebel's Dilemma*. Ann Arbor, MI: University of Michigan Press.

Lichbach, Mark I. (1997) "Contentious Map of Contentious Politics." *Mobilization*. 2(1): 87–98.

Lijphart, Arend (1996) "The Puzzle of Indian Democracy." *American Political Science Review*. 90(2): 258–268.

Lilly, Peter (2006) *Dirty Dealing: The Untold Truth about Global Money Laundering, International Crime and Terrorism*. New York: Kogan Page.

Lipnack, J. and J. Stamp (1986). *The Networking Book: People Connecting with People*. London: Routledge & Kegan Paul.

Lipset, Seymore (1959) "Some Social Perquisites of Democracy: Economic Development and Political Legitimacy." *American Political Science Review*. 53(1): 69–105.

Lipset, Seymore (1963) *Political Man*. New York: Doubleday.

London, Perry (1970) "The Rescuers: Motivational Hypotheses about Christians Who Saved Jews from the Nazis." In L. Berkowitz and J. Macauley (eds.) *Altruism and Helping Behavior: Social Psychological Studies of Some Antecedents and Consequences*. New York: Academic Press: 241–250.

Loveman, Brian and Thomas M. Davies (1985) *Guerrilla Warfare: Che Guevara*. Lincoln, NE: University of Nebraska Press.

MacCaffery, Edward J., Daniel Kahneman, and Matthew L. Spitzer (1995) "Framing the Jury: Cognitive Perspectives on Pain and Suffering Awards." *Virginia Law Review.* 81: 1341–1420.

Mack, John E. (1984) "Cultural Amplifier." Paper presented to the Committee on International Affairs at the Fall Meeting of the Group for the Advancement of Psychiatry. White Plains, New York.

Macpherson, C. B. (1962) *The Political Theory of Possessive Individualism: Hobbes to Locke.* Oxford: Oxford University Press.

MacStiofain, Sean (1975) *Memoirs of a Revolutionary.* Edinburgh: Gordon Cremonesi.

Maddock, Richard C. and Richard L. Fulton (1966) "Marketing to the Mind: Northern Ireland." *Crime, Law, and Social Change.* 20: 273–292.

Maleckova, Jitka (2005) "Impoverished Terrorists: Stereotype or Reality?" In Tore Bjorgo (ed.) *Root Causes of Terrorism: Myths, Reality and Ways Forward.* London: Routledge.

Maliniak, Daniel, Amy Oakes, Susan Peterson, and Michael J. Tierney (2007) "Inside the Ivory Tower." *Foreign Policy.* March/April.

Maloba, Wunyabari O. (1993) *Mau Mau and Kenya: An Analysis of Peasant Revolt.* Bloomington, IN: Indiana University Press.

Mao Tse-Tung (1961) *Mao Tse-Tung on Guerrilla Warfare.* Trans. Samuel B. Griffith. New York: Praeger.

Marcus, George E., W. Russell Neuman, and Michael Mackuen (2000) *Affective Intelligence and Political Judgment.* Chicago: University of Chicago Press.

Marcuse, Herbert (1964) *One Dimensional Man: Studies in the Ideology of Advanced Industrial Society.* Boston: Beacon Press.

Marighela, Carlos (1985) *Manual of the Urban Guerrilla.* Chapel Hill, NC: Documentary Publication.

Martin, Roger (1980) *Pigs and Other Animals: A True and Thought-provoking Story of Violence, Brutality, and Perversion in our Jails!* Arcadia, CA: Myco Publishing.

Mascarenhas, Anthony (1986) *Bangladesh: A Legacy of Blood.* London: Hodder and Stoughton.

Maslow, Abraham (1968) *Towards a Psychology of Being.* New York: Van Nostrand Reinhold.

Matthews, R. C. O. (1984) "Darwinism and Economic Change." *Oxford Economic Papers.* 36: 371.

McAdam, Doug (1982) *Political Process and the Development of Black Insurgency 1930–1970.* Chicago: University of Chicago Press.

McAdam, Doug, Sidney Tarrow and Charles Tilly (1996) "To Map Contentious Politics." *Mobilization: An International Journal.* 1(1): 17–34.

McClosky, Donald N. (1985) *The Rhetoric of Economics.* Madison, WI: University of Wisconsin Press.

McGartland, Martin (1997) *Fifty Dead Men Walking.* London: Blake.

McGirk, Tim (2004) "Terrorism's Harvest." *Time Asia.* August 2.

McKittrick, David (2001). *Lost Lives.* London: Mainstream Publishers.

McLellan, Vin, and Paul Avery (1977). *The Voices of Guns: The Definitive and Dramatic Story of the Twenty-two-month Career of the Symbionese Liberation Army.* New York: Putnam.

McRae, Kenneth D. (1990). "Canada: Reflections on Two Conflicts." In Joseph Montville (ed.) *Conflict and Peacemaking in Multiethnic Societies.* Boston: D. C. Heath: 197–218.

Mehra, Ajay (2000) "Naxalism in India: Revolution or Terror?" *Terrorism and Political Violence*. 12(2): 37–66.

Mehra, Ajay (2006) "The Thin Edge of the Naxal Wedge." *The Indian Express*. 14 April.

Merari, Ariel (1990) "The Readiness to Kill and Die: Suicidal Terrorism in the 1980s—A Chronology of Events." In W. Reich (ed.) *Orgins of Terrorism: Psychologies, Ideologies, Theologies, States of Mind*. Cambridge: Cambridge University Press: 192–207.

Merari, Ariel (2005) "Social, Organizational, and Psychological Factors in Suicide Terrorism." In Tore Bjorgo (ed.) *Roots of Terrorism: Myths, Reality and Ways Forward*. London: Routledge: 70–86.

Merari, Ariel and N. Friedlander (1985) "Social Psychological Aspects of Political Terrorism." *Applied Social Psychology Annual*. 6: 185–205.

Midlarsky, Manus I. (1982) "Scarcity and Inequality: Prologue to the Onset of Mass Political Revolution." *Journal of Conflict Resolution*. 26: 3–38.

Midlarsky, Manus I. And Kenneth Roberts (1985) "Class, State, and Revolution in Central America: Nicaragua and El Salvador Compared." *Journal of Conflict Resolution*. 29: 163–195.

Milgram, S. (1974) *Obedience to Authority: An Experimental View*. New York: Harper & Row.

Miller, Judith (1996) *God Has Ninety-nine Names: Reporting From A Militant Middle East*. New York: Simon & Schuster.

Minh, Ho Chi (1961) *The Selected Works of Ho Chi Minh*. Hanoi: Foreign Language Publishing House.

Mintz, Alex, Nehemia Geva, Steven Redd, and Amy Carnes (1997) "The Effects of Dynamic and Static Choice Sets on Political Decision Making: An Analysis Using the Decision Board Platform." *American Political Science Review*. 91(3): 553–566.

Mishal, Shaul and Abraham Sela (2000) *Palestinian Hamas: Vision, Violence, and Coexistence*. New York: Columbia University Press.

Mitchell, J. Clyde (1956) *The Kalela Dance: Aspects of Social Relationships Among Urban African in Rhodesia*. Manchester: Manchester University Press.

Mitchell, Richard P. (1969). *The Society of the Muslim Brothers*. London: Oxford University Press.

Mohanty, Manoranjan (1977) *Revolutionary Violence: A Study of the Maoist Movement in India*. New Delhi: Sterling Publishers.

Mohanty, Manoranjan (2005) "The Course of Naxalism." *Himal Southasian*. September–October, 1–5.

Mohanty, Manoranjan (2006) "Challenges of Revolutionary Violence: The Naxalite Movement in Perspective." *Economic and Political Weekly*. 22 July: 3136–3168.

Moloney, Ed (2002) *A Secret History of the IRA*. New York: W. W. Norton.

Monroe, Kristen (1996) *The Heart of Altruism: Perceptions of a Common Enemy*. Princeton, NJ: Princeton University Press.

Moore, Will (1998) "Repression and Dissent: Substitution, Context, and Timing." *American Journal of Political Science*. 38(3): 851–873.

Moran, Daniel (2001) *Wars of National Liberation*. Washington DC: Smithsonian History of Warfare Series, HarperCollins.

Morgan, Robin (2002) "The Demon Lover Syndrome." *MS*. 13(3): 17.

Morrow, James (1997) "A Rational Choice Approach to International Conflict." In N. Gava and A. Mintz (eds.) *Decision Making on War and Peace*. Boulder, CO: Lynne Reinner: 11–32.

Moussalli, Ahmad S. (1992). *Radical Islamic Fundamentalism: The Ideological and Political Discourse of Sayyid Qutb.* American University of Beirut.

Mueller, Dennis (1979) *Public Choice.* New York: Cambridge University Press.

Mueller, John (2005) "Rather Unusual Propositions about Terrorism." *Terrorism and Political Violence.* 17(4): 487–506.

Mukherjee, Kalyan and Rajendra Singh Yadav (1980) *Bhojpur: Naxalism in the Plains of Bihar.* Delhi: Radha Krishna Prakashan.

Mukherjee, Partha N. (1979) "Naxalbari Movement and the Peasant Revolt in North Bengal." In M. S. A. Rao (ed.) *Social Movements in India.* Vol. I. New Delhi: Manohar Publications: 17–90.

Muller, Edward N. (1985) "Income Inequality, Regime Repressiveness, and Political Violence." *American Journal of Sociology.* 50: 47–61.

Muller, Edward N. and Karl-Dieter Opp (1986) "Rational Choice and Rebellious Collective Action." *American Political Science Review.* 80: 471–487.

Munson, Henry, Jr. (1988) *Islam and Revolution in the Middle East.* New Haven, CT: Yale University Press.

Musgrave, A. (1981) "Unreal Assumptions in Economics: The F-Twist Untwisted." *KYKLOS.* 34: 377–378.

Nagata, Judith (1981) "In Defense of Ethnic Boundaries: The Changing Myths and Characters of Malay Identity." In Charles F. Keyes (ed.) *Ethnic Change.* Seattle, WA: University of Washington Press.

Napoleoni, Loretta (2003) *Modern Jihad: Tracing the Dollars Behind the Terror Networks.* New York: Pluto Press.

Napoleoni, Loretta (2005) *Terror Incorporated: Tracing the Dollars Behind the Terror Networks.* New York: Seven Stories Press.

Narayan Swami, M. R. (1994) *Tigers of Lanka: From Boys to Guerrillas.* New Delhi: South Asia Publishing.

Naroll, Raoul (1964) "On Ethnic Unit Classification." *Current Anthropology.* 5: 283–312.

Nassar, Jamal R. (1991) *The Palestine Liberation Organization: From Armed Struggle to the Declaration of Independence.* New York: Praeger.

National Commission on Women Report. Delhi: Radha Krishna Prakashan. http://ncw.nic.in/pdfreports/Gender%20Profile-Chhattisgarh.pdf.

Naylor, R. T. (1997) "Mafias, Myths, and Markets: On the Theory and Practice of Enterprise Crime." *Trans-national Organized Crime.* 3(3): 2–18.

Naylor, R. T. (2002) *Wages of Crime: Black Markets, Illegal Finance and the Underworld Economy.* Ithaca, NY: Cornell University Press.

Nelson, R. R. and S. G. Winter (1982) *An Evolutionary Theory of Economic Change.* Cambridge: Harvard University Press.

Newberg, Andrew and Mark Waldman (2006) *Why We Believe What We Believe: Uncovering Our Biological Need for Meaning, Spirituality, and Truth.* New York: Free Press.

Newberg, Andrew, Eugene d'Aquili, and Vince Rause (2001) *Why God Won't Go Away: Brain Science and the Biology of Belief.* New York: Ballantine Books.

Newman, Saul (1991) "Does Modernization Breed Ethnic Political Conflict?" *World Politics.* 43(3).

New York Times (1990) "Evolution in Europe: Bishop Rebukes IRA for Car Bomb Attacks." 28 October.

New York Times (2007) "Madrid Bombing Suspect Denies Guilt." 15 February.

Nofal, Mamdouth, *et al.* (1998) "Reflections on Al-Nakba." *Journal of Palestine Studies.* 28(1): 5–35.

O'Ballance, Edgar (1967) *The Algerian Insurrection, 1957–62.* Hamden, CT: Archon Books.

O'Brien, Connor C. (1988) *God Land: Reflections on Religion and Nationalism.* Cambridge, MA: Harvard University Press.

O'Donnell, Guillermo (1993) "On the State, Democratization and Some Conceptual Problems." Working paper No. 192. University of Notre Dame: The Helen Kellogg Institute for International Studies.

O'Duffy, Brendan (2007) "LTTE: Liberation Tigers of Tamil Elam." In Marianne Heiberg, Brendan O'Leary, and John Tirman (eds.) *Terror, Insurgency, and the State.* Philadelphia: University of Pennsylvania Press: 189–228.

O'Leary, Brendan (2007) "IRA: Irish Republican Army (Oglaigh na hEireann)." In Marianne Heiberg, Brendan O'Leary, and John Tirman (eds.) *Terror, Insurgency, and the State.* Philadelphia: University of Pennsylvania Press: 189–228.

O'Leary, Brendan and Andrew Silke (2007) "Conclusion: Understanding and Ending Persistent Conflicts: Bridging Research and Policy." In Marianne Heiberg, Brendan O'Leary, and John Tirman (eds.) *Terror, Insurgency, and the State.* Philadelphia: University of Pennsylvania Press: 387–426.

O'Leary, Brendan and John Tirman (2007) "Introduction: Thinking about Durable Political Violence." In Marianne Heiberg, Brendan O'Leary, and John Tirman (eds.) *Terror, Insurgency, and the State.* Philadelphia: University of Pennsylvania Press: 1–18.

Oberoi, Harjot S. (1987) "From Punjab to 'Khalistan:' From Territoriality to Metacommentary." *Pacific Affairs.* 60(1): 26–41.

Oberschall, Anthony (1973) *Social Conflicts and Social Movements.* Englewood Cliffs, NJ: Prentice Hall.

Oberschall, Anthony (2004) "Explaining Terrorism: The Contribution of Collective Action Theory." *Sociological Theory.* 22(1): 26–37.

Olson, Mancur (1968) *The Logic of Collective Action.* Cambridge, MA: Harvard University Press.

Olsson, P. A. (1988) "The Terrorist and the Terrorized: Some Psychoanalytic Considerations." *Journal of Psycho-history.* 16(1): 47–60.

Ostrom, Elinor (1998) "A Behavioral Approach to the Rational Choice Theory of Collective Action: Presidential Address." *American Political Science Review.* 92(1): 1–22.

Overgaard, Per Baltzer (1994) "The Scale of Terrorist Attacks as a Signal of Resources." *Journal of Conflict Resolution.* 38(3): 452–478.

Overstreet, Gene D. and Marshall Windmiller (1959) *Communism in India.* Berkeley, CA: University of California Press.

Paige, Jeffrey M. (1970) "Inequality and Insurgency in Vietnam: A Re-Analysis." *World Politics.* 23: 24–37.

Palast, Gregory (2002) *The Best Democracy Money Can Buy.* London: Pluto Press.

Pallister, David and Owen Bowcott (2002) "Banks to Shut Doors on Saudi Royal Cash." *Guardian.* 17 July.

Palmer, David S. (1995) "The Revolutionary Terrorism of Peru's Shining Path." In Martha Crenshaw (ed.) *Terrorism in Context.* University Park, PA: Pennsylvania State University Press.

Pape, Robert A. (2003) "The Strategic Logic of Suicide Terrorism." *American Political Science Review*. 97: 343–361.

Pape, Robert A. (2005) *Dying to Win: The Strategic Logic of Suicide Terrorism*. New York: Random House.

Paranzino, Dennis (1972) "Inequality and Insurgency in Vietnam: A Further Re-Analysis." *World Politics*. 24: 565–578.

Pareto, Vilfredo (1968) *La liberté économique et les événements d'Italie*. London: B. Franklin.

Pavier, Barry (1981) *The Telengana Movement 1944–51*. New Delhi: Vikash Publishing House.

Pearlstein, R. M. (1991) *The Mind of the Political Terrorist*. Lexington, MA: D.C. Heath.

Pedahzur, Ami, A. Perliger, and Leonard Weinberg (2003) "Altruism and Fatalism: The Characteristics of Palestinian Suicide Terrorists." *Deviant Behavior*. 24: 405–423.

Perkins, John (2004) *Confessions of an Economic Hit Man*. San Francisco: Berrett-Koehler.

Perrucci, R. and M. Pilisuk (1970) "Leaders and Ruling Elites: The Interorganizational Bases of Community Power." *American Sociological Review*. 35: 1090–1157.

Pew Research Center (2002) *What the World Thinks 2002: How Global Publics View Their Lives, Their Countries*. Washington DC: The Pew Research Center.

Pfaffenberger, B. (1988) "Sri Lanka in 1987: Indian Intervention and Resurgence of the JVP." *Asian Survey*. 28(2): 137–147.

Phelps-Brown, E. (1972) "The Underdevelopment of Economics." *Economic Journal*. 82: 73–86.

Pinker, Steven (2002) *The Blank Slate: The Modern Denial of Human Nature*. New York: Viking.

Pitt, J. C. (ed.) (1981) *Philosophy in Economics*. Dordrecht: Reidel.

Popkin, Sam (1979) *The Rational Peasant*. Berkeley, CA: University of California Press.

Popper, Karl (1960) *The Poverty of Historicism*. Boston: Beacon Press.

Popper, Karl (1968) *The Logic of Scientific Discovery*. New York: Harper & Row.

Post, J. M. (1995) *Bosnia: What Happened*. Boston: Addison Wesley.

Post, J. M. (1997) *Political Paranoia: The Psychopolitics of Hatred*. New Haven, CT: Yale University Press.

Post, J. M. (1998) "Terrorist Psycho-logic: Terrorist Behavior as a Product of Psychological Forces." In W. Reich (ed.) *Origins of Terrorism: Psychologies, Ideologies, Theories, States of Mind*. Washington DC: Woodrow Wilson Center Press: 25–40.

Post, J. M. (2003) " 'When Hatred is Bred in the Bone:' Socio-cultural Underpinnings of Terrorist Psychology." Proceedings from an International Expert Meeting in Oslo.

Post, J. M. (2004) *Leaders and Their Followers in a Dangerous World: The Psychology of Political Behavior*. Ithaca, NY: Cornell University Press.

Post, J. M. (2005) "The Socio-cultural Underpinnings of Terrorist Psychology: When Hatred is Bred in Bones." In Tore Bjorgo (ed.) *Root Causes of Terrorism: Myths, Reality and Ways Forward*. London: Routledge: 54–69.

Post, J. M. (2006) "The Psychological Dynamics of Terrorism." In Louise Richardson (ed.) *The Roots of Terrorism*. London: Routledge: 17–29.

Power, Samantha (1999) *Leave None to Tell the Story: Genocide in Rwanda*. Paris: Human Rights Watch.

Prinz, Jesse (2004) *Gut Reactions: A Perceptual Theory of Emotion.* New York: Oxford University Press.

Prunier, Gérard (2005) *Darfur: The Ambiguous Genocide.* Ithaca, NY: Cornell University Press.

Qasim, Muhammad (2002) *The Ulama in Contemporary Islam: Custodians of Change.* Princeton, NJ: Princeton University Press.

Qin, J., J. Xu, M. Sageman, and H. Chen (2005) "Analyzing Terrorist Networks: A Case Study of the Global Salafi Jihad Network." In R. Kimmel, N. Sochen, and J. Weickert (eds.) *Lecture Notes in Computer Science: Vol. 3459–2005. Intelligence and Security Formatics.* Heidelberg, Germany: Springer Berlin: 287–304.

Quorchi, Muhammed, Samuel Maimbo, and John F. Wilson (2003) *Informal Funds Transfer Systems: An Analysis of the Hawala System.* International Monetary Fund, 24 March.

Qutb, Sayyid (1993) *Milestones.* Kazi Publications.

Radlauer, Dan (2002) "An Engineered Tragedy: Statistical Analysis of Casualties in Palestinian–Israeli Conflict September 2000–September 2002." ICT (24 June) http://www.ict.org.il/.

Ram, Mohan (1971) *Maoism in India.* New Delhi: Vikash.

Ramet, Sabrina (1996) *Balkan Babel: The Disintegration of Yugoslavia from the Death of Tito to Ethnic War.* Second edition. Boulder, CO: Westview Press.

Rao, Amiya and B. G. Rao (1992) *The Blue Devil: Indigo and Colonial Bengal.* New Delhi, New York: Oxford University Press.

Rapoport, David C. (1977) "The Politics of Atrocity." In Yonah Alexander and Seymore Maxwell Finger (eds.) *Terrorism: Interdisciplinary Perspective.* New York: John Jay Press: 17–33.

Rapoport, David C. (1984) "Fear and Trembling: Terrorism in Three Religious Traditions." *American Political Science Review.* 8(1): 658–677.

Rapoport, David C. (1992) "Terrorism." In M. E. Hawkesworth and Maurice Kogan (eds.) *Routledge Encyclopedia of Government and Politics.* Vol. 2. London: Routledge.

Rapoport, David C. (2005) "Four Waves of Terrorism." In Dipak K. Gupta (ed.) *Terrorism and Homeland Security.* Belmont, CA: Wadsworth.

Rapoport, David C. (2006) "Before the Bombs there were Mobs: American Experiences with Terror." UCLA, unpublished manuscript.

Rasch, William (2004) *Sovereignty and its Discontent: On Primacy of Conflict and the Structure of the Political.* London: Birkbeck Law.

Ray, Rabindra (2002) *The Naxalites and Their Ideology.* Second edition. New Delhi: Oxford University Press.

Ray, Sibnarayan (2002) *In Freedom's Quest: A Study of the Life and Works of M. N. Roy: Vol. II: The Comintern Years (1922–27).* Kolkata: Minerva Associates Publications.

Redd, Steven B. (2003) "The Poliheuristic Theory of Foreign Policy Decision Making: Experimental Evidence." In A. Mintz (ed.) *Integrating Cognitive and Rational Choice Theories of Foreign Policy Decision Making.* New York: Palgrave Macmillan: 101–126.

Redding, W. C. (1972) *Communication within the Organization: An Interpretative Review of Theory and Research.* New York: Industrial Communication Council.

Redman, Deborah (1993) "Adam Smith and Isaac Newton." *Scottish Journal of Political Economy.* 40(2): 2100–2130.

Regin, Deric (1969) *Sources of Cultural Estrangement*. The Hague, The Netherlands: Mouton & Co. Publishers.

Reich, William. (1998) "Understanding Terrorist Behavior: The Limits and Opportunities of Psychological Inquiry." In W. Reich (ed.) *Origins of Terrorism: Psychologies, Ideologies, Theologies, States of Mind*. Washington DC: Woodrow Wilson Press: 261–279.

Reuter, Peter (1983) *Disorganized Crime: Illegal Markets and the Mafia*. Cambridge, MA: MIT Press.

Rex, John (1995) "Ethnic Identity and Nation State: The Political Sociology of Multi-Cultural Societies." *Social Identities*. 1(1): 24–25.

Ricolfi, Luca (2005) "Palestinians, 1981–2003." In Diego Gambetta (ed.) *Making Sense of Suicide Mission*. Oxford: Oxford University Press: 77–131.

Robb, John (2007) *Brave New War: The Next Stage of Terrorism and the End of Globalization*. Hoboken, NJ: John Wiley & Sons.

Roberts, Kevin (2004) *Lovemarks: Future Beyond Brands*. New York: Power House Books.

Robins, R. S. and J. M. Post (1997) *Political Paranoia: The Psychopolitics of Hatred*. New Haven, CT: Yale University Press.

Robinson, Joan. (1962) *Economic Philosophy*. London: Watts.

Roger, Miranda and William Ratliff (1993). *The Civil War in Nicaragua: Inside the Sandinistas*. New Brunswick, NJ: Transaction Publishers.

Rogers, Steven (2003) "Beyond Abu Sayyaf." *Foreign Affairs*. 83(1): 5–21.

Rose, Richard (1990) "Northern Ireland: The Irreducible Conflict." In Joseph V. Montville (ed.) *Conflict and Peacemaking in Multiethnic Societies*. Boston, MA: D. C. Heath, Lexington Books.

Rose-Ackerman, Susan (1996) "Altruism, Nonprofits, and Economic Theory." *Journal of Economic Literature*. 36 (June): 701–728.

Rosendorf, Peter and Todd Sandler (2004) "Too Much of a Good Thing? The Proactive Response Dilemma." *Journal of Conflict Resolution*. 48(4): 138–151.

Rotberg, Robert I. (2002) "The New Nature of Nation-State Failure." *Washington Quarterly*. Summer.

Rotberg, Robert I. (ed.) (2004) *When States Fail: Causes and Consequences*. Princeton, NJ: Princeton University Press.

Rotella, Sebastian (2004) "Jihad's Unlikely Alliance: Muslim Extremists Who Attacked Madrid Funded the Plot by Selling Drugs, Investigators Say." *Los Angeles Times*, 23 May.

Roy, Ashish K. (1975) *The Spring Thunder and After*. Calcutta: Minerva Associates: 74–75.

Rubin, Trudy (2007) "Bombing Meant to Provoke Revenge." *San Diego Union Tribune*. 6 June: B6.

Ruby, C. L. (2002) "The Definition of Terrorism." *Analyses of Social Issues and Public Policy*. 2(1): 9–14.

Rudra, Ashok (1974) "Usefulness of Plan Models: An Assessment Based on Indian Experience." In Ashok Mitra (ed.) *Economic Theory and Planning: Essays in Honour of A. K. Das Gupta*. Calcutta: Oxford University Press.

Rummel, Rudolph J. (1994) *Death by Government*. New Brunswick, NJ: Transaction Press.

Rushdie, Salman (2001) "This Is About Islam." *New York Times*. Sunday, 11 November.

Russell, C. A, and B. H. Miller (1983) "Profile of A Terrorist" In L. Z. Freedman and Y. Alexander (eds.) *Perspectives on Terrorism*. Wilmington, DE: Scholarly Resources, Inc.: 45–60.

Russett, Bruce M. (1964) "Inequality and Insurgency: The Relation of Land Tenure to Politics." *World Politics*. 16: 442–454.

Ruttan, Vernon W. (2002) "Imperialism and Competition in Anthropology, Sociology, Political Science, and Economics: A Perspective from Development Economics." In Shoshana Grossbard-Shechtman and Christopher Clague (eds.) *The Expansion of Economics: Toward a More Inclusive Social Sciences*. Armonk, NY: M. E. Sharpe: 49–67.

Sachs, Carolyn J. and Lawrence D. Chu (2000). "The Association between Professional Football Games and Domestic Violence in Los Angeles County." *Journal of Interpersonal Violence*. 15(11): 1192–1201.

Sageman, Marc (2004) *Understanding Terror Networks*. Philadelphia: University of Pennsylvania Press.

Samanta, Amiya (1975) *The Left-Extremist Movement in West Bengal*. Calcutta: Allied Press.

Samuelson, Paul A. (1938) "A Note on the Pure Theory of Consumers' Behavior." *Economica*, 5: 61–71.

Samuelson, Paul A. (1954) "The Pure Theory of Public Expenditure." *Review of Economics and Statistics*. 36: 387–389.

Samuelson, Paul A. (1965) *Foundations of Economic Analysis*. New York: Athenium Press.

Sanderson, Thomas M. (2004) "Transnational Terror and Organized Crime: Blurring the Lines." *SAIS Review*. 24(1) Winter–Spring: 49–61.

Sandler, Todd and Walter Enders (2004) "An Economic Perspective on Transnational Terrorism." *European Journal of Political Economy*. 20(2): 301–316.

Sandler, Todd and H. E. Lapan (1988) "The Calculus of Dissent: An Analysis of Terrorists' Choice of Targets." *Syntheses*. 76: 245–261.

Sandler, Todd, J. T. Tschirhart, and J. Cauly (1983) "A Theoretical Analysis of Transnational Terrorism." *American Political Science Review*. 77: 36–54.

Sarraj, E. (2002) "Why We Blow Ourselves Up." *Time Magazine*. 159(14), 8 April: 35–42.

Satz, Deborah and John Ferejon (1994) "Rational Choice and Social Theory." *Journal of Philosophy*. 91: 71–87.

Scarborough, Rowan (2003) "Drug Money Sustains al-Qaeda?" *Washington Times*. 29 December.

Schacht, Richard (1970) *Alienation*. Garden City, NY: Doubleday Company.

Schama, Simon (1989) *Citizens: A Chronicle of the French Revolution*. New York: Vantage Books.

Schelling, Thomas C. (1978) *Micromotives and Microbehavior*. New York, London: W. W. Norton.

Schelling, Thomas C. (1991) "What Purposes Can 'Internaational Terrorism' Serve? In R. G. Frey and Christopher W. Morris (eds.) *Violence, Terrorism, and Justice*. New York: Cambridge University Press.

Schlesinger, Jr., Arthur (1965) *A Thousand Days: John F. Kennedy in the White House*. Boston: Houghton Mifflin.

Schmid, Alex P. (2004) "Terrorism: The Definitional Problem." *Case Western Reserve Journal of International Law*. 36 (2 & 3): 375–419.

Schmid, Alex P. (2005a) "Links Between Terrorism and Drug Trafficking: A Case of Narco-Terrorism?" Paper presented at International Summit on Democracy and Security. 8–11 March, Madrid.

Schmid, Alex P. (2005b) "The Links between Transnational Organized Crime and Terrorist Crimes." *Transnational Organized Crime*. 2(4) Winter: 40–82.

Schmid, Alex P. and Albert J. Jongman (1988) *Political Terrorism: A New Guide to Actors, Authors, Concepts, Databases, Theories, and Literature*. New Brunswick, NJ: Transaction Books.

Schmid, Alex P. and Jenney de Graaf (1982) *Violence as Communication: Insurgent Terrorism and the Western News Media*. Beverly Hills, CA: Sage Publications.

Schneider, J. and J. M. Post (2003) *Know Thy Enemy: Profiles of Adversary Leaders and their Strategic Cultures*. Second edition. Maxwell Air Force Base, AL: USAF Counterproliferation Center.

Schneidman, E. S. (1985) *Definition of Suicide*. New York: Wiley.

Schneidman, E. S. (1999) "Perturbation and Lethality." In D. G. Jacobs (ed.) *The Harvard Medical School Guide to Suicide Assessment and Intervention*. San Francisco, CA: Jossey-Bass.

Schuessler, Alexander (2000) *A Logic of Expressive Choice*. Princeton, NJ: Princeton University Press.

Schumpeter, Joseph (1939 [1912]) *The Theory of Economic Development: An Inquiry into Profits, Capital, Credit, Interest, and Business Cycle*. Trans. R. Opie. New York: Oxford University Press.

Schwartz, David C. (1973) *Alienation Theories and De-alienation Strategies*. Middlesex, UK: Science Review, Ltd.

Sears, D. O., L. A. Peplau, J. L. Freedman, and S. E. Taylor (1998) *Social Psychology*. Sixth edition. Englewood Cliffs, NJ: Prentice Hall.

Seeman, Melvin (1959) "Alienation and Estrangement." In A. C. Campbell and P. E. Converse (eds.) *The Human Meaning of Social Change*. New York: Russell Sage Foundation: 467–527.

Sela, Avraham and Moshe Ma'oz (eds.) (1997) *The PLO and Israel: From Armed Conflict to Political Solution 1964–1994*. New York: St. Martin's Press.

Selbourne, David (2005) *The Losing Battle with Islam*. New York: Prometheus Books.

Seligson, Michell A. (1966) "Agrarian Inequality and the Theory of Peasan Rebellion." *Latin American Research Review*. 31: 140–157.

Sen, Amartya K. (1967) "Isolation, Assurance and Social Rate of Discount." *Quarterly Journal of Economics*. 81: 112–124.

Sen, Amartya K. (1977) "Rational Fools: A Critique of the Behavioral Foundation of Economic Theory." *Philosophy and Public Affairs*. 6: 317–344.

Sen, Amartya K. (1984) *Collective Choice and Social Welfare*. New York: W. W. Norton.

Sen, Amartya K. (1987) *On Ethics and Economics*. Oxford: Basil Blackwell.

Sen, Amartya K. (1990) "More than 100 Million Women are Missing." *New York Review of Books*. 37(20) 20 December.

Sen, Amartya K. (1999a) *Development as Freedom*. New York: Knopf.

Sen, Amartya K. (1999b) *Commodities and Capabilities*. Delhi, New York: Oxford University Press.

Sen, Amartya K. (2006) *Identity and Violence: The Illusion of Destiny*. New York: W. W. Norton.

Sen, Sunil (1972) *Agrarian Struggle in Bengal*. Bombay: People's Publishing House.

Sengupta, Somini (2005) "Where Maoists Still Matter," *New York Times*, 30 October.

Sengupta, Somini (2006) "India's Unrelenting 'People's War': 25-year Maoist Fight Plagues Countryside." *International Herald Tribune*. 13 April, p. 1.

Sengupta, Uttam (2006) "Hilltop View of Rebels: Jhumra is Like Siachen, Says Officer." *The Telegraph*. Calcutta. Monday, 7 August.

Seton-Watson, Hugh (1977) *Nations and States: An Inquiry into the Origins of Nations and the Politics of Nationalism*. Boulder, CO: Westview Press.

Shah, Niaz A. (2007) "Self-defence in Islamic Law." Yearbook of Islamic and Middle Eastern Law. 12.

Shaw, E. D. (1986) "Political Terrorists: Dangers of Diagnosis and Alternative to Psychopathological Model." *International Journal of Law and Psychiatry*. 8: 359–368.

Shelley, Louise and John Picarelli (2002) "Methods, Not Motives: Implications of the Convergence of International Organized Crime and Terrorism." *Police Practice and Research*. 3: 305–318.

Shepsley, Kenneth A. and Mark S. Bonchek (1997) *Analyzing Politics: Rationality, Behavior, and Institutions*. New York: W. W. Norton.

Sherif, M. (1935) "An Experimental Study of Stereotypes." *Journal of Abnormal Psychology*. 29: 371–375.

Sherif, M. (1966) *Group Conflict and Cooperation: Their Social Psychology*. London: Routledge & Kegan Paul.

Sherif, M. and C. Hovland (1961) *Social Judgment: Assimilation and Contrast Effects in Communication and Attitude Change*. New Haven, CT: Yale University Press.

Silke, Andrew (1998a) "Cheshire-Cat Logic: The Recurring Theme of Terrorist Abnormality in Psychological Research." *Psychology, Crime, and Law*. 4: 51–69.

Silke, Andrew (1998b) "The Lords of Discipline: The Methods and Motives of Paramilitary Vigilantism in Northern Ireland" *Low Intensity Conflict & Law Enforcement*. 7(2): 121–156.

Silke, Andrew (1999) "Rebel's Dilemma: The Changing Relationship between the IRA, Sinn Fein and Paramilitary Vigilantism in Northern Ireland." *Terrorism and Political Violence*. 11(1) (Spring): 55–93.

Silke, Andrew (2005) "Fire of Iolaus: The Role of State Counter-Measures in Causing Terrorism and What is to be Done." In Tore Bjorgo (ed.) *Root Causes of Terrorism*. London: Routledge: 241–255.

Silke, Andrew and Max Taylor (2000) "War Without End: Comparing IRA and Loyalist Vigilantism in Northern Ireland." *Howard Journal of Criminal Justice*, 39(3): 249–266.

Simon, H. A. (1979) "Human Nature in Politics: The Dialogue of Psychology with Political Science." *American Political Science Review*. 79(2): 293–304.

Simon, Herbert (1987) "Making Management Decisions: The Role of Intuition and Emotion." *Academy of Management Executives*. 1(1): 57–64.

Simon, Herbert, Joanne Morreale and Bruce Gronbeck (2001) *Persuasion in Society*. Thousand Oaks, CA: Sage Publications.

Singh, Khuswant (ed.) (1981). *Muhammad Iqbal: Shikwa & Jawab-i-Shikwa. Complaint and Answer. Iqbal's Dialogue with Allah*. London: Oxford University Press.

Singh, Prakask (2006) *The Naxalite Movement in India*. New Delhi: Rupa & Co.

Siqueira, Kevin (2005) "Political and Militant Wings within Dissident Movements and Organizations." *Journal of Conflict Resolution*. 49(2): 218–236.

Siqueira, Kevin and Todd Sandler (2006) "Terrorist Versus the Government: Strategic

Interaction, Support, and Sponsorship." *Journal of Conflict Resolution.* 50(6): 878–889.

Sivan, Emmanuel (1985) *Radical Islam: Medieval Theology and Modern Politics.* New Haven, CT: Yale University Press.

Skar, Harald Olav (2007) "PLA CPN (M): People's Liberation Army of the Communist Party of Nepal (Maoist)." In Marianne Heiberg, Brendan O'Leary, and John Tirman (eds.) *Terror, Insurgency, and the State.* Philadelphia: University of Pennsylvania Press: 359–386.

Skocpol, Theda (1979) *States and Social Revolutions: A Comparative Analysis of France, Russia, and China.* Cambridge: Harvard University Press.

Smelser, Neil J. (1963) *Theories of Collective Behavior.* New York: The Free Press of Glencoe.

Smelser, Neil J. and Seymore Lipset (1966) *Social Structure and Mobility in Economic Development.* Chicago: Aldine Press.

Smith, Adam (1937 [1759]) *The Theories of Moral Sentiments.* New York: Modern Libraries.

Smith, Adam (1981 [1759]) *The Theory of Moral Sentiments.* D. D. Raphael and A. L. Macfie (eds.) Indianapolis, IN: Liberty Funds.

Smith, Adam (1982 [1776]) *An Inquiry into the Nature and Causes of the Wealth of Nations.* Indianapolis, IN: Liberty Classics.

Smith, Anthony D. (1983) *Theories of Nationalism.* Ithaca, NY: Cornell University Press.

Smith, Thomas W. (1995) "The Order of Presentation and the Order of Understanding in Aquinas's Account of Law." *Review of Politics.* 57(4) (Autumn): 607–640.

Smock, David (2004) "Ijtihad: Reinterpreting Islamic Principles for the Twenty-First Century." *Special Report No. 125.* Washington DC, United States Institute of Peace. http://www.usip.org/pubs/specialreports/sr125.html

Snow, David A. and Robert D. Benford (1992) "Master Frames and Cycles of Protest." In Aldon Morris and Carol McClurg Mueller (eds.) *Frontiers in Social Movement Theory.* New Haven, CT: Yale University Press.

Sober, Elliott and David Wilson (1998) *Unto Others: The Evolution of Psychology of Unselfish Behavior.* Cambridge, MA: Harvard University Press.

Solow, Robert (1986) "Economics, Is Something Missing?" In W. N. Parker (ed.) *Economic History and Modern Economist.* Oxford: Basil Blackwell: 21–29.

Solsten, Eric (ed.) (1993) *Cyprus: A Country Study.* Fourth edition. Federal Research Division, Library of Congress; Washington, DC: The Division: Headquarters, Dept. of the Army.

Spencer, Herbert (1879 [1967]) *The Evolution of Society: Selections from Herbert Spencer's Principle of Sociology.* Chicago: University of Chicago Press.

Stanley, W. (1996) *The Protection Racket State, Elite, Politics, Military Extortion, and Civil War in El Salvador.* Philadelphia, PA: Temple University Press.

State Failure Taskforce, http://globalpolicy.gmu.edu/pitf/

Steedman, Ian (1977) *Marx After Sraffa.* London: Unwin Brothers.

Steedman, Ian and U. Kraus (1986) "Goethe's Faust, Arrow's Possibility Theorem and the Individual Decision Taker." In Jon Elster (ed.) *The Multiple Self.* Cambridge: Cambridge University Press.

Stern, Jessica (1999) *The Ultimate Terrorists.* Boston: Harvard University Press.

Stern, Jessica (2000). "Pakistan's Jihad Culture." *Foreign Affairs.* Nov/Dec 79(6): 115–127.

Stern, Jessica (2003a) *Terror in the Name of God: Why Religious Militants Kill.* New York: Ecco.

Stern, Jessica (2003b) "The Protean Enemy." *Foreign Affairs.* July–Aug.

Stevenson, Jonathan (1996) "Northern Ireland: Treating Terrorists As Diplomats." *Foreign Policy.* 105: 125–40.

Stigler, George J. and Gary Becker (1977) "De Gustibus Non Est Disputandum." *American Economic Review.* 67(1): 76–90.

Stohl, Cynthia and Michael Stohl (2007) "Networks of Terror: Theoretical Assumptions and Pragmatic Consequences." *Communication Theory.* 17: 93–124.

Stohl, Michael (1987) "Terrorism, States, and State Terrorism: The Reagan Administration in the Middle East." *Arab Studies Quarterly.* 9: 162–172.

Stohl, Michael (2005) "Expected Utility and State Terrorism." In Tore Bjorgo (ed.) *Root Causes of Terrorism: Myths, Reality, and Ways Forward.* London: Routledge: 198–214.

Stoker, Donald (2007) "Insurgencies Rarely Win—And Iraq Won't Be Any Different." *Foreign Policy.* January/February.

Stone, John (1995) "Race, Ethnicity, and the Weberian Legacy." *American Behavioral Scientist.* 38(3): 396.

Stossel, J. (2004) *Give Me A Break.* New York: HarperCollins.

Streeten, Paul (1967) "The Use and Abuse of Models in Development Planning." In K. Martin and J. Knapp (eds.) *The Teaching and Development Economics: Its Position in the Present State of Knowledge.* London: Frank Cass.

Strenz, T. (1988) "A Terrorist Psychosocial Profile: Past and Present." *FBI Law Enforcement Bulletin.* 11: 91–111.

Sundar, Nandini (2006) "Bastar, Maoism, and Salwa Judum." *Economic and Political Weekly.* 22 July: 3187–3192.

Suny, Ronald (1993) *The Revenge of the Past: Nationalism, Revolution, and The Collapse of the Soviet Union.* Stanford, CA: Stanford University Press.

Swami, Parveen (2007) *India, Pakistan, and the Secret Jihad: The Covert War in Kashmir, 1947–2004.* London: Routledge.

Swan, T. (1962) "Circular Causation." *Economic Record.* 421–426.

Swarup, Shanti (1966) *A Study of Chinese Communist Movement.* Oxford: Clarendon Press.

Sweetser, Eve and Gilles Fauconnier (1996) "Cognitive Links and Domains: Basic Aspects of Mental Space Theory." In Gilles Fauconnier and Eve Sweetser (eds.) *Spaces, Worlds, and Grammar.* Chicago: University of Chicago Press.

Sweezy, Paul (1981) *Four Lectures on Marxism.* New York: Monthly Review Press.

Tajfel, H. (1970) "Aspects of Nationality and Ethnic Loyalty." *Social Science Information.* 9: 113–44.

Tajfel, H. (1978) *Differentiation Between Social Groups: Studies in Inter-group Relations.* London: Academic Press.

Tajfel, H. (1981) *Human Groups and Social Categories: Studies in Social Psychology.* Cambridge: Cambridge University Press.

Tajfel, H. (ed.) (1982) *Social Identity and Inter-group Relations.* Cambridge: Cambridge University Press.

Tajfel, H. and J. C. Turner (1986) "The Social Identity Theory of Inter-group Behavior." In S. Worchel and W. G. Austin (eds.) *Psychology of Inter-group Relations.* Chicago: Nelson-Hall: 7–24.

Tal, David (ed.) (2001) *The 1956 War.* London: Frank Cass Publishers.

Tarrow, Sidney (1994) *Power in Movement: Social Movements, Collective Action and Politics*. New York: Cambridge University Press.

Taylor, M. (1988) *The Terrorist*. London, Washington: Brassey's Defence Publishers.

Taylor, Charles and Michael T. Hudson (1973) *World Handbook of Political and Social Indicators*. New Haven, CT: Yale University Press.

Taylor, Charles and Michael Jodice (1982) *Annual Events Data*. Inter University Consortium. New Haven, CT: Yale University Press.

Taylor, M. and E. Quayle (1994) *Terrorists' Lives*. London: Brassey's Defence Publishers.

Thomas, Hugh (2001) *The Spanish Civil War*. Fourth revised edition. New York: Modern Library.

Thompson, T., M. Townsend, M. Bright, and M. McMahon (2005) "Terror Suspect Gives First Account of London Attack." *Observer*. 31 July.

Tichy, N. (1981) "Network in Organizations." In P. Nystrom and W. Starbuck (eds.) *Handbook of Organizational Design*. New York: Oxford University Press. Vol. 2: 203–224.

Tilly, Charles (1978) *From Mobilization to Revolution*. Reading, MA: Adison Wesley.

Tilly, Charles (1993) *European Revolutions 1492–1992*. Oxford: Basil Blackwell.

Tilly, Charles (2004) "Terror, Terrorism, Terrorists." *Sociological Theory*. 22(1): 5–13.

Tripp, Charles (2002) *A History of Iraq*. Cambridge: Cambridge University Press.

Trotsky, Leon (1959) *The Russian Revolution: The Overthrow of Tzarism and the Triumph of the Soviets*. New York: Doubleday Anchor Books.

Tudge, C. (2002) "Natural Born Killers." *New Scientist*. 174: 36–9.

Tullock, Gordon (1971) "The Paradox of Revolution" *Public Choice*. 11: 89–99.

Turco, R. (1987) "Psychiatric Contributions to the Understanding of International Terrorism." *International Journal of Offender Therapy and Comparative Criminology*. 31(2): 153–161.

Tyson, Laura (2001) "It's Time to Step Up the Global War of Poverty." *Business Week*, 3 December.

Underhill, Paco (2000) *Why We Buy? The Science of Shopping*. New York: Simon & Schuster.

United Nations General Assembly (2001) "Convention against Transnational Organized Crime." New York: United Nations Publications: 25–26.

United Nations Office on Drugs and Crime 92006) *Glossary of Money Laundering Terms*. http://www.unodc/money_laundering_glossery.html#M.

van Woerkens, Martine (2002) *The Strangled Traveler: Colonial Imaginings and the Thugs of India*. Chicago: University of Chicago Press.

Varese, F. (2001) *The Russian Mafia: Private Protection in a New Market Economy*. Oxford: Oxford University Press.

Varshney, Asutosh (2002) *Ethnic Conflict and Civil Life: Hindus and Muslims in India*. New Haven, CT: Yale University Press.

Venieris, Yannis P. and Dipak K. Gupta (1983) "Sociopolitical and Economic Dimensions of Development: A Cross-Section Model?" *Economic Development and Cultural Change*. 31(4): 727–756.

Victoroff, Jeff (2005) "The Mind of the Terrorist: A Review and Critique of Psychological Approaches." *Journal of Conflict Resolution*. 49(1): 3–42.

Volkan, V. D. (1988) *The Need to Have Enemies and Allies: From Clinical Practice to International Relations*. Dunmore, PA: Jason Aronson.

Volkan, V. D. (2000) "The Political Economy of Protection Rackets in the Past and the Present." *Social Research*. 67: 709–744.

Volkav, V. D. (2002) *Violent Entrepreneurs: The Use of Force in the Making of Russian Capitalism*. Ithaca, NY: Cornell University Press.

Volkan, V. D. (2004a) *Blind Trust: Large Groups and Their Leaders in Times of Crisis and Terror*. Pitchstone.

Volkan, V. D. (2004b) *Bloodline: From Ethnic Pride to Ethnic Terrorism*. Boulder, CO: Westview Press.

Voll, John O. "Northern Muslim Perspective." In Joseph Montville (ed.) *Conflict and Peacemaking in Multiethnic Societies*. Boston: D. C. Heath: 389–410.

Wade, Nicholas (2007) "Aping Empathy: Did Human Morality Evolve from Primate Social Behavior?" *San Diego Union Tribune*. 19 April: E1.

Walker, Thomas (2003) *Nicaragua: Living in the Shadow of the Eagle*, Fourth edition. Westview Press.

Wallerstein, R. S. (1995) *The Talking Cures: The Psychoanalyses and Psychotherapies*. New Haven, CT: Yale University Press.

Ward, B. (1972) *What's Wrong with Economics?* London: Macmillan.

Weimann, Gabriel (2006) *Terror on the Internet: The New Arena, The New Challenges*. Washington DC: United States Institute of Peace.

Weinberg, Leonard and William L. Eubank (1987) "Italian Women Terrorists." *Terrorism: An International Journal*. 9: 241–262.

Weinberg, Leonard, Ami Pedahzur and Sivan Hirsch-Hoefler (2004) "The Challenges of Conceptualizing Terrorism" *Terrorism and Political Violence*. 16(4): 777–794.

Welldon, J. E. C. (1883) *The Politics of Aristotle*. Trans. 1905. New York: Macmillan.

Wells, Jonathan, Jack Meyers, and Maggie Mulvihill (2001) "War on Terrorism: Saudi Elite Tied to Money Group Linked to bin Laden." *Boston Herald*. 14 October.

Wendt, Alexander (2004) "The State as a Person in International Theory." *Review of International Studies*. 30: 289–316.

Whelpton, John (2005) *The History of Nepal*. Cambridge: Cambridge University Press.

White, Garland F., Janet Katz, and Kathryn E. Scarborough (1992) "The Impact of Professional Football Games Upon Violent Assaults on Women." *Violence and Victims*. 7(2): 157–171.

White, Robert (1989) "From Peaceful Protest to Guerrilla War—Micromobilization of the Provisional Irish Republican Army." *American Journal of Sociology*. 94: 1277–1302.

Wilkinson, Paul (1971) *Social Movements*. New York: Praeger.

Wilkinson, Paul (1974) *Political Terrorism*. New York: Wiley.

Wilkinson, Paul (1977) *Terrorism and Liberal State*. London: Macmillan Press.

Wilkinson, Paul (ed.) (1981) *A British Perspective on Terrorism*. London, Boston: Allen & Unwin.

Williams, Phil and Ernesto U. Savona (1995) "Introduction: Problems and Dangers Posed by Organized Crime in the Various Regions of the World." *Transnational Organized Crime*. 1(3) Autumn: 25.

Wilson, Edward O. (1975) *Sociobiology: The New Synthesis*. Cambridge: Belknap Press of the Harvard University Press.

Wolfenstein, E. (1967) *The Revolutionary Personality: Lenin, Trotsky, and Gandhi*. Princeton, NJ: Princeton University Press.

Woo, H. K. H (1986) *What's Wrong with Formalization in Economics?* Newark, CA: Victoria Press.

Woodward, Bob (2002) *Bush at War*. New York: Simon & Schuster.

Woodward, Bob (2006) *State of Denial*. New York: Simon & Schuster.

Worldwatch Institute (1993a) *Progress Toward a Sustainable Society*. Washington DC.

Worldwatch Institute. (1993b) *Supporting Indigenous Peoples in the State of the World*. Report on Progress Toward a Sustainable Society, Washington DC.

Wright, Lawrence (2004) "The Terror Web: Were the Madrid Bombings Part of A New, Far-reaching Jihad Being Plotted on the Internet?" *New Yorker*. 2 August.

Wyne-Edwards, V. C. (1962) *Animal Dispersion in Relation to Social Behavior*. Edinburgh: Oliver and Boyd.

Yachury, Sitaram (2006) "Learning from Experience and Analysis: Contrasting Approaches of Maoists in Nepal and India." *Economic and Political Weekly*. 22 July: 3168–3171.

Yergin, Daniel (1991) *The Prize: The Epic Quest for Oil, Money, and Power*. New York: Simon & Schuster.

Yotopoulos, P. and J. B. Nugent (1976) *Economics of Development: Empirical Investigations*. New York: Harper & Row.

Zakaria, Fareed (2003) *The Future of Freedom: Illiberal Democracy at Home and Abroad*. New York: W. W. Norton.

Zimbardo, Phillip (1969) *The Cognitive Control of Motivation. The Consequences of Choice and Dissonance*. Glenview, IL: Scott, Foresman.

Zimbardo, Phillip (2007) *The Lucifer Effect: Understanding How Good People Turn Evil*. New York: Random House.

Zimmermann, Matilde (2001) *Sandinista: Carlos Fonseca and the Nicaraguan Revolution*. Durham, NC: Duke University Press.

Zirakzadeh, Cyrus E. (2002) "From Revolutionary Dreams to Organizational Fragmentation: Disputes Over Violence Within ETA and Sandero Luminoso." *Terrorism and Political Violence*. 14(4): 66–92.

Index

Printed in the United States
121004LV00002B/106-138/P